Wooden Boat

An Appreciation
of the Craft

Wooden Boat

An Appreciation of the Craft

Editors of
WoodenBoat Magazine

Addison-Wesley Publishing Company

Reading, Massachusetts • Menlo Park, California
London • Amsterdam • Don Mills, Ontario • Sydney

Ye who would pass by
and raise your hand against me,
hearken ere you harm me.
I am the heat of your hearth
on the cold Winter nights,
the friendly shade screening you
from the Summer sun
and my fruits are refreshing draughts
quenching your thirst as you journey on.
I am the beam that holds your house,
the board of your table,
the bed on which you lie
and the timber that builds your boat.
I am the handle of your hoe,
the door of your homestead,
the wood of your cradle
and the shell of your coffin.
I am the gift of God
and the friend of man.

— in a park in Portugal

Design by Sherry Streeter, Brooklin, Maine

Set by Camden Type 'n Graphics, Camden, Maine, in Mergenthaler Baskerville

Frontispiece: The Gokstad Ship, Universitets, Oldsaksamling, Oslo, Norway

Much of the material in this book originally appeared in *WoodenBoat* Magazine, P.O. Box 78, Brooklin, Maine 04616

ISBN 0-201-09280-8

ABCDEFGHIJ-WZ-898765432

Dedication

The success of *WoodenBoat*, and therefore the publication of this book, would not have been possible without the physical and spiritual support and assistance of all those who have worked here over the years. The rewards during the lean years were meager indeed, and the frustrations many. No one ever complained. Now, as always, it is the people who make the difference, who make the magazine so special. So it is to all of you who have lent heart and soul, that this book is dedicated.

Norman Abrams, Spike Africa, Judy Allen, Kathy Allen, Susie Allen, Judith Andras, Susan Campbell Allen, Peter Anderheggen, James Arbuckle, Lynne Blair, Maynard Bray, Karen Bryant, Lorna Bryant, John Buchanan, Jennifer Buckley, John Burke, Patricia Conn, Marjorie Conterio, Jane Crosen, Barbara Curtis, Cynthia Curtis, Zilla Daniel, Thomas Darge, Mary Jo Davies, Jane Day, Terry Driscoll, David Eastman, Gail Fordham, Mark Gaier, Susie Garfield, David Gerstel, Richard Gorski, Katie Greene, Lynnette Grey, John K. Hanson, Jr., Shirley Hewitt, Ray Higgs, Verona Holden, Richard Jagels, David Kasanof, David Keith, Lucia del Sol Knight, George Kuchenbecker, Roshanna Kesselman, Michelle Lamprell, William Lamprell, Jr., Dick Lerner, Robin Lincoln, Cabot, Heidi and Zachary Lyman, Ryck Lydecker, Daniel MacNaughton, Lea Malmquist, Lynn McVicker, Jacqueline Michaud, Debbie Miltner, Mitchell, Melanie Moore, Erik Morch, Nick Nicholson, Peggy Nicholson, Margaret Page, William Payne, John Pazereskis, Randall Peffer, W. Lyman Phillips, Royce Randlett, Jr., Milanne Rehor, Judith E. Robbins, Karen Roy, Marcia Schwartz, John Servais, Roxanne Sherman, Kristin Smith, Marcie Smith, Mike Smith, Tim Snider, Dennis Solomon, Peter H. Spectre, George Spindler, Sophie Spurr, Sheri Morey Steele, Sherry Streeter, Sally Tompkins, Jim Tolpin, Matthew Walker, Stephen Ward, Elizabeth Webster, Ann Starr Wells, Dick West, Kimberly White, Barbara Woycke

Because the production of this book required time and energy above and beyond the call, it is only fair that we acknowledge the efforts of those who labored long and lovingly over it:

Kathleen Brandes, Maynard Bray, Jennifer Buckley, Camden Type 'n Graphics (Connie and Doug Leavitt), Jane Crosen, Terry Driscoll, Robin Lincoln, Karen Roy, Peter H. Spectre, Sherry Streeter, and Norma Whitman. We offer our gratitude to Anne Eldridge, our editor at Addison-Wesley, for her unfailing support and encouragement.

—*JW*

Contents

Introduction

I AM OFTEN ASKED how I "got the idea" for *WoodenBoat* magazine, and how it all started. From a vantage point of eight years' time, and with the publication of this book, it seems appropriate to recount at least a few of the details of the time and place in which the magazine was born.

Having determined that I liked building small wooden boats for a living, I had settled, in 1972, with my wife, Susie, and infant son at the head of a high-tide cove in Pembroke, Maine, not far from the Canadian border. We had chosen eastern Maine because there we could afford land on the shore, and somehow, that seemed to me to offset the isolation of the place. (It turned out not to be true, but that isolation came to play a part.)

As a still-wet-behind-the-ears boatbuilder, I felt quite out of touch with the more solidly experienced boatbuilders who lived and worked a couple of hours and more to the westward. My apprenticeship, such as it was, had been in yacht repair, under the immensely capable influence of Jack Jacques at the Dutch Wharf Boat Yard in Branford, Connecticut. My time there was more significant to my experience than all the boat and boatyard work that I had done prior to that. It was there that I really began to understand the limits and potentials of wood in boats, and thus, where the process toward *WoodenBoat* really took form. My boatbuilding work was a rather strange blend of yacht and small boat construction, influenced, obviously, by the large-yacht repair work, and by the small-boat construction work of John Gardner. Unfortunately, both influences were far away from Pembroke. Few yachts ventured that far Downeast, and few boatbuilders were left there. So, I found myself working in a kind of experiential vacuum. I needed to be more in touch with the boatbuilding industry. I needed access to experience.

My initial idea was to establish a newsletter for the trade, a simple means of creating a network, which did not then exist, among professionals. Taking a cue from the journals in the medical profession, I suspected that those who engaged in boatbuilding and repair could benefit from a regular sharing of insight and experience. And such sharing, it seemed, could do much for the industry's health and longevity.

Yet, the more I contemplated the idea, the less feasible it seemed. What was really needed, I finally reasoned, was a combination trade *and* consumer publication, a full-fledged magazine.

The truth of the matter is that I did not know enough not to think big. It seemed to me that in spite of the fact that most magazines did not cover wooden boats at all, there was surely enough interest out there to support a new publication, especially if it could be kept simple in concept and execution. (I shudder, in retrospect, at my notion of simplicity.) So, the idea of *WoodenBoat* magazine was born. My ability to think about anything else was severely limited. In spite of our lack of knowledge, experience, and money, I was relentless in my determination to pull it off.

Though I knew nothing about paper, printing, or graphic arts, I did believe in the power and purpose of magazines. I began by writing to about a dozen magazine printers, describing my ideas, posing my questions, trying to sound as if I could pull it off. To most of the printers, my obvious naivete was enough to prevent them from responding at all. Two printers, however (one of whom ended up printing the first two issues), took me seriously enough to respond, and both were enormously helpful in providing me with advice and assistance. Each step brought me a little closer to an understanding of the process, and I began to be able to speak the language. I asked incessant questions of everyone I could find with any experience at all, and I listened carefully to the answers.

With the help of friends who could write, we collected the contents for the first issue. Our enthusiastic friend Tom Darge taught me what an art director was, and then introduced me to one, Norm Abrams, whose taste I liked. Norm's knowledge and experience, combined with his willingness to rescue me from my graphic disorientation, made the creation of the first issues very easy. It was late spring 1974, and we had the summer to produce enough copies of the magazine to introduce it at the Newport, Rhode Island, Sailboat Show in September. It was an occasion we could not miss, for the place would be overflowing not only with the normal showgoers, but also with crowds of spectators who were in Newport to watch the America's Cup races.

Knowing nothing about the capitalization requirements of new magazines, we weren't at all disappointed to have been able to raise $14,000 through the sale of our boat and through generous loans from two friends. Indeed, it seemed like a fortune. Had we undertook such things, we would have been well advised to test the idea of the magazine with some direct mail advance promotion, but there was neither time nor money to do that, and no apparent source of names of likely prospects. Instead, I was banking on the naive assumption that if we could get the issues printed, we could sell them. So, print them we did. On August 1, a little more than six months after deciding to go ahead with the idea, we took the artwork for that first issue to the printer. Nearly three weeks later, with a mixture of feelings that ranged from unrestrained excitement to uncontrollable dread, we rolled up to their door with a U-Haul truck to pick up 12,000 copies of *WoodenBoat* No. 1.

By some freak of the word-of-mouth system, we had already received two subscription orders. That left us with only 11,998 copies of the magazine to sell, so we packed the bulk of those into Susie's mother's garage, took a few copies around to friends to show them off, and waited, somewhat nervously, for the Newport show.

Somehow, at Newport, the idea — and the magazine — took hold. Although we did not do a landslide business, the response was overwhelmingly positive. Two hundred blessed souls forked over their nine dollars for a year's worth of *WoodenBoat*. (Many of those told me later that they never expected to see a *second* issue, much less a sixth.) More than 400 single copies were sold at the show as well, and most of those buyers later turned into subscribers. We began to see that if we could get it in front of the right people, it could succeed. So, Tim Snider in New England and Bill Payne in California packed cartons of issues into their cars and began to sell them to stores wherever they could. The issues almost invariably sold well, and with the rapidly increasing exposure, the magazine began to be talked about and sought after. We did two more boat shows that fall and then returned to Brooksville, Maine, where we had moved from Pembroke, to work on the second issue. As it happened, that second issue, due out in November, didn't appear until February 1975, and it took us about a year to catch up to the schedule, but no reader ever complained.

We built a small cabin to be our home and office. It was rather a shanty of a place, 24 by 30 feet, without power, phone, or running water. The magazine operation occupied a part of one end. But it was growing. By Christmas of 1975, we had about 3,000 subscribers. I still didn't know what I was doing.

I learned my lessons slowly and painfully. I made a lot of mistakes, and yet, in spite of them, *WoodenBoat* grew. It took a little more than a year to sell those first 12,000 copies, but it pointed up a crucial fact: that the back issues of the magazine could continue to have value. In fact, if it hadn't been for that, we might never have survived the financial burden. It also took a year for me to realize that one cannot run a business in one's living room while trying to raise a family in the same room. It is economical, but it is neither sensitive nor intelligent, and the burden on the family is not worth it. Moving the magazine out of the house seemed to suggest that we be a little more businesslike on other fronts, which was difficult for me, but I began to get the hang of it. We were well on our way.

There were still obstacles ahead. We moved first to a small house in the village that we had to vacate for the summer. We then moved down the street to a house that we arranged to rent and eventually buy, on the assumption that we wouldn't have to move again. But just as the winter of 1976–77 was beginning to release us from its grip, that house burned to the ground. So, with a lot of charred books and papers, we moved, like a band of refugees, from place to place until September 1977, when we were offered a house in Brooklin big enough to accommodate our growing staff, which numbered 10. There we stayed, very comfortably, until June 1981, when we numbered 20. By then we had acquired, apparently by divine intervention, our present place.

Our place is an old estate that was slightly run down from five years of neglect and more than its share of vandalism. But it is as if it were made for *WoodenBoat*. We are at home and comfortable, and we have come far from the cabin in the woods.

The story of *WoodenBoat* as it continued — and continues today — is an intricate one, full of the personalities of a lot of wonderful people. On behalf of those people, I must say that we have done well. We have gone from those first two subscribers to a circulation of over 70,000, and we are still growing. We have tried to remain purposeful but not greedy, efficient but not inhuman. I have loved nearly every minute of it, and nearly everyone who has been associated with it.

The creation of the issues from which the contents of this book have been selected has not been without pain, but for the most part, it has been exciting.
　　　　　　　　　　　　　　　　—Jon Wilson

The Soul of a Wooden Boat

Jon Wilson

IN 1979, CoEvolution Quarterly, a magazine based in California, published a special issue on the oceans. The magazine's editors wanted to know why someone would "invest his last penny in a magazine initially published out of the back of a truck — a magazine declared by most sages to be dead before it started and doomed to be shredded for mattress stuffing soon after, since 'wooden boats are obsolete and nobody cares anymore.'" That was five years after WoodenBoat magazine's initial publication, yet it was the first time Jon Wilson had ever gathered together his thoughts and feelings on the subject. Some time later, Jan Adkins asked Jon to contribute a chapter for his Wood Book, so Jon revised the CQ article. The revised version appears here.

A handsome Whitehall skiff contrasts with the full-dressed yachts tied at the Seaport dock.

WOODEN BOATS remind me a lot about what we've forgotten — or perhaps never knew. With rare exception, their shapes and structures reveal the accumulated experiences of thousands of years. They have pleasing shapes, for the most part; the material itself practically demands it. As if the grace of the forest trees were bequeathed in abundance to every plank sawn. And each plank, in turn, has carried with it the duty to lie gracefully in place, resisting to the end any move toward the awkward and angular. That duty was once well understood. Designers, builders, and just plain lovers of boats could respond in awe to the nature of wood and let their hearts and hands be guided by it.

Today we see too little. Our yearnings for more seem nostalgic, romantic, and unreasonable. But it has little to do with the past, more to do with the quality of the current creative spirit. At one time, no boats were built except by hand and eye alone. Experience and intuition guided the shapes of craft. The Viking and Polynesian traditions, almost literally poles apart in their needs and resources, contain remarkably unique craft, whose structure and design were governed largely by the resources at hand. It was imperative to their success that they understood the limitations and the possibilities of the woods with which they worked, and in their understanding they created shapes that best enhanced those elements. Not only did that creative synthesis work well for its time, but the shapes thus created — the traditional craft of those seafaring nations — still leave us in awe.

When I look around at the stock plastic boats that are currently on the market, I wonder whether they leave anyone in awe *now*, much less 10 years from now. But they serve their purpose — it just happens not to be *my* purpose.

So, what do the traditions and the future of wooden boats represent for us today? Certainly more than leisure-time diversions and delights and certainly more than an annual series of headaches over chipped paint and open seams, greasy bilges and soggy berths. But I'm in the business of celebrating the existence of boats built of wood, and in affirming the future of that existence, so my focus may seem to be biased. I guess it is, for I truly believe that wooden boats have a lot to teach us about our purpose on the planet. (I also believe that about music, houses, clear thought, sharing, and love.)

Picture this: A quiet man walks into an ancient wood to fell an old oak that stands with widespread branches. There's an old stand of cedar down in the swamp below, and when he's finished getting out the crooks from the limbs of the oak, and measured and cut that long, straight butt, he's going down to fell a couple of them.

His axe and his saw are clean and sharp, and he's been looking forward to this day for some time. The trees were marked last summer, perfectly suited to the building of a 19-footer, a sailing skiff whose model he carved out on a couple of June evenings and that sat on the mantel for months while he eyed her shape from every angle, living with her, as he knew he'd have to when she was done.

His work is purposeful and reverent — he moves through the wood with gratitude and care, delighting in this time with the very trees that will soon become lumber for the boat. He's in no hurry, for the lumber will be stacked for the winter and summer, drying slowly and comfortably — getting used to not being trees anymore, preparing for life as a boat.

On this crisp fall morning, he has felled and limbed up an oak and three cedars. The seeds of both have come down with the branches, and carefully he gathers them. The best will be sown in his infant woodlot; the rest will be scattered where the growth is thin. He believes in wood, and he knows its nature. He plants for the next generation, and the one beyond that. Not to be remembered, because he won't be, but to give back to the earth, in return for her gifts.

If tomorrow's a good day, the neighbor will bring in his horses and skid out the logs. On the last trip the sledge will bring out the brush for kindling, and chunks for long fires. The wood will be quiet again, with four fewer trees, four more stumps, a little more sunlight, and the green tips of a few cedar branches spread around.

The sawyer will come to pick up the logs and saw them with care for the boatwright. When he returns, his truck will be stacked high with lumber, and together they'll put it in the shed to dry.

The winter and summer will pass while the man waits patiently. The lumber will dry and shrink a bit as it yields the moisture from its innermost fibers. On the ends of a few cedar planks near the door, some small checks will occur — the draft has dried them too fast. But no matter, they're long enough still to get out good planks.

The mornings are frosty again when the time is right. With axe and saw, chisel and plane, he shapes the keel, stem, and sternpost. The carved model guides his hand in the certainty of experience and intuition. He trusts them implicitly — never falters on the way — and shapes the timbers with just the right balance of lightness and strength. The boat is, after all, to be agile and strong. His work is purposeful and unhurried. The upswept limb on the old oak is now the gentle sweep of the stem, and the straight-grained stock provides keel and sternpost. Bolted together, the backbone stands ready for frames and planks, and with battens and clamps her shape is defined. The stock for the frames is sawn out and made ready. Too stiff to be bent, it will lie in the steambox for an hour or so while the fibers are cooked just enough. Then, one at a time, they'll be rushed to the boat, clamped into place, and left to cool to their new shape. It's quick work, and easy, too. With enough moisture in the wood, and wet enough steam, you can tie a knot in a freshly cooked oak frame.

The fragrance of new oak pervades the shop now, but tomorrow the shavings from new cedar planks will take over, their pungent aroma filling the place. And in less than two weeks the hull will be planked, as the idea takes form in reality.

Now the details will go a little more slowly as the boatwright considers his alternatives inside and on deck. Three thwarts? Four? Benches? Side decks? With a hull to step into he can feel the subtleties of great and small changes and doesn't begrudge the time spent in considering. When the questions are answered and alternatives chosen, he moves along swiftly. Paint for the surfaces easily worn, varnish for those that will show it off best, and oil for floorboards that must not be slick.

Solid spars shaped from a woodlot spruce will be oiled to give them a sensible finish. A sailmaker friend cuts and sews a cotton sail, and someone leaves a pair of oars rescued from a lifeboat no longer in service. The knowledge of a lifetime, and lifetimes before, has gone into this craft. She has grown from an idea into a living being, infused with the creative energy of the forest and work of a man. She has sprung from the earth's elements just as surely as the man who built her has. As the days grow longer and warmer, she waits with her builder, just as impatiently.

Then comes the day. The weather is warm, the tide is right, and she feels water beneath her for the first time. Afloat at last, this is the moment they've worked for, as the new sails fill and draw. Out of the harbor and across the great bay they sail, this man and his boat. Working together, they discover what she can do, reaching, running, and climbing to windward. In the late afternoon the wind drops for a while, and before it picks up again he has sculled her home.

She is lively and responsive, with plenty of sail for the days with light breezes, and plenty to reef when the wind pipes up. What began as a vague thought has become a clear idea — a dream brought forth. She is lovingly modeled, lovingly built, and lovingly cared for. The hours of work are returned to him a hundred times over in pleasure. Rare is the day that he doesn't sail her, if only for an hour. And rare is the hour aboard that doesn't restore his spirit and affirm his love for the boat.

The soul of a wooden boat is an elusive thing. One can feel its presence in a derelict craft almost as much as in a well-loved one. But defining it is quite another thing. For me it is found in the blend of energies invested by the designer, the builder, and the owner. If all three investments have been made with love and care, the soul of the boat seems stronger.

There are very few things that we can dream into being, build with our own hands, and enjoy for a lifetime. There are fewer still that we can buy from someone else. Wooden boats shine among them, in spite of some bad press in recent years.

It's said that wooden boats leak and rot, are a horror to maintain, and are too expensive to build anymore. Indeed, they're said to be dying out. Although most who own and iove wooden boats must disagree, those who aren't sure why they're still attached to them are in grave danger of switching their allegiance. Such people have often been the victims of inexperience and misinformation, or they may have discovered that the care of living things requires deeper commitment and responsibility than the care of a plastic facsimile does, and have neither the time, money, nor interest for such complication. Moreover, there are some very bad wooden boats in the world, examples of poor design, construction, and maintenance. The most lavish amount of love and care for such boats may at best only slow the process of deterioration. On the other hand, there are some wooden boats nearly a century old that are still going strong for their owners.

The care of such fine creatures has become almost an occult science to some, perhaps because some of the elementary aspects of care and maintenance have been forgotten or obscured among the promotional boats for today's miracle products — best suited to today's miracle boats.

Well, what about the rest of us? Perhaps the key to understanding lies in the continuing recognition of the wooden boat as a living thing; recognizing surface problems as symptomatic of deeper problems. Sometimes simple, sometimes not, all they require is attention. For instance, there's an area on the topsides of the hull where the paint blisters and peels every year, creating the otherwise unneeded work of having to scrape, sand, and spot with paint before doing the entire hull. One owner will find it a frustrating and unavoidable part of the ownership of a wooden boat, while another will explore the problem methodically. To begin with, it is undoubtedly a case of excessive moisture in the wood. Since wooden hulls need to evaporate moisture from the planking into the interior, it's very important that the structure be well known to good designers. But it wasn't always so. There have been many boats built whose ceiling (inner hull skin) is fitted tight from cabin sole to sheer clamp with nary a gap in it. Such a structure looks neat and adds stiffness but prevents good ventilation, and without that, the wood becomes too saturated, and paint won't adhere. More often, the problem is a hanging locker, or a sealed-up compartment inside, that was left unventilated through oversight or carelessness. Cutting some openings so that air can circulate through the spaces between the frames will promptly allow the planking to breathe, and soon paint will adhere again. Trapped moisture — vapor or water — is the main problem in wood boats. In the right quantities it can peel paint and varnish, make a perfect place for rot, cover the interior with mildew, and turn rich mahogany to a spongy black mass. The ways to trap it are poor joinery, inexperience with structures at sea, total dependency on weird miracle substances, and inattentive or inexperienced maintenance.

The uninformed believe that the wood itself is at fault, as if by some malevolent decree, the wooden boats of the world have it in for their owners. Not so; they only need love and care, which for some is too high a price.

Another common woe is the chronic leaker. The boat that the owner is afraid to leave for more than a week, because the water will be over the floorboards or cabin sole. Or the boat that is tight as a drum at the mooring but leaks like a basket in a seaway. Well, before we jump to any conclusions, we need to remember that in all likelihood, the boat in question was tight as a drum when she first touched water. There's no need for a properly built wooden boat to leak at all, and there are plenty of fine examples with dusty bilges to prove it. But for various reasons, some boats, large and small, begin to work themselves apart as the years go by. Not that they *must*, but they *do*. The causes for such working can be anything from fastenings that are too light or are corroded, to broken frames, to poorly fitted floor timbers, to a design that failed. The root causes are usually simple and unnoticed by the average owner. Yet, as the hull begins to work, the effect is felt elsewhere in the boat as that thrust is transmitted throughout her. But faulty elements don't mean that the boat is a hopeless case, any more than two broken legs mean that a man will die.

What is not always clear, however, is that the price of repair — in the hospital or the boatyard — is usually unpredictable, usually high, and requires a skilled artisan whose temperament can make the difference in the job. But remember, we're talking about living beings here. We're talking about love and trust, confidence and courage. If you attempt to care for your wooden boat without these things, she becomes a burden to the spirit. If she is not understood, and loved for what she is, you'll never be happy with her. The parallels are surely obvious.

Most of us are willing to let life teach us much, and the lessons we learn aren't always so comfortable. Sometimes, although we see ourselves as salty romantics, born to the sea, we discover that life on the sea is just like life ashore, and find ourselves unfulfilled and sometimes frustrated by the burdens of care and responsibility for our boats. Perhaps we need a change.

Certain boats need certain owners. The ownership of a tired little vessel demands an incredible will. A will that takes over as the structure weakens, a resolve that can never fail. And it's perfectly reasonable. Some boats are held together by the will of their designers and builders. Those that are not must depend on their owners. They are never separate from their owners, but extensions of them.

The soul of the wooden boat is only intact when its elements are. Living close to the boat gets one deeply in touch with it, and care and attention yield beauty and pleasure. We, the owners, are integral parts of that soul, and no boat survives without love. But, neither does any other living thing.

The Man Who Planted Hope

Jean Giono

HERE IS one of those wonderful essays that seems to have a life of its own. Peter Anderheggen, a teacher and now head of the WoodenBoat School, showed the piece to Jon Wilson back in the late 1960s. At that time the story was published in pamphlet form by the Friends of Nature in Brooksville, Maine. In 1976, the story was reprinted by the CoEvolution Quarterly *with this intriguing illustration by Tom Parker. Realizing that our readers weren't necessarily conversant with the idea that* anything is possible, *even planting a forest singlehandedly, we knew we should publish the article as well, to give this remarkable story further exposure. This was our first real departure from publishing material about the boats themselves and enabled us to place a narrow subject into larger perspective.*

FOR A HUMAN character to reveal truly exceptional qualities, one must have the good fortune to be able to observe its performance over many years. If this performance is devoid of all egoism, if its guiding motive is unparalleled generosity, if it is absolutely certain that there is no thought of recompense and that, in addition, it has left its visible mark upon the earth, then there can be no mistake.

About 40 years ago I was taking a long trip on foot over mountain heights quite unknown to tourists in that ancient region where the Alps thrust down into Provence. All this, at the time

I embarked upon my long walk through these deserted regions, was barren and colorless land. Nothing grew there but wild lavender.

I was crossing the area at its wildest point, and after three days' walking found myself in the midst of unparalleled desolation. I camped near the vestiges of an abandoned village. I had run out of water the day before, and had to find some. These clustered houses, although in ruins, like an old wasps' nest, suggested that there must once have been a spring or well here. There was, indeed, a spring, but it was dry. The five or six houses, roofless, gnawed by wind and rain, the tiny chapel with its crumbling steeple, stood about like the houses and chapels in living villages, but all life had vanished.

It was a fine June day, brilliant with sunlight, but over this unsheltered land, high in the sky, the wind blew with unendurable ferocity. It growled over the carcasses of the houses like a lion disturbed at its meal. I had to move my camp.

After five hours' walking I had still not found water, and there was nothing to give me any hope of finding any. All about me was the same dryness, the same coarse grasses. I thought I

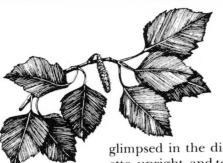

glimpsed in the distance a small black silhouette, upright, and took it for the trunk of a solitary tree. In any case I started toward it. It was a shepherd. Thirty sheep were lying about him on the baking earth.

He gave me a drink from his watergourd and, a little later, took me to his cottage in a fold of the plain. He drew his water — excellent water — from a very deep natural well above which he had constructed a primitive winch.

The man spoke little. This is the way of those who live alone, but one felt that he was sure of himself, and confident in his assurance. That was unexpected in this barren country. He lived not in a cabin but in a real house built of stone that bore plain evidence of how his own efforts had reclaimed the ruin he had found there on his arrival. His roof was strong and sound. The wind on its tiles made the sound of the sea upon its shores.

The place was in order, the dishes washed, the floor swept, his rifle oiled; his soup was boiling over the fire. I noticed then that he was cleanly shaved, that all his buttons were firmly sewed on, that his clothing had been mended with the meticulous care that makes the mending invisible. He shared his soup with me and afterward, when I offered my tobacco pouch, he told me that he did not smoke. His dog, as silent as himself, was friendly without being servile.

It was understood from the first that I should spend the night there; the nearest village was still more than a day and a half away. And besides, I was perfectly familiar with the nature of the rare villages in that region. There were four or five of them scattered well apart from each other on these mountain slopes, among white oak thickets, at the extreme end of the wagon roads. They were inhabited by charcoal-burners, and the living was bad. Families, crowded together in a climate that is excessively harsh both in winter and in summer, found no escape from the unceasing conflict of personalities. Irrational ambition reached inordinate proportions in the continual desire for escape. The men took their wagonloads of charcoal to the town, then returned. The soundest characters broke under the perpetual grind. The women nursed their grievances. There was rivalry in everything, over the price of charcoal as over a pew in the church. And over all there was the wind, also ceaseless, to rasp upon the nerves. There were epidemics of suicide and frequent cases of insanity, usually homicidal.

The shepherd went to fetch a small sack and poured out a heap of acorns on the table. He began to inspect them, one by one, with great concentration, separating the good from the bad. I smoked my pipe. I did offer to help him. He told me that it was his job. And in fact, seeing the care he devoted to the task, I did not insist. That was the whole of our conversation. When he had set aside a large enough pile of good acorns, he counted them out by tens, meanwhile eliminating the small ones or those that were slightly cracked, for now he examined them more closely. When he had thus selected one hundred perfect acorns, he stopped and went to bed.

There was peace in being with this man. The next day I asked if I might rest here for a day. He found it quite natural — or, to be more exact, he gave me the impression that nothing could startle him. The rest was not absolutely necessary, but I was interested and wished to know more about him. He opened the pen and led his flocks to pasture. Before leaving, he plunged his sack of carefully selected and counted acorns into a pail of water. I noticed that he carried for a stick an iron rod as thick as my thumb and about a yard and a half long. Resting myself by walking, I followed a path parallel to his. His pasture was in a valley. He left the little flock in the charge of the dog and climbed toward where I stood. I was afraid that he was about to rebuke me for my indiscretion, but it was not that at all: this was the way he was going, and he invited me to go along if I had nothing better to do. He climbed to the top of the ridge about a hundred yards away.

There he began thrusting his iron rod into the earth, making a hole in which he planted an acorn; then he refilled the hole. He was planting oak trees. I asked him if the land belonged to him. He answered no. Did he know whose it was? He did not. He supposed it was community property, or perhaps belonged to people who cared nothing about it. He was not interested in finding out whose it was. He planted his hundred acorns with the greatest care. After the midday meal he resumed his planting. I suppose I must have been fairly insistent in my questioning, for he answered me. For three years he had been planting trees in this wilderness. He had planted 100,000. Of these, 20,000 had sprouted. Of the 20,000 he still expected to lose about half to rodents or to the unpredictable designs of Providence. There remained 10,000 oak trees to grow where nothing had grown before.

That was when I began to wonder about the age of this man. He was obviously over 50. Fifty-five, he told me. His name was Elzeard Bouffier. He had once had a farm in the lowlands. There he had had his life. He had lost his only son, then his wife. He had withdrawn into this solitude, where his pleasure was to live leisurely with his lambs and his dog. It was his opinion that this land was dying for want of trees. He added that, having no very pressing business of his own, he had resolved to remedy this state of affairs.

Since I was at that time, in spite of my youth, leading a solitary life, I understood how to deal gently with solitary spirits. But my very youth forced me to consider the future in relation to myself and to a certain quest for happiness. I told him that in 30 years his 10,000 oaks would be magnificent. He answered quite simply that if God granted him life, in 30 years he would have planted so many more that these 10,000 would be like a drop of water in the ocean.

Besides, he was now studying the reproduction of beech trees and had a nursery of seedlings grown from beech nuts near his cottage. The seedlings, which he protected from his sheep with a wire fence, were very beautiful. He was also considering birches for the valleys, where, he told me, there was a certain amount of moisture a few yards below the surface of the soil.

The next day we parted.

The following year came the War of 1914, in which I was involved for the next five years. An infantryman hardly had time for reflecting upon trees. To tell the truth, the thing itself had made no impression upon me; I had considered it as a hobby, a stamp collection, and forgotten it.

The war over, I found myself possessed of a tiny demobilization bonus and a huge desire to breathe fresh air for a while. It was with no other objective that I again took the road to the barren lands.

The countryside had not changed. However, beyond the deserted village I glimpsed in the distance a sort of greyish mist that covered the mountaintops like a carpet. Since the day before, I had begun to think again of the shepherd tree-planter. "Ten thousand oaks," I reflected, "really take up quite a bit of space." I had seen too many men die during those five years not to imagine easily that Elzeard Bouffier was dead, especially since, at 20, one regards men of 50 as old men with nothing left to do but die. He was not dead. As a matter of fact, he was extremely spry. He had changed jobs. Now he had only four sheep but, instead, a hundred beehives. He had got rid of the sheep because they threatened his young trees. For, he told me (and I saw myself), the war had disturbed him not at all. He had imperturbably continued to plant.

The oaks of 1910 were then 10 years old and taller than either of us. It was an impressive spectacle. I was literally speechless and, as he did not talk, we spent the whole day walking in silence through his forest. In three sections, it measured 11 kilometers in length and three kilometers at its greatest width. When you remembered that all this had sprung from the hands and the soul of this one man, without technical resources, you understand that men could be as effectual as God in realms other than that of destruction.

He had pursued his plan, and beech trees as high as my shoulder, spreading out as far as the eye could reach, confirmed it. He showed me handsome clumps of birch planted five years before — that is, in 1915, when I had been fighting at Verdun. He had set them out in all the valleys where he had guessed — and rightly — that there was moisture almost at the surface of the ground. They were as delicate as young girls, and very well established.

Creation seemed to come about in a sort of chain reaction. He did not worry about it; he was determinedly pursuing his task in all its simplicity; but as we went back toward the vil-

lage, I saw water flowing in brooks that had been dry since the memory of man. This was the most impressive result of chain reaction that I had seen. These dry streams had once, long ago, run with water. Some of the dreary villages I mentioned before had been built on the sites of ancient Roman settlements, traces of which still remained; and archaeologists, exploring there, had found fishhooks where, in the 20th century, cisterns were needed to assure a small supply of water.

The wind, too, scattered seeds. As the water reappeared, so there reappeared willows, rushes, meadows, gardens, flowers, and a certain purpose in being alive. But the transformation took place so gradually that it became part of the pattern without causing any astonishment. Hunters, climbing into the wilderness in pursuit of hares or wild boar, had of course noticed the sudden growth of little trees, but had attributed it to some caprice of the earth. That is why no one meddled with Elzeard Bouffier's work. If he had been detected, he would have had opposition. He was undetectable. Who in the villages or in the administration could have dreamed of such perseverance in a magnificent generosity?

To have anything like a precise idea of this exceptional character one must not forget that he worked in total solitude: so total that, toward the end of his life, he lost the habit of speech. Or perhaps it was that he saw no need for it.

In 1933 he received a visit from a forest ranger who notified him of an order against lighting fires out of doors for fear of endangering the growth of this *natural* forest. It was the first time, the man told him naively, that he had ever heard of a forest growing of its own accord. At that time Bouffier was about to plant beeches at a spot some 12 kilometers from his cottage. In order to avoid traveling back and forth — for he was then 75 — he planned to build a stone cabin right at the plantation. The next year he did so.

In 1935 a whole delegation came from the Government to examine the "natural forest." There was a high official from the Forest Service, a deputy, technicians. There was a great deal of ineffectual talk. It was decided that something must be done and, fortunately, nothing was done except the only helpful thing: the whole forest was placed under the protection of the State, and charcoal burning prohibited. For it was impossible not to be captivated by the beauty of those young trees in the fullness of health, and they cast their spell over the deputy himself.

A friend of mine was among the forestry officers of the delegation. To him I explained the mystery. One day the following week we went together to see Elzeard Bouffier. We found him hard at work, some 10 kilometers from the spot where the inspection had taken place.

This forester was not my friend for nothing. He was aware of values. He knew how to keep silent. I delivered the eggs I had brought as a present. We shared our lunch among the three of us and spent several hours in wordless contemplation of the countryside.

In the direction from which we had come, the slopes were covered with trees 20 to 25 feet tall. I remembered how the land had looked in 1913: a desert... Peaceful, regular toil, the vigorous mountain air, frugality and, above all, serenity in the spirit had endowed this old man with awe-inspiring health. He was one of God's athletes. I wondered how many more acres he was going to cover with trees.

Before leaving, my friend simply made a brief suggestion about certain species of trees that the soil here seemed particularly suited for. He did not force the point. "For the very good reason," he told me later, "that Bouffier knows more about it than I do." At the end of an hour's walking — having turned it over in his mind — he added, "He knows a lot more about it than anybody. He's discovered a wonderful way to be happy!"

It was thanks to this officer that not only the forest but also the happiness of the man was protected. He delegated three rangers to the task, and so terrorized them that they remained proof against all the bottles of wine the charcoal-burners could offer.

The only serious danger to the work occurred during the War of 1939. As cars were being run on gazogenes (woodburning generators), there was never enough wood. Cutting was started among the oaks of 1910, but the area was so far from any railway that the enterprise turned out to be financially unsound. It was abandoned. The shepherd had seen nothing of it. He was 30 kilometers away, peacefully continuing his work, ignoring the

War of 1939 as he had ignored that of 1914.

I saw Elzeard Bouffier for the last time in June of 1945. He was then 87. I had started back along the route through the wastelands; but now, in spite of the disorder in which the war had left the country, there was a bus running between the Durance Valley and the mountain. I attributed the fact that I no longer recognized the scenes of my earlier journeys to this relatively speedy transportation. It took the name of a village to convince me that I was actually in that region that had been all ruins and desolation.

The bus put me down at Vergons. In 1913 this hamlet of 10 or 12 houses had three inhabitants. They had been savage creatures, hating one another, living by trapping game, little removed, physically and morally, from the conditions of prehistoric man. All about them nettles were feeding upon the remains of abandoned houses. Their condition had been beyond help. For them, nothing but to await death — a situation that rarely predisposes to virtue.

Everything was changed. Even the air. Instead of the harsh dry winds that used to attack me, a gentle breeze was blowing, laden with scents. A sound like water came from the mountains; it was the wind in the forest; most amazing of all, I heard the actual sound of water falling into a pool. I saw that a fountain had been built, that it flowed freely and — what touched me most — that someone had planted a linden beside it, a linden that must have been four years old, already in full leaf, the incontestable symbol of resurrection.

Besides, Vergons bore evidence of labor at the sort of undertaking for which hope is required. Hope, then, had returned. Ruins had been cleared away, dilapidated walls torn down and five houses restored. Now there were 28 inhabitants, four of them young married couples. The new houses, freshly plastered, were surrounded by gardens where vegetables and flowers grew in orderly confusion, cabbages and roses, leeks and snapdragons, celery and anemones. It was now a village where one would like to live.

From that point I went on foot. The war just finished had not allowed the full blooming of life, but Lazarus was out of the tomb. On the lower slopes of the mountain I saw little fields of barley and rye; deep in that narrow valley the meadows were turning green.

It has taken only the eight years since then for the whole countryside to glow with health and prosperity. On the site of the ruins I had seen in 1913 now stand neat farms, cleanly plastered, testifying to a happy and comfortable life. The old streams, fed by the rains and snows that the forest conserves, are flowing again. Their waters have been channeled. On each farm, in groves of maples, fountain pools overflow on to carpets of fresh mint. Little by little the villages have been rebuilt. People from the plains, where land is costly, have settled here, bringing youth, motion, the spirit of adventure. Along the roads you meet hearty men and women, boys and girls who understand laughter and have recovered a taste for picnics. Counting the former population, unrecognizable now that they live in comfort, more than 10,000 people owe their happiness to Elzeard Bouffier.

When I reflect that one man, armed only with his own physical and moral resources, was able to cause this land of Canaan to spring from the wasteland, I am convinced that, in spite of everything, humanity is admirable. But when I compute the unfailing greatness of spirit and the tenacity of benevolence that it must have taken to achieve this result, I am taken with an immense respect for that old and unlearned peasant who was able to complete a work worthy of God.

Elzeard Bouffier died peacefully in 1947 at the hospice in Banon.

A Boatbuilder's Garden

George Putz

GEORGE PUTZ, one of the editors of The Mariner's Catalog, *came in one day and said he'd like to write an elaborate piece on silviculture — the whole bit — from selecting trees, to tending and harvesting wood, to learning where you might find what you need to do the job right. George is one of those people who can wade his way through piles of source material and talk for hours with experts in their fields and still extract the essence of the subject at hand — he understands the whole system without becoming distracted by the background noise. He spent the best part of a winter assembling and assimilating the material for the article, which we published in two parts. We don't have room for the extensive bibliography and listing of sources that originally accompanied the article, but there are always back issues . . . .*

As a direct result of this article, Countryman Press of Vermont contracted with George to write a book on silviculture, and American Forests *magazine asked him to write a regular column.*

A PERSON who decides to build a wooden boat changes his life forever — not because of the boat, but because of the wood. Yet almost everyone's great boat is in the past, or the future. What remains always present and fresh are the skills and experience of joining the stuff, wood, and the trees from which it comes, and the community that nutures trees, the forest.

As with all natural experiments, civilization must try out consuming bigness. But all such experiments must sooner or later find the limits of their strategy of exploitation. It does not make any difference whether the resources dry up because of drought, flood, famine, disease, volcanic eruption, or excess consumption; the result is the same — extinction, or at the least a very serious changing of form.

As far as wooden boatbuilding is concerned, the notion that trees and forests are renewable resources is, simply, completely ridiculous. And the decisions that are and shall be directing our national behavior toward trees and forests are out of our hands. For these reasons, all woodworkers, and wooden boatbuilders most particularly, must be increasingly responsible for their own resources, now and in the future.

Our concern here is for the economics and the plant and forest dynamics that underlie, and are the rationale for, good woodlot management practice. We must also consider the present and future market contexts that are bound to affect woodland owners, and look at the basic elements of silvicultural practice.

We are only now beginning to understand what trees are, and this understanding is rapidly changing the wood products industry's attitude toward them. Not until 1970 did anyone bother to dig up an entire tree with scientific care. This was done by three College of Forestry professors at Syracuse University, who dug up a 39-year-old red pine to see what they would see. Carefully, by hand, they dried and weighed every hair's-breadth rootlet. They found that 18½ percent of the dry weight of the tree (and, yes, they weighed every needle!) was below ground. This has silvicultural implications we'll discuss later.

The work of a tree is to produce carbohydrates with which to maintain life processes, and from which to manufacture woody tissue for the growth of the roots, bole (trunk), branches, twigs, and leaves or needles. There are thousands of substances produced by trees, and things trees do with those substances — indeed, every species is, in part, a species by virtue of its particular combinations. But all trees share the primary work of making molecules of cellulose, stringing them into long fibers, bundling and twisting the long fibers together, and then gluing the bundles themselves together with a bind substance, usually lignum. If one's primary interest in trees ends there — the efficient manufacture of wood fiber — one's attitude is restrictive, to say the least.

The wood products industry is progressively coming to view wood as simply fiber, or as aggregates or constituents slightly above or below the fiber level. It is their version of bottom-line thinking. This is not to be criticized out of hand, for such thinking has vastly increased the efficiency of wood resource utilization. But any view of trees that is limited to a single use will naturally come into conflict with the views of others, especially those who hunger after select boatstock.

Consider that a tree may produce: food, fiber of several sorts, drugs, dyes, gums, and resins from its roots; oils, dyes, specialty fibers, animal food, and soil compost from its leaves; cork, tannins, drugs, yet more fiber, and fuel from its bark; essential oils and honey nectar from its flowers; and, of course, the food and chemicals from its fruits and seed — all besides the wood in the bole and the branches. All these products, potential and actual, go by the board when a tree is dropped and converted for its timber or fiber alone. One resources economist calculated that an average mature hardwood tree produces $36,000 worth of goods and services in its lifetime, if such goods and services were to be acquired by other means at current costs.

A tree, left alone and in the open, can be described as an annually incremented cone of tissue. The manufacture of this tissue takes place through photosynthesis — the action of sunlight on leaf cells containing chlorophyll — which converts nutrient substances from the soil, carbon dioxide from the air, and water, into cellulose, lignum, and all the enzymes, proteins, etc., necessary for plant life — indeed, for all life on earth. Oxygen is given off as a by-product. Trees, then, to function properly must do everything they can to maximize the amount of light striking their green leaves or needles. Thus a tree standing in the open deposits its new tissue about equally along its bole. Its general cone shape is a function of new growth, and its branches at the top are always smaller than the lower old growth. This cone of wood is surrounded by a broader cone of branches and needles.

In a competitive setting, however, it is not good strategy for the tree to maximize sunlight by using its growth energy to broaden the cone. Its optimum strategy is to grow upward, to keep up with, if not surpass, the surrounding trees. There is much crowding and jostling in the early period of new or reseeded growth, as anyone who has walked through a 10-year-old stand of trees knows. As competition among trees reduces the light striking the lower levels, "natural pruning" occurs. The trees shut off growth energy, and eventually any sustaining energy at all, to their lower branches, which die, eventually decaying and falling from the bole. Once this process begins, all competitive trees — those that don't lose the battle and die entirely — as a matter of course begin their cone increment deposition at the lower end of the second third of the tree's total bole height. This is how straight, parallel-sided, clear sawlogs are created. The place of primary tissue development is always moving up the bole. Conclusion: clear stock requires a forest.

One hundred twenty thousand seedlings to 120 trees. You can almost hear the strain of competition, see them reach for the sky. A forest is a war zone among trees and associated plants. As with any war, there is a context in which it must be considered to be understood. A general principle among ecologists is that the more stressed an environment is, the greater the tendency for that environment to contain very large populations of very few species. There is an inverse relationship between population and variety. For example, an acre of ledge in the ocean near the Arctic Circle may host 10,000 individuals each of, say, three bird species. On the other hand, an acre of jungle in the tropics might host one or two of many scores of species. Forest zones are similar. The more environmentally stressed and uniform an environment, the fewer species there are.

Forest ecologists divide the United States into many primary associations, or forest areas, with 10 of them found east of the Mississippi. Each area is delimited by a fairly straightforward set of environmental characteristics, including temperature range, moisture cycle, elevation, soil type, and, of course, species occurrence.

Ordinarily a forest is described in terms of its dominant upper canopy species, but a forest is three-dimensional, and each forest type has its characteristic subdominant understory species and associated shrub and ground cover species. There is, furthermore, the fourth dimension of time. Each forest area has its own way, its own particular sequence of species appearance and development as they increase their range into new areas or, more commonly, recover from disasters or disturbance. Each forest area has its own specialized warfare.

Except for the tropical and subtropical species, such as cypress, the mahoganies, and teak, almost all of the species that boatbuilders use are represented in either the "mixed-meso-phytic hardwoods" or the "boreal forest," and can be gardened. The tropical and subtropical species cannot, because their regimes are not sufficiently understood. Tropical forests store their nutrients in their biomass — within the trees and plants themselves — while our North American temperate forests store most of their nutrients in their soils. (This is because the tropical regime is bacteria based, while our temperate regime is fungus based.) When you take a mahogany, you also take all the nutrients in the local system. When you take the oak or cedar, you removed only a very small portion of the nutrients in the local system. Tropical silviculture may be an impossibility.

Paleobotanists estimate that about half the forests that were standing at the dawn of the Neolithic Age are standing now. The lost half was consumed in 8,000 years, but keep in mind that soil degradation has occurred in the temperate forests yet standing. Of the continental United States forest area, about 70 percent of the area standing when Columbus landed remains forested, but with the same proviso. The quality of this 70 percent is generally much lower than the original, being in third and even fourth growth in many areas, especially east of the Mississippi.

There was a lot of wood here when the white man came, and a lot remains. But for the most part we are indifferent to it when we don't actually hate it. Alexis de Tocqueville, in his *Democracy in America*, written in the 1830s, mentions the Americans' loathing of trees, their great preference for the open spaces so hard won from the forests. And there are many journal and diary entries from the 1790s and well into the 19th century recounting death and injury from limbs that crashed down onto farmers and passersby from giant virgin hardwoods that had been girdled and left to stand and rot in the grain fields.

The mixed hardwood forest that these trees represented had been there millions of years — 60 million years in the case of the Allegheny and Cumberland regions. A given stand of fully mature trees would have been growing for about 800 years in the association seen by a colonist. In other words, it takes a climax hardwood

forest stand about 800 years to reach anything like final stability after any radical disturbance. To be sure, reforestation *per se* takes place quickly; trees can reach cutting size in less than a century. But the final climax stability — with all the climax species represented, all ages for continuous recruitment represented in the stand, and all soils fully built — takes much longer. This becomes important later on when we consider how a stand of trees should be managed and harvested — whether to "thin," say, or "release cut" rather than "clearcut." Ignorance of the dynamic differences between virgin and reverted or secondary growth is responsible for much hogwash in the literature and conventional wisdom among environmentalists, and even among many professional foresters, who categorically denigrate clearcutting as an appropriate harvesting method.

Softwoods are a different matter. Most pines are pioneer species that require regular alteration of their environment by fire or wind to continue growing and regenerating. Without fire or wind, or human nurture, these pines are soon replaced by later dominants in the natural growth sequence of forest development, though white pine is one of the few important exceptions. White pines can occur as a climax dominant in mixed and pure stands, much to the boatbuilder's good fortune. But most other pines are pioneer, not climax, creatures and so are troublesome, as we'll see.

The boreal forest, which stretches in one form or another from coast to coast, mostly above 40 degrees latitude, but also at lower latitudes on higher elevations, is a climax association. But its environment is more stressed than other U.S. forest areas. There are more of fewer species, and the boatbuilder's garden, with introduced species in such areas, must be considered and tended with more care. Whether one is considering the boreal on the East Coast, with red, white, and black spruce as canopy dominants, balsam fir as the subdominant understory species, and eastern larch and white cedar in the lowland wet covers; or the boreal on the West Coast, with Douglas fir or Sitka spruce as the canopy dominant, with hemlock or red cedar as the codominant understory, the silvicultural considerations are basically the same. There will be less flexibility in the choice of species, more susceptibility to weather hazards, more intelligence required in the effort. But, as a forest, the boreal association reaches nearly final stability earlier. In effect, it requires less recovery work after distur-

bances than does a hardwood association and is generally able to stand high levels of stress, whether manmade or natural.

Hardwood or soft, the fundamental antipathy the average citizen feels toward the forest (except, perhaps, for some romantic notions — but, then, romanticism kills lots of things) is reflected in the simplifications that make up our understanding of what a tree is and what forests are, and how wood is to be used. When a commercial forester clearcuts a wild stand, and then replants a single species — say he cuts mixed hardwoods for furniture and veneer stock, pulp, and firewood, and then replants red pine — the effect is that of trading an orchestra for a solist. The hassles and inefficiencies of the orchestra are eliminated, and the efficiency of *fiber* growth is greatly increased, but he is stuck with all the idiosyncrasies of the bloody solist. A common cold can ruin the concert.

The stand that once cared for itself, each species taking and giving to the forest environment, now becomes prone to insects, blights, and drought, which can invade and ruin with impunity. The monocultural species takes and gives only what it is programmed to, and the once-extant subtleties of the soils and habitat are dissipated quickly. Efficient, modern monocultural systems create a tremendous environmentally expensive simplification. Many individual woodlot owners are guilty of the same thinking when they concentrate on only one species or one use for the wood harvested.

A tree is no more the basic unit of the forest than a bee is the basic unit of the hive, or a particular organ the basic unit of the organism. The forest *is* the basic unit. A forest of all one species is no more a forest than a hive of all drones a hive, or a person of just stomachs a person. No matter how efficient our wood use becomes, if simplification of the forests is inherent to the understanding of efficiency, then the fundamental understanding of forests as a self-managing system of warfare is ignored. Man must then become a combatant in the growth process itself, as he has in agriculture by engaging in the ever-escalating spiral of having to fertilize, and to use herbicides, fungicides, and insecticides. Go ahead and make structural flakeboard out of limbs and tops, use computers for "Best Open Face" (BOF) sawmilling, employ "Edge Glue and Rip" (EGAR) to make large pieces out of small pieces, use stumps for paper, use limbs, twigs, and needles to make alcohol, use aspen pellets for livestock food (yes!), burn chips or even gasify wood to make electricity or oil, design skidders, dozers, stackers,

chippers, delimbers, and even chainsaws to be safer and quieter or less damaging — do it all! But this will not improve the basic unit, the forest, one iota.

The forest products industry thinks of efficient conversion of fiber. They are using everything they have. There is a threat that the government will capitulate in our parks and wildlands when we are on the ropes later on. With their cuts will go our boatstock for the next 200 years.

On the average, wood is eight times more energy-efficient than alternatives in all its applications. And, in the words of the American Forest Institute:

...the last moment to do something dramatic about timber supply in 1980 was about the spring of 1955. And to the average citizen in 1955, the year 1980 was just a little this side of infinity.

Most Americans are up to their necks in 1974 problems, and not really prepared emmotionally or physically to deal with problems of timber supply in 1990.

Any boatstock any reader will ever use is growing now, and it has been growing for a long time. We must find it, tend it, improve it, protect it, and nurture it for those who will follow in our wake. We must practice silviculture in forests. But first a few words about the similarity between silviculture and agriculture.

A farmer is, by definition, a culturalist, an agriculturalist, devoted to nurture and propagation for purposes of production. What is there in what the agriculturalist does, or thinks, or uses, that seems so often to cause degradation eventually? What is there in this irony of agriculture that we can learn to avoid in our silviculture?

Silviculture, the intentional nurture and propagation of tree growth, is like agriculture in a more subtle way than the simple raising of wood plants. It is the nature of the plants chosen to become raised intentionally that gives agriculture its unique properties of high production on the one hand, and susceptibility to various disasters on the other.

The original way food-producing grains, legumes, and fruits were obtained was by gathering, obviously, and whether the earliest agriculture was created by a stroke of genius, or through a long process of intuitive or inadvertent selection is moot. The point is that all species that eventually were farmed successfully were *weedy pioneer heliophytes*. These are three critical words: "Weedy" means rank in the sense that the plants will grow anywhere

where their minimal requirements of growth are met. "Pioneer" means that they occur very early in the natural sequence of succession in soil that has been stressed or disturbed. Cut, scrape, inundate, or otherwise disturb a patch of soil, and it is the pioneers that will first inhabit the patch. "Heliophyte" means sunloving. The plants thrive in open sunlight and are intolerant of, and retarded and soon killed by shade.

All three of these qualities of agricultural species subject them to danger, and so too their propagators. Agriculture came into being when people learned to weed these productive weeds — to eliminate the hardier competition and to fertilize the desirable, less hardy weeds. But, look at the other logical as well as actual problems that this creates. When a high-production weed exists naturally, it is, necessarily, quite rare. So, its predators are rare, not only the big ones — the birds and animals able to eat it — but also the smaller ones — bugs, microorganisms, and the like. Once these food plant species are propagated, however, and concentrated, so too are the predators invited to lunch on a much large scale than would occur naturally. Pest predation, and the need to control it, increases dramatically. And when these pests, not to mention natural weather cycles, get the upper hand, which is bound to occur periodically, the increased population, a product of the improved resource base, is bound to suffer fatal shortages.

It is the nature of agriculture to be ensconced in danger. Weedy pioneer heliophytes of high productivity are designed by nature to be prone to suppression. To keep them from being suppressed takes hard work.

It is much the same for those species of trees being selected for modern commercial silvicultural production. As with all plant types, trees do not live by themselves. Naturally occurring monospecific communities are relatively rare, and occur only under special circumstances. The typical tree lives and thrives in a community of other trees, different kinds of trees — each occupying a particular niche in the forest environment, using these soil ingredients instead of those, occupying this slope, elevation, and moisture content instead of that, here in the canopy level instead of there. Each species uses the offerings of the environment differently, holds its biomass for differing periods of time, and contributes back to the soil the products of special characteristics when it dies and decays. All the while, of course, each species hosts different populations of microor-

ganisms, insects, mosses, ferns, fungi, lichens, birds, and other animals, as both food and homes.

Now, just as weedy pioneer heliophytes are the first to occupy ideal agricultural soils when they are stressed or altered, so weedy pioneer heliophytic trees are the first to occupy stressed or altered forest soils. Except for ash and a couple of the pines, none are used, or fit to be used, in boatbuilding, and of these only white pine had much favor, and that mostly for decking. All are subject to the same consequences of cultural propagation as the agricultural species. They are designed that way.

Whether a stand of trees is cut for that little schooner you have always wanted, or to get out another edition of your local newspaper, is immaterial as far as the forest soil is concerned. What is material to the soil is that it saves itself from leaching and erosion. The increases in soil losses created by deforestation are astounding.

In stream water, itself increased 30 to 50 percent because the trees are not there to transpire water, nutrient runoff on a northern hardwood slope will increase 300 to 1,000 percent, and particulate matter, soil itself, by as much as 16,000 percent for one to two years until growth is reestablished. The weedy pioneers — the alders, aspens, pincherries, raspberries, and all the stuff that makes producing tree lovers heartsick — invade the ground, cover it, and begin the long reorganization necessary to allow another forest to grow.

Peeking out of these exploitative weedy plants, here and there, are the more tolerant species, biding their time until, eventually, their much more conservative growth strategies come to dominate the cover, closing the sunlight and life out of the early pioneer enthusiasts. This is called secondary succession, and its processes must always be kept in mind by the boatbuilder's gardener. If the weedy pioneer heliophytic syndrome of constantly struggling to arrest the succession in favor of a selected few species is to be avoided, greed must be kept in check. The gardener must ignore the fact that the value of the standing crop on his land could be increased tenfold. But we are ahead of ourselves.

Get hold of some woodlands. Get control of it. If you cannot own it outright, get a lease on it that will hold good for at least two working generations — 99 years is a standard in the legal biz. Size of the woodlands is not as important as location and variation in the slopes and soils. In ideal conditions, a woodlot of 10 acres will be able to supply a boatbuilder all his (her) life. But 50-plus acres will probably be necessary to get the desirable variety of growth conditions. Get a lawyer and explain to her (him) that your needs are *commercial*, even though very long term, and get her to research and exploit every avenue your town, county, and state offers to protect commercial forest land from excessive (unendurable) taxation and from pressures to use your woods in ways detrimental to the growth of the kinds and shapes of wood you will need. Also, get the woodlands into your will, to be left to the very best recipient possible, tendering it with whatever covenants and restrictions you think have a chance of being observed.

Then, *write to* and *visit* a professional forester, before you allow him to visit your forest. This is to avoid the nodding-head syndrome, a very dangerous disease that afflicts all professional people — its external symptoms being a nodding of the head while you explain your particular needs and insights, his head meantime dominated by all manner of presuppositions, most of which boil down to "I've-been-in-this-business-for-28-years-and-you're-just-a-turkey . . . ."

Go ahead and admit to the forester that you are crazy. But also make sure he understands that your goal is to exploit the forest very slowly, that you want to treat standing trees for special kinds of growths, that you want to introduce new species, possibly exotic to the local forest, and that you would like the forest to manage itself as much as possible, such as by the use of companion planting, much like that employed in organic vegetable gardening.

When your forester has stopped nodding his head, and he has a look that may indicate that he is thinking, let him "cruise" your woods and make up for you a map showing standing species diversity, age classes, slopes and drainage, soils, and a standing timber assessment — including the current timber values in those trees that may be "over-mature" for their type and soils, or otherwise endangered.

With the aid of these conversations and that map, get to know your woods personally. Find out the history of your woods from previous owners, old folks, and town records. Look for old field fences, walls, cellar holes, and road-beds. Follow them, and note their effects on the standing growths — there are always effects, and they tell you how to behave toward them. For example, reverted fields once used for hay or crops are almost always deficient in potassium and phosphorus. Check out, follow, or perambulate all the surface waters, and get to know the *ecotones*, those narrow bands of mixed associations that exist between different forest types.

Finally, since many boatbuilders and fine woodworkers we know talk to trees, there just has to be something in it. Go ahead. Other people won't hear you, and there are *those* trees, bound, by the way, to introduce conflicts with your forester, who always calls trees old enough to talk "over mature."

Whatever decisions you make regarding the loquacious ancients, you will be cutting trees, beginning immediately, not only to acquire the building stock you'll need in the near future — say, the next five years — but also to clean and thin your woods for healthy growth, to open areas for the introduction of new species, or to produce good natural seed beds, and to make some cash on non-boatstock sawtimber and fuel wood.

Milling Your Own

Bob Darr

MANY BOATBUILDERS harvest their own trees for lumber — especially crooked wood for grown frames and knees — but until the advent of the chainsaw mill, few had the facilities to mill lumber to specification. We heard that Bob Darr, a California boatbuilder with a passion bordering on fanaticism for using local woods for building boats, had considerable experience milling his own lumber. We asked Bob to share with us his methods for making planks and timber directly from logs without having to get involved with a commercial sawmill. With Bob's advice and the proper tools, even small-time boatbuilders can make use of local woods, which are easily found, inexpensively acquired, and satisfying to use.

I CAN RECALL with anxious amusement some of my first lumber-cutting expeditions, which were undertaken with hardly any experience but with plenty of enthusiasm. It's a wonder that my friends and I weren't killed or injured.

On one of these adventures, three of us were cutting some beautiful laurel trees that had fallen under a load of snow two years before. The trees were in a remote area, and we had to cut them into suitable logs and haul them to a small mill in a neighboring town.

Above — The author stands with a pair of flitches sawn with the Alaskan mill. A little time and a little care yield just what he needs for his boats.

The Alaskan mill, ready for the harness.

Above — The top of the felled log is dubbed off with an adze to accommodate the 2 x 12 plank on which the guide rollers will travel.

Right — The plank is tried.

After crosscutting them with a dull, ancient chainsaw, we pulled them up the canyon using blocks and tackles, with my truck hauling the working end along the dirt road. We towed the logs up from tree to tree, using a 400-foot length of 2-inch Dacron line, heavy blocks, and strops made of steel cable. By setting and resetting our lines, we soon had them all to the top and had to consider how we were going to get the logs to the mill. There were five of them — the heaviest weighed close to a ton — and we didn't have a suitable truck. The solution finally struck me: I would rent a truck. I adroitly dodged the rental agent's questions about what I was moving and was soon on my way back to the logs with a regular house-mover's truck.

It was not an easy task getting the big truck up those dirt roads, and I tried not to think about what it would be like to come back down with all that weight aboard. It was early spring, and there were places in the road cut by streams, some nearly 2 feet deep; landslides made the road impossibly narrow in other places. But nothing can match the enthusiasm of youth. We were soon on our way down with

the first load, creeping slowly in low gear, delighted with our success.

We got the first load to Rico Calvi's mill in Occidental (California) late in the afternoon. Rico's mill, a large circular saw, was dismantled as it always is until the rains stop in the late spring. We had come to drop off the wood, which he would cut later. Rico heard us pulling up and walked out to greet us. He must have been at least 75 or 80 years old then, with long white hair and an extremely gentle face and manner. He was carrying a newborn lamb in his arms, and with the late afternoon golden light, he looked like nothing less than a prophet from the *Old Testament*. He started laughing when he realized what we were doing with the U-Haul truck. We backed up to the spot he indicated for unloading, and he watched us, smiling, as we struggled with the big logs, all of us very tired by then. Finally, when he was convinced that we weren't going to get them out, he jumped into the truck with a peavey and a length of pipe, and asked us to get out of the way. He then rolled out the logs effortlessly by putting the pipe roller under them.

Later, we sat around and talked. He told us how pepperwood (this is what he called laurel) was once commonly used, even in boatbuilding, and how the trees at higher elevations were superior to the ones on the coast. My own experience has since confirmed this.

At other times, before I purchased my Alaskan mill, I used to take logs to Wes Hulbert in Tomales for milling. He had a standard old Belsaw (still available from the company) hooked up with a flat belt to an old Chevy or something that smoked like mad. There was a loading ramp near the mill, and once the logs were off the truck, the work was just about done. I'd give this type of mill a fairly high recommendation if you have the space and want to set up a somewhat permanent operation to cut a lot of wood. The company is reliable and the equipment is well proven. The mill has to be set up correctly and does require other gear — including a good truck and flat land with good access — but its big advantage is speed and simplicity. If everything is set up just right, you can produce a lot of lumber, though you are limited to logs 2 feet in diameter and 14 feet long unless you modify the standard mill. The current cost for a Belsaw mill is under $3,000, not including the power source, which can be as little as 25 h.p. from an old car or truck.

But three or four years ago, I decided to buy an Alaskan mill. I was tired of hauling big logs around to mills, and the danger and extra expense were getting to me. I liked the idea of a portable mill that could reduce the logs to manageable flitches and leave the rest to compost in the forest.

A chainsaw mill is actually only a simple metal framework that is attached to a conventional, though powerful, chainsaw equipped with a special ripping chain. By adjusting the distance between the rollers on the frame and the chainsaw bar, you can cut any thickness of plank that you want. This is done by pulling the mill through the log instead of running the log through the mill. My mill was made by Granberg Industries in Richmond, California, and though some mills use two chainsaw engines, one on each end of the bar, I opted for a single, very powerful Stihl 090 chainsaw engine on a 4-foot bar. If I ever want to, I can put another engine on the opposite end, but I haven't seen a need for it yet.

Clearly, though, a chainsaw mill is not the kind of mill to set up for commercial work. It's too slow and involves too much maintenance. It is, on the other hand, the best thing I've found for my boatbuilding lumber needs. The mill and its accessories can be stored under my workbench and can be loaded within 15 minutes into my old pickup. Voilà! — we're off to the hills or to some old lady's backyard for the locust tree. You can sharpen it yourself, and if you're cutting eucalyptus, that might mean three or four times in a day. It's the very best thing that I know of to cut knees or sweeps, which I used to have to do with an adze and a bandsaw.

But aside from being slow, the chainsaw mill does have some other faults. It will try to break down on you every third cut. Either the chain will loosen or the carburetor will foul. The machine vibrates terribly, and I suspect you can get bursitis if you handle one too often. Having a two-cycle engine, it naturally smokes a good bit.

I used the mill for a couple of years by holding the throttle and pulling it as recommended with a partner on the other end; then I started thinking about a harness to get some distance from the vibration and especially from the fumes. I worked out a simple harness that consists of a wooden bar with ⅜-inch line running from each end of the mill to each end of the bar, where adjustable clove hitches can be tied. Also leading from the bar is a throttle cable or a similar gear cable to control the throttle on the chainsaw engine. The Stihl 090 actually has a spot in its mechanism designed for a cable hookup, but you can find a way to make a cable work on any engine. I start the saw on the log, set myself up in the harness, and just lean back

Above — The plank rests comfortably atop the log.

Left — The depth of cut (thickness of flitch) is set.

Below — The harness lines make fast to the handle, through which is mounted a remote throttle control.

and watch. One man on the harness can make a faster and more even cut than two men pulling the saw through without the harness, and it's safer and far less tiring.

Let's take a look at the whole process from tree to boat, so you can see what's involved. First, consider your needs. If you intend to build a boat, or you're planning a big restoration, or even hope to build some furniture, any of these jobs will require a lot of expensive wood. Since the chain mill and its gear will cost under $2,000, you may decide, as I did, that it is a worthwhile investment, particularly if your life is centered around woodworking. I have paid for my mill many times over in the savings I've made cutting my own wood, and I've ended up with superior wood in the bargain.

Now, you have to find the trees you need, not always an easy task. One way is to keep your eyes and ears peeled for anyone deciding to get rid of that white oak in their front yard, or the black acacia that's choking out the sunshine. Over the years, I've found that the best way is to go to farmers and ranchers who have a lot of land and trees, explain my requirements, and ask for their trees. I even take pictures of my work to show them. When they understand what I am doing, it is amazing how many of these people will pitch in and try to help. They don't always want money in exchange, either. I usually try to trade some service for the tree, often cutting up a bunch of firewood, or doing some clearing. Don't go to see them with the attitude that you deserve something for nothing, or you won't get very far. If you're honest from the start, these people will respond in kind.

When you have the tree lined up, here is what to take along to do the job correctly: The mill, already sharpened; sharpening gear; an extra chain; goggles; earmuffs; a fuel can (filled); extra two-cycle oil; a hose to siphon gasoline; plenty of chain-lubricating oil; screwdrivers and a wrench set; hammers; wedges; an axe; a peavey; pick and shovel; handsaws; a perfect 2 x 12 plank, 4 feet longer than your longest cut; nails; chalkline and level; rope with a couple of suitable blocks; a come-along; pipe rollers; a fire extinguisher; a small first-aid kit; some money; food and drink; the boat plans, with dividers and rule; seedlings.

You also need a pickup truck, and it's best if this is neither new nor in poor working order. The brakes must be good. Try to get to the site early so that you don't feel pressured by time. Whenever possible, I take someone with me to assist in case of an injury in a remote area.

You can determine which way you want the tree to fall either by considering the way it's leaning or by planning the cut properly. If the tree is going to fall near a road or a house, get someone with experience in felling to help you out the first time. I usually make a small wedge cut on the side I want the tree to fall, not more than a third of the way in. I'll then cut straight in toward the middle of the wedge cut from the other side until the tree seems almost ready to fall — usually you hear some serious creaks from the tree. You can then use some wedges on this last cut and even bias them so that when you drive them in, they push the tree more one way than another. So pound in the wedges and wait for someone to shout "TIMBER," then move back out of the way in case the tree decides to spring back at you.

This explanation is somewhat simplified, and different situations may require additional maneuvers. You may have to top the tree first so branches won't hit a line or a house. Through experience, you will learn to vary the depth of the wedge cut, depending on the angle of the tree and where you want it to go. But read up on the subject of tree felling before you tackle it for the first time.

The tree is down. You can now come out from wherever you were cowering and see what the damage is. Did the tree break anywhere? It's time to cut off the limbs and haul them out of the way so that you can see the whole trunk. Remember, it's dangerous to leave branches around when you're carrying sharp tools.

Once you've decided on how you're going to divide the log, determine how it is supported on the ground. It is very easy to trap the chainsaw bar in the wood if you're not thinking about each cut. If the piece to be cut is free (completely in the air), then make a cut from underneath to about halfway through the log. Meet this cut with one from above, and the piece will fall off nicely.

Usually you must be more careful, since the log will want to collapse right where you're making the cut. You can avoid this by making the first cut from the underside, as before, but not as deep — only a quarter of the way up. Then come down from the top until the bar disappears, and pound a wedge in behind it to prevent binding. Often you'll have to dig under the tree with a pick and shovel, because you don't want the chain from the saw to touch *any* dirt, or you'll have to resharpen it.

With a little experience, you'll find that you can cut any tree down and into sections without much trouble. The hard part comes when you have several logs lying there waiting to be hauled away to a mill or to be cut up on the spot with the Alaskan mill. And there's the task of cleaning up your mess.

You can, alone, get a half-ton log into the back of your truck if you've brought along the right gear. By backing the truck up to the log's end, you can load it in by rolling it back and forth with the peavey onto pieces of blocking. Keep adding pieces of blocking until the log end is above the height of the truck bed, back the truck under it, shove a pipe roller under the beast where it's touching the truck bed, then pull it in with the come-along. Remember to watch your feet and be very careful.

When loading large slabs, I make a ramp to the truck bed with a couple of 6 x 6s, then just roll the slabs up on pipe lengths, again pulling with the come-along. It helps to have a wire strop on hand to be set up as a noose that can be led from the underside of the log or slab.

One of the big advantages of the Alaskan mill is that you can cut the wood into more manageable pieces that can usually be loaded by hand if a couple of people are present. If you've decided to own or borrow (God knows that I'd *never* lend out mine, however) a chain mill, I'll get on with the next step. Because there is so little involved in setting up a harness, which makes the work safer and more comfortable, I'm going to describe how to run a mill that way.

I mention in the list of equipment a plank that is 4 feet longer than any cut that you are planning to make. This plank should not be just some old construction lumber, but instead should be a carefully selected plank, 2 x 12, absolutely straight when you buy it or after you've trued it up. Store it carefully between logging journeys, because you'll need this plank to make every cut. Whatever errors are in it will be duplicated in your flitches.

After turning the log for a while and studying it, decide which side would be the best one to start the cut from. You should choose the flattest side — the side that is most closely parallel to the heart in the log. I try not to use the heart in my work, because experience shows that this is where a lot of checking and twisting problems originate. In fact, if I can, I make my first cut right through the heart, then make consecutive cuts from either of the two halves.

The plank is sometimes difficult to position for the first cut. You must measure from the heart of the log to the top of the plank at each end and make sure that the measurement is the same, which often means that one end of the plank will have to be built up with wedges or the other end of the log adzed down a bit. Use a string line to make sure that everything is kept straight and true. Sixteen-penny nails can be used to keep everything in place; be sure the plank is really solid or the weight of the mill will warp the cut. Allow an equal overhang at each end of the log.

Set the measurement on the chain mill, fire it up for a warmup, turn it off again, then set it on the plank at the end where you want to begin the cut. Since the mill is heavier on the engine side, you must balance the mill by adding lead weight to the other side until it will ride smoothly on its own. Check the fuel and chain oil and make sure that the throttle cable connection is secure. Fire up the engine and start pulling on the harness, keeping things in balance as the chain bites in. After your cut is about a foot long, come back and put a couple of small wooden wedges in the kerf on either side so that the chain and bar aren't pinched. Do this also

at the middle of the cut, and just before you come through at the end of the cut.

Once you've made the first cut, the others will be a lot easier to set up because of the flat surface. Set them up exactly the same way, but instead of using 16-penny nails, use nails that will only protrude a half inch or so into the slab being cut, and be sure never to forget the length of the nails in your calculations. Don't forget to add in the thickness of the plank on each cut.

That's about all there is to using an Alaskan mill, except a few small hints, like keeping the chain sharp and making sure that it is getting enough oil. I recommend buying a sharpening jig. Get the manual type, because it can be used in the middle of the forest and doesn't take off as much metal as the electric variety.

When you bring your beautiful pieces of wood home, it's time to consider seasoning them. Even if you have cut wood to be bent, you should let the wood sit for a couple of weeks at least. There is a good deal of information available about seasoning wood, so I won't go into this topic at any great length here. But I would like to emphasize that some woods are more stable than others, just as some cuts of wood are more stable than others. Vertical-grain stock is the most dimensionally stable of any plank cut. Some woods are difficult to stabilize, and it may be helpful to soak these in salt water.

I first heard of this method from my father, who told me that in the past, large fir trees intended for spars were buried in the mud near the shore so that the incoming tide would cover them. After several months, they were moved onto land for drying out. I have bundled slabs of wood, weighted them, and sunk them under the dock near my shop. Perhaps the salt leaches into the wood and acts as a stabilizing factor. When the wood is out of the water, the salt seems to prevent too much moisture from leaving the wood too rapidly, thereby avoiding splitting and warping. In the case of some woods, freshwater soaking can be used to change the color of the wood. One example is California laurel, which will turn an almost black color prized by certain furniture makers in the Northwest. Remember, in any case, that the wood needs the usual drying time after it has been soaked. *Never* leave the wood to season without painting the ends, and don't leave it out in the open without a cover. Once you start using the wood, say, in a backbone or as framing, keep the finished work painted with oils to prevent any more rapid seasoning.

Cutting and milling your own lumber can be a rewarding experience — be prepared, be thoughtful, and be careful!

Pete Culler's Workshop

Maynard Bray
Jon Wilson

*P*ETE CULLER WAS *a boatbuilder in Hyannis, Massachusetts, who after years of experience could create just about anything connected with wooden boats — from mixing his own paint to forging his own fittings. What's more, he had the time and temperament to fashion many of his own tools, which, along with those he found necessary to purchase, constitute a fascinating collection most appropriate for the art of boatbuilding. Shortly after Pete died in 1978, Maynard Bray, Jon Wilson, and* WoodenBoat's *photographer, Benjamin Mendlowitz, went through Pete's shop with his long-time friend George Kelley. They spent an entire day talking about the different tools, why they were made, and how they were used. Shortly after this, the tools were moved to Mystic Seaport Museum, thanks to the generosity of Pete's good wife, Toni. It was she who gave us the opportunity to see and photograph the shop. Although we missed the benefits of having Pete himself talk about the shop and tools, we captured the place and its contents essentially as he had left them.*

CAPTAIN PETE CULLER made a fantastic contribution to the renewal of interest in traditional small craft among many of us. His writing in *National Fisherman, The Mariner's Catalog, The Telltale Compass,* and *WoodenBoat* has been widely read and deeply appreciated. His three books, *Skiffs and Schooners; Boats, Oars, and Rowing;* and *The Spray* (all published by International Marine, Camden, Maine), are testament to his knowledge and experience.

The little boats he designed and built (several of which he took to Mystic Seaport's annual Small Craft Workshop) were the inspiration for many who finally got out of their armchairs to "do it themselves," and Pete was always most encouraging on such projects.

His large designs are just as impressive. The well-known schooner *Integrity,* designed and built for Waldo Howland, the schooner *John F. Leavitt,* designed to carry freight under sail, leave a rich legacy for all of us.

He was perfectly contented and always busy. From his own shop alone emerged more than 50 small boats, and many more designs, all of which were sold through the Concordia Company in South Dartmouth, Massachusetts. Concordia took care of the paperwork and supplied the boatbuilding materials, allowing Pete to keep his overhead low and his life simple. His hourly rate, even billed through Concordia, was a bargain, and he could probably have had plenty of work if he had charged double for his services, but he dismissed such thoughts. To encourage the ideas of resourcefulness, craftsmanship, integrity, and simplicity — the themes of his life — meant far more to him than any amount of money, and encourage he did.

In the hope that some of Pete Culler's resourceful thinking may rub off, we're pleased to take you on an illustrated tour of Pete Culler's wonderful shop.

Opposite — Pete Culler's shop was part garage, part workshop. He built small boats on the second floor and "launched" them onto his pickup truck.

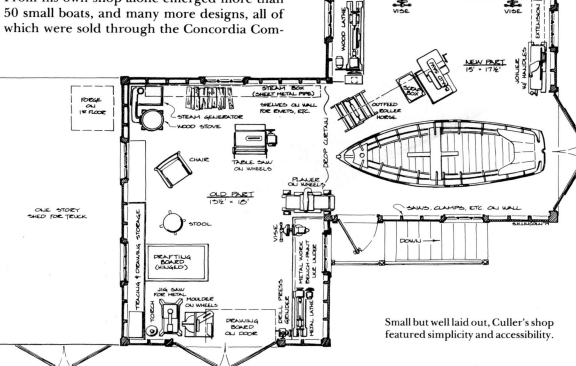

Small but well laid out, Culler's shop featured simplicity and accessibility.

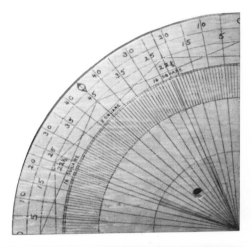

" *Usable iron and steel go to waste like wood these days. Much excellent tool steel hits the scrap pile. Working tool steel brings to mind the picture of a craftsman of much skill and training — few think they dare attempt it. Yet, to make simple things takes little skill; more skill develops as you go. Besides, the stock is junk, and free, so you can afford mistakes in learning. Now, if you get taken up by this sort of thing, and a forge is available, possibilities are unlimited, as is the stock to work with. A garage that works on big vehicles often has broken truck springs out back. This is prime stuff for big tools. Need I say more?* **"**

— *Pete Culler in* Mariner's Catalog Vol. #1

Below — The photograph shows the shop's "heating plant" (a pot-bellied stove with a 35-gallon economizer on top) and the "steam generator" (a welded, wood-fired affair that, with its array of internal tubing, can start putting out steam only minutes after a fire is lit). The steambox itself is made of galvanized sheet metal ducting and shows in the upper right.

Above — His kit of caulking tools was kept in this covered wooden firkin. Because caulking irons must be kept clean, smooth, and rust-free if they are to work properly, they were generally kept in cans with oiled cotton.

Left — Pete's imagination was always restless, and one day it brought forth this protractor, which is marked for 8-siding and 16-siding spars and oars. With it, he could determine the width of each face for any diameter and make up a perfect taper gauge.

Above — Pete was as much at home with sawn-frame vessels as he was with delicate Rushton canoes. He had grown up with the tilt-head bandsaws, called shipsaws, once common in large commercial yards, and he set about to rework his own 16-inch bandsaw for more convenient bevel work. After adding a big, easy-to-read quadrant and a right-angle drive to get the table-tilting crank within easy reach of the operator, he could saw out the changing bevel on a small boat's transom by himself in about the same way as with the old-time shipsaw.

Left — This table saw was equipped with wooden wheels and could be moved easily around the shop. As shown, it sits where the boats were set up and built — usually right-side up if they were round-bottomed, with their keels blocked up off the floor to a convenient working height.

Above — A nail tray of his own devising gave him easy access to many combinations of sizes, from the smallest to the largest, and was portable enough to use at the boat or the beach.

Right — This blacksmith shop occupied the back corner of the dirt-floored, lean-to garage where Pete's venerable green Jeep pickup was kept.

Below — In this corner of the shop, most of the serious woodworking took place. The bandsaw is nearby (at the left in the photo) and the bench is fitted out with a couple of good wood vises. The firkin sitting on the bench holds Pete's caulking tools, and the lathe next to it is set up to sharpen skip-tooth "disposable" bandsaw blades.

Above — The woodstove, just out of the picture to the right, made work at this drafting table fairly comfortable, even in the dead of winter.

Right — A short piece of narrow-gauge railroad track has been cut and ground to a pleasing and functional shape to become a fine little anvil for bench-top use.

Left — An old file was used as the iron in this handsome hand router. All his tools were marked with Capt. Pete's initials, R.D.C. (for Robert D. Culler).

Top right — Worn-out files have good steel in them, and Pete could see no reason to throw them away when they got dull; he'd just draw out their temper and fashion them into some kind of cutting tool, like these carving knives, and then harden them up again so they'd hold their edge. Tool handles were gotten out of scraps of hardwood by turning them on the wood lathe.

Right — Baby planes, each made with a different use in mind — and each made to a slightly different shape.

Below — With the gift of creating things that were beautiful and with a never-ending store of new ideas in his head, Pete would rarely make anything the same way a second time. Even boats he built to the same set of plans would come out slightly different in their details and paint schemes. There is only one hand plane like this one in the shop, but what a beauty it is.

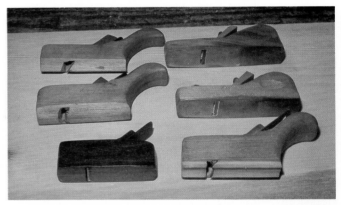

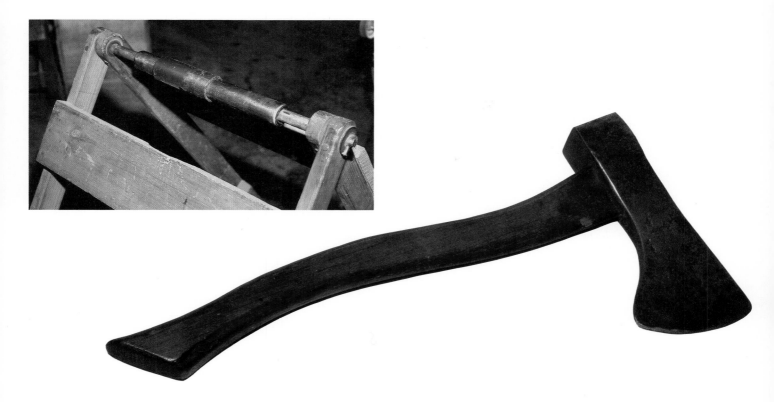

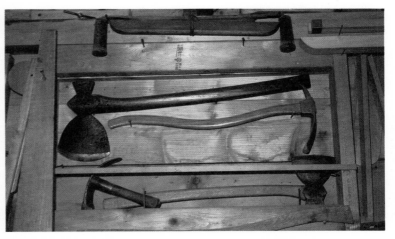

Above — This little axe was made from the steel of an old automobile spring; the handle was shaped to suit Pete's swing.

Top — Concentric rollers on this outfeed horse allow the timber or plank to traverse — a handy feature if you're sawing out a curved shape on the badsaw. The horse itself maybe raised or lowered by changing the spread of its legs and may be collapsed altogether for storage.

Above — The craftsman's workshop is filled with the tools he acquires over a lifetime, and each of those here must have a great story behind it. A drawknife, two broadaxes, a gutter adze, purchased from Woodcraft Supply, to which Pete had added a horn to improve its balance, and a small cooper's adze for closer work, ready to be used again. At the bottom is his pattern for an adze handle.

Left — Why buy an expensive bench vise when you can make a far more beautiful one out of wood?

Right — This templating tool was made from some sheet copper scraps and wooden "fingers," which are kept in line, as they slide back and forth, by wide grooves on the underside of each and matching tongues on top. A bit of work to make, but also a challenge to his endlessly creative nature.

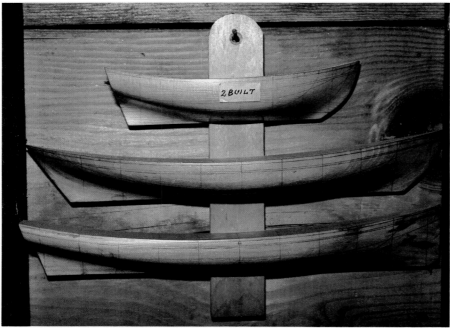

Left — Starting with a very rough sketch, Pete worked out the shape of each design in three dimensions by means of a half model. When the model suited him, he would draw up the lines on paper and complete the plans. Mounted together here are a tender, a double-ender, and a Whitehall type. The stations, buttock lines, waterline, and top strakes are drawn in.

Below — As the half model developed, Pete could study the proportions of the full shape by placing the model on his sheet of highly polished metal. This mirrored the image beautifully without the distorting effect of mirrored glass, which would also reflect the thickness of the glass. Viewed from several angles, the full shape would reveal any subtle problems that needed to be worked on.

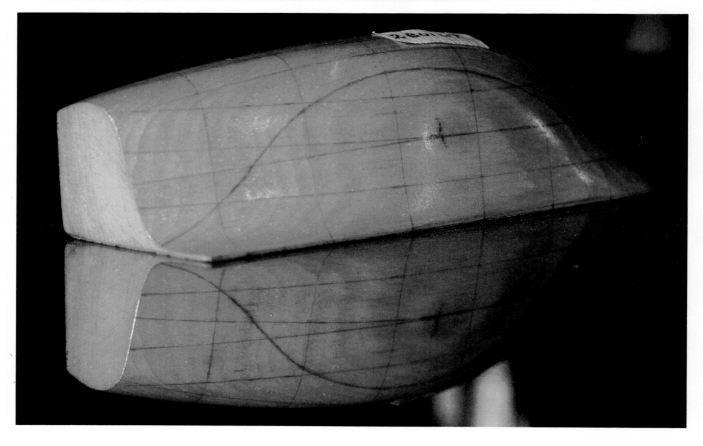

"It's sometimes said that the table saw is the basic machine for woodworking; maybe so for a cabinet shop, but definitely not for boat work. I say own a table saw if you can, but not at the expense of more useful tools."

— *Peter Culler in* Skiffs and Schooners

Right — With a piece of galvanized flat bar and some scrap hardwood, there seemed to be more challenge and satisfaction in making his own sliding bar clamps.

Left — Designing was a big part of Pete's activity in later years, and the boats he drew ranged from 8-foot punts to a 125-foot coasting schooner. His drafting table was small, but it was laid out so he could work around three sides of it. The wooden ships' curves, some of which are shown here, were made by Pete; in fact, he even made his own scale rules, which read from right to left, a convenience to a left-hander like Pete. Just before he died, he wrote in *Mariner's Catalog #6* a wonderful description of his approach to boat design.

Below — Within easy reach at the back of Pete's workbench is an enviable collection of beautiful socket chisels, an oilstone mounted in a block whose height and beveled top make it easy to use, spokeshaves for any need, one of Pete's special homemade rules — this one with centering measurements and nail sizes — and an assortment of crooked knives.

From Rags to Riches

Matthew Walker

MATTHEW WALKER, one of our most avid and articulate supporters, wrote us regularly from the West Coast with ideas, comments, and criticisms. Occasionally he also sent photographs, which were always good. At one time he worked at Tom Wylie's modern shop in Alameda, California, a high-tech wooden boatbuilding yard. On a trip across the Bay to Sausalito, he stumbled across an obscure yard specializing in traditional plank-on-frame boat construction. Matthew was struck by the extraordinary differences between the two levels of boatbuilding technology expressed within a few miles of each other. In his story, the traditional yard was kept anonymous at the request of the boatbuilders who worked there (they weren't sure they could handle the publicity), but in a subsequent WoodenBoat *article on the same boatyard, they were revealed to be the Sausalito Shipwright's Co-Operative, whose experience has since encouraged the formation of other cooperatives around the country.*

Successful old-style boatbuilding — two Sprays and a mammoth ship saw. The hull at the left will be carvel planked; the one to the right is lapstrake planked.

I F SOMEONE told me, "I don't want to build a wooden boat because I don't like wood!" now *that* would be someone with their head screwed on correctly. I couldn't argue with that someone, no sir, not for a minute, 'cause everyone's entitled to their opinion, even a fool. My only complaint is against those irrational souls who say one of two things: "I can't afford it," or "I can afford better."

Now, to those who sadly rattle the old penny-jar, shake their heads, and fire up hope for the wooden boat of their dreams, my answer is: Don't give up! You'd be surprised how easily good wood can be acquired, and at minimal expense, too. Of course, building your own boat would take time, so if you can't break away from that fascinating job of yours, not even on

weekends and occasional evenings, then don't mess with it — nothing is more discouraging than a good idea left unfinished. And there's no doubt that you'll end up spending some money, no matter what material you choose for construction, so I won't pretend you can build "for nothing." Just don't tell me you "can't afford it" unless you've covered all the possibilities . . . .

Ideas: Ask around, does anyone sell "used lumber" nearby? Is somebody you know tearing down an old barn? Is there an orchard up the street that's being cleared? Have you checked local boatyards for salvageable wrecks? Hell, why not tiptoe across the street at night and saw a chunk off your neighbor's front porch? I won't tell if you don't . . . .

More ideas: Do you know anyone who might want to split the cost of a used, high-quality bandsaw? A planer? Start a boatbuilding "club," and share your tools (but choose your friends wisely). Get together and buy in volume — you'll save a lot that way. Buy someone's old boat and rebuild it . . . recycle!

All of this merely to prepare you for some bad news . . . do you see this picture here, the one on the opposite page? Well, I have promised not to tell where I got this. The picture must speak for itself.

Perhaps you can understand my regret. Imagine me rolling down the highway, seeing the same old suburban sights (yawn, scratch, scratch), when all of a sudden, what's that I see? No doubt about it, it's a boat, a wood boat, and a big one! So I go down an alley, through a

Successful new-style boatbuilding — a cold-molded light displacement racing yacht and the owner's land transportation.

Builders clamping mahogany "ringing frame" into wall jig.

Keelson is bolted into place over frames and stations.

fence, around the corner, through a junkpile, and there they are, *two* of them! One boat is in frame (that's the one I saw from the road), and the other, hidden under a shed, is much further along . . . .

A dog greets me, hoisting up a sleepy head just long enough to snort and put it down again. The occupants of a rabbit hutch crowd up against the wire mesh and think carroty thoughts. A chicken coop erupts loudly, settles down, and lots of little round hens' eyes watch me pass. There is, high above the drone of flies in the compost-heap, another sound, something very familiar . . . .

A shirtless, sun-browned young man comes quickly down the ladder. He nods to me, walks over to a bench, grabs a pencil, walks back to the ladder, and disappears up into the boat. Everything around me, at first glance, seems utter chaos — sawdust, dirt, weeds, and debris — but the eye can make sense of it. The crazy-quilt of scrap metal overhead keeps one dry, tools here, paint there, and that mound of old canvas has a rowboat peeking out, showing off a brand-new paint job.

"Hi." A voice from above.

"Hi. Saw the boats from the road. Can I have a look around?"

"Sure." The young man descends to the ground, then busies himself as I have my look around. But I am fairly bursting with questions, and he is, however casually, watching me. So I walk back to where he stands planing a piece of wood.

Second layer of diagonal veneers being stapled over the first. Picture shows second layer with and without 2-inch strips in place. Visible at top of picture are stapler and coiled plastic air-hose, also bronze staples, razor-knives, and metal straightedge. Another stapler is visible at lower right.

Using battens and a block-plane, the major deck-beams are faired to their designed curves.

The complete process of "gold-leaf" transom lettering, as performed by Al "Rembrandt" Gerundo, of Alameda, California. It's done on the transom of an all-wood, high-performance, custom racing yacht intended as a production prototype that costs "somewhere between one or two hundred thousand, depending on customer options." When was the last time you saw 24-karat gold-leaf applied, much less on such a vessel?

"What kind of boats?"

"Fishermen."

"Sails or engine?"

"Oh, sails, for sure. But they'll have engines, too."

I turn, noticing a dusty, framed print hanging on a post, and ask, "Any particular model? What plans did you use?" A weathered old face, seen often in books about the sea, looks calmly out from the dark print, and I slowly recognize Captain Joshua Slocum himself as I hear the answer . . . .

"*Spray.* Both of them."

Well, Slocum would be proud, let me tell you. The man who, in 1894, rebuilt a decrepit old oysterman, a fat little New England sloop no more than 37 feet overall, and with it sailed the first singlehanded circumnavigation of the earth, would be very proud indeed.

"Listen, how would you feel about a magazine article about these boats?"

"Sure, fine, wouldn't mind a bit. I ought to bring it up at the next meeting, though."

"Meeting?"

"We're a cooperative. The others might not want the publicity, you know. A bunch of sightseers around here would be a pain."

"A cooperative . . . ."

"We each pay $15 a month, share tools, books, the planer, bandsaws, jointer . . . and that."

"That" took my breath away. Towering 8 feet tall, painted dark green with ornate yellow trim, its great black motor and drive-belts hidden behind a safety-cage, stood the finest old "ship's saw" I have ever, ever seen, an absolute beauty with a counterbalance and heavy worm-gear adjustment for *everything*, a bed that stayed level while the carriage tilted . . . an enormous, ancient creation, the sheer mechanical magic of which made it far more than an ordinary boatbuilder's bandsaw.

"God . . . damn!"

"Nice, eh?" He paused to oil a bearing. Then he punched a button, let the saw reach operating speed, and slid a piece of seasoned oak under the sharp blade, almost as if it wasn't there . . . it seemed like a lesson in cutting butter.

"Fifteen dollars a month?"

"Well, there's a lot of us."

How much did you spend on the boat so far?"

"Oh, maybe $300. I don't know what the other one cost. Sawn frames and treenails helped; used screws and bolts only where I had to." He walked back to the stern and said, "See these? I cut and squared some hard copper wire for these little rivet nails, and I used pennies for

washers." Sure enough, honest Abe Lincoln was diligently holding the transom together, his face gracing scores of homemade "burrs," or "clinch rings."

"Where'd you get the lumber?"

He walked forward to a frame that seemed darker than most. "This one and a couple of others are pieced together from an old tug down on the mud." He pointed at the stem. "Old hotel." The planking was all scrap lumber, except below the waterline. "That I bought at a salvage yard, cheap." And so on . . . .

It was getting dark, the sun easing down behind the hills. I wrote down directions for returning, suggested that my magazine-article idea be brought up at the next cooperative meeting ("a lot of people need to know that this can be done"), and promised to bring my cameras next time. "I'll be back."

So much for those of you who "can't afford it." Yet, how does one answer someone who supposedly "can afford better" than wood construction, someone with the money to buy or build anything on the market? Until recently, wood was at a disadvantage. Traditional plank-on-frame work, at least in large vessels, is limited by the scarcity of heavy timber; while the forests of North America were once almost so thick that a squirrel (a real crazy one) could have started west in New York, jumping from tree to tree, and never coming to earth until he hit San Francisco, today the idea of large, cheap, expendable wood ships is pure fantasy. In smaller craft, however, quality plank-on-frame construction lives on, especially in cruising boats, "character" vessels, and a variety of commercial fields.

That's all well and good, you say, but what about modern, light-displacement boats, specifically racing sailboats? It has already been shown that cold-molded wood construction can produce beautiful, easily maintained, and highly competitive smaller sailboats at a reasonable price. Thomas Wylie, Gary Mull, and the Gougeon brothers are among several designers and builders out to prove the point, and they are succeeding.

What brings me back to the original question — what about the sailor who wants it all, and *can* afford it? Is it now possible to get size, competitive speed, low maintenance, luxurious accommodations, strength, and beauty in a wooden sailboat? Here I'll let facts speak for themselves, because I'm dealing with what many experts in the boating industry consider to be "the last frontier" in production boatbuilding, a development fully as important as the introduc-

tion of fiberglass 20 years ago: the return of the luxury racing "yacht" — in wood.

The pictures shown on these pages (except page 34) are of a 42-foot cold-molded, racing sailboat built by Thomas Wylie Design Group of Alameda, California. The first Wylie 42 was commissioned by Elliot Siegel of Chicago, Illinois, will very definitely be competitive under the International Offshore Rule, will be named *No Go 8*, and is worth well over $100,000.

The construction of *No Go 8*, after detailed lofting, began with a "strongback" . . . thick, heavy lumber assembled into a rigid, ladder-shaped, and level framework over which the hull was built upside down; the strongback provides both support and accurate reference points. Large mahogany "ring-frames" were then laminated, as were spruce deckbeams and a full-length mahogany keelson. The frames and beams, having been clamped and glued to proper contours on floor or wall jigs protected with waxed paper, were then tapered, planed, radiused, and sanded, after which they were bonded to the perimeters of internal bulkheads cut from Bruynzeel mahogany plywood. Gougeon Brothers' epoxy resin glue (WEST System) was used throughout.

Vertical posts and diagonals were next set up on the strongback to locate permanent bulkheads and temporary plywood stations (to be cut out after planking). The keelson was positioned overhead along the centerline, then glued, clamped, and bolted to frames. Before fairing and beveling began, gaps formed along the intersections of keelson and frames were filled with laminated mahogany. The transom and floors were then fitted into place.

One noteworthy aspect of *No Go 8*'s construction is that much of the boat's interior was installed before planking began; engine beds, hanging lockers and shelves, bunks, and galley — all were put in while the hull was still a mere skeleton. Once you get used to working upside down, the accessibility provided by this sequence makes sense (there is no climbing in and out of a finished hull, carrying large sections of wood).

A more subtle reason for this method is that *No Go 8*'s "modular" interior must do structural duty as well. In a racer, any excess weight is a potential handicap to speed, so even the ordinary hanging lockers serve to stiffen the boat. Besides connecting one bulkhead to another, most of the interior is also securely attached to the hull. The result is a lightweight, rigid system of boxes, much like a "monocoque" racing car or aircraft fuselage. The easiest way to accom-

plish this result is, first, to let the outboard edges of all interior panels extend beyond their intended dimensions until the frames, keelson, etc., are faired and beveled, then to install and trim interior components so that they will everywhere touch the future inside surface of the hull. After provisions are made for access and proper drainage, the spruce sheer clamp is laminated in place, the boat is planked, and interior panels are bonded to the hull with an epoxy "fillet."

No Go 8 was strip-planked longitudinally with Port Orford cedar measuring ⅝ inch by 1 inch. One edge of each strip was rounded to a (convex) 5/16-inch radius, the opposite edge hollowed to a slightly greater radius; the effect produced, when the strips are glued and stapled together (and to the frames), is very much like tongue-and-groove floor paneling, only curved. At this point, after fairing with block planes, one has constructed what is essentially a "plug," or mold, over which a series of cold-molded boats might be built. The difference in the Wylie 42 is that the plug becomes a permanent part of the boat; final diagonal planking on *No Go 8*, thinner than would be the case on an equivalent cold-molded boat without longitudinal strips, was thus four ⅛-inch layers of western red cedar, stapled and glued carefully to avoid air pockets, each layer bonded at a 90-degree angle to the one below and in some areas reinforced with carbon graphite fiber. The entire hull was then covered with thin fiberglass cloth and clear resin, followed by wet-sanding and polyurethane; the deck (a laminate of 9, 6, and 4 mm mahogany plywood) is finished likewise.

The sophisticated design and accommodations of the Wylie 42 surpass even such industry standards as the C & C Custom 42 and Nautor Swan 431 cruiser/racers, among others. With modern cold-molded work, wood is now dimensionally stable, free from rot and leakage, and, assuming good workmanship, just as strong, light-weight, and low-maintenance as any other material now in use. One further advantage is that a wood vessel doesn't have to be ashamed of its appearance. There is nothing funnier than boat advertisements saying, "You won't see any fiberglass below decks . . . it's all covered with beautiful wood." True enough, all those fiberglass, steel, and aluminum yachts are carrying around a lot of extra weight, just so their interiors don't give them away!

Rags to riches . . . you can easily afford it, and now you can't buy any better.

How to Build *Piccolo:*
A Seaworthy Sail & Paddle Canoe

Bob Baker

*I*N DECADES PAST, *most boating magazines regularly featured articles on how to build a particular boat, including full specifications and plans. The articles became more infrequent as production-line boats predominated and amateur boatbuilding declined. In the belief that amateur and small-scale commercial endeavors form the bedrock of wooden boatbuilding, WoodenBoat has attempted to foster the free exchange of information. We therefore took up the practice of publishing how-to-build articles, of which quite a number have appeared to date, and undertook to market scaled boatbuilding plans of appropriate designs.*

Piccolo, one of the boats in our how-to-build series, came about as the result of our desire for a sailing/paddling canoe that looked good, performed well, and would be seaworthy enough for crossing open bays. We had hoped it would be half-decked, but such was not possible if the boat was to be kept within the weight limits of portability for one person. We are proud to have commissioned Bob Baker of Westport, Massachusetts, to design and build Piccolo, and we expect to continue with such projects with other builders in the future.

THE WONDERFUL One-Man Boat, or, more accurately the Perfectly Respectable Two-Person Boat, started out as a very simple proposition. "What is needed," said Jon Wilson, "is a 12-foot boat for one person, light enough to be easily carried, and very car-toppable, to be propelled with a double paddle." So four of us sat down in *WoodenBoat*'s office on a cold, rainy day in November to talk about it. The fellow in the easy chair pointed out that it is great good fun to go to sea with a friend; someone sitting on the floor thought it would be nice to steer her with foot pedals; and someone else wanted the beast to sail. Not bad for one 12-foot canoe-

Making the molds.

Above—Setting her up.

Laminating the stem.

Joining the stem and keel.

type thing. At least nobody wanted six berths, a head, and a galley.

I was just a little leery of trying to carry two large people safely in a normal 12-foot canoe hull, so I threw out the whole clinker-built canoe concept and started from scratch. The principal dimensions were easy. I stretched her out to 12 feet 8 inches to give her more lift in the ends without making the deckline too full. Thirty inches beam is about all that can be managed comfortably with a double paddle, so that's what she has. The end result is a very fine-lined, burdensome hull with some pretensions of seakeeping ability. She has heavy stems to take banging on rocks and things, and since there is no centerboard, she has a relatively deep keel the length of her. The keel was given quite a bit of rocker to improve her turning ability.

The rig, since you could hardly expect to get up and run around the boat to handle it, had to have as few moving parts as possible, having everything lead to within easy reach of one person, and be short enough so that all the spars would stow comfortably inside the boat. Also, it had to be large enough to drive the boat, as I wanted her to really sail, not just look like she might. The ketch rig seemed obvious from the start. You can get a reasonable amount of area in the two sails, spread out fore and aft to balance the deep ends and set low enough not to overpower her. The standing lug is ideal. All it requires is a halyard, a downhaul, and a sheet. Lead the halyard and sheet to jam cleats within reach of one person and you're in business. Jam cleats are used so you can dump the whole mess in an emergency.

So what we came up with is a boat that weighs 51 pounds stripped, paddles easily, and sails very well. She will carry about 400 pounds in decent weather, will keep the sea out in bad weather with one aboard, and in general will do whatever is required of her. With her long keel, she will run straight in any combination of wind and wave, but she will not be much interested in turning on her heel. And she isn't a dewdrop sailer, as she draws about 8 inches loaded. I certainly would not recommend her for whitewater work, but for poking around rivers and harbors, and along the coast in decent weather, she does very well.

So, having committed the whole mess to paper, leaving out a few small details that were subject to change without notice, I got an OK from The Editors and we commenced to build her. Since I had never designed or built a hull of this nature before, I rather expected a few surprises.

The first surprise came in lofting—the long,

easy lines of the hull don't leave you much room for error. We found ourselves moving the battens by 32nds to make them come fair. Generally, if a batten doesn't run through an intersection just where it should, you can nudge it with your toe and set another nail. Not so here. The nudge will produce a hump or a hook without half trying. The point here is not to scare you before you start, but rather to be sure you loft the boat very carefully.

Take your time. The offsets are correct, I believe, since I picked them up from our own lofting. The lines are drawn to the inside of the planking, so you don't have to deduct anything, but the inner rabbet and the bearding line must be drawn to allow for ¼-inch planking. I took the angle of the plank to the keel at the midship section and used that as a constant angle for the back rabbet. So instead of a 90-degree angle, you have one a little shallower, which effectively leaves you a little more wood between the rabbets in the stems. This is not necessary, but every little bit helps here. Enough said about the lofting. It's perfectly straightforward as long as you're accurate.

Now that the boat is laid out on the floor, you begin to see that she is really a very small boat, but don't worry — you can fit into her.

In picking up patterns, the Mylar method seems to work very well. Trace the pieces on Mylar and cut the patterns out with scissors. The Mylar is stiff enough to be drawn around.

Molds are gotten out of pine planed on two sides for accuracy. I built the boat upside down on a building horse that gets used for everything here. It consists of two pieces of 2-inch by 6-inch spruce, 16 feet long, separated by 4-inch by 4-inch posts set on the floor. It's tall enough to provide a comfortable working height. The molds then have a centerpiece that fits tightly down between the rails of the horse. On this, it is a relatively simple matter to square and true the molds. The ends of the molds can, of course, be carried to the floor in the usual way. There is no need to bevel the molds, as the strain on them is not great and the corners — edges — won't cut into the planking. Bear in mind that the molds forward of amidships are set on the after side of the station mark, and the molds aft are set on the forward side of the mark.

The stems, or the stem and the post, are made of spruce to keep the weight down. If you have access to spruce knees, fine. Otherwise, the stems must be laminated. The laminations should follow the inner, rather than the outer, line of the stem. This allows for a little less bend, but it will keep the plank fastenings from falling

The backbone in place.

Checking for fairness.

The garboards clamped in place.

The garboard fastened.

Below — Hanging the broadstrake.

Fastening the broadstrake.

Below — Patterns show the shapes of the planks.

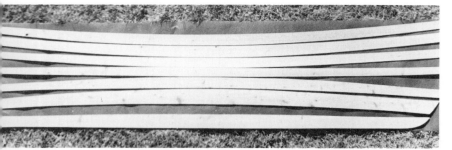

in the same line of grain. Since the two ends have very nearly the same rake, one jig will do for both the stem and the post, or you can make one thick stem and saw it in half. One-eighth-inch laminations seem to be good. Epoxy does a grand job of sticking things together, but it sure can get messy!

While the stems are curing, get out the keel and keel batten. Again, for the sake of weight, I used ash. One plank I used had a sweep to it that just matched the rocker, so the keel was sawn to shape, but the keel could have been sprung to shape just as easily. The grain in the keel batten should be as straight as possible, since ash tends to warp as it dries. To save a little more weight, taper the keel from ¾ inch at the rabbet to ½ inch at the bottom. Stems are also tapered to a ½-inch face. The keel and batten are screwed together, using 1-inch #8 bronze screws, one at each end and one 2 inches forward of the station marks. That will keep them out of the way of the frame fastenings. Clean up the stems so they are sided ¾ inch, cut them to shape, and rabbet them. They are fastened to the keel with two screws and epoxy. When the epoxy has set up, you can clean up the rabbet where the stem meets the keel and cut the back rabbet in the keel.

Set the backbone assembly into the molds and check each mold to be sure everything is all right. The easiest way to keep the keel where it belongs is to wedge it down with posts from the ceiling. If, for some reason, you can't do that, use small angle brackets screwed to the batten and to the molds. It's hard to get the screws out after she's planked, so don't use the brackets if you don't have to.

With the molds set in place and the keel on them, run four or five light, springy ribbands over the molds to check the setup for fairness. Let the ribbands run naturally over the molds and hold them down with a single round-headed screw at each mold. Any unfairness will show up like a sore thumb, and the offending mold must be raised, lowered, shaved, or padded to rectify the situation. At this point, checking for fairness is more a matter of eye than measure, although a few quick measurements can help you decide what's wrong.

So, with everything together and placed where you want it, you can start thinking about the planking. Having been brought up with eastern white cedar, I consider it the best stock there is. And, of course, the best of it comes from Massachusetts, Rhode Island, and Connecticut. The only trouble is that it's nearly impossible to find clear stock in any size, so I'll admit to a few alternatives. The eastern cedar from the Carolinas is a little brittle and in center cuts has a tendency to split right down the middle. Northern, or Maine, cedar is quite acceptable if you don't mind lots of knots. A knot at the edge of a plank — or worse, half a knot — can be disastrous. Western red cedar does like to split, and Port Orford and Alaskan cedar are both a bit heavy. However, all the cedars are quite usable.

I suppose your planking stock choice depends on personal preference and what you are used to. If you haunt the local mills long enough, you may find just what you want in your own backyard. Just remember that you are dealing with ¼-inch stuff. If a plank or a species is going to be a bad actor, it will act twice as badly in very thin sizes. When push comes to shove, you can plank with spruce from the local lumberyard. Pick the piles for reasonably clear, tight stock, and you're home free. All these planks can be gotten out in one length, so get stock 10 inches wide and 14 feet long, if possible. A nice piece of mahogany for the sheer plank sets off the lines of the boat to advantage. Honduras mahogany is heavy — like oak — but Philippine will do well, as will a piece of Spanish cedar, if you can find it.

In lining off the molds for the planks, please take a little extra time to get your planks visually correct. Avoid planks much over 4 inches wide, as they will split more easily than narrow ones. Also avoid any tendency toward downward hooks in the ends. You should have wider planks in the bottom and topside, narrow ones at the turn of the bilge. Try to get one plank to run through the tightest part of the turn from end to end. Always bear in mind that the shape of the planks in a clinker-built hull can make or break the appearance of the finished boat.

If you wish, you can measure my planking diagram and go from there. Notice that my garboard and second plank are both 4½ inches wide when you include the ½-inch lap. This leaves 3½ inches unsupported, but I got away with it, and you can too, if you're careful. After the boat has been lined off to your satisfaction, you can start planking.

The garboard is the only plank that will require soaking. The twist at the ends is just too great to take a chance on, so fit the planks roughly and soak them thoroughly. I dropped ours in the river for the night. Clamp them up on the molds and stems, and go away to let them dry out again. This is a good time to get out frame stock, which will be ¼-inch by ½-inch ash, not necessarily straight-grained, but not with the grain running out badly either. Cut the frames on a table saw, plane them out by hand

Planing the sheerstrake fair.

Below — Planking complete and off the molds.

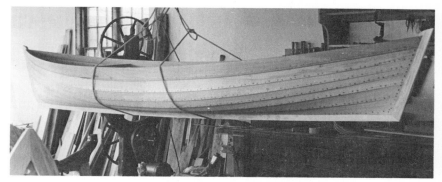

Clenching the laps.

Marking the frame centerlines on the sheer clamp.

With three frames clamped in place, the clench nailing begins.

Below — Sheer clamps are sprung in place, clamped, and clench nailed through the sheerstrakes.

The spruce shelves notch over the frames against the top of the second plank down.

Below — The thwarts notch snugly over the shelves, to which they are fastened.

on the bench, and chamfer off the inside corners. The frames are one length from gunwale to gunwale, so 6-foot stock is in order.

When you are sure the garboards have dried out, make the final fits, cut the bevel for the lap at the ends, and fasten them in place. The planking is so thin that the only acceptable lap is a dory lap. Shiplap won't do. Start the lap about 18 inches from the end of the plank. For fastenings, use ¾-inch #6 bronze screws in the stems and ⅝-inch copper tacks in the keel batten, about 2 inches apart. *Always* bore a hole the size of the fastening's shank in the planking. If you don't, the thin cedar will almost certainly split. I know from experience. Bore into the keel batten with a drill two sizes smaller and not quite the full depth of the tack.

Incidentally, I believe the planking for this boat should be very dry. Presumably, the boat will not be in the water long enough at any one time to do much swelling, but since this boat will most likely be on top of a car at highway speeds, she will dry out quickly. To keep her from opening up, use dry wood.

All right, the garboards are fastened and it's time to bevel the laps for the next plank. Use a short piece of straight stock, place one end on the mark for the top of the next plank, and plane the outboard face of each garboard until the piece lies flat. Do this at every mold and then connect the flats. Real care is required in beveling, and without it, the next plank cannot be spiled. The fastenings will pull the two planks together whether the bevels are perfect or not, and if the bevels are wrong, you will put a terrible strain on the planks. So go gently.

With the bevel cut on the garboards to your satisfaction, get out the second plank. I found out from experience that the planking is so limber that putting it in a vise to plane the edges is less than satisfactory. Instead, clamp it flat on the bench top with the edge hanging out. Hold your plane — a small modelmaker's plane is ideal — in one hand and plane the edge true. When clamping in the new plank, start amidships and work fore and aft. This will make the plank lie fair with no bulges. So check the fit, cut the bevels at the ends, clamp it up again to check the fit of the bevel the whole length, make any corrections, and clamp it up again for fastening.

It is up to you whether or not you put flexible compound in the laps. If you feel there are bumps and humps in the joint, run in a very thin film of Life-Calk or a similar compound. If you feel you've done a good job and all is smooth and true, don't put anything in the joint.

Now you have to measure out the spacings for the fastenings and frames. The frames are to be 3 inches on center, which means there will be a frame on every station line and three in between. Mark frame locations on the lap of the plank you've just clamped on. I used plank fastenings 1 inch apart, so there are two fastenings between frames. Mark those on the lap. The fastenings go in the center of the lap, but for safety, stagger the line of fastenings ⅛ inch apart. This will provide a space ³⁄₁₆ inch from the edge of the plank to the first line of fastenings, ⅛ inch between, and ³⁄₁₆ inch to the edge of the other plank. With all this marked on the lap, bore for the plank fastenings, but not for the frame fastenings. Here again, bore for the shank size of the ⅝-inch copper tacks.

The planks are clench nailed, or clench tacked, if you prefer. If you've never tried clench nailing, practice first on some scrap stock. The point of the tack should be placed diagonally across the grain, and as the tack is driven home, the point should *turn up and in* toward the main part of the plank, rather than down toward the edge. Don't try to set the head any more than flush with the surface of the plank. It's not necessary to go farther, and the hammer head can crush the plank.

After you have fastened in the first pair of planks above the garboard, get out and fit the next pair. When getting out planks for any boat, I think it's a good idea to make the first plank for, say, the starboard side, the second for the port side, and alternate sides all the way up. This way, you can even out any small discrepancies in the molds and your plank lines will come out even. It's even more important in this canoe, where a little error makes a big difference. As you add planks, keep track of the plank lines to be sure both sides are going up evenly, especially at the ends, where a difference really shows up.

Now having fitted the next pair of planks to perfection, clamp them one at a time and mark them carefully for your fastenings. Remember that the frames must be kept parallel to the station lines or molds, or square to the keel, as you prefer to think of it. Remember to stagger the fastenings or run the risk of splitting the plank. Keep all this in mind as you go, and the line of fastenings will come out beautifully straight and even all the way up the side.

When you get to the plank below the sheer plank, stop a minute and consider something new. The sheer plank, whether it is spruce, cedar, or mahogany, will look very good with a nice ⅜-inch bead cut in the lower edge of it. When the bead is cut, though, there is very little wood left between the bead and the rest of the plank, so it is not safe to fasten through the

Fitting the mast step.

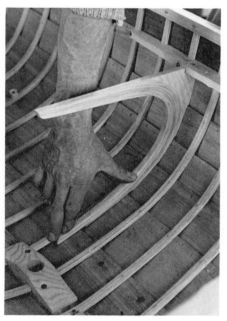

Hanging knees notch over the planking.

Below — Thwarts, shelves, and knees tie the structure together.

Above — Looking forward, showing the foot pedals in place.

Floorboard pairs are cleated together beneath and held down with turnbuttons.

Above — Backrests are sawn out of cedar, and four stiffeners are riveted to the after sides.

The push/pull tiller can rest in the notch cut in the backrest.

bead. Therefore, to get good fastening room, you must increase the width of the lap from ½-inch to ⅞ inch, adding the equivalent of the ⅜-inch bead. Then you can fasten above the bead in safety.

Cutting the bead is no great problem, but it is a good idea to grind a little off the inside corner of the plane iron so it doesn't cut the groove too deeply. At the ends, where the plank is beveled, you will have to let the plane run out and cut the bead progressively less deeply by hand, or you will cut right through to the other side of the plank.

With the bead cut, you can hang and fasten the sheer plank, take off all the clamps, and stand back to admire your handiwork, but there are two more things to do before she can be taken off the molds. First, bore for all the frame fastenings, which will be 1-inch #13 *nails*, not tacks. They are larger by one drill size than the tacks, so bore accordingly. These holes must be in nice straight lines or the fastenings will come through the sides of the frames, or worse, clear of them.

One last thing. Fit stretchers inside the hull from sheer to sheer at, or close to, stations 2, 4, 9, and 11. Now you can let go whatever is holding the keel down and wiggle her up off the molds. This will require one person to lift at each end. Set her in a padded cradle of some sort on a pair of sawhorses, and take a good look at what you've done.

Any fastening that isn't properly clenched can be taken care of now. Then she should be sanded thoroughly inside and given a good dose, on the inside only, of linseed oil cut in half with turpentine. The next project will be to fit the sheer clamps, so let the oil soak in overnight so you don't get it all over you and your work.

Now that the oil has had a chance to soak in properly, let's continue. The first thing to do is mark a centerline for the frames. Use a limber batten or a piece of broken bandsaw blade, bend it into the boat gunwale to gunwale, and draw a line through all the predrilled holes. This is one of the two places where a friend is a great help. Chances are that the line won't pass nicely through all the holes but as long as it comes close, you're in business. If it doesn't even come close to some holes, you will have to plug and redrill them.

Next thing is the sheer clamps. Some people call them "inwales," but that seems to me to be a cumbersome name. A sheer clamp is just what its name implies — it clamps everything together at the sheer. The *Piccolo*'s clamp is a piece of ½-inch by ¾-inch spruce long enough to go from the stem to the sternpost in one length. (I went to the local lumberyard and picked through the piles of 2 x 6 framing stuff until I found a good clear one.) Cut one end to fit nicely against the side of the stem, start bending and clamping at the bow, and work aft to the stern, making sure the clamp lies tightly against the sheer plank all the way. At the stern you can cut the clamp to length by eye and then plane it to fit tightly against the side of the post — so tightly that it wedges a bit.

When the sheer clamp is nicely fitted and all clamped in, mark the centerline of each frame on the underside of the sheer clamp, then take it out and cut the taper at each end for the breasthooks. Set it aside and do the same for the other one. You can notch the clamp for the frame heads now or wait until later; it doesn't make much difference.

At this point, someone is sure to ask why I use a closed or capped gunwale rather than an open gunwale; that is, one with a lighter sheer clamp fastened on the inside of the frame heads and open between. I believe the closed gunwale makes a tighter, stronger, and better-looking job. However, if an open gunwale is your desire, you can make the clamp thinner — 5/16 inch by 3/4 inch — and deal with it accordingly. Obviously, neither type can be fitted until after the boat is framed, so let's get on with that.

Before you start framing, refer to the construction plan and locate and mark lightly the position of the four shelves in the boat. These are fastened with rivets at every other frame, so mark these holes on the outside of the boat and do not put the frame fastenings into them until later.

Presumably you have already cut and planed the frame stock and have made half a dozen extra frames for breakage. The night before you start framing, put the whole bundle of frames to soak either in the bathtub or in any other container that is long enough. A 6-foot piece of plastic drain pipe capped at one end works well. You can frame singlehanded, but it's painful. You'll be a lot happier if you can find a friend to help.

So in the morning get up steam in the box and have at it. The procedure is to bend in three or four frames starting in the center of the boat, and then clamp and nail them. Then bend in three or four more, working alternately fore and aft. As each frame goes in, bore for and drive a 3/4-inch ring nail through it and into the keel. These nails should be staggered about 1/4 inch on each side of the centerline to keep the keel from splitting. The usual way to make a frame lie flat against the planking is to give it a good rap on the head to drive it down, but don't

Rudder and tiller rigged and ready. Note the mizzen sheet lead.

Tiller/yoke detail.

Halyard and downhaul detail.

do it to these delicate ones or you'll start a crack somewhere.

Although it doesn't take very long to write or read about framing, the job seems to go on interminably. Various people have helped me frame, and most have quit from boredom, so pick your friend with care.

The frame heads are cut off on an angle, ³⁄₁₆ inch below the sheer out against the plank and ½ inch below it on the inside. Make a jig from a short length of scrap from the sheer clamp to mark them all evenly. The frames are cut this way to leave the most frame and take the least out of the notch in the sheer clamps. Having done this, notch the clamps to take the frame heads and bend the clamps one at a time into the boat. These are fastened with 1-inch copper nails driven from the inside at each frame, as well as a couple of nails beyond the frames at each end. Clench the nails up over the sheer plank so the guards will hide their ends.

The breasthooks will go in next. Naturally grown crooks of apple, ash, and oak are best. The breasthooks are small, so you can saw them out of a rough limb with a small bandsaw or worry them out with a handsaw. Try to get both breasthooks out of the same crook so the grain and color will match at the two ends. If you can't find a crook or don't want to cope with cutting one, the shape can be laminated, or as a last resort, you can use straight-grain hardwood. But be aware that straight-grain stuff has very little strength when used as a knee and should be avoided if possible.

The breasthooks should be fitted to stand just a little above the top of the sheer clamps so they can be dressed off to a slight crown. They are fastened with a rivet through their ends and two bronze screws along each side. Now with a small plane, well sharpened and set close, clean up the tops of the sheer planks and plane the breasthooks to a slight crown. Bore a ³⁄₈-inch hole in the after breasthook to make a fairlead for the mizzen sheet.

Guard rails come next. I made these of ash to save a little weight, but oak is perfectly good. Or, if your sheer plank is a light-colored wood, Honduras mahogany might look fine. Try not to use a softwood, as the guards will chafe quickly. The guards are ⁵⁄₁₆ inch by ½ inch, planed half round. Cut them to fit exactly and nail them in place with ¾-inch ring nails. Where the guards feather out to nothing on the stem and sternpost, use a small ½-inch screw rather than a nail, which might cause the guards to slip.

The shelves are spruce, ½ inch thick, molded 1⅛ inches and sawn to shape. They fit in flush with the top of the second plank and are riveted through all at every other frame, starting at their ends. The after shelf, since it spans an even number of frames, requires two rivets in a row, and it doesn't make any difference which end of the clamps they are driven in.

The strength of the hull would probably be improved by making the shelf in one length from the bow to the stern, but such a shelf would also add to the weight of the boat and would certainly be nasty to fit. I don't believe the added strength is worth the effort, but try if you like.

Of the four thwarts, the two in the ends are cedar and the middle two are ash. The three that are mast thwarts are 3 inches wide at the ends and swell out to 3½ inches in the middle. The fourth one, since it doesn't do much except hold the boat apart, is 3 inches all the way across. The ends of the thwarts are notched over the frames, and their undersides are relieved to fit down about ³⁄₁₆ inch over the

The Breasthook
The natural-crook breasthooks are handsome and strong. The detail at left shows how they are fitted (before the guard rails). The photo sequence at right illustrates the process of cutting out a pair of breasthooks from a crook. First, the pattern is rough-traced so that a flat can be sawn along one side so that a slab can be sawn off, leaving plenty of surface for the pattern. Next, the other side is slabbed off, leaving plenty of thickness from which to obtain two breasthooks. The two can now be sawn to shape.

shelves. The thwarts must be fitted with some care, since they take the side thrust of the rig.

There are two fastenings at each end of each thwart driven down into the shelves. I used a combination of screws and bolts to be sure the thwarts don't come out. Three thwarts can be fastened now, but don't fasten the after main-mast thwart yet, because it is easier to fit the two hanging knees with the thwart removed.

The knees are ½-inch spruce laminated and fitted very carefully to the planking, jogged at the laps. Since the bend is very tight, I found the laminations had to be a skinny ⅙ inch or they broke. Here again, it is much easier to glue up a single thick lamination (about 1¼ inches thick) and then saw it in half, instead of making two thin ones.

The knees are positioned tightly against the forward side of the frames. Use one rivet on the lower end of each knee and a ¾-inch ring nail at each lap. Be careful here, as these fastenings are very close to the frame fastenings. With the knees fastened to the planking, the thwart is set down over them and fastened on each end to the shelves. Again, use one rivet through the end of the knee, with two or three screws through the thwarts into the knee outboard of this.

The mast steps are ash, 1 inch by 1¾ inches by 6 inches. The holes for the masts are 1 inch in diameter, and the three steps are each notched over the frames to sit tightly on the keel. Two screws, each offset from the center-line at each end, hold them down. Be sure to cut a drain for the mast holes so they won't hold water.

From here on, we'll be getting into the picky part of this little beast. These are finicky little details that are hard to explain and time con-suming to make, but have patience — we're making progress and the end is in sight.

This is a good time to add the stem bands and to sand and oil the outside. The stem bands are ½-inch half-oval brass. At the top of the stem and sternposts, bend the brass over and flatten it as much as you can. Then, with a file, shape the flattened part to match the shape of the stemhead. Bore and countersink for ½-inch #6 screws to be spaced about 8 inches apart. For the oil, use either a linseed and turpentine mix if you intend to varnish, or one of the new pene-trating oil finishes. One word of caution: When the can says "Use with adequate ventilation," it means just that! Penetrating oil can be pure misery in an unventilated space.

And so back to the inside. Floorboards are made as indicated; use leftover plank stock and pieces of broken frames. They can be clench nailed together with ⅝-inch tacks. The two pieces that carry the foot brace are ¾-inch by 1⅜-inch cedar or spruce, whatever you have. These are screwed on top of the floorboards and must be notched over the frames and the partner knees. The foot brace is just a ¾-inch by 1-inch stick cut to ¾ inch square at the ends, and it is dropped into the notches in these pieces. The floorboards are held down with two turnbuttons made of scrap frame stock.

This boat would be quite simple to finish out if only one person were to paddle her. But as soon as you introduce the second person, you are faced with making three adjustable posi-tions for the back rests. The rack, for want of a better name, that holds the backrests is made of ½-inch ash and shaped as shown. Bear in mind that the width across the boat from the notch on the other side has to be the same in all three positions. Therefore, the racks must taper with the beam of the boat. Fasten the racks with ¾-inch #6 screws.

Backrests are relatively simple. I curved them like a chair back to be a little more comfortable, but they could be made flat if you wish. Get them out of 1½-inch cedar or spruce and carve in the curvature. The end result should be ⅜ inch thick.

Four hardwood cleats are riveted across the back; this should help prevent it from splitting. The forward backrest fits in either position in the forward rack, while the after one fits in just one place. The latter, when standing vertically, will be against the thwart. Note that the backrests must tilt back fairly far, so relieve the top and bottom of the notches in the racks accordingly. Enough. If you get through that, you can get through anything.

Now you need three fairleads and three jam cleats. These are all of ½-inch by 1-inch ash. Rivet them through the thwarts, since they take a fair amount of strain.

In addition to the two jam cleats on the after thwart, there are two pins for the mainsheet lead. These are ⅛-inch brass rod — brazing rod is good — about 2 inches long. Hammer a slight head on them and drive them into holes that are a whisker too small so they can't fall out.

Two fairleads must be made for the yoke lines. They are also ½-inch ash and are open so the lines can be dropped in. Make them according to the drawing and fasten them on the face of the frame, tightly against the clamp, with one ¾-inch #6 screw.

At this point, everything that is going into the boat is in, so you can apply whatever finish you desire inside and out and set her aside to dry while you make such accessories as the foot pedals.

Foot pedals are cut as shown out of ½-inch ash and fastened to the foot brace with 2-inch butt hinges. The bottom of each pedal is cut at a 45-degree angle so the pedal will tip aft as well as forward. The keyhole slot in the top outer corner is to take a knot in the end of the steering yoke lines, so relieve the back of the round part to make the knot seat securely.

The rudder design is self-evident. It is made of ½-inch mahogany, oak, or ash — anything that is hard and strong. If you make it in two pieces, use two or three drifts of ⅛-inch brass rod and glue the two pieces together with epoxy. Taper the blade to ¼ inch at the after edge.

This canoe was billed originally as a complete do-it-yourself project for which you had to buy nothing but basic materials. This is true as long as you know something about working metal. If you don't, then our billing is almost true. The rudder hangers are fabricated of strap brass and brass tubing. I went to my friend Tony-the-Blacksmith for these, since he knows more about such things than I do. If you want to try to make them yourself, the four gudgeons are simple enough. But easy? I'm not so sure.

Each gudgeon consists of a ½-inch length of ⁵⁄₁₆-inch-inside-diameter brass pipe or tubing and a length of ⅙-inch by ½-inch brass strap bent around and sweat-soldered to it. Since there is no particular strain on the joint, soft solder will do, but hard solder will be better. Fit one pair carefully to the sternpost and one pair to the rudder. They are attached with two rivets each. Countersink the holes in the straps so the rivet heads can be filed off flush. The rudder is hung with a length of ¼-inch brass rod headed over on its upper end so it won't drop through, and long enough so the rudder will ride up when you go aground.

The rudder yoke is ½-inch oak or ash shaped pretty much to suit yourself as long as you stay within the overall dimensions. When you have the yoke shaped, ship the rudder and try the yoke to be sure it clears the post. The yoke is held in place with a ⅛-inch brass pin through the rudderhead.

Tony Millham also made a brass hook for the tiller. He did such a beautiful job that I hesitated to put it on the boat. You could very well put it on the mantel to be admired. He made the hook with two pieces hard soldered together. The plate is a piece of ⅛-inch stock cut to shape and draw filed to remove excess stock where it is not needed for strength. The hook was drawn from a piece of ¼-inch rod, with a knob forged on the end; it was bent to shape. After it had been soldered to the plate and cleaned up, you couldn't find the joint.

You can make the hook the same way Tony did, but file the taper into the hook before it's bent. Hard soldering, I guess, is easy enough if you know what you are doing. Another method, of course, is to whittle a wooden pattern of the hook and have it cast at a foundry.

When you have the hook made, by whatever method, it is riveted onto one end of the yoke. This, by the way, is the weakest part of the boat. If you jam the tiller when you are getting it on or off, you stand a chance of cracking the yoke. The whole assembly is strong enough to do its intended job as long as you use a little care in getting the tiller on and off.

Speaking of tillers, this one works by being pushed or pulled. It is made of ash, ¾ inch by 1 inch and long enough to reach from the yoke to amidships in the boat. Taper it to ¾ inch square at the inboard end and round the last 18 inches for a comfortable handgrip. The hole for the hook is ⅜ inch, deeply countersunk on

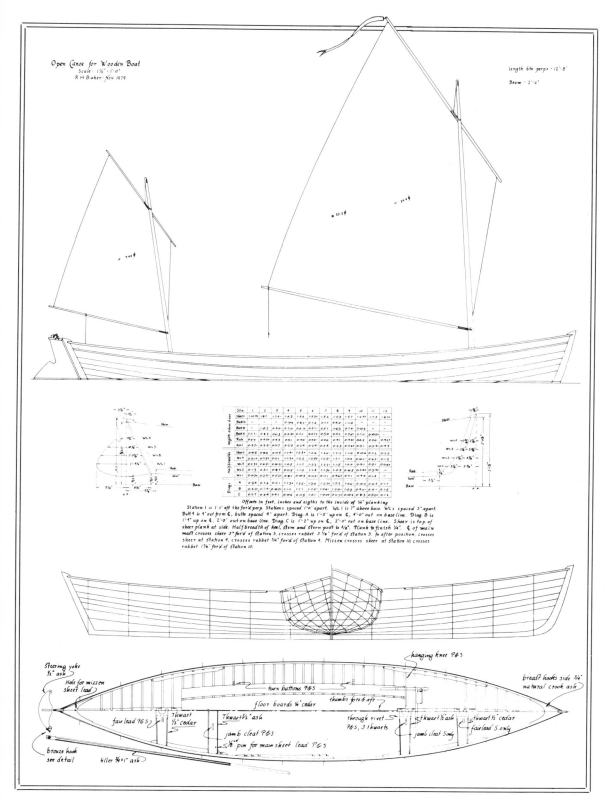

both sides so the tiller will swivel when dropped over the hook. I had a piece of ash on hand with a gentle sweep to it, so I used it for the tiller. The sweep serves no useful purpose except to add to the overall appearance of the boat.

The first time we went sailing, we found that the tiller, if left unattended, had a tendency to drop overboard and stream out behind the boat. Very embarrassing! So I cut a fairly deep, round notch in the top of both backrests near their outboard ends. This notch retains the tiller very nicely. To make doubly sure the tiller stays put, a rope grommet is placed over it and is tied to a thwart.

So there is the hull, complete with all its fittings. Now we need spars.

One of the features of this rig is that it enables one to reduce sail without working too hard at it. Therefore, both masts are designed to fit in any of the three mast thwarts, thus allowing three possible sail combinations. The mizzenmast would look ridiculous if it were the same diameter as the main, so its large diameter is carried only to the height of the highest thwart, and then the diameter is reduced to an appropriate size. Out of the boat, the mizzen looks like a stretched-out tenpin, but in the boat, it's fine.

All the spars can be gotten out of a 2-inch by 10-inch rough spruce staging plank 10 feet long. Go to the lumberyard and pick over their pile of staging planks until you find a decently clear one that measures a fat 2 inches thick.

The masts are straightforward spar making, except for the swelling at the foot of the mizzen; please note that the holes for the halyards are bored at an angle to the centerline of the hull. This provides a fairlead to the yard, which is hung on the port side. With a gouge, relieve the lower side of the hole to make a nice round lead, or "dumb sheave," for the halyard. Don't forget the small wooden jam cleat at the foot for the downhaul. This goes on the centerline and is fastened with a couple of small-diameter screws.

The yard and boom for each sail are the same diameter and very nearly the same length, so don't get them confused.

You have a couple of options for the jaws. I had some kinky apple branches around, so that's what I used. The jaws are only ⅜ inch thick, so the grain must follow the curve or they can be broken easily. A piece of oak with the right kink will do, but stay away from all softwoods. There is no great strain on the jaws in service, but banging around in the boat and on shore can do them in. The other alternative for the jaws is ½-inch brass half-oval, which should be bent to shape a bit oversize and padded with leather or jute twine. Don't forget to bore a ¼-inch hole athwartships at each end of the yards and booms for lashing, and a ¼-inch hole through the boom jaws for the downhauls. Give the whole works two or three coats of paint or varnish and set all the spars out to dry.

Now you have built everything there is to build, and it's time to rig her. A good place to begin is with the steering yoke lines. These are ¼-inch spun Dacron, long enough to lead from the yoke to the foot pedals with a little to spare. They lead down through the yoke with a nice stopper knot on top. A Matthew Walker knot

with a star-shaped leather washer underneath looks well. You can, of course, burn the running ends, but a nicely done drum whipping looks better. The running ends lead forward under the two after thwarts, through the open fairleads, and finish with figure-eight knots on the forward side of the keyhole slots in the pedals. Since there are two positions for the foot brace, you need two knots. Adjust these so that, with tension on the lines, the pedals are leaning slightly forward. After you have used them for a while, you can fine-tune them to your own taste.

I used ¼-inch spun Dacron for both halyards, as it stays limber wet or dry. The halyards are spliced to the yards just behind the jaws. If you used brass jaws, you may have to use small bee blocks to keep the halyards from working forward. They should be about 6 inches aft of the mast. The main halyard leads through the masthead hole, down to the thwart, aft through the fairlead, and through the hole in the jam cleat. Be sure the halyard is long enough so you can tie a stopper knot in its end and still get the yard down into the boat. Now rig the mizzen halyard, which comes down through the fairlead and forward to the jam cleat.

For downhauls use light stuff — ³⁄₁₆ inch or so. These are spliced around the booms, through the holes in the jaws, and led through the hole in the jam cleat. The mainsheet is more ¼-inch Dacron spliced around the boom and through the clew grommet. It leads around one of the pins in the after thwart and then to your hand — it must never be cleated, as that invites disaster. The mizzen sheet of ³⁄₁₆-inch stuff is spliced around the boom directly above the hole, forward through the fairlead at the foot of the mast, and to the jam cleat on the after thwart. This sail is so small that you cleat it safely with no worry.

One last thing. The main needs a nicely made streamer, about 2 inches wide and 3 inches long, attached to the end of the yard.

I should throw in here a few quick thoughts on the paddle. The best length for this boat seems to be 8 feet 6 inches, although 8-foot ones do very well. Since there just isn't room for you and 8 feet of paddle in the boat when sailing, a two-piece jointed paddle is a necessity. In *Sensible Cruising Designs*, L. Francis Herreshoff has a design for a very nice double paddle. Some more 2-inch spruce staging plank would make a good one, but you will have to buy the ferrules for the joint.

So that's about it. Find yourself a friend, pack a good picnic, and go see what the other side of the river looks like.

Sailing Together Around the World

Mary Maynard

*T*HE DREAM *of building a boat and sailing off into the sunset has certainly become a cliché by now. Yet very few dreamers actually pull it off, primarily because building a boat appropriate for long-distance voyaging and then breaking away from shoreside obligations are considerably more difficult than the mind's eye makes them. But the Maynards had the vision to begin (the first step) and the perspicacity to finish (the toughest part) the construction of a replica of Joshua Slocum's* Spray. *Then they launched her and sailed off on the adventure we all envy. Theirs is a classic realize-your-dream tale and a lesson to all of like mind. When Mary Maynard offered the story to us, we were delighted to publish this fine piece.*

MY HUSBAND AND I decided to build a copy of Captain Joshua Slocum's *Spray* for many reasons. We felt a *Spray* would be a comfortable, roomy boat to cruise with our three children. Its workboat finish would be inexpensive to build and easy to maintain. We believed in Slocum and in his descriptions of handling *Spray* and of her seakindly qualities. And, as a romantic clincher, the original *Spray* had been owned in Noank, Connecticut, the village in which we were living.

So we began. I supported our family with my job as a newspaper reporter, and George closed his woodcarving shop and refused further orders. Working from the drawing in our paperback copy of Slocum's *Sailing Alone Around the World*, George expanded and faired the hull lines.

A replica of Joshua Slocum's *Spray, Scud* has visited some of the same waters as the original.

Some old Noankers doubted that such a boat could be built today. "You can't get good white oak no more," they said, recalling the days when pasture oaks, good for knees and framing members, grew nearby. Undaunted, George drove inland to George Franklin Miner's farm in North Stonington. Miner agreed to cut curved logs for deckbeams and floor timbers, and straight-grain oak for frames, stem, sternpost, and rudder.

Yellow pine for planking was no longer shipped into Noank, so again we had to go to the source: Spicer's Lumber & Piling Company in Church Creek, Maryland, which supplied first-class boat boards to Chesapeake Bay boatbuilders. We purchased 2,000 board feet, 1½ inches rough, about 17 feet long, in flitches up to 24 inches wide. In our yard, we stacked the boards with spacers and covered the pile with a tarp. To prevent checking, I painted the ends of each board with a thick goo of pine tar and old paint, and within a month the boards were properly seasoned.

Meanwhile, George lofted the lines full size on plywood sheets, made blueprints, firmed up scantling measurements, and decided how to build and install the framing. In general, he followed old-time Noank practice with gleanings from Slocum. Long sessions with builders Jack Wilbur, Fred Cousins, and Major William Smyth provided a wealth of experience on which to draw.

On May 28, 1971, we raised a glass of wine to the 6-inch by 8-inch oak keel that was finally shored up true to the baseline. The pause didn't last long, for the next day, up went the oak stem, fastened with ½-inch-diameter steel rods. A tenon on the 6-inch by 12-inch by 9-foot oak sternpost was fitted into a mortise in the keel and secured athwartships with an oak dowel; heavy white oak deadwood completed the backbone of the boat we had decided to name *Scud*. The transom, 2-inch by 6-inch white oak planks bolted to a frame of oak 2 x 3s, was secured with six ½-inch galvanized bolts athwartships through the 2 x 8 horn timbers and the sternpost.

It took only two days to set and plumb the molds, which were made of spruce 1 x 6s. Ribbands of 1-inch by 2-inch spruce doubled to form 2 x 2s on 10-inch centers, were faired and nailed to the molds.

To some people, our ship began to resemble the Ark. "When's the rain coming, Noah?" became a familiar query. So when they asked the inevitable, "How big is it?" George responded in Biblical fashion, "Twenty-one cubits and a span long, 8 cubits and a hand wide, and 2 cubits, a span and a hand deep." (That is, 36 feet 9 inches on deck, 14 feet 2 inches beam, and 4 feet 6 inches draft.)

Framing provided an opportunity to include our neighbors in the building. George loaded the steambox (a long cedar box attached by a hose to a gas-fired hot-water heater) with the 1⅞-inch by 2-inch frames, and steamed them for two or three hours. Friends would arrive with their tools to help clamp the hot frames and nail them to the ribbands.

George hand-planed the planking to 1⅜ inch thickness — except for the garboards, which were 2 inches thick. (Buying the lumber milled at a slight extra cost would have saved weeks of work, but we realized this too late.) He lined off the topside planks to 4 inches amidships, tapering to 3 inches at the hood ends. Below the waterline, the planks were put on as wide as possible — up to 14 inches wide on the flat run in the stern. George worked mostly alone, except when he needed help installing the bow and stern planks, which required steaming.

The fastenings were 4-inch galvanized boat nails, clinched inside. Eight ¼-inch bolts held the butts to 2-inch-thick oak butt blocks. All this was done under the watchful (and often critical) eyes of landlubbers. One day, as George and I were wrestling with a hot plank that had to take a 90-degree bend in 14 feet, two men whom we had never seen before drove up and began poking around. After watching us clamping, kicking, wedging, shoring, hammering, and cursing the stubborn plank into place, one man remarked: "What do you do when it all falls down?" It didn't.

When only the deadwood and topsides were planked, George fitted the sawn floor timbers. In the midsection of the boat, the largest floors were 8 inches deep and 4 inches thick and extended from 4 feet to 6 feet athwartships. It would have been much quicker and easier to have put in the floors before planking by just dropping the lower ribbands, but George was afraid — incorrectly — that the frames might lose their shape. Later, he removed the frame from the most curved part of the boat, waited, then bolted it back in. It fit perfectly, proving to his satisfaction that the steamed frames were exerting no stresses trying to straighten themselves out.

Children, passing to and from school daily, kept things light. They inspected the work and passed judgment: "You did a lot of work today, Mr. Maynard." "I'm glad you're putting on a worm shoe so the worms will have a place to live too," or "You must be awful strong to do all that. I'd hate to get in a wrestle with you."

All exposed oak was painted several times during construction with an equal mixture of linseed oil, Stockholm tar, and turpentine. This minimized the problems of shrinkage and twisting as the relatively green oak dried out in the framing of the vessel. Bolts in the joints were taken up as the oak continued to season. Where the transom planks shrank and opened up, pine wedges were glued in before painting.

Less than a year after the keel was laid, the shutter plank went in. We painted the inside of the planking with Cuprinol and filled the deep bilge pockets aft with gravel and hot pitch. Cypress strips, 1 inch by 2 inch, from a dismantled water tank, were nailed in for a ceiling.

All winter and spring a battle had raged over what kind of deck to put on. The traditionalists demanded a plank deck. Friends with a gaff-rigged schooner advised fiberglassed plywood, based on their experience trying to keep a plank deck tight in the tropics. I wanted dry bunks for myself and the kids. George, concerned with aesthetics and also the practical side of living aboard with a family, was undecided. He even penciled a running tally on the side of the boat, gathering the votes of all the sidewalk superintendents, but he relied on the judgment of the old-time boatbuilders. Major Smyth described schooner voyages to Venezuela in the 1920s, when the crew lived under the canvas-covered cabin, not under the leaky deck. "Don't tell anyone I said this," he confided one day, "but there's this new product that will work, called 'fiberglass' . . . ."

George capitulated, and two layers of ½-inch exterior-grade plywood (the lofting boards) with the butts staggered, were epoxied and nailed into the deckbeams, then covered with a layer of polyproplylene cloth and polyester resin. The outer edge of the plywood was covered with an oak rubstrake bedded in synthetic rubber. (Four years later, George overlaid the deck with a layer of 4-inch by ¾-inch Australian hardwood, bedded in bitumin and nailed. We all helped pitch the seams.)

With the deck finished, the audience turned to the subject of caulking. "Who's he going to hire?" they wondered. Oblivious to the speculation, George peered over old-timer Howard Davis' shoulder one afternoon as Davis was caulking the *Nellie*. George's observations and Davis' running commentary on "caulkin' Noank style" were sufficient apprenticeship. On nine successive days, as George caulked our boat, an innovative mockingbird ran through his entire repertoire trying, unsuccessfully, to imitate the ringing music of the caulking mallet. After launching, when spiders were spinning

Less than a year after the keel was laid, the planking was complete.

webs in the bilge, we heard indirectly that Davis was pleased with his teaching.

When a crane came to lift "Noank's Ark" onto a flatbed truck for a trip to the Noank Shipyard, the Flood arrived — the first northeaster of the year. Though it was pouring rain and blowing, a festive spirit prevailed; as *Scud* was towed past the local store, proprietor Jimmy Abruzzi pitched good-luck pennies onto the deck, and someone produced rum in paper cups.

During the previous 18 months, the attitude of our neighbors had changed from an unspoken "How can that boy from Chicago presume to build a New England boat?" to "You ought to see the big project Maynard's got over there." Out of attics and barns articles appeared: adze handles, a huge bandsaw, an antique thickness planer, and a portable electric plane. Models, photos, and books about Slocum and *Spray* were loaned. Gear from other ships arrived: a spar from the Noank schooner *Kathryn*, a 130-pound fisherman anchor, iron ballast bars from the full-rigged ship *Joseph Conrad*, the wheel from Ellery Thompson's dragger *Eleanor*, teak decking from the sandbagger *Annie*, a canvas lugsail from the steamer *Exemplar*'s lifeboat, and a 12-inch portlight from the Baltic trader *Gundel*. Flags, logbooks, a vintage sextant, a Seagull outboard, and innumerable bits and pieces of other people's dreams became part of *Scud*.

On November 11, 1972, about 200 villagers, most of whom had contributed time, moral support, advice, or equipment, braved the cold rainy weather to see *Scud* launched. Our bilge pump, from the 106-year-old Noank sloop *Emma C. Berry*, was hardly necessary, for *Scud* tightened right up. Those who came to the night-long pump-watch had nothing to do but party.

The next day, *Scud* was towed to Groton Long Point lagoon, where George installed the interior. The woodburning stove kept things cozy all winter, although the ice thickened to 6 inches around the hull.

Below decks was finished off fisherman-style. The main cabin contained the stove, wood lockers, galley, kitchen table, settees, and bunks for our three children (then 8, 9, and 11). A crawl-through cargo space with shelved lockers, and five 42-gallon water tanks separated the two cabins. In the aft cabin were the navigation gear, a settee, lockers, and the skippers' double bunk, only inches from the wheel. The forepeak, which had its own hatch, was for gear and sail storage. (Later, when our sons grew, the forepeak was converted for their use, and their old bunks now hold sails.)

George copied the sail plan from *Sailing Alone Around the World* and scaled rigging details from old photos of *Spray*.

As with most home building projects, *Scud* took twice as long and cost twice as much as we had planned. Our original estimate of $3,500 and 18 months' time turned out to be closer to $7,500 and 31 months from lofting to sailaway. But sail away we did.

In 20,000 miles of sailing, we find *Scud* behaves identically to Slocum's descriptions of *Spray*'s performance: comfortable, able, and fast. On our ocean passages we average about 110 miles a day — with good winds we made 370 miles in 48 hours in the Pacific. The 1,000-mile crossing from the Azores to Gibraltar was made in seven days flat, most of the time double-reefed. *Scud* clawed off a lee shore (Keeling-Cocos Island) in a Force-8 gale with full sail set, shipping green water over the lee rail only once.

Like *Spray*, *Scud* will self-steer accurately with the wheel lashed in beckets; she balances and self-steers under any combination of sails and on any point of sail, but she is steadiest with a flying jib set on a pole lashed beyond the bowsprit and the wind on the quarter. A change in wind strength or direction requires putting the wheel up or down a spoke. At sea we usually made adjustments once a day, after the noon sight.

Scud is an anachronism with no electronics gear or engine, but we have no fuss, no muss with diesel oil, fuel bills, or equipment breakdowns. It also means we are not, and cannot be bound to a schedule other than that of wind and weather. We sat for nine days in the Doldrums whistling for the wind, but such is, and always has been, the way of pure sailing ships. We regret not having an engine only when becalmed in the lee of the land, when beating to windward

into a narrow harbor, or when contemplating a daysail with guests. Seldom have we changed our destination because we couldn't sail there.

Our 16-foot oars are *Scud*'s only auxiliary power, replacing a 6½-h.p. Seagull outboard that broke down early in the trip. We use them in very light airs to shoot quickly through the eye of the wind, pulling on one oar and backing the other. We can row *Scud* at ½ knot in calm water, and that often provides just enough speed to give us steerageway.

With practice, and *Sailing Alone Around the World* as our guide, we are learning to get the best from our sails. Our 1,100 square feet of working sails (jib, staysail, main, and mizzen) are heavy, 11-ounce triple-stitched Dacron. We had sailed 2,000 miles before we first set our light-weather (7 ounce) 300-square-foot jumbo jib, instead of the two smaller headsails. We have since added a featherweight drifter, which also doubles as a mizzen staysail. We have replaced our picturesque dipping lug mizzen with a leg-o'-mutton sail, which sets better when close-hauled and is easier to handle.

The gaff mainsail is less of a problem than we had feared: to prevent it from slatting and flogging in a calm, we secure the boom in three directions. It is tied down with ½-inch line to the rail just aft of the shrouds. The end of the boom is guyed forward to a block and tackle at the stemhead and is kept steady by the mainsheet pulling aft.

When we're blasting to windward in a seaway, *Scud* sails on her bottom, not her ear. We heel no more than 15 degrees, regardless of wind strength. Consequently, we need no fiddles on the table, no pot clamps on the stove, and no bunkboards. This stability simplifies sail-handling.

A new panel reefing system makes it possible to reef the main, or shake out a reef, without dropping the sail. When hove-to under double- or triple-reefed main and backed staysail, *Scud* takes the seas just forward of the beam and lies quietly, drifting slowly to leeward.

We are learning the tricks Slocum knew: we tack cargo-schooner fashion, by backing the jib and hauling the mizzen to weather; we try to let the tides work for us by riding them up a channel or across a bay, and once, we drifted up an Australian creek with the flood tide, dropping the anchor just before we reached the dock. The bow stopped and the tide carried our stern around, so we nestled up to the dock facing downstream. We sometimes spin *Scud* out of a snug berth using lines and sail by releasing the bow line, letting the jib fill and turn us away, then casting off astern. Twenty-ton *Scud* can be

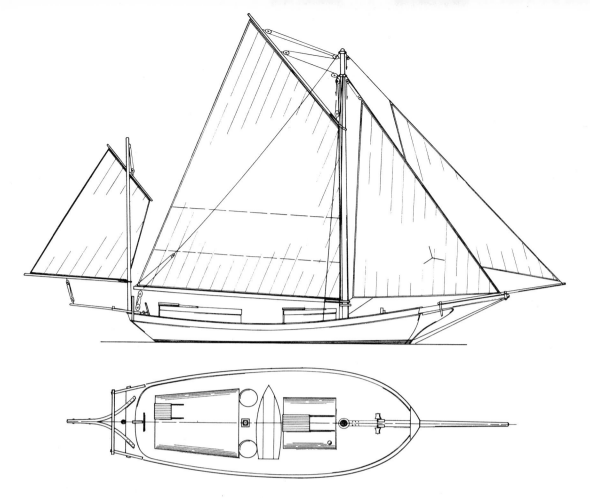

Scud's sailplan
and deck
arrangement.

maneuvered easily in a harbor with lines: we frequently change moorings or shift along a dock by warping, for it gives us more control than sail power or someone else's engine. Kedging into tight places is another way we avoid sailing into trouble.

We depend upon our ground tackle to keep us secure in port. From the catheads hang two 130-pound fisherman anchors, one rigged with 180 feet of ½-inch chain, the other with 50 feet of chain and 120 feet of 1½-inch nylon. In coastal waters we also carry on deck two 40-pound kedges, each with 200 feet of ½-inch line. In sandy anchorages, the 60-pound Danforth replaces one bower. We raise the anchors with a crab windlass and a Spanish burton.

Scud began her voyage with two sets of main shrouds, ½-inch galvanized wire set up on deadeyes and Dacron lanyards. After 12,000 miles, George renewed the shrouds and, because a connecting bolt had broken, he added a third shroud for safety. He parceled and served them full-length with tarred marline — periodic retarring keeps them corrosion-free and weather-tight. At present we have no mizzen shrouds, taking the halyard aft and to weather to provide a running backstay for the mast. We have sailed with mizzen shrouds, but they girt the sail.

Scud has no winches; sheets and halyards are rove through tackles to give sufficient mechanical advantage. The luff of the jib (or jumbo jib) is tensioned, after the sail is raised, with a block and tackle at the tack; a handy billy can be clapped on the jibsheet for more power.

Originally the halyard blocks were shackled to 1-inch eyebolts through the mast, but these sheared enroute. Now, all blocks aloft are shackled to tabs on 3-inch by ¾-inch steel bands clamped around the masthead.

Scud has suffered no dry rot. Because she is a wooden boat, we take normal precautions against worms — painting with soft copper paint every six months and taking great care not to scratch or bang the bottom. In American Samoa, George cut out an 8-inch-long teredo worm that had grown in our bow planking in less than six months. He also repaired worm damage in the rudder and sternpost where the rudder continually chafed off the paint and exposed the wood. He sheathed the problem areas with thin copper to prevent further damage.

We find sailing and maintaining an engineless boat to be a learning experience. There are always little improvements to make, better ways to handle gear. We know what Slocum meant when he said that he learned more seamanship on *Spray* than on any of his previous ships.

A Second Tri

Meade Gougeon

Her windward hull held high, *Rogue Wave* undergoes sea trials. At the time she was built, she represented the latest thinking in both trimaran design and cold-molded construction.

*T*HIS ARTICLE *was one part of a many-faceted section we published on multihull history and development in wood. We published the piece because we wanted to provide a perspective on the evolution of catamaran and trimaran design in this country, while at the same time pointing toward the future of wood in light, fast multihulls.* Rogue Wave, *the trimaran discussed here, was designed by Dick Newick, one of the finest multihull designers at work today, and built by the Gougeon Brothers in their WEST System, a modern adaptation of cold-molded wood construction. Such a method, pioneered by author Meade Gougeon and his brothers Jan and Joel, and featuring the use of specially formulated epoxy resins, represents a side of the technology of wooden boatbuilding that is most assuredly part of the future.*

After sailing Rogue Wave *successfully in a number of ocean races, Phil Weld, the owner, had yet another cold-molded trimaran (*Moxie*) built and went on to win the 1980 singlehanded transatlantic (OSTAR) race in record time.*

I N 1972, when we were beginning to popularize our Wood Epoxy Saturation Technique (WEST) system of wooden boat construction, we heard rumors that Phil Weld of Gloucester, Massachusetts, had hired Dick Newick to design a giant 60-foot ocean-racing trimaran. We called and made our pitch, but the job had alrady been given to an eastern yard. The tri was to be built of fiberglass foam sandwich — a popular material at the time. Weld called his new boat *Gulf Streamer* and sailed her very hard for the next few years.

Four years later I met Phil at the 1976 World Multihull Symposium in Toronto. He had just lost *Gulf Streamer* a few months before, having flipped her upside down in mid-Atlantic and survived in her interior for five days before rescue. Even though he was still depressed, he talked of buying a used multihull or perhaps building a new one. I told him that if he planned to build, we would like to take a look at the job. A month later we got a call from Dick Newick, who asked if we'd like to build another 60-foot version of *Gulf Streamer*. After a visit by Dick and Phil, and several telephone calls, we agreed to a contract, and in the fall of 1976 we started the construction of *Rogue Wave*.

Dick Newick had designed *Gulf Streamer* "right" in the first place. There were no major design changes for the new version, save that she was now to be built of wood; only minor alterations were to be made to the cabin and hull shapes. This was to be the largest wooden structure we had ever built. Even Dick Newick, who had built many boats out of wood, had never engineered a wooden structure this large.

Structurally, multihulls must deal with many complex engineering problems that do not have to be dealt with in monohull sailboats. Whenever two or more hulls are permanently connected and subjected to a raging seaway, a number of problems occur simultaneously. Strong forces try to separate the hulls from one another, and racking or twisting forces — the worst and least-understood force — create problems that begin to fatigue materials. It was obvious that a lot of attention would have to be given to critical areas of the structure.

Gulf Streamer suffered a number of problems that we corrected in *Rogue Wave*. At 17,000 pounds, *Gulf Streamer* was about 4,000 pounds over the weight desired by the designer. She sat low in the water at the transom, causing undue amounts of drag; yet, she was very strong and never had any structural damage through her thousands of miles of heavy-weather sailing — a tribute to her designer and builder. But she was also a flexible boat, and the consequence of this was her inability to keep a taut forestay. This prevented her from being as fast as her designer had expected her to be, though she had done well in some races. Another factor was simple aesthetics: her interior was not very pretty, and the nicest thing that anybody had to say about it was that it was functional.

Our primary construction goal for *Rogue Wave* was to build a boat strong enough to withstand any sea condition on any ocean in the world. Our second goal was to provide a solid, rigid (and beautiful) structure that would not flex when subjected to high loads or heavy seas. And, finally, we wanted *Rogue Wave* to have a bare-boat weight of 12,000 pounds — a full 5,000 pounds, or 30 percent, lighter than *Gulf Streamer*.

Rogue Wave must have the distinction of being the largest wood structure ever built relying solely on adhesive bonding as the major fastening method for its thousands of pieces and parts. In the entire structure, probably fewer

Beneath the smooth, apparently one-piece exterior lies an intricate network of plywood, timber, veneer, and epoxy. This is a view of the main hull taken from the port outrigger. Construction of the interior is well along, and the fairing shells on the cross beams are just being started.

The resemblance to airplane technology is striking. Shown are two of the port cross beams under construction.

than 200 screws were used; these were applied primarily in areas where more pressure was needed than could be easily supplied with staples. We used five different types of air-powered staple guns. Staples temporarily connect all of the wooden parts together so that adhesive bonding can take place. Most of the staples are left in place, and while they do help somewhat in acting as fasteners, we do not count on them. Rather, we rely almost entirely on our glue bonds to transfer all loading between individual parts. The net savings in fasteners for a boat of this size is significant. And the benefits of the bonded joint, with its high point loading, is unquestioned at this time. *Rogue Wave* is the best example to date of the success of this concept.

Both the main hull and the two outriggers were built using an aircraft-type construction technique. Large sawn-plywood web frames were used to support longitudinal stringers, which were set on edge to give maximum support to the hull skin. In this case we used 9-ply, ½-inch mahogany and spruce plywood. This

supported Sitka spruce stringers, which measured 1½ inches by ⅝ inch. The beauty of this light-framework system is that it becomes the mold over which the final skin is laminated, which makes relatively efficient construction possible for this size of boat. The outer skins on all three hulls were ½ inch thick and laid up in double-diagonal fashion at approximately 45-degree angles from the horizontal. Two layers of 5-ply, ¼-inch okoume-spruce plywood were used.

The curves on all of the hulls were very fair and gentle. This allowed us to bend the thicker ¼-inch ply, completing the skin construction in only two laminations, instead of four laminations of ⅛-inch veneers. Because of the tremendous amount of surface area involved in building three large hulls, this saved us a great deal of labor. Pure veneer lamination might have been a bit stiffer and stronger than two layers of ¼-inch ply, but, in our judgment, the savings in labor more than offset this advantage. The hull surface area, including supporting stringers and web frames, averages 1.6 pounds per square foot.

The keel was laminated up with one layer of ¾-inch mahogany, and thin plywood was sandwiched between each lamination to prevent splitting. The main hull's sheer clamps were made up of two laminations of ¾-inch by 4-inch Sitka spruce. The outrigger sheer clamps were three laminations of ⅝-inch by 3-inch white ash. Because the outrigger hulls are more prone to damage than the main hull, this extra strength is a practical consideration.

Once we had completed three strong, rigid hulls, the fun really began. The problem was to connect all these hulls together in a strong, accurate, and beautiful manner. The latter was as difficult a part of the project as any. Aesthetics is primarily the designer's function. The same rules that apply to art, architecture, and product design apply to multihulls. In the evolution of form following function, Newick's designs have brought the beauty of multihulls a long way from the early days. As the engineering has responded to the boats' capacity for speed and efficiency, a natural beauty and grace has emerged. In this *Gulf Streamer-Rogue Wave* design, Dick Newick has given us a multihull that is very pleasing to the eye. Building in that configuration was another matter.

The three hulls of *Rogue Wave* were connected with three structural beams, each nearly 35 feet in length, and constructed separately from the main hull. The beams contained major structural bulkheads that were glued into

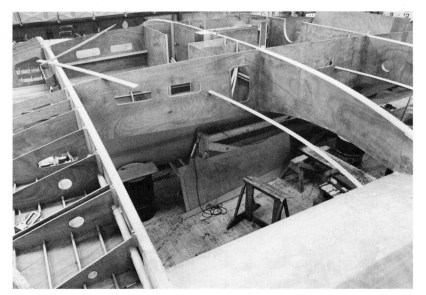

the boat, and when finished, they became an elaborate truss framework system sandwiched between two giant plywood skins. It happened as follows: One skin was shaped and a number of structural members were attached. Then it was installed in the main hull before the remaining internal members were connected between the beams and bulkheads. When the second skin was laminated over this completed internal structure, a strong and rigid beam/bulkhead was created. The ply took the primary shear loads, and the internal framework handled the direct tension and compression loading. Once the beam installation was complete, the outriggers were decked over, and then the frames for the elaborate beam fairings were begun.

Even though there are two separate cabins with a cockpit between, they were built together to form a large anti-torsion box girder that withstands twisting loads and provides fore-and-aft stiffness. This makes it possible to maintain a taut forestay and prevents headsail sagging. The problem of inefficiently setting headsails has afflicted many modern multihulls, and it has been a difficult one to solve. While the IOR keelboat fleet has long been aware of the sagging forestay problem, and for many years has attempted to build solid, rigid systems to prevent deflection of the boat structure, the multihull movement has developed this concern only recently. Lack of torsional resistance has also been a difficult problem for multihulls. We feel that this unique flowing cabin design, together with the WEST System, provides the answer to both problems.

The cabin walls, made from ½-inch plywood, acted as sheer webs between the three beams, preventing them from torqueing against one another. They could not move individually, no matter what loads were imposed. When the main cabin roof was installed, the "box" was completed. It was a very interesting part of the structure, because it was built using a honeycomb sandwich 3½ inches thick. The bottom of the cabin roof sandwich was constructed separately on the shop floor with all of the framework installed. Once the interior ceiling was fitted into place, the honeycomb core material was glued in place and a final layer of ⅜-inch-thick 5-ply mahogany plywood was laminated over to complete the sandwich. The purpose of the 3½-inch-thick cabin roof was to provide a higher floating level in the event of capsize, and better livability inside the inverted structure. The resulting composite also provided an extremely rigid, lightweight cabintop

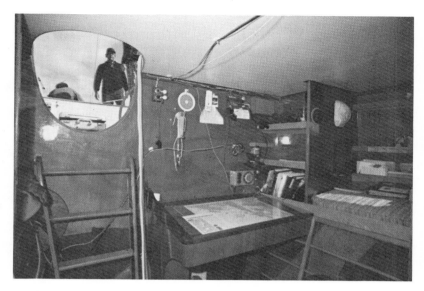

surface that did not rely on heavy interior framework.

Every attempt was made to make a beautiful as well as easily lighted interior. The ceiling is the only painted part of the interior — this was done before it was hoisted into place — and is intended to reflect the minimal lighting, powered only by a single solar cell panel. Eight different types of wood were used on the interior, and some were chosen because of their light color. White ash was used for all the trim on bulkheads, cabinets, and bunks. Sitka spruce and Gaboon, finished in high-gloss varnish and accentuated by a white ceiling, made interior lighting very easy.

The proper sealing of the interior, together with providing the base for a high-gloss finish, was achieved by using a prefinished system that we have refined over several years. Whenever possible, we precoated and presanded individual parts before they were incorporated in the boat's structure. It's a lot easier to do these operations at the workbench than in a cramped interior. Furthermore, coating and sanding around the stringers and frames is extremely time-consuming. If the parts are sanded and coated individually in a nice atmosphere, the quality of the finish will always be much higher. When we assemble the parts, excess glue is carefully cleaned away so that the mating parts blend into one another with very little final sanding needed. When the entire boat is assembled, a final check is given to all of the surfaces to be varnished (or painted). After cleaning off any dust and dirt that might have accumulated, we apply a coat of high-gloss varnish, giving a surface that looks as though it had received five coats of hand-rubbed varnish.

One of the greatest challenges of *Rogue Wave*

The navigator's area. The berth extends outboard of the main hull, a portion of which is visible in the lower right.

From some angles *Rogue Wave*'s interior resembles that of an airplane fuselage, except that nearly every structural member is varnished wood.

was building the six beam fairings, each pair of a different shape. The beauty of the boat comes from the designer's lines in these fairings, and we had to construct them in such a way that they flowed properly from one part of the hull to the other. The technical difficulty in doing this lies in the lofting of the fairing, which cannot be done in a normal fashion from a centerline as one would loft a hull. The fairings curve in several directions, and translating drawings into completed shapes became something of an eyeball proposition.

In addition to being a flowing sculpture, the fairings must also withstand tremendous punishment from heavy wave action, and still be rather light. They are designed to take aft shear loads in the event the outrigger were to collide with something solid enough to stop the entire boat. Accomplishing these goals was further complicated by the fairings' large surface area, which needed to be well supported. A frame-and-stringer construction similar to that in the hulls was used. It supported two laminations of 3/16-inch Gaboon mahogany plywood, which make up the total 3/8-inch outer skins.

Another interesting feature of *Rogue Wave* is the construction and placement of her wooden water and fuel tanks. There are two water tanks, of 40 gallons each, mounted beneath the floor. They are separate tanks, not built integral to the skins, so they can be removed for cleaning and inspection. Both of these tanks were built using the WEST System. They had taped seams, generous fillets, and internal baffles to control surging in a seaway. Even the 40-gallon diesel fuel tank, located forward of the engine compartment, is made of wood.

Rogue Wave's exterior finish was completed with the application of a minimum-thickness (three coats) epoxy coating. As called for in the designer's specifications, all of the hulls were covered with polypropylene cloth to provide high abrasion resistance. After sanding the epoxy, and using primers and surfacing putties over her 3,000 square feet of surface area, we painted her with a special linear polyurethane enamel made for us by International Paints. This paint was unique because it could be applied with a roller and brush and still produce a high-gloss quality equal to that of spraying. Not only was *Rogue Wave* too large a structure to spray-paint in a practical manner, but we considered sprayable linear polyurethane too dangerous to use because of the fumes. The final finish was extremely hard and durable, with impressive resistance to marring and scratching. This type of paint can greatly re-

duce the maintenance requirements of large wooden boats, and we hope that *Rogue Wave* is capable of going five years before having to be repainted. If she had to be painted every year, the time, inconvenience, and cost would probably make owning her prohibitive.

We estimated that we could build the wooden hull structure to weigh around 10,000 pounds. On launch day, the boat weighed 11,075 pounds — less mast, boom, rigging, and centerboard. This included the engine, however, and its accessory hardware, the steering system, and all the other sail-handling hardware. Deducting the weight of all of these items, we figure the wood structure alone weighed around 9,500 pounds. Completely rigged, *Rogue Wave* weighed 12,000 pounds. Consider a monohull weighing 12,000 pounds. It would probably be 35 feet long and be designed to sail at six to eight knots. *Rogue Wave* is 60 feet long, has a 34-foot beam, and is designed to sail at 15 knots plus; indeed, she is capable of 25 to 30 knots in ideal conditions.

Rogue Wave, basically a very simple boat, is cutter-rigged. Her most sophisticated gadgetry is her hydraulic system, with three separate hydraulic rams — one on the backstay, one on the inner forestay, and one on the auxiliary forestay for light-air headsails. These are linked to a central hydraulic pump that allows the skipper to adjust the tension of these individual stays as he desires. Any one of these rams is capable of inducing 4,000 pounds of tension, which certainly prevents the leading edge of the jibs from sagging-off in heavier airs. The stiff hull structure, combined with this hydraulic system, gives *Rogue Wave* highly efficient windward ability. For example, shortly after launching, Phil Weld and one crew left Gloucester, Massachusetts, for St. Maarten in the Caribbean. It was a tough 1,500-mile beat, almost dead to windward, and *Rogue Wave* sailed a particularly fast passage of less than 10 days. She averaged over 6 miles per hour along the rhumb line, and over 9 miles per hour along the legs.

Rogue Wave was a most satisfying project for us. An additional benefit from the owner's standpoint is that she cost no more to build than did *Gulf Streamer* (dollars adjusted for inflation). It appears that with our present level of knowledge, our accumulated experience, and technology, we can build custom one-off boats a lot better, and at lower cost than any competing boat system. It reinforces our belief that wood is indeed the boatbuilding material of the future.

Designer's Comments

ORDERS FOR big trimaran designs are rare, especially two from the same client! Boat number one for Phil Weld had been enough of a success that it was the pleasure she had given, and the survival potential after her capsize, that stuck in his mind as he contemplated her replacement.

Before we sat down to discuss his new design, I had sketched several approaches to the Welds' requirements for a fast, comfortable cruiser for four or five, with good solo and two-man racing potential. We kept coming back to minor modifications of the *Gulf Streamer* design, and finally agreed that either she had been pretty close to what we wanted the first time, or we had simply run out of new ideas.

Rogue Wave is lighter but more burdensome than her glass predecessor, and much stiffer structurally. She also has as fine a finish as can be found on any yacht (varnished engine room and all). Her 34-foot beam exceeds the length of most yachts, but it is just as easy to get used to — except in the most crowded harbors — as is her effortless 9 knots with 39-h.p. diesel, and often double that under sail. Improvements over *Gulf Streamer* include better safety features to absorb grounding shock on the main daggerboard, a swing-up skeg/rudder unit, two Peter Spronk-style offshore heads, and a much larger galley. The rig had been largely perfected already — a truly solo 60-footer for one (good) sailor!

Most sailors now realize that multihulls are fast off the wind, but no diehard lead lugger should bet more than he can afford to lose when challenging *Rogue Wave* to a windward race.

When the pioneers of the ballasted tradition were still experimenting with ways to preserve the oxhide "planking" of their coracles, the Pacific islanders were exploring a fifth of the globe's surface in craft that have been just recently "discovered" elsewhere. They had no metal, but they knew wood and fiber lashings and they knew the sea. If the ancient Polynesians had discovered epoxy and Dacron sailcloth, perhaps our own idea of "traditional" would be a whole lot different.

In any event, modern materials, combined with Polynesian, Micronesian, and Melanesian traditions, are giving some of us a great deal of pleasure.

— Dick Newick

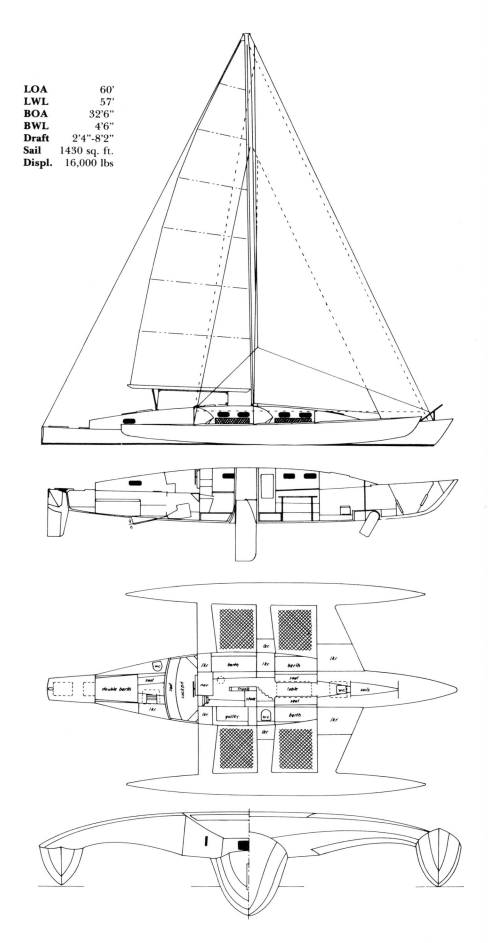

LOA	60'
LWL	57'
BOA	32'6"
BWL	4'6"
Draft	2'4"-8'2"
Sail	1430 sq. ft.
Displ.	16,000 lbs

In the Classic Spirit

Jon Wilson

The 21' Philbrick runabout is a thoroughly modern boat built with the latest techniques, but it has the style of the classics of Hacker and Gar Wood, Century and Chris-Craft.

*P*AUL LIPKE, *a young fan of wooden boatbuilding who toured hundreds of boatshops around the country to write his book* Plank on Frame, *first suggested a story on Don Philbrick. We are always interested in publishing material about both the craftsmen who build wooden boats and the excellence of the craft that they build. So when Jon Wilson went to San Francisco in April 1979, he arranged to spend a day at Philbrick's shop with Brian Dowley, the photographer. This small-scale production shop turned out contemporary classics in wood as if there were no other way to build them. As for Don, he was a classic man himself — possessing the inquiring mind of an engineer and the skill of a superb boatbuilder.*

*I*T MAY BE the quietest production boatshop there is. Four boats are in different stages of completion, and four men divide their time among them. There is no assembly line, but there is a method, and Don Philbrick is the man who sees that the method is followed. The atmosphere is neither stifled nor mechanical, but efficient and respectful, because Don Philbrick knows his stuff. He ought to — he's been building and repairing runabouts for 45 years, right there in Oakland, California.

The shop is a long, split-level frame building

with a tin roof, a few windows, and a small storage lot outside. The front is overshadowed by a freeway and the back opens out into the Oakland Estuary. Maybe it's the freeway traffic that makes the shop seem quiet by comparison, or maybe it's the fact that the shop is so long, but whatever the reason, one has the feeling of entering another world there. If you time it right, you walk through the shop seeing these four boats under construction, and at the end is an absolutely breathtaking fifth one, a finished mahogany runabout 21 feet long, awaiting delivery to another ecstatic customer. You can't help exclaiming, and Don can't help repeating that they really have to be seen to be believed. He's right. The pictures are nice, but the boats are far more than that.

One is first tempted to say, "This really takes you back to the heyday of the runabouts." But this is no replica for nostalgia buffs. It is a beautifully proportioned runabout for today — strongly influenced by Hacker and Gar Wood, reminiscent of others like Century and Chris-Craft, but distinctly different. The chromed emblems on the topsides, just a few inches forward of the transom, read *Philbrick* in a script style he developed himself. He is justifiably proud of his boats, and he keeps an eye on every detail. As we look over the tucked-and-rolled naugahyde seat covers, he allows that the job wasn't what it should have been on this boat, and he points out a place where the material wasn't pulled quite tight. But it won't leave his shop until it's right. As for me, I can hardly stop stroking the 10-coat finish.

It all began in Oakland. His school years were filled with the news of the record-breaking runabouts of the period, and he and his friends devoured every boating magazine they could find. He loved them all, but John Hacker's work really stood out from the rest, and ideas began to take shape in his mind. During his last year in high school, he worked at Swanson's Yard on the Estuary, planking the hulls of the cruisers 30 feet and up that were being turned out there. But it wasn't for him. Immediately after high school he went into business for himself, designed an 18-foot runabout, and built it on speculation. It was 1934, and the finished boat made enough of an impression that he turned to building on order, which was to continue uninterrupted until 1966. It wasn't only runabouts (he was also involved in a creamery business with his father for 13 years), but he was always at it. When the time came to choose between boats and cows, he had no trouble. Besides, not every boatbuilder could also make great ice cream!

The wheel and instruments are custom-crafted items.

His work ranged from simple 12-foot outboard skiffs all the way up to a 52-foot houseboat with parquet floors and a fireplace. (It was meant to be a paddle-wheeler, but the paddle wheel was never built.) In between these were the runabouts and some inboard-powered hydroplanes.

He was well into the racing scene then, trailering his runabouts all over the West Coast to the regular 5-mile course races. One year (he forgets which one), he and his boat took the high-point trophy out there, which isn't bad for a racer who designed and built his own craft.

He studied no naval architecture but picked up drafting and fairing on his own. The shapes come out of his head, but he's never modeled a boat first. Nor is he in the habit of laying down the boats full size. Instead, he drafts out the shape he wants to a scale of 3 inches to 1 foot and fairs it up, and then he scales the measurements off for molds and patterns. He has laid down only one boat full size but sees no point to it for his particular use. He recently departed from his common scale to draft a 27-foot runabout that he's developed, and on this the scale is half.

The lines of the afterdeck of the Philbrick runabout blend well with the receding wake.

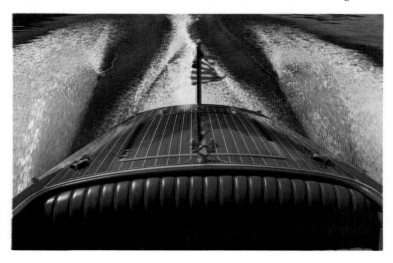

Sometime in the early 1950s, he decided that the racing scene was becoming tiring, and he simply stopped. There was plenty of building and restoration work to do, and traveling around with his boats was no longer so much fun. He had never advertised, but the work was always there, and he used the time refining his thinking as well as his building methods. There is no finer teaching aid in wooden boats than the repair business, and Don Philbrick immersed himself in it. His reputation as a knowledgeable craftsman and experienced racer brought business from all corners, and every problem in the repair business was translated into a solution in the construction business.

But the timing was wrong. The sentiments of the 1960s were away from wood and craftsmanship and toward mass production, and Don wasn't about to try to buck that tide. But people still wanted unique boats. In 1966 he built a 20½-foot "convertible" runabout, cold-molded in three layers of vertical-grain spruce, epoxy glued. That alone would have been interesting enough for the mid-1960s, but he took it further. He went out into his yard, where he had two 1957 Chrysler Imperials. From them he removed the windshields, the convertible tops, and the electric side windows. Using his genius for conversion, he cut and combined the tops and windshields into one and installed

The sides are planked with ⅜" Honduras mahogany and the bottom is laminated with two layers of marine fir plywood.

them, along with the fully powered pushbutton side windows, in the boat! Everything still functions, but the owner doesn't use the boat much, so it's rarely seen about.

It was shortly after this that he decided to retire from building. There was still as much repair work as he wanted, but the interest in new wooden boats had declined, leaving only a few true enthusiasts, all of whom were disappointed when Don decided to put away his patterns.

He kept it up for 10 years, until finally, in January of 1977, he decided to get back into production. The interest in such craft was again on the increase, he had been getting more and more inquiries, and a friend of his was interested in going into partnership. For some time, Don had been thinking about a refined shape, some new production methods, and the great resurgence of interest, so he jumped back in with both hands.

The boat was the current 21-footer, and he had no sooner begun when the news began to travel. Barbary Coast Yacht Brokers in San Rafael heard about it and headed for the shop, and there was the boat, big as life. It wasn't long before they had an agreement to buy the boat and to commission several more, to be promoted and sold through the brokerage.

The 21-foot model is standard, and every component is patterned. The boats are framed and planked upside down, then turned over for interior work and finishing. The final weight of the boat is about 2,600 pounds equipped, which is considered light for a runabout of this length. But they are by no means weak, and the remarkable weight is one of the things that makes the boats so attractive, because they perform well in a variety of conditions. Indeed, that's exactly how Don Philbrick arrived at the design and the construction methods.

The backbone is edge-grain fir, upon which are fastened Philippine mahogany sawn frames. These are tied together with plywood gussets, glued, and Anchorfast nailed. The sweeps are long and gentle from the transom to about 18 feet forward, and the frame spacing there is just over 28 inches on centers. The forward three feet converge quickly toward the stem, and the spacing here shortens to 22 inches.

The bottom is laminated in two layers of marine fir plywood (¼ inch and ⅜ inch, totaling ⅝ inch). The joints are staggered and land on alternate frames, fastened down with brass wood screws. After the heads of the screws are surfaced with a nonshrinking plastic putty, the bottom is sheathed with two layers of fiberglass cloth and epoxy resin, which is turned up over the chines and then feathered out smooth.

In the early days, Don had used single thick bottoms, but around 1940 he began using plywood inner skins with mahogany planks glued over. But the problems with shrinking and swelling persisted, until in 1953 he changed over to solid plywood in two layers. It was strong and stable, but he found that people needed just a bit more durability, so in 1958 he went to the additional step of sheathing with glass. Although the resins have improved, the plywoods haven't, in Don's view, but he remains satisfied with the quality of the marine grades.

The plywood bottom is rabbeted into the mahogany chine logs, which extend outboard an inch or so from transom to stem, creating an integral spray rail and providing a perfect surface for the side planking to run by.

The sides are well engineered. When the frames are in place on the form, lines are struck for ⅜-inch plywood seam battens, which are let in to them, glued, and fastened. Since everything is patterned, even the butts are scheduled, and plywood blocks are set in place. Then comes the ⅜-inch Honduras mahogany planking. Glued edge-to-edge and to the battens, they are also fastened with brass screws that are countersunk and plugged. The butt joints are just that, but also glued (end grain to end grain), and to the plywood battens and blocks. There are six planks to a side, averaging 3¾ inches wide amidships. The lowest plank measures just over 5 inches wide, because it runs down by the chine logs, where it is then planed flush. This is a weak area in a lot of runabouts, but Don feels he has the problem licked with his construction process.

In the early days, resorcinol glue was the only adhesive he would trust in his boats. In spite of the demands it made in temperature, fit, and clamping pressure, he felt there was nothing better. But the epoxies changed all that. With the technology advancing apace, he had more and more options available, and he knew how to take advantage of them. He needed, most of all, a durable end product that could stand the loads imposed on a high-performance craft. But just as important to him were its ability to stand on vertical surfaces (such as seam battens and frames) without running off, and a practical pot (working) life. In the end, he got all three (including an eight-hour pot life) in a specially made formulation from Smith & Co., 1220 South 49th, Richmond, California.

The transom is the same construction: single-layer, batten seam, glued and screwed. All planks are mahogany except the lowest, which is plywood that is sheathed. The transom planks run by the side planks, and the end grain exposed is then covered by a ¹⁄₁₆-inch by 2½-inch chrome binding strip. It's a quick, sure method, and it has continued to hold up well.

The rounded stem face is sculpted from four ¹³⁄₁₆-inch mahogany laminates, which are glued and fastened to a plywood plate into which the plywood seam battens are fitted, and over which the planking lies. Battens and planks are trimmed flush with the plate, and the stem is then attached for final shaping and fairing. Inside, the plate is tied to the keel through a built-up plywood knee, which is sided 2¼ inches and runs 20 feet aft to the first pair of frames.

Deckbeams are sawn from ¾-inch plywood and are doubled at each seat back. Covering boards and kingplank are doubled mahogany, glued and fastened, and the straight-laid decking lies over plywood. Everything is epoxy glued, but in the seams of the laid decking is a bead of white Life-Calk, a polysulfide. Quarter- and stemhead-joints in the covering boards are mitered and glued, and other joints are glued butts. Such joints wouldn't work if the entire undersides weren't glued as well, but so far they've created no problems, according to Don. Occasionally a customer will prefer that the laid decking be bleached blond, but most of the boats are totally dark mahogany.

The interior is framed out with a Philippine mahogany grid, the entire interior is primed and painted a neutral grey, and then the plywood seats and floors are built. The hull is ceiled with ¼-inch plywood, which is later upholstered, as are the seats themselves.

After the exterior is planed and sanded to perfection, the finishing process begins. A mahogany filler stain is rubbed in, and then come the coats of sprayed acrylic enamel. Don has built a spray booth for the operation, which works beautifully. Lighted at the top and sides with plenty of fluorescents, it is painted white for additional reflected light. When a boat is sprayed, they hose down the walls with water, close the doors, and turn on the exhaust fan to the outdoors. Dust and fumes are drawn out while new air is drawn in through a series of wall filters. With such a setup, the spraying can go quickly. Depending on the needs of the boat and Don's mood, he'll put up to 10 coats of enamel on, rubbing between coats to keep out the little imperfections. When enough coats have been put on, he just lets the boat sit for two weeks while the enamel sets up.

Acrylic enamel is a two-part material whose catalyst can make the finished coating more or less flexible. Don prefers the more flexible formulation, knowing the nature of wood in boats.

Don Philbrick reveals the 240-h.p. Ford V-8 that moves his runabouts along at over 40 knots.

When the two weeks are up, they go at the boat with polishing compound, working it down to a hard, mirror-smooth finish. Maintenance will require only a regular rinsing with fresh water (no detergents). Don says he knows the finish thus cared for will last five years, and if it ever needs to be refinished, it will strip easily with paint remover. The current interest in linear polyurethane coatings hasn't made much of an impression on Don. He hasn't tried it yet and isn't really interested in doing so until he has the time and space to experiment.

Hardware and trim on the Philbrick boats is almost all custom-made. The motif is chrome on brass or bronze. The only aluminum in the boat is found in the frame of the laminated Nardi sports-car wheel. Cleats, chocks, vents, the stem guard, and even the instrument bezels are fashioned under Don's supervision. The half oval that surrounds the cockpits is annealed and bent to shape before being plated with chrome, and every piece is checked first for flaws. If something more is needed, Don will work up a pattern and have the item cast at a nearby foundry. Surprisingly, he uses no bedding under any of the hardware, finding it unnecessary.

The standard power plant in the 21-footer is a 351-cubic-inch, 240-h.p. Ford V-8. Because the best place for it in this boat is at the after end, Don uses a V-drive unit to keep the propeller shaft angle at the required 11 degrees below horizontal. At sea level, it will drive the boat at 44 m.p.h. At Lake Tahoe, 6,000 feet high, it is only 34 m.p.h.

He has influenced stock propeller design on the basis of his testing and experience, and he continues to try to improve different aspects. Currently, he has a rudder and rudderstock configuration that calls for a keyed stainless steel stock, around which is cast a manganese bronze rudder, forming a one-piece unit. The engineering and patterns sprang from his own mind, and the unit is cast, like his other custom hardware, at the nearby foundry.

One of the most distinctive Philbrick touches on these runabouts is found in the exhaust ports through the transom. Instead of the usual round ports with wide flanges (which are fairly simple to produce and install), he forms the copper pipe into a more oval shape. Then, he houses the ports within a continuation of the bumper rails, which run aft where the topsides tumble home. The whole assembly wraps right around the transom and sides and is bedded in Life-Calk and bolted through the hull with stainless steel bolts. Bedding is used here instead of glue, because, if the boat went hard against a pier, the breaking away of the rail might damage some of the planking. He obviously has it figured out.

Today there are three full-time builders, plus Don, working quietly and methodically on the new boats. There are two others who work part-time doing the restoration work, which continues to pour in. You could, if you had the time and money, walk into the shop and buy an unsold one (if there were any), place an order for the standard model, or talk over the possibilities of a custom-built job to someone else's design.

Most of the business is at Lake Tahoe, where interest in such craft (and the money to afford them) is abundant. But there are also Philbrick boats in such places as New York, Florida, and Texas. If Don has his way, there'll be a lot more. He has the technology at hand, the resource available, and a ready labor force. At the drop of a hat he could step up production with no loss in quality, and if all goes well, he will probably do just that.

The Genius of N.G. Herreshoff

Maynard Bray

M AYNARD BRAY'S passion for and appreciation of the work of Nathanael Herreshoff remained an untapped resource for us at WoodenBoat *for a long time. His desire to "get it right" (for eventual publication in a book) seemed to preclude any hope of ever "getting it down" (at least for magazine editors, who seem to want to get it all now, not later). But Maynard finally grew impatient with boat lovers' general lack of insight into the true genius of Herreshoff. A visit to the Herreshoff Museum in Bristol, Rhode Island, for some specific photographs proved to be all the catalyst Maynard needed, and he sat down to set the record — at least part of it — straight. The resulting article clears the way to an understanding of the extent of NGH's genius as it was applied to small- and medium-sized sailboats — the role, for instance, of design as a function of straightforward yet durable construction — and an indication of the usefulness of this information today. Maynard continues to add to his appreciation of Herreshoff's techniques and insights, and we expect to publish more in the future on this revolutionary yacht designer.*

N.G. Herreshoff's reputation as a designer of fast sailing yachts began in earnest with the 46-foot-waterline-class sloop *Gloriana* in 1891.

THE NAME HERRESHOFF, even today, appears somewhere between the covers of nearly every issue of almost every boating magazine published in this country. There are good reasons for such a legend, despite the fact that the key figure behind it died over 40 years ago, and the Herreshoff Manufacturing Company closed its Bristol, Rhode Island, doors for the last time shortly after World War II.

When they were new and competing for the "auld mug," the big sophisticated *America's* Cup sloops dominated the lion's share of yachting news. There were five successful Cup defenders launched between 1893 and 1914, all designed and built by Herreshoff, who in the same period produced some runners-up as well. It was these spectacular and highly publicized craft, probably more than anything else, that placed their creator, Nathanael Greene

Herreshoff, at the head of his profession. Also receiving their deserved share of attention were his big metal-hulled two-masted schooner-yachts, one of which, *Katoura*, at 162 feet, was even bigger than the Cup boats and has the distinction of being the largest sailing vessel ever built by the yard. And there were the steam yachts up to 145 feet, and torpedo boats up to 175 feet, along with the engines and boilers that powered them; there were one-design racing sailboats of all sizes up to 106 feet; there was exquisite and innovative hardware cast or forged by the yard; there were superior sails — the first crosscut ones ever; there were hulls of steel and bronze, as well as ones of wood.

All of this and more resulted in a legend that just goes on and on. Today, most of what might be called Herreshoff's major work survives only on paper in the form of drawings, photographs, and written material. Fortunately, there is plenty of that and most of it is readily accessible. For example, there are many books and articles by the late L. Francis Herreshoff, a son and well-known designer in his own right. Among these books is a full-length biography of N.G. Herreshoff and the boats he designed. There is the Herreshoff Marine Museum at Bristol — started largely by the efforts of another son, Sidney, and kept going after his death a few years ago by family, friends, and members — whose purpose is to collect, preserve, and exhibit Herreshoff-related material. And there is the magnificent collection of Herreshoff Manufacturing Company drawings at the Hart Nautical Museum at MIT, in Cambridge, Massachusetts.

In a sense, it's curious that boats that must have seemed like incidental work at the time have survived the longest. Quite a number of the small and medium-sized wooden sailboats built in those shops from the models and drawings of N.G. Herreshoff are still around and in good condition, even though they are generally past the half-century mark. Their existence and their still-to-be-admired beauty and speed under sail have brought into being a kind of reverent fraternity of owners and enthusiasts. Back when these boats were built, they were considered small, and they lived in the shadows of larger and more spectacular craft. Even in the years that followed, they have never, in my opinion, been closely examined in print for what they really are: beautiful creations of a man and a shop capable of producing complex engineering marvels but who had the wisdom to keep the boats extraordinarily simple. It is hard to understand the continuing preoccupation with Herreshoff's major yachts — contemporary writers still seem to focus on them. They are romantic curios in this day and age, and the likes of them are probably gone forever. On the other hand, many of his small craft can still be examined, and some of what it took to design and build them, once understood, can be put to use in boats being produced today.

Sailing yachts of 40-foot waterline and less, designed by N.G. Herreshoff and built by the Herreshoff Manufacturing Company, are studied here — what they are and how they were built. It's important to know not only why they looked so pretty, sailed so well, and lasted so long, but also to examine the methods used to build them. It was a highly refined and surprisingly standardized system, different in many respects from that used by most other yards.

Although the Herreshoff Manufacturing

Company had been in business about 25 years when the 20th century dawned, and it was by that time very much living up to its name of manufacturing boats on a semiproduction basis, its heavy involvement with sailing craft had only been going on for about 10 of those years — heralded into being by the unbeatable sloop *Gloriana* in 1891. Before that time, steam yachts, launches, and a few steam-powered military craft, along with the boilers and engines for them, were the company's mainstay (169 power, only 11 sail between 1868 and March 1891). Quite a few small and medium-sized sailing craft came out of the shops in the 1890s, however, besides the big attention-getting ones. By 1900, the tally shows that only 41 more powerboats had been built, compared with 125 sailing craft, and of these 125, 109 were 40 feet or less on the waterline.

Primarily, these 109 boats consisted of rather small craft of the type then in vogue — open racing boats with long ends and deep fin keels, and of the same general appearance as Captain Nat's own sloop *Dilemma*, which came out as the first fin-keeler in 1891. The 18-foot and 21-foot-waterline classes were going strong then, and quite a few one-of-a-kind boats were created to fit those measurement rules. The country's first major one-design class, a dozen Newport 30-footers (42 feet overall), came out during this decade. They were hot stuff at the time, with very lightweight hulls, lead-ballasted fin keels, and plenty of sail area. With balanced spade rudders, they could turn on a dime, and I suspect that they could give today's racing machines of similar size a good run for their money.

Another class that came into being about the same time was the Buzzards Bay 15-footer (24½ feet overall), which first appeared in 1898 and proved so popular that production continued on and off for the next 30 years. These were decked craft without cabins, and although designed for racing, were great boats to sail in just for the fun of it. Some are still around, dearly loved by their owners.

The 1890s saw the first Herreshoff-designed and built America's Cup defenders *Vigilant, Defender,* and *Columbia* come into existence, along with a couple of other big ones. *Navahoe* in 1893 was the first of these big metal-hulled beauties, ordered no doubt because of the resounding success of Herreshoff's *Gloriana* of 1891 and of *Wasp* the year after that. Except for these two 46-foot (on the waterline) sloops, Captain Nat had no background in the design of large sailing yachts when, in the single winter of 1892–93, he produced not only *Navahoe*, but *Colonia* and *Vigilant* as well — all about 130 feet overall. That his early small sailing craft had to become, in effect, testing models playing an important role in the development of the first big racing sloops is another reason to look closely at them.

Captain Nat and the shops continued to find eager buyers for a wide range of sailing craft after 1900, and at no time after 1891 did power-boats constitute a majority of their peacetime output. From the beginning of 1900 to the beginning of 1917 (when most work on pleasure craft came to a halt because of World War I), the Herreshoff Manufacturing Company produced some 280 additional sailing craft — all but 40 of them 40 feet on the waterline or less — and only 94 more powerboats. The sailboats during this time consisted of many more one-designs than before, so although Captain Nat's design work was still a monumental achievement, one has to keep in mind that only about a quarter of these sailing craft represented brand new designs.

The Universal Rule for measuring and hand-icapping sailboats was adopted by the leading yacht clubs about 1904, and its widespread influence resulted in better boats thereafter. Fuller hull lines and shorter overhangs made them roomier and more seakindly, while smaller sail-plans made them far easier to handle. Needless to say, they were inherently stronger as well. Captain Nat, as dissatisfied as anyone with the earlier length-and-sail-area rule, had first suggested the formula that was to become the Universal Rule, and with such a head start, he immediately set about designing the nicely modeled craft that the rule encouraged. Undoubtedly his finest designs for these craft were developed during the 1904–1917 period, and that is why so many of that age survive today. There are the New York Thirties and Forties (and Fifties, if one wants to stretch our arbitrary 40-foot limit a bit). There is Captain Nat's own *Alerion III* and the boats that she spawned: the Newport 29s, Buzzards Bay 25s, the Fish class, and the familiar 12½-footers. There were early S-boats, R-boats, Q-boats, and P-boats, all of a more moderate model than the long-ended freaks of the 1890s.

When peace returned and the booming 1920s dawned, the company was in no position to take advantage of the potential. Captain Nat was in his 70s and had sold most of his interest in the business. His blind and energetic brother, J.B. (for John Brown), who always ran the business end of things so well and for so long, had died in 1915, and the company was without an effective leader. The plant was probably overcapitalized for the work then available, and its syndicate of yachtsman-owners (who had attempted to keep things going after J.B.'s death) had not done well. With more money to be made elsewhere, they put the entire plant up for auction in 1924, at which time the majority of it was obtained by the Haffenreffer family. Under this new and dedicated ownership, and with the sometime help of Captain Nat, the full-time talent of his oldest son Sidney, and the work of many of the old-timers who had grown up with the place, the Herreshoff Manufacturing Company kept going through the Depression and on to the end of World War II. I suspect the profits, if any, were small without the original partners running things. Nat and J.B. left mighty big shoes to fill — impossible ones, really — and the times were different. Money was harder to come by in the 1930s and people generally wanted smaller boats with low prices instead of custom designs of high quality. The place had to compete in this price war with other yards; it could no longer call the shots. It was a time of even more one-design activity with large numbers of small boats being built. Sailboat hull numbers went from No. 819 in 1917 to No. 1511 in 1941, mostly due to one-designs such as 12½-footers, MIT dinghies and S-boats. The powerboats gained but 37 during this time, not counting those built for military service during the two wars. Although fewer in number, there were some really fine designs from this period.

The year 1946 saw the delivery of the plant's last recorded boat, No. 1521 — a Fishers Island 31-footer named *Memory*. The so-called north and south construction shops, which had given birth to so many fine yachts and most of the other buildings on the water side of Hope Street, were demolished shortly after the war. When Harry Town, a former employee, bought the place in the 1930s, it became known as the Herreshoff Yacht Yard and went on to build some boats in the east construction shop. Pearson Yachts was the next owner, then Grumman. (I think it was Grumman that saw fit to raze the east shop about a dozen years ago.) More recently, the Herreshoff Marine Museum has been able to acquire the now-vacant waterfront land and one of the nearby buildings. But all in all, that part of Bristol is quite different now from what it was 75 or 80 years ago.

So much for the company's history — its beginning, middle, and end. The middle years, the ones a decade or two following the turn of the century, are the ones of greatest interest as far as sailing craft are concerned. They bear a closer look. Back then, the output of the shops and the men in them, according to L. Francis,

In 1892, when this picture was taken, the 39-foot by 164-foot north construction shop was almost new. This was where most of the wooden-hulled yachts would be built. Whitewash was used inside the shops as an effective way of heightening the natural light coming through the windows. At the left is a bracketed walkway about halfway up the height of the north wall; at the far end of this walkway, or gallery, is the shop foreman's office.

was at its highest standard. He rightly identifies the crew as being the best asset of the organization, claiming that the personnel of a yacht yard is of far more importance than the machinery or the plant layout, and that the whole crew at that time was the finest lot of men he had ever seen in any manufacturing business. He says further:

"The employees in 1900 and the next few years were usually less than two hundred, [but] the production was great. This was because the company had developed certain methods of building that were particularly efficient, and because the works were especially well managed. It seems remarkable today that such a small crew of men could turn out so much work. You must remember, however, that things were quite different then: the men went to work at seven in the morning and, excepting for the noon hour, worked right through to six at night. I well remember the appearance of the works lit only with open gas lights on the long winter evenings. There were fewer holidays then for the workers of the Herreshoff Manufacturing Company, and as I remember it, they were New Year's, Fourth of July, Labor Day, Thanksgiving, and Christmas. Of course they worked all day Saturday.

"The men of those days were strong and tough; sometimes after this ten-hour day they would work overtime at a slight increase in pay, and I recall one man who worked twenty-four hours straight. This was a sparmaker, Jim Davidson, who made a new mast for one of the Newport Thirties which had carried hers away in a race and wanted a new spar for the next race with, I think, only a day between races.

Many of the men neither smoked nor drank and were as hard and muscular as athletes in training. They were able to work hard, and liked it; they could saw or plane continuously for hours without stopping to rest, and that is one of the reasons they built so many yachts in 1900 with a small crew. But they also had the know-how and made every stroke count. They gloried in accomplishing a good day's work, and I glory now in having known and seen those Samsons and Vulcans at work, but I fear the mold they were cast in is lost and that we will never have such accomplishments again.

"The workmen at this time were paid less than fifty cents an hour, generally, although the Herreshoff Company at that time was noted for its high rate of pay."*

Much has been written about the taciturn personality of Nathanael Herreshoff. Little has been said about how busy the man must have been during his most active years — being driven by important customers who wanted their yachts on time, by a big work force with an insatiable appetite for design information, and by an older brother who kept bringing in contract after contract for which Nat was expected to do the designing. With so much of the future of the place and its people depending on him, it is little wonder that newsmen and other casual acquaintances found him abrupt with their small talk. In reading over some of his correspondence, it is apparent to me that he was quite human; it's just that there were many times when he was too busy or preoccupied to carry on a conversation. Of him, L. Francis says:

*Excerpted with permission from *Capt. Nat Herreshoff, the Wizard of Bristol,* Sheridan House, 1953.

79

"Even though we are able to account for the manner in which the workmen built their yachts so fast those days, I fear no one will ever account for how Captain Nat got the designs out for them, for he certainly designed more yachts than anyone had before or has since, and went into much greater detail. As an example of his great productiveness, at the last of his life the Herreshoff Manufacturing Company had on file about eighteen thousand drawings for most of which he had drawn or laid out the principal proportions in pencil and he often kept three or four draftsmen inking his drawings. The models he made would have been a creditable lifework for anyone in quantity alone, leaving aside the quality. Although we know that for many years he worked twelve hours a day and most Sundays and holidays, still his accomplishments were amazing.

"In looking over Captain Nat's drawings one cannot help but be impressed with the amount of calculation and concentrated thought that went into them. It is no exaggeration to say that most all of them are extremely ingenious and could have been made only by a person of much experience who could concentrate steadily on his work and who lived a very long life."*

Let's take a look at what "manufacturing" a boat at Herreshoff's meant. Basically it meant building her upside down with a mold for every frame. Just where Captain Nat got the idea for doing things this way has probably been lost to history, but L. Francis says it was first tried out in 1876 when building the racing catboat *Gleam*. Screws for plank fastenings were introduced at the same time. And while it wasn't long before they caught on elsewhere, it has always been puzzling to me why the basic upside-down building method, which the screws complemented so well, was not adopted more widely by other yards. Assembly-line boatshops often used this method, at least to a certain degree, but at Herreshoff's nearly every boat up to about 65 feet — regardless of whether there was to be one hull or a hundred — was framed and planked in the upside-down position. The frames would be steam-bent around and set up on individual molds, and because this made the frames inaccessible on their inside faces for riveting or clench-nailing, the planks were fastened to them with screws. Being downhand work, the task of planking was a relatively easy one, as were the steps of planing, smoothing, and caulking that followed. With the men and their tools for the most part supported by the inverted hull itself, far less staging was required

—a considerable saving in materials, labor, and shop space.

Only the planked-up part of the hull would be built upside down; after planking, the hull would be turned over and set on its waiting deadwood and ballast keel for bolting. Provided there is an efficient way to flip the hull over after planking, which there was in those shops thanks to overhead traveling cranes and chain hoists, this is a fast and logical system for building boats.

By building several boats alike, the "manufacturing" expertise of the company really came into its own. That meant that a single set of frame molds, a single set of hardware and ballast keel patterns, and a single lofting along with the usual templates that went with it could be used to build many boats, with their initial cost being amortized over all that were of that particular one-design class. As might be expected, Herreshoff built great numbers of these class boats to a variety of designs. Numbers and sizes ranged from over 400 of the 12½-footers (sometimes called Bullseyes) to the four big sloops of the New York Yacht Club 70-foot class, whose hulls measured 106 feet overall. The famous class of New York Thirties (43½-feet-overall sloops) are typical of Herreshoff's production-line approach to boatbuilding. L. Francis describes how 18 identical boats were produced during the winter of 1904-05:

"There were generally three of them side by side in this production row, the first one upside down over her molds being planked; the next one turned rightside up having her deck laid and interior built; while the last one had been set on her lead and was being finished off and painted. After they really got in production, these boats shifted along in the production line at the rate of one a week, or in other words, one was completed each week and was taken away to the storage yard on a special wide-wheeled low gear hauled by horses. Of course, most all of the parts of these boats were prefabricated and there was a pattern for each plank and other principal parts which were gotten out about 18 at a time."*

Keeping the construction of the boats simple and somewhat standard, even though their size and shape varied a good deal, was also what "manufacturing" was all about. What this really meant was that boats were built more easily if all were designed by the same person — someone who appreciated the fact that beauty and performance could go hand in hand with simplicity. No designer was ever more capable of this than N.G. Herreshoff. Surprising as it may seem, a study of any one of his designs reveals

*Excerpted with permission from *Capt. Nat Herreshoff, the Wizard of Bristol*, Sheridan House, 1953.

instance after instance of things laid out in the most straightforward way consistent with the task they had to perform. If a design was complicated, rest assured it was only because the performance standards were high. Things were never complicated or unnecessarily elaborate just for the sake of complication. His extensive use of what we think of today as custom hardware has fogged this picture somewhat. Making fittings of metal by casting, forging, or machining was about as easy for Captain Nat then and there as making things of wood. At his disposal were patternmakers, foundrymen, blacksmiths, and machinists — as well as boatbuilders. All he did was take advantage of that potential to produce some of the most functional, beautiful, and astonishingly simple marine hardware ever. Nat Herreshoff has often been thought of as a gifted and prolific engineer with the eye of an artist, but I'm not sure many realize that he also had the design philosophy of a Shaker craftsman.

Wood for boatbuilding at the turn of the century, and even up until Herreshoff's went out of business, could be had in long, clear lengths of whatever species was thought best. The white oak and longleaf yellow pine in particular, if the surviving boats are any indication, were virtually flawless and had a lot to do with why these boats are still around. Because of its size and volume, the business justified a large inventory not only of oak and pine, but also of other boatbuilding woods. There was teak, butternut, cedar, cypress, white pine, mahogany, Sitka spruce, Port Orford cedar, and Douglas fir in sufficient quantity and of sufficient quality to make selecting the right piece for the job at hand a real pleasure. There was a timber pond at hand for curing big oak timbers without danger of their checking, and a big band resaw with which to manufacture efficiently thick cants and timbers into thinner planking stock. In 1924, at the time the company was auctioned off, the wood inventory read as follows.*

87,000 bf	longleaf yellow pine
21,000 bf	Oregon pine (Douglas fir)
5,600 bf	Eastern white cedar
3,200 bf	Port Orford cedar
5,600 bf	oak (in dry storage)
1,237 bf	teak
1,000 bf	Philippine mahogany
500 bf	white pine
350 bf	butternut

Manufacturing rough-sawn wood into finish dimensions through the use of various machinery was primarily the job of a millman who would, on order, get out planks and timbers to specified sizes. The boatbuilders in turn put the shapes, bevels, and curves on the planed-up stuff coming out of the mill and went on to fit and fasten it on the boat. Millwork generates a lot of waste in the form of shavings, sawdust, and scraps, and keeping the milling operations in a separate shop left the floors of the building shops quite free of this debris. With their inside walls and ceilings whitewashed, and with the floors swept and things generally put away when not in use, the building shops appear in photos more like hospital operating rooms than a run-of-the-mill boatshop. Where many men worked on a job at once, this orderliness must have been a major factor in maintaining a high level of productivity.

*Henry S. Anthony & Co. catalog describing the plant and its physical assets for the voluntary liquidation sale held August 21 and 22, 1924.

one — It's hard to imagine better working conditions — good natural lighting, some heat from the nearby steam pipes, plenty of space around the boat, and a setup that could be reached from a convenient working position. The keel is in two lengths, with the deadwood acting as a butt strap to reinforce the joint between. The missing forwardmost molds will not go in until the fairing and rabbet cutting in way of the keel/stem scarf are complete. A portion of these molds with frames already bent around them show at the far right, and next to them (the rear of the stem) is the setting-up form for the transom planking.

The Building Process

The Fishers Island 23s (34 feet overall) were designed by Sidney Herreshoff, and 14 of them were built between 1932 and 1938. This is the first one, *Tronda* (Hull No. 1212). She, like the others of her class and quite a number of additional smallish craft, was built in the so-called east construction shed, which was directly across Hope Street from the plant's waterfront buildings.

two — Single thickness mahogany planking was used on this class of boats, close fitted without caulking in the fashion of European builders. Except for the bunging (which is underway) and prime-painting, the hull appears about ready to turn over.

Using long lengths rather than short ones joined together saves time in fitting, especially if the joint has to be a fancy scarf. But if much curve is required, the use of long pieces can be wasteful of material, unless the curved shape is achieved by steam-bending. For example, a boat's stem may be plenty strong if made up of two or three pieces scarfed together, but there is far more work involved than in making it from a single length. The same thing is true of keels and covering boards, sheer clamps and coamings. Herreshoff excelled at steam-bending and exploited the process to the utmost. Keels for most of the sailboats were of the plank type, steamed and bent over the molds as they were set up on the building floor. The steam-bent frames used there were commonplace, but

Herreshoff bent the stems as well — around a form using a backing strap and a tackle. The transoms, if curved, were made from oak planks, which responded well to being steamed and then forced over a properly shaped form. The oak covering boards, because of being steam-bent, have their grain running along their curved shape, instead of across it on the bias near the ends, and they contain a minimum of time-consuming joints. Generally, covering board stock was gotten out to a little more than twice the required thickness of the finished pieces and bent against blocks nailed to the shop floor. The extra thicknesses meant that the stock would be more stable when bent, unlike a flat shape. Resawing and thickness planing later gave birth to a matched pair of curved

three — Flipping over a hull by means of a couple of endless slings rove through blocks (pulleys) is as simple a method as one could hope for. But doing it this way depends on some reliable means of lifting, obviously not a problem here. There were cranes like the ones shown in all three of the major building shops, and any pair of them could take the weight of a "little" boat like this without even puffing. Enough molds are left in to retain the hull's shape and to strengthen it in way of the two lifting slings until the boat is brought fully upright and moved over, and is resting on her keel.

four — The entire weight of this boat is taken by the two wheel-equipped bearers that roll on rails. When she is ready to be taken away, it will be by way of the big sliding door and a special yard trailer called a low gear. Staging on the near side has been removed for the photographer, and perhaps the same thing is true of the work crew. Even though out of sight in this picture, they have made good progress in the three weeks or so since the boat was set up and the first photograph was taken. Here, the deck and its canvas covering have been laid, the cabin sides and coamings are in place, and the starboard toerail looks like the next order of business.

covering boards. Coamings were often seen as continuing forward in one piece, curving to meet at their forward ends. Tillers, sheer clamps, bilge stringers, seat knees, and even harpins (the shelf-like timbers that provide full-width support for the side decks in place of deckbeams) were also made up from straight-grain stock by means of steam-bending.

Near-perfect wood must be had if it is to bend without breaking, and in this regard the extensive use of pieces formed by steaming went hand in hand with having a stockpile of good oak.

Having the rest of the material at hand when needed was, compared with most yards, easy for the Herreshoffs because it consisted largely of raw material from which things could be made instead of a supply of store-bought specialty items. They were concerned about iron to be forged, brass and bronze to be cast and machined, sailcloth to be sewn, oil and pigment from which paint could be made. So much of the manufacturing was under its own roof, it's no wonder a customer could order a major new yacht in the winter and expect to sail her in the spring.

It was times like these when a heavily capitalized yard like Herreshoff's had an advantage over the smaller shop. It appears that as long as there was a demand for high-quality yachts, and as long as the company was "especially well managed," the Herreshoff Manufacturing Company was very profitable, if not downright lucrative. While other yards were struggling along with outside designers (each of whom had his own pet way of drawing a plan and constructing a boat), and putting up with store-bought standard hardware, had no inventory of first-class seasoned wood, and were without comparable facilities and tools, Herreshoff consistently built great numbers of prestigious boats for the carriage trade. With such a demand, it is doubtful if J.B. and N.G. ever felt pressured into competing with other builders in terms of price. The surviving cost records clearly show that, by comparison with other boats of the same size and type, these Bristol-built beauties cost plenty.

Planning the design and construction so that the bulkheads, bunks, iceboxes, self-bailing cockpits, galleys, and lockers could be built elsewhere in the shops and then quickly scribed down and installed in the ceiled-up hulls before they were decked, was also a key factor in "manufacturing" a boat at Herreshoff's. Generally speaking, all the joinerwork, including the

bulkheads, was nonstructural and landed on the continuous bow-to-stern hull ceiling.

The deck structures, such as cabin trunks, hatches, and companionways — like the interiors — were also designed to be subassembled. They were then fitted and fastened after the decking was laid. This system of doing things had the double advantage of keeping large numbers of workers from interfering with each other on board the boat and of allowing these parts to be built in other shops, where the work could be done more conveniently, comfortably, and productively. Separate cabinet and joiner shops were certainly not unique in big yacht-building yards, but a well-thought-out design in which building efficiency is as important to the designer as performance and appearance was indeed rare. A new design, even though vastly different in appearance and shape from those that preceded it, was adaptable to the same methods of construction and made use of many of the same materials, details, and fittings. Easy

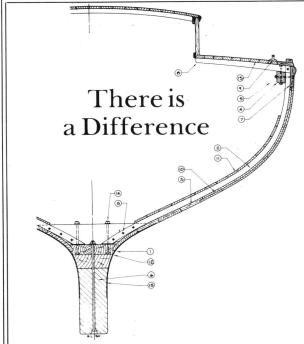

There is a Difference

MANY BOATS properly carry the name Herreshoff. Not only did Captain Nat (as NGH was called) design boats, but so did two of his sons, Sidney and L. Francis, as well as others of the family. A grandson, Halsey, is still very much in the yacht design business today. So when you're speaking of a Herreshoff-designed boat, you have to be careful to identify which of the Herreshoffs you're talking about; there is quite a difference in the nature of their work.

Compounding this problem of identity is the fact that boats are still being produced in all manner of materials that use the name Herreshoff in their ad-

vertising copy — sometimes with legitimate reason and sometimes simply to add some rather groundless prestige. And adding still more to the confusion are misled owners who claim, generally in classified ads, that their boats are Herreshoffs, when in reality these craft have no connection with that lineage whatsoever.

While Nat Herreshoff was an incessant experimenter — and was continually trying out new ideas on his customers' boats — he had, by 1900, adopted certain characteristic features that appear again and again in his small sailing craft. There were exceptions, to be sure, but I'm talking here about the distinguishing features that made the boats easy to build, gave them good performance and a long life, and nowadays can be used to identify a genuine Herreshoff-built boat from one that isn't. If you're ever asked for an opinion on whether a boat was designed by Nathanael and built by the Herreshoff Manufacturing Company, these are some of the things to look for:

1 — A so-called plank type of keel that has been steamed and sprung into place. It is of uniform thickness but tapers in width, being narrow at the bow and stern and widest in the center over the ballast keel. A little of its lower edge will be visible below the rabbet line for most of its length on the outside of the boat.

2 — Tapered (small at the head, big at the heel) steam-bent frames that are more or less square in cross section. In the small craft, such as dinghies, 12½-footers, Fish-class boats, and S-boats, the frames are not tapered.

3 — Planking that is fastened to the frames by flat-head wood screws whose heads have been puttied over in small craft and covered by bungs in larger ones.

for the designer and draftsmen (since great detail was needed only where there were changes), and easy for the men building the boat in that much of what they did on the new boat was the same as what had been done on the earlier ones. In looking at the drawings, it appears that things were standardized enough to make building the boats easy within the limits of the customer's requirements and Herreshoff's own propensity for trying out new ideas. It seems that by 1900 he was generally quite satisfied with his past ways of building boats and tried to keep from surprising his workmen with new concepts.

Captain Nat grew up when the changeover to outside ballast was made and played an active part in eliminating ballast carried in the bilge. He recognized early the advantages of keeping a sailboat's hull weight to a minimum so she could carry a greater percentage of her displacement as an outside lead ballast keel — and throughout his career he always seemed to be way ahead of other designers in this respect. Because the weight or center of gravity was low, Herreshoff boats could consistently carry their sail to advantage in stronger winds. Rating rules of the day set limits, of course, on what a designer could and could not do in terms of the sail area allowed on a hull of a certain size and shape, and these restrictions represented a challenge to designers and encouraged them to develop the fastest boat for a given rating. A well-shaped hull having the minimum resistance was an important factor, but so was a hull with a low center of gravity. And the only way to get that was to shave every last pound of unnecessary weight off the boat's structure and rig and get it down low. I've probably oversimplified the facts a bit, because there were limits applied to the ratio of ballast to displacement, but there has always been a need to produce a lightweight hull and rig of adequate strength in any high-performance sailing craft. At this Nat Herreshoff excelled.

4 — Sheer clamps of nearly square cross section whose outboard edges have been continuously beveled along their length to fit against the changing flare of the frame heads. The upper surfaces of the clamps were kept about level to make good landing for the deckbeams. Through-bolts showing square nuts were used for fastening both the frames and beams to the clamp. There is normally a good-sized chamfer on the lower inboard corner of Herreshoff sheer clamps.

5 — Deckbeams and plank-type floor timbers are fastened to every frame. Bolts or rivets are used at the floors, flathead wood screws at the deckbeam ends.

6 — A lead rather than iron ballast keel held on with bronze bolts.

7 — Oak, teak, or hard mahogany sheerstrakes and covering boards. Sometimes the sheerstrakes were specially molded to incorporate an integral guard rail, a feature rarely used by other builders.

8 — Absence of fore and aft carlings under the sides of cabins or coamings so that the ends of the deckbeams are clearly visible.

9 — Custom-cast bronze hardware, which usually includes the familiar Herreshoff bow chocks and hollow wide-base cleats.

10 — A band of double planking in medium- and larger- size wooden yachts that extends from the rabbeted lower edge of the sheerstrake to well below the turn of the bilge amidships, where it joins the single-thickness bottom planking by means of a rabbet as well. Bottom planking in these boats is generally longleaf yellow pine; the double planking is usually of a softwood such as cedar or cypress on its inside (thinner) layer, and of yellow pine, western fir, or mahogany on the outside.

11 — Ceiling, if used, will run in a continuous band uninterrupted by bulkheads and other joinerwork from a few frames aft of the stem to a few forward of the transom. The upper edge of this band is spaced down from the sheer clamp about one frame space. The bilge stringer is often omitted in ceiled-up boats.

12 — Only very rarely is there a knuckle outside at the lower edge of the garboard — a common feature in many boats of other builders. Most Herreshoff-built boats are shaped to give a continuous and fair curve from the bottom corner of the ballast keel all the way up to the deck edge. This usually involves contoured ballast keels and deadwood.

13 — Decking is usually of pine or cedar, and it may be either in narrow strips sprung in parallel to the covering board or in wider ones that run fore and aft parallel to the centerline. A rabbeted covering board would be used in the latter case to give support to the ends of the deck planking. Deck seams were sometimes caulked and sometimes made up with tongue-and-groove or ship-lapped edges. Unless the yacht is a big one with laid decks of scrubbed white pine or teak, you'll probably find her deck covered with canvas laid in white lead paste and sandwiched under the cabin, coamings, and toerails.

14 — The boat will be virtually free of iron or steel fastenings, with the exception of the nails holding the decking to the beams (quite common) and the bolts connecting the floor timbers to the frames (rare, usually found only in the later boats). Galvanized steel carriage bolts were also used on occasion in boats after 1925 or so, as fastenings for the deckbeam ends to the sheer clamps.

15 — Several external bronze straps that help hold the ballast keel onto the hull will be found in all but the smallest of keel-type sailing craft. These straps are let in flush and are located on frame lines.   — MB

The Remarkable Sloop *Shadow*

Jon Wilson

*O*UR INTEREST IN *revealing the roots of yacht design methodically in* WoodenBoat *led to the establishment of a series on the subject. In the early years of serious yacht design, a schism developed between those who favored wide, shallow craft and those who preferred narrow, deep boats. The two schools of thought merged ultimately in a classical design compromise, and the classical compromise sloop of that era was* Shadow, *designed by Nathanael Herreshoff at the age of 23. As one of NGH's most successful early designs,* Shadow *was the product not*
of a singular brainstorm, but rather of a short lifetime of experiences that produced a perspective on the yachts and working craft of the day. She not only represents one of the first and best compromise yachts, but also provides an excellent example of design as a product of both observation and experience. We chose to publish the story of Shadow *both to chronicle her creation and career and to attempt to demystify her ability and that of her designer. It's simple, really — when awareness and experience are complemented by a keen mind, excellence will emerge.*

TO UNDERSTAND the story of *Shadow*, we must have some understanding not only of the time and place in which Nathanael Herreshoff, at 23, carved her elegant model, but of the elements that came to bear on his experience to that point. For *Shadow* was no ordinary yacht, although in her early days, no one seemed to take particular notice of her. Yet in spite of her remarkable qualities, neither was she anything but the product of the logical and progressive mind of a young man who observed his surroundings with care. So the story really begins in those surroundings, which were the waters of Narragansett Bay, specifically Bristol, Rhode Island, some 10 miles north of Newport, halfway up the Bay to Providence.

The history of yachting at Newport is full of glitter and extravagance — a rich tradition in more ways than one. So much so that the deeper history of Narragansett Bay has been obscured from popular study. By comparison with what is known of traditional working craft of the coast of Maine, for example, little is known of the traditional craft of lower Narragansett Bay, for only a handful of examples, models, and sketches survived of such types as the Newport Shore boat, the Newport catboat, the Narragansett Bay sloop, and the early Newport or Point boat.

But the tradition was there. It had been there since before the late 1600s, when the town of Bristol was organized, perhaps in hopes of rivaling its English counterpart as a major seaport. And one can't help but consider the implications of Bristol's own early traditions upon the Herreshoff family, whose history in the town begins just after 1800. Located as it was, between New York and Boston, a more industrious impulse was required for Bristol to make a place for itself in the world of commerce. According to the historical tradition, Bristol, as well as other Rhode Island ports, flourished well into the mid-19th century, when the nature of commerce and transport began to change in this country. According to L. Francis Herreshoff, in his *Capt. Nat Herreshoff, The Wizard of Bristol*, as many as 15 Bristol ships were engaged in foreign trade by 1690, and between 1700 and 1800 the town produced not only these standard vessels of commerce, but also privateers and slave ships. The latter two types depended for their success, of course, on their ability to outsail almost anything else afloat.

Even in the early youth of Nathanael Herreshoff, shipbuilding was a significant aspect of Bristol's economy, but the times were changing. The rewards of commerce had opened the way for the pursuit of pleasure, and "yachting" was slowly gaining in popularity. When Nathanael was born in 1848, only one yacht club — New York — had a formal organization in this country. At the end of the Civil War, there were only nine organized clubs. But by 1871, the year *Shadow* was built, there were no fewer than 28.

They must have been heady years for those early sailors and boatbuilders. Designing boats on paper had not yet been heard of in this country, though that would soon change with the appearance, also in 1871, of A. Cary Smith's *Vindex*. When boatbuilders carved their models, they did so not to admire them, or to talk about them, but to *build* them. They had neither the time nor the inclination for empty theorization. Their tradition grew out of the working boats of their locale: the shallow centerboard boats around New York, where the waters were relatively shallow and calm, the deep-keel craft around Boston, where seaworthiness was more of an issue and the water was generally deeper, and the variations in between. Narragansett Bay was the home of one of those variations: the Newport, or Point boat, a deep-keel type that figures heavily in the evolution of *Shadow*'s distinctive shape.

The Newport boat is one of the earliest-known small craft of Narragansett Bay. The hull was seen by Howard Chapelle as distinctly related to the radical Bermuda sloops of the early 1800s, and by W.P. Stephens as related to the English cutters of the late 1700s. Whatever its origins, it had become something unique unto itself prior to 1830, and according to Chapelle, by 1850 the type was being replaced by the shoaler centerboard sloops and catboats.

Opposite — Shadow glides along in light airs while all but the man who tends the jib topsail sheet relax. She was steered with a horizontal wheel, favored by many of the early designers but not too popular among many owners.

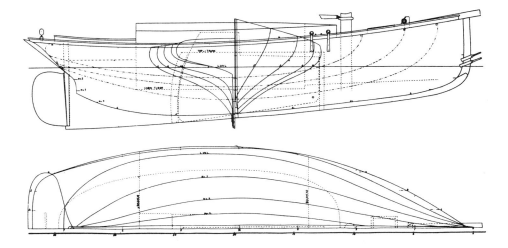

The lines of *Shadow* as taken off and drawn by W.P. Stephens and John Hyslop, and published in the July 28, 1887, issue of *Forest and Stream*.

Such was the influence of the New York builders upon the shape of yachts and working craft alike in those days. Such was the passion for swiftness.

The Newport boats were generally deep, short-ended craft of around 20 to 25 feet overall, rigged with a single mast (stepped a little farther aft than on a catboat), and a loose-footed, short-gaff sail. A removable bowsprit fitted over the stemhead and was held in place by means of a solid rod bobstay with a hook that fastened to an eye or staple on the side of the stem just above the waterline. To this bowsprit was hooked a jib, set flying, for light and moderate breezes. Like all working boats of the time, they were inside-ballasted and of ample beam, and an average Newport boat carried several tons of stone ballast very low. The combination of these elements made them versatile and weatherly boats and capable of standing up to considerably more wind and sea than the boats built on the New York models.

Because of those qualities, it is easy to see how they might have influenced Charles Frederick Herreshoff, Nathanael's father, to build one, *Julia*, for his family's use sometime around 1833, the year he was married to Julia Lewis. This boat was the first of several *Julia*s, and although she has never been referred to specifically as a Newport boat, she has been described as being typical of the boats of the Bay, and further details about her seem to support the conclusion. If the record serves correctly, this same *Julia* was still participating and doing well in the friendly races on the Bay in 1853.

In any case, *Julia* was a part of the Herreshoff family for some 20 years, and she was undoubtedly the boat in which Nathanael was first taken out as a boy, it being the primary means of

transportation around the Bay, as well as the boat for sport. And the sport was growing, for Bristol, located rather at the center of the Bay, became the gathering place for all who loved to race together. Charles Frederick Herreshoff was among them. Indeed, as time went on, it seems that his life grew closer and closer to the water, and farther from the workings of the family farm. And it's no wonder, for those must have been exciting days.

It was into this scene that Nathanael was born in 1848, the seventh of nine children. The world (or at least Bristol) was a beautiful place then. The possibilities for experimenting around the water were endless. It was a time when resourcefulness was passed on by necessity, and rowing and sailing were learned as children learn to ride bicycles nowadays.

For a few years, it appears that the children played the way all children do, but there was plenty to feed the insatiable curiosity of them all as Charles shared with his children the delights of the Bay and its islands. By the time he was 14, in 1855, Nathanael's older brother John (J.B.) was building the little V-bottomed *Meteor* for himself in his own shop. It was during this period that he was stricken with blindness, a turn of fate that had much to do with the nature and number of responsibilities that gradually fell to Nathanael, who was seven years younger. Although their father remained a companion and teacher to J.B., it was Nathanael who had now to begin to see for *two* people, and to see *every detail*, for J.B. had an untiring mind, and there's no doubt that Little Natty had little rest. By the time he was 11, he was able to lay down the shapes for the molds of *Sprite*, modeled by his father and J.B. together (and now on display at the Herreshoff Marine Museum in Bristol).

Nathanael was also becoming quite a helmsman on the Bay and a veteran of voyages as far away as New York.

At 18, J.B. was in the business of building small boats, and utilizing more than ever the developing talents of Nathanael. By 1863, J.B. had developed his business enough to hire a crew and to acquire a sawmill for the production of lumber. The business thrived, and the building of small boats gave way to the building of small yachts, modeled primarily by J.B. and his father at first, with the sailplans and other drafting requirements being handled by Nathanael. But the young man was also demonstrating his ability to translate his observations about the way boats performed to the process of modeling, and it appears that his father and brother were beginning to depend more and more upon his instincts — so much so that in 1864, at age 16, Nathanael modeled a 35-foot centerboard sloop. Two of these were built on the model, and the second, *Violet*, went to Boston under the ownership of Eben Denton, an active yachtsman who played his part in extolling the virtues of the Herreshoffs to his cronies. In any case, it appears that *Violet* is the first yacht for an outside customer whose model is attributed solely to Nathanael. Had he wanted to, he could surely have joined his brother in partnership then and there, but he had already set his sights a bit higher, and in the fall of 1866, he was enrolled at the Massachusetts Institute of Technology in the mechanical engineering curriculum. For as curious and capable a mind as his, it is likely that the resources at MIT held his interest for quite some time, although he was able to gather, during the year, with the members of the newly formed Boston Yacht Club (of which Eben Denton was a charter member), there to talk boats and sailing without interruption.

Considering his thorough knowledge of the subject, his experience in modeling and constructing boats, and his apparent facility with math, the Club asked Nathanael to construct a set of measurement rules and a table of time allowances for the members' boats. Such a table would allow the boats of the Club to compete together, though their particular dimensions (sail area was not considered) might vary considerably. To the participants in the sport, the creation of the time allowance tables brought a consistent standard to bear on rating, and suddenly the competition could become more meaningful. It was the first such table published in this country and was a profound contribution to the sport.

It is a remarkable feat for an 18-year-old to be constructing such tables in the absence of very much reference data, and it reveals something of the depth of his understanding of hull shape and performance characteristics. But that understanding was second nature to him, or so it seems, and his fascination appears to have been with the further development of the steam engine. In 1869, so the records say, he left MIT and returned to his native Rhode Island, where he worked as a draftsman for the Corliss Steam Engine Company of Providence. It is doubtful that his responsibilities were limited to drafting for very long, with as thorough a mechanical background as he had, and he surely spent time in the pattern and machine shops there as well. Indeed, it was in the pattern shop at Corliss that he carved out the model of *Shadow*.

It appears that J.B., with characteristic ambition and ability, was bringing in customers for Herreshoff yachts as fast as he could, and that Nathanael's expertise in the modeling and drafting of these was so highly sought by him that the younger brother was beginning to burn the midnight and weekend oil. In November of 1870, he produced *Shadow*'s model. Her profile above the waterline looked much like the centerboard sloops of the time, but below, she was unusual. She was deep — nearly a foot deeper, as modeled, than other contemporary Herreshoff sloops of approximately the same waterline length, the reason being to get her ballast as low as possible. The turn of the bilge was quite high, nearly all above the waterline, while below that line, her midsection was extremely hollow. She was equipped with a unique Herreshoff contrivance, the shifting ballast car, which traveled on a track in the cabin and provided a significant amount of leverage to weather. She was built during the winter of 1870–71, by J.B., for Dr. E.R. Sisson of New Bedford, who, curiously enough, owned her but one season — and therein lies a short tale.

What little appears in the historical records about *Shadow*'s first season suggests that Dr. Sisson was never at ease with her unusual shape. Indeed, according to Nathanael Herreshoff's recollections, the new owner refused, at first, to accept the yacht as built, because in model it departed so substantially from the shoaler sloops of the time. But no man was a match for the larger-than-life personality of J.B. Herreshoff, and one can easily imagine that it took little convincing; Dr. Sisson had a new sloop.

He apparently sailed her in several races during the season of his ownership, and she was acknowledged to be a fast sailer, though not especially so. Given her remarkable performance in subsequent years, it is perhaps safe to say that the good doctor's heart was not in it. Or, perhaps he was unable to put together the kind of crack crew that could make *Shadow* fly. In any case, by the spring of 1872, she was in the hands of Charles S. Randall, also of New Bedford. One can only surmise that Dr. Sisson was glad to be rid of her. But a remarkable exchange of letters about *Shadow*'s origins appeared in *Forest and Stream* some 16 years later, when the yachting public had finally awakened to her phenomenal achievements.

August 18, 1887

I think it no more than fair that a true statement of how the *Shadow* came to be built should be given to the public. Dr. E.R. Sisson, who is considered one of the best local yachtsmen hereabouts, employed his brother-in-law, Nathan Sears, a boat builder, to cut a model for a sloop yacht, which the doctor talked of building. The model was executed and accepted by Dr. Sisson, who gave Mr. Sears the dimensions. The doctor being desirous that the Herreshoffs should build the yacht, a run was taken down to Bristol, when the subject was brought to the attention of these celebrated builders, who informed him that they never built yachts after any other person's model. The doctor wishing to build from the dimensions in his model, asked if they would build on the lines named by him (Sisson), they to cut a model. This the brothers consented to do, and when the lines were given them they ridiculed the idea of building a yacht of the dimensions named, saying that a yacht built according to the plans would prove useless as far as speed was concerned. They rather demurred from undertaking the task but the doctor insisted, and the Herreshoffs agreed to build for a certain sum. The yacht was finished, and when Dr. Sisson went to Bristol to take possession he found that they had charged him several hundred dollars more than agreed, and he would not take her. Finally the Herreshoffs, who had little faith in the craft, came down from their high horse and Dr. Sisson took the yacht as per contract. He brought her to this port, named her *Shadow*, and while owned by him sailed her in several races, when she was proven to be a fast sailer. In justice to Dr. Sisson, I think this brief sketch of how the *Shadow* came to be built should be stated, as a perusal of the article in the *Forest and Stream* would lead yachtsmen to think that the Herreshoffs were the originators of this fast sloop, which has such a wonderful record. Take the lines of the far-famed *Puritan* and compare them with those of the *Shadow*; and it will be seen that they are an outcome from the plans originating with Dr. Sisson, the *Shadow* being the first deep draft centerboard yacht built in the country.

— Lewis Temple in *New Bedford Standard*

September 15, 1887

Mr. N.G. Herreshoff writes to the *New Bedford Standard:*

My attention has been called to an article in your issue of Aug. 18, over signature of Lewis Temple, in which the invention of the yacht *Shadow*'s lines is claimed for Dr. Sisson. I am not usually swayed by what is printed in newspapers, nor do I think this claim, false as it is, will be credited by any yachtsman; but this seems a case where one's duty to the public itself demands that the truth should be known. I modeled the *Shadow* in each and every particular, and her then peculiar lines had been in process of development in my mind for more than a year before I knew such a person as Dr. Sisson existed. One year before the *Shadow* was built I cut two preliminary ones of her same character — notably a schooner yacht about 90 feet long, which model can be seen. If I remember rightly, her name, *Shadow* was suggested by Mr. John Hussey, of your city, some time before she was launched. It is true that there was a time of dissatisfaction on the part of Dr. Sisson when the *Shadow* was finished and about to be delivered. He at first refused to accept the yacht because her builders had departed so far from the usual type, or to use his words as I remember them, 'were experimenting at his expense.'

February 1, 1888

We publish the following at the request of Mr. Lewis Temple, whose first statement in regard to *Shadow* has been questioned. The letter was sent by Mr. Temple, some time since, but was not received until recently.

To the Editor of the *New Bedford Standard*: It seems to be a knotty question as to the origin of this celebrated sloop model. Had I known that Mr. Lewis Temple was to have published his article of 'credit to whom credit is due,' in reference to the origin of the *Shadow*, I should have asked him not to; but in the main what he said is true, the Herreshoffs to the contrary, especially about the high horse. Mr. N.G. Herreshoff said to me while his brother John B. Herreshoff was building the *Shadow*, and one year and a half afterward, that he did not think as much of the *Shadow*'s model as he did of the *Clytie*'s. As far as my knowledge goes in the matter of lines held by present and semi-past modellers, there is but little that is new. Most of us remember the Baltimore clippers of some years since; compare these lines with the present and you find nothing but a modification. A little more depth, more canvas, and leaded keel, and you have it about all. I acknowledge, as I always have, that John B. Hussey suggested the name *Shadow*, and feel sure that no one knows better than he how suggestive that name was of the little intrinsic value she proved to me.

— Very truly, E.R. Sisson

The possibility exists, of course, that Dr. Sisson and his brother-in-law did, in fact, produce a model with *Shadow*'s general characteristics, that is, a beamy, deep centerboarder. But if such were the case, he should have been more than pleased with the resulting yacht.

Charles S. Randall was of somewhat different persuasion. To make a success of his new sloop, he would have to learn her strengths from the man who modeled her, so he invited Nathanael Herreshoff to sail *Shadow* in a match race early in the season. Many years later, Nathanael recalled the race in a letter to C.H.W. Foster:

My first race under the Eastern Yacht Club flag, was in

Though the wind is dropping fast, there is still an opportunity to appreciate the phenomenal amount of canvas that *Shadow* could carry, including the spinnaker poled out to starboard to catch the faintest breath. By the time this photo was taken, in August 1887, she had become something of a legend.

early summer of 1872 when I sailed *Shadow* against Malcolm Forbes' *White Cap*. *Shadow* was designed by me and was of rather unusual type. She was 35½' on deck, 33½' waterline, 14'4" beam, and 5'6" deep. Draft without centerboard was about 4'9". The garboards were quite low and nearly 6" hollow, and all the ballast was contained inside. The yacht was built for a Dr. Sisson of New Bedford in 1871 by John B. Herreshoff and at the time I sailed her was owned by Mr. Randall, also of New Bedford. *White Cap* was designed by Bob Fish and built for the Livingston Brothers in 1867 or '68, and like most of Fish's designs was of a quite shallow centerboard type and very fast. Her dimensions were very nearly the same as *Shadow*'s.

The race started outside of Marblehead Rock in a quite moderate SSE breeze — which gave a beat to windward. *White Cap* started a little ahead and she began gaining slightly. Our club topsail was too large and could not be sheeted flat, so after getting sail needles and twine ready we lowered it and sewed in a reef along the foot. By the time we had it reset *White Cap* was out to windward fully ⅛ mile. But we began gaining and had a very substantial lead at the weather mark which we held to the finish. This race and another in Buzzards Bay later in the season indicated the advantages of a hull with greater displacement even with all

the ballast inside. . . . . *Shadow* was later bought by Dr. John Bryant and under his handling was an unbeatable yacht for 15 years, until Edward Burgess designed *Papoose* for Charles Adams and his brother with nearly all ballast outside. She outsailed *Shadow* easily.

Although Nathanael could make her go, it seems as if Randall couldn't quite get what he wanted out of her, so he sold her the following year to Caspar Crowninshield, a fellow member of the Eastern Yacht Club. Under his two-year ownership (1873–74), *Shadow* doesn't appear to have placed in any races, although she seems to have entered a few. Perhaps Crowninshield didn't care much for racing but preferred a more leisurely kind of sailing. Or perhaps, like his predecessors, he couldn't quite get what he wanted out of her. Sometime after the season of 1874, he sold her to yet another member of the Eastern Yacht Club, Tucker Daland. Under his ownership, *Shadow* began to establish herself, and it would seem that he was the first owner who truly understood what he had in this unusually deep centerboarder. Indeed, it was probably he who made her *deeper*, for someone had done so by the spring of 1875, increasing her draft from 4 feet 9 inches to 5 feet 4 inches. Perhaps he decided that the shifting ballast car was too much of a nuisance, removed it, and substituted more weight in the bilge for the leverage of the ballast car. It would have required the addition of relatively little more lead inside to bring her down 7 inches, and the modification must have been considered successful, for her draft never changed again, as far as is known. Her ballast, incidentally, had been specially cast to fit as low as possible in the bilge.

Of the two organized regattas in which *Shadow* participated during the season of 1875, she gained firsts in both elapsed and corrected time. Although it's not known how stiff the competition was in her class that year, it wasn't getting any easier to win, with the ever-increasing interest in the sport. And the Eastern Yacht Club seems to have been where the best boats were gathering, east of Cape Cod, so the standards of the day were demanding. As for conversation on the veranda, it had already begun to focus upon the question of keel versus centerboard, or narrow and deep versus wide and shallow. So new was the question that the word "compromise," as it was later to be applied to *Shadow*'s hull form, was not yet in use. She was simply referred to as a deep centerboarder. The world had still not awakened to her remarkable attributes, but, by and large, could think only in extremes, and toward the shallow ones at that. According to W.P. Stephens, about the only articulate proponent of depth-as-opposed-to-beam was C.P. Kunhardt, editor of *Forest and Stream*, who wrote a comprehensive treatise on the subject of initial versus ultimate stability in the October 1875 issue of *The Aquatic Monthly*. It was considered to have fallen on deaf ears, for the majority of budding yachtsmen seemed to want speed and were ignorant not only of the dangers of wide, shallow hulls in the wrong conditions, but of the traditions that had created the fast and weatherly boats east of New York. They were incapable, in fact, of translating their enthusiasm into experience, the crucial ingredient.

To wit: It was in 1875 that the famous centerboard schooner *Mohawk* was launched at New York. With a waterline length of 120 feet, she drew only 6 feet of water. The following year, she capsized in a gust of wind while at anchor with her fore, main, and topsails set. Five people were trapped and drowned below.

But though the capsize was a great tragedy, it was surely a catalyst in the moderation of the extremists. In the years that followed, the partisans of each form grew more equal in number, and the stage was set for the full-fledged cutter-sloop controversy.

More importantly, perhaps, the stage was set for *Shadow*, the sloop that was ahead of her time, to come into her own. By the beginning of the 1877 season, *Shadow* had been purchased from Tucker Daland by Dr. John Bryant, an active sailor, a friend of Edward Burgess, and a newly elected member of the Eastern Yacht Club. It was under his ownership, which lasted 20 years, that *Shadow* became so widely celebrated — first for her singular, if controversial, victory over the Scottish cutter *Madge* in 1881, then later, when the term "compromise" hull became part of the popular vocabulary and she was discovered to have been one all along. In truth, her success had as much to do with the men who sailed and cared for her as it did with the man who modeled her.

Dr. Bryant loved *Shadow* as she had never been loved, and he was deeply committed to keeping her in the best condition for both racing and cruising. As yachting grew, so did the number of yacht clubs and regattas, and *Shadow* was there, showing her stern to almost all who raced against her. Though Dr. Bryant was an excellent sailor (he was later to be one of the afterguard on the Cup defenders *Puritan*, *Mayflower*, and *Volunteer*), he entrusted the sailing of *Shadow* in races to Captain Aubrey Crocker, a Cape Cod skipper with sharp instincts and long experience, who was later to skipper the aforementioned Cup defenders. With "Cap'n Aub" and a consistent and enthusiastic crew, *Shadow* established a record without precedent. When she met *Madge* in 1881 at Newport for the famous race, she had been under Bryant's ownership for four years. Her record to that point, out of 49 races, was 39 firsts, seven seconds, and three thirds.

She was 10 years old, and now acknowledged by the contemporary press as being the finest example of the American sloop on the water. For the members of the Eastern Yacht Club, who had watched *Madge* clean up in New York waters, here was a chance to show off their best. The choice was obvious: it would be *Shadow* and *Madge* in a pair of match races. Not only would it be a race between cutter and sloop, but between foreigner and native. It would be a matter of honor.

The cutter versus sloop controversy was nowhere more evident than in the pages of *Forest and Stream*, whose editor, C.P. Kunhardt, was a deeply entrenched cutter crank. He didn't think very much of the merits of the American sloop as compared with those of the English cutter. For, although the "planks-on-edge" were more the product of rating rules than good sense, he subscribed to the principles on which the cutters were based, namely, less beam and more depth for their length than their American counterparts. In fact, his impatience was less for *Shadow* and other deep sloops than for the skimming dishes, the proponents of which were as obstinate in their defense of their type as he was fanatical in his attacks. Yet, his lone voice was barely audible in the noise and excitement of light-draft racing around New York Bay. Ironically, it was that noise and excitement that brought *Madge* to New York, where she put the sloops to shame, and later, to Newport, where her races with *Shadow* marked the beginning of a new era in yacht design.

It has been said that C.P. Kunhardt himself was in large part responsible for seeing that *Madge* was shipped to American waters, here to prove once and for all that the cutter was the better boat. It's possible, of course, but perhaps more plausible that some kindred souls at the Seawanhaka Yacht Club arranged the occurrence with her owner, James Coats, and remained anonymous in their endeavors. In any case, she arrived in mid-August 1881, in the care of her captain and Mr. W.L. Blatch, a friend of Coats's and a member of the New York Yacht Club. By mid-September, Blatch and a committee from the Seawanhaka Yacht Club had arranged a series of races on New York Bay between *Madge* and the best of the light-draft sloops, *Schemer* and *Wave*.

The story goes that *Madge* had been spending her time sailing impromptu matches in the Bay with numerous centerboarders and losing them on purpose by sailing with her staysail backed and her bilge half full of water, and dragging 20 fathoms of chain in the mud. As far as is known, it was no more than a story, but the cutter did, indeed, play possum, and very convincingly. The excitement of overconfidence was abundant, and when the day of the first race arrived, the vast majority of gambling men put their money on the crack centerboard sloops.

They figured *Madge* to be beaten easily, and they were wrong. She swept over the courses like a thoroughbred, knifing through the same seas that stalled the beamy sloops. Though in a calm-to-moderate breeze and sea she could foot no faster than the sloops, she could point much higher, and thus weather the marks more quickly and easily. Of course, the sloop men thought surely they had the cutter on the downwind runs, for they could trice up their centerboards and fly, while *Madge* would have to drag her lowslung ballast through it. But it was not so. The cutter seemed to run just as fast.

Officially, *Madge* sailed five races in New York in 1881. In fact, the fifth race was without a competitor, as *Schemer* had sprung her rudder and was unable to sail the course; she willingly forfeited the prize money rather than postpone the race, which the cutter sailed alone. Her uninterrupted victories were by margins of from five to 12 minutes, elapsed time, over the 40-mile course, and corrected time increased the margins to between 17 and 23 minutes. To the patriotic sloop men, it was a shocking defeat. As a number of yachting writers pointed out, it was fortunate that the competition was not for the *America*'s Cup.

The contemporary press conceded the victories in no uncertain terms, and the majority of the writers seemed full of admiration and praise for the cutter. The light-draft "traps" had been soundly defeated, and the wave of patriotic pride gave way to disappointment. C.P. Kunhardt was beside himself with pleasure, for he had been vindicated. The pages of *Forest and Stream* were full of his self-satisfied prose.

The *New York Times* for October 1, 1881, carried the most concise summation of events:

The performances of the Scotch cutter *Madge*, which has so significantly and painfully beaten the American sloops against which she has been matched, are adapted to create a variety of feelings in the American yachting breast. When she made her appearance here it was the almost universal belief that her owner had come a long way for the sake of a bad beating. Experienced yachtsmen looked at her and said that she might be regarded as a good boat by British yachtsmen, accustomed to the short and nasty seas of the English and Irish Channels, but that she was utterly unsuited to our waters. Nevertheless, this little British yacht has beaten our fastest sloops, and without the least necessity of availing herself of the time allowance to which she was entitled.

If the best of New York felt the sting of defeat, the best of Boston were anxious for the fray. There was no question that the eastern

In the Massachusetts Yacht Club annual regatta for 1890, *Shadow* leads *Nomad,* a sloop designed in 1884 by A. Cary Smith.

sloops were deeper, heavier, and generally more wholesome than New York's light drafts, and many of the more knowledgeable believed that they could provide stiffer competition for *Madge*. Indeed, even Kunhardt himself did not dismiss that possibility out of hand, for *Shadow*, the best of them all, had an enviable record and a crack crew.

On Saturday, October 8, *Madge* dropped her mooring off Staten Island and sailed for Newport to rendezvous with *Shadow*. The Newport races would be different from the New York races in that the two types represented would be less radically different in character. Both were fast and weatherly in a variety of conditions; both had the ability to stand up under a full press of canvas; both were essentially noncapsizable; both had behind them an impressive list of victories.

The races, scheduled for Friday and Saturday, October 14 and 15, 1881, were to be over two courses. The first was to be 10 miles to windward and back, or 20 miles altogether, with no time allowance, and the second, a triangle of 10-mile sides, or 30 miles, with *Shadow* allowing a handicap of just over three minutes to *Madge*.

Aboard *Shadow*, Dr. Bryant followed his usual practice of turning the sloop over to "Cap'n Aub" Crocker for the races. Aboard *Madge*, Captain Robert Duncan, who had so

skillfully taken New York by surprise, prepared to show the cutter's stern to yet another victim. But it was not to be so that day, for *Madge* carried away one of her spreaders while rounding a mark and lost the first race to *Shadow*. On Saturday, however, with her spreader repaired, *Madge* returned to defeat the sloop. [Kunhardt's account of the races is excerpted on the next page]

Kunhardt had been twice vindicated now. But his writings were so openly biased that it was difficult for some sloop men to be sure of the meaning of the results. Knowing that his own word would not be good enough for his bitter opponents, he published a letter from *Madge*'s skipper, and one from a Boston observer. He also published letters upholding *Shadow*'s victory that tended to make their authors sound totally irrational. Not one appeared from Dr. Bryant or Captain Crocker.

Unfortunately, the two boats never raced again, though there was often talk of organizing new matches. It hardly mattered; *Shadow* and *Madge* were both wholesome, handy, and swift examples of their respective types. In a sense, the fluke of a victory by the sloop provided the more entrenched sloop fanatics with a mechanism for adapting their prejudice to the new thinking that resulted. And new thinking it was, for almost overnight the periodicals of the time were full of announcements of deeper

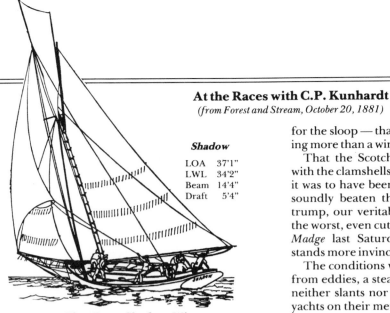

At the Races with C.P. Kunhardt
(from Forest and Stream, October 20, 1881)

Shadow

LOA	37'1"
LWL	34'2"
Beam	14'4"
Draft	5'4"

First Race, Shadow Wins

The *Shadow* is probably the finest example of the American sloop extant. She was brought to the line in the most perfect condition and was fully alive to the keenness of the races in store for her. She had the advantage of a thoroughly trained crew of quick-witted amateurs who had successfully worked her across the finish in the lead a great number of times.

It was noteworthy that *Shadow* was not any too good in even a little sea, and we believe her modeler, Mr. Herreshoff, if requested to design a boat particularly good in rough water would follow out the modifications we have been counseling. With these the *Shadow* would have been a better boat for all-round work than she is.

Madge would have won but for the accident to her spreader, and running out of the wind after breaking tacks with her opponent as a last desperate effort to hunt for luck. The accident got the cutter's crew, supplemented by some green Newport hands, into a mess with her canvas.

Of course with a lame leg the cutter could not point as is her wont, or rather the sloop pointed just as high, which she could not have done had *Madge* not been so badly winged at the most critical moment, when the turn up home had just begun.

Whenever the two yachts had things alike the cutter overhauled and weathered the sloop in an unmistakable way which guaranteed a win for the stranger should even terms ever be had. The pot went to *Shadow* legitimately enough, but the race, if anything, served to mark the cutter as a little the better of the two, and in a series of races we believe *Madge* would be able to more than cope with *Shadow* on even terms, let alone making her time off the big sloop, to which she is properly entitled.

Second Race, Madge Wins

The cutter has met a sloop without a peer in America, a sloop in the most perfect racing condition, tooled by a crew as smart and live as ever took a yacht over a course, and that same sloop, in as fair a race as was ever sailed, has succumbed to the fine form, big displacement and Gosport wings of the truly "Invincible *Madge*." Tally six for the cutter and but one for the sloop — that solitary relief to monotony, nothing more than a win on a most patent fluke at that.

That the Scotch cutter should have made sport with the clamshells of New York was bad enough, but it was to have been expected. That she should have soundly beaten the "wonderful *Shadow*," our best trump, our veritable right bower in case it came to the worst, even cutter men hardly dared to hope. Yet *Madge* last Saturday surpassed herself, and now stands more invincible than ever.

The conditions were perfect. An open course free from eddies, a steady, solid working breeze offering neither slants nor puffs, just enough sea to put the yachts on their mettle, no accidents, no "errors," and both competitors close aboard in the same wind and water all over the course. No fairer test could have been had. Under such circumstances we looked for a complete reversal of the accidental results of the day previous, and the cutter did not disappoint her friends.

Madge, 10 tons
Shadow, 12.5 tons

Start	First Mark	Second Mark	Finish
11:26:49	1:05:00	2:34:25	3:43:05
11:23:50	1:05:45	2:40:55	3:49:09

Shadow, Dr. Bryant, Eastern Y.C., therefore wins by 22 m. 42s.

An instructive table, indeed. A clear gain of 2m. 44s. on a beat ten miles to windward. A clear gain of 5m. 45s. on a ten mile reach and nearly an even thing squared away, the sloop with her board triced up, showing more sail, and the cutter not driven for the best.

Madge

LOA	46'
LWL	39'9"
Beam	7'9"
Draft	7'8"

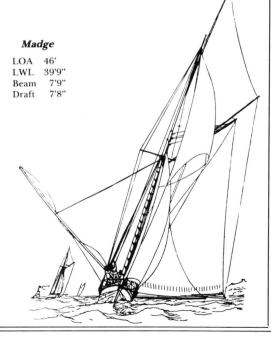

boats being designed and built. The orders for pure cutters abounded, as yachtsmen rushed to follow the example set by *Madge*. Some designers began experimenting with a form that came to be called the "compromise cutter," which could be described as a deep and narrow centerboarder. As for the builders of light-draft sloops, their orders were for more and more depth. Good sense was beginning to prevail, although the cutter-sloop controversy was anything but over. Kunhardt knew only too well that *Shadow* was a unique American sloop, that there was not another like her, and that his mission was not yet accomplished. *Madge* had won the battle for him, but not the war. She had proven that she could traverse a course in short order no matter what the weather, and perhaps that she could finish a day's run an hour or so before a sloop if the run was mostly to windward. Interestingly, that attribute so impressed Dr. Bryant that he ordered a longer topmast and larger club topsail for *Shadow* for the 1882 season.

It would be difficult, from our limited vantage point, to assess the performance improvements made by that change, because *Shadow*'s record remained a fairly consistent five wins out of six starts, on the average. But there would have to be gains, for her low ballast gave her tremendous power. Perhaps some gain was psychological. After all, he could not help but have been influenced by *Madge*'s awesome ability, in a breeze, to stand up to a whole sail sheeted flat as a board. To look up and see his own towering cloud of canvas drawing would be a thrill beyond compare. But *Shadow* was one of the few (if not the only) centerboard sloops that could safely accommodate such an increase.

We see her today as a "compromise" type; in her day she was simply a "deep centerboarder." The word "compromise" as a description of hull form was not then in use, primarily because the *notion* of compromise was unacceptable to all but those of solid experience, who knew it to be an integral and inevitable aspect of practical yacht design. It was not so much a matter of making sacrifices as it was of balancing gains and concessions, of *combining* qualities rather than reducing them. When he modeled *Shadow*'s exquisite hull, young Nathanael Herreshoff combined an unusual set of elements. That he did so with such success may have surprised even himself. Compromise, in the positive sense of the word, had been part of the process. Compromise, in the negative sense, is what sloop

fanatics feared. They needed to believe in their boats, and since there was nothing to compare with *Shadow*, she remained the boat to beat.

In August 1883, *Wave* sailed east from New York for a match that both owners had sought since their matches with *Madge*. She made the passage under her cruising rig and her racing spars and sails were shipped by express. Through a series of mishaps, an incomplete outfit arrived, and late, at that. The result was that only two disappointing and inconclusive races could be held before the match had to be called off due to lack of time. Predictably, *Wave* fared well in the light breezes of the races, but an accurate evaluation was impossible. It was generally concluded that in such conditions she would move faster through the water than *Shadow*, but that the latter would point higher. A stronger breeze might have favored her in speed, simply because she could carry sail longer, but *Wave* was a bigger boat in every respect but draft. With that disappointing result to show for her effort and expense, she sailed again for New York.

It might be useful to recall at this point that while she regularly beat everything in her class, whether keel or centerboard, *Shadow* was not a racing machine. She was a cruising boat that raced for the sport and performed consistently well. For the 1883 season she took seven firsts out of eight starts; for 1884 it was four firsts and four seconds out of 11 starts. For 1885 it was two firsts out of only three starts, which might suggest that Dr. Bryant, Captain Crocker, and the sloop's crack crew were tiring of the game, but the opposite was true. Their friend Edward Burgess had designed a moderately deep centerboard sloop named *Puritan*, which had been selected to defend the *America*'s Cup against the cutter *Genesta* that year. *Puritan*'s skipper was none other than "Cap'n Aub" Crocker, and her afterguard, the crew of *Shadow*. That the combination was successful is a matter of history, and their success was repeated twice with the Cup defenders *Mayflower* and *Volunteer* in 1886 and 1887. In *Forest and Stream* the fires of the cutter-sloop controversy were fanned, as the deep cutters *Genesta*, *Galatea*, and *Thistle* fell victim to our moderate centerboarders. It was during this period that the term "compromise" began to be applied to the Burgess boats, as they combined attributes of the centerboard sloop in hull form and attributes of the cutter in rig. As time went on, it came to mean anything that lay somewhere between the two types.

In the fall of 1886, *Shadow* found herself in the midst of another cutter-sloop controversy — ironically, with another Watson-designed plank-on-edge, the little 5-ton *Shona*. She was shipped from Scotland to the United States by her owner, C.H. Tweed of Boston, for pleasure sailing out of Marblehead. Tweed was a part owner in the cutter *Clara* as well, which was raced by Captain John Barr. Though *Shona* was not on the racing circuit, it was only natural that she participate in regattas about Marblehead. One in particular, on September 4, 1886, found her matched against *Shadow*, though they were not sailing in the same class. In tonnage the sloop was considerably larger, but their waterline lengths were nearly identical.

Forest and Stream, reporting on the regatta, described the unintended match:

> The little cutter *Shona*, sailed by Capt. John Barr and a crew drafted from *Clara*, was dodging right along the line as the gun fired, and was off like a flash, swinging her No. 2 topsail. She was followed 11 seconds later by *Shadow*, carrying club topsail, with Capt. Aubrey Crocker at the Wheel.
>
> The course gave them a beat out to Half Way Rock, then a long run up the coast to a stakeboat off the Spindle, at the entrance to Swampscott Harbor, then a long thrash to windward, back to Half Way and a run home.
>
> *Shadow* and *Shona* easily distanced the others and had it hot and heavy between them, both boats being handled for all they were worth. *Shona* seemed to have a trifle the best of it beating out of the harbor, but at the Spindle they were close together, and some work was indulged in, the cutter got the best of it, and spun out a little lead on the beat back, which she rather increased running home, and finally won by 3m 16s corrected time [3m 23s elapsed], after one of the best races ever sailed here.

It would appear to have been a fascinating turn of events, but although a few entrenched cutter cranks found ammunition for their cause in *Shona*'s victory, and a few centerboard men were doubtless embarrassed by it, not much was made of it in the press. The inference drawn is that it was simply an exciting race, that wind and sea conditions were ideal for *Shona*, and that there was little significance in the result. One of *Shadow*'s crew members, Edward Hawes, did write to *Forest and Stream* that *Shona* had gained her lead by standing a bit farther offshore, where she "took perhaps a trifle better breeze, or less tide, perhaps. . . ." In any case, *Shadow* found her revenge on June 23rd of the following year in the Eastern Yacht Club regatta, when she simply walked away from the saucy but overpowered little cutter.

A stiff breeze was blowing as the race began, the topmasts were down on both boats, and reefs were tucked into the mainsails. The course was an equilateral triangle of 36 miles off Marblehead. As *Forest and Stream* reported:

> At the start and in the rough water, *Shona* had the best of *Shadow*, but as soon as the time came to shake out the reefs, the latter left her all day. The little cutter sailed on through what was for her a tremendous sea, but she was nowhere beside the larger and more powerful boat.
>
> *Shadow* beat *Shona* by 15 minutes, and though in the late races the little cutter had been badly handicapped by a very poor suit of new sails, she can never hope to sail on even terms with a boat so much larger as *Shadow*, to say nothing of the new *Papoose*.

So, the pride of the sloop was restored, if, indeed, it had ever been lost, but the end of an era was upon her, marked by the appearance of *Papoose*, the boat that inspired a whole new direction in design.

Designed by Edward Burgess for Charles Francis Adams III, *Papoose* was intended for both racing and cruising. Although *Shadow* had been undisputed champion of her class for more than a decade, Burgess thought he could design a keel sloop that could beat the old centerboarder without resorting in any way to extremes in form. If he was successful in his endeavor to combine such speed and comfort on a waterline length of 36 feet, he would be on to something unique.

On June 17, 1887, the occasion of the Dorchester Yacht Club regatta, the opportunity presented itself, and the new era was ushered in. *Shadow* was soundly defeated. In *Forest and Stream* for June 30, W.P. Stephens wrote:

> The question of board vs. keel is already settled for all who have watched the races of the last few years and seen how closely the extreme boats, though handicapped in other directions, have pushed the best results of 50 years' experience with centerboard boats; and today the best informed and most liberal friends of the compromise boats admit that for speed the board is inferior to the keel. Coming events cast their shadows before, and in the complete defeat of the fastest centerboarder of her size ever built, a boat with a reputation held against all comers for 16 years, and sailed by a crew that has handled her in many victorious races, the wise ones see a forecast of the contest of next September. The new boat *Papoose* is virtually a small *Thistle*, a keel boat of wide beam and great depth, but with a form such as has never yet been found in the many previous efforts about Boston to combine these two elements. Fresh from the builder's yard, with new sails and gear stiff and unwieldy, and sailed by her owner, a young man just in the midst of his college examinations, she beat the famous *Shadow* with Captain Crocker at the wheel, by 10 minutes in 20 miles, the wind being light and the water smooth. There were no flukes, the race was seen by many, and it has set all Boston to wondering just how the moral can be applied to *Mayflower* and *Thistle*. This is but the beginning of an attempt to bring to bear in the designing of keel boats untrammeled by extraneous conditions, the same skill and knowledge that has been expended on centerboards and we

are content to leave the result to the near future, confident that the old dogma of the inherent excellence of the centerboard to windward is nearly disposed of, and in the meantime can do no further harm.

For 16 years *Shadow* had been practically invincible. For 10 of those years Dr. John Bryant had seen to it that she was sailed at her best. She was still the finest example of the American sloop on the water, and rapidly becoming the only example. Ironically, only a month prior to the Dorchester regatta, W.P. Stephens and John Hyslop were at Dr. Bryant's home in Cohasset taking off *Shadow*'s lines for publication in *Forest and Stream*. We are lucky that they succeeded, for we were assured not only of her shape being preserved, but also of a contemporary description of her. Being a cutter crank himself, W.P. Stephens was a believer in the ultimate correctness of keel craft. But when he and John Hyslop arrived in Cohasset and gazed upon the remarkable shape of the center-

boarder hauled up on the railway, they must have been mightily impressed. *Forest and Stream* was a contemporary weekly not given to considering the past, yet even as the new era was being ushered in by the remarkable *Papoose*, Stephens saw fit to devote considerable space to the remarkable *Shadow*. Her lines, a rough sailplan, and a list of dimensions accompanied the following essay:

Of late years the name of Herreshoff has been so closely associated with steam that the earlier successes of the firm are little thought of, none of the latter efforts of the famous brothers have brought more fame, nor more deservedly, than the yacht *Shadow*, whose lines never before published, we give herewith. Built in 1871, she is still in the racing after 17 years, during which time she has fully proved her superiority to all the centerboard boats of her class, while today, when the American centerboard sloop has disappeared from racing, *Shadow* alone remains to represent the type. Why she has held the first place for so long, and why she still is in the racing, when the rest have withdrawn in favor of more modern craft, are questions of the greatest interest, but the answer to both is evident on an inspection

By September 1, 1887, when this photo was taken, the Burgess-designed *Papoose* had ushered in a new era.

of the lines. Speaking broadly today, when all minor distinctions have disappeared in the great issue of sloop vs. cutter, *Shadow* may be taken as a typical American sloop; but if we look into her characteristics more closely and compare her with the best boats of her day, the sloop of 15 years since, the great difference between them is apparent. The draft for a yacht of *Shadow's* length at that time was about 3' or 3'6", while the leading characteristics were shoal body, moderate deadrise and a hard bilge. In marked opposition to these are the distinctive features of *Shadow*, an extreme draft of 5'4", a great proportionate depth of body, a large angle of deadrise and a light bilge, while her lead ballast stowed close to the skin was very much lower than in the flatter boats. With this strong combination of initial elements selected, the builders added their skill and knowledge in arranging all minor details of the design, so that the boat was not only of a far more advanced type, but she realized more fully the inherent advantages of her type. Her large area of load water plane, great depth of body and the consequent low position of her ballast and high center of buoyancy insured a maximum of stability, while the form itself is easy with fair waterlines and clean run on the buttock lines.

While her record entitles her to be called a racing boat, *Shadow* has been used by all her owners as a cruising craft, and she has good accommodations for a boat of her type. The cabin is large, with double berths on the two lockers and about 5'6" headroom. The centerboard rises through the trunk as shown, the opening being closed by a hinged lid when the board is lowered. The galley is fairly roomy, though of course lacking in the matter of height. There is a large cockpit aft, the steering being done with a wheel. The rig is that of a sloop with single jib, a storm jib being set on a shifting stay, set up at will to the eye on the band of the preventer bobstay. The jib sheets lead from an eyebolt between the shrouds, through block on jib, then through fairleader on rail, as shown, and to cleat aft. The present topmast houses and is rather long for the old sloop rig, but in other respects there is little departure from it. It would be interesting to know all the influences that worked on the builders to produce a boat so different from the majority at that time, but the accounts all vary. At any rate they produced a boat that was not only better than any of her contemporaries, but that has held her racing life after the others have ended theirs and withdrawn from the contest. *Shadow* was built at Bristol, Rhode Island, in 1871, for Dr. E.R. Sisson, of New Bedford. He sold her to Mr. C.S. Randall of the same city, who in turn disposed of her to Mr. Tucker Daland. For the past dozen years she has been owned by Dr. John Bryant, of Boston, a member of the E.Y.C. who with other amateurs, has sailed her in most of the races open to her during that time. Her skipper for some years has been Capt. Aubrey Crocker, of *Puritan* fame, and to his skill and care a part of her success is certainly due. *Shadow* enjoys the distinction of winning the only match lost by the cutter *Madge*, beating the latter in one race off Newport in 1881, and losing one race to her.

Evolution is a curious phenomenon: If a new breed emerges while one of the fittest of the old breed survives, the latter becomes a kind of outcast in time.

Papoose and the boats that followed her evolved quickly into what became the very popular 40-foot class, which, within two years, boasted 19 yachts. In combination with the modification of rating rules and new thinking, hull forms became characterized by long overhangs, and the 40-footers led to the 46-footers, epitomized by such triumphs as *Gloriana* in 1891 and *Wasp* in 1892. Plumb stems and "stubtails" disappeared from the scene. The exemplary American sloop *Shadow* had outdistanced nearly all of her kind, and still she was ready for more. But the competition had been retired. By 1891, it was becoming difficult to find a match for her.

Had she been nothing more than a racing machine, Dr. Bryant might have had to sell her. But she had always been a comfortable cruising boat as well, so he was forced to give up nothing but the competition, such as it was.

Shadow remained his pride and joy until 1897, when, after having owned her for 20 years, he sold her. It is doubtful that anyone could have put as much heart and soul into caring for her as John Bryant had, and though information on her last years is sparse, a few things are known.

She probably changed hands a number of times, her history and significance growing more obscure with each transaction. Between 1900 and 1905, she had at least two owners, both of whom were Boston residents. One story holds that subsequently she was sold to an owner who used her as a fisherman. We do know the nature of her end, and we quote one last time from *Forest and Stream* for April 25, 1908:

> The disastrous fire that on April 12 swept over a part of the town of Chelsea, Massachusetts, destroyed the once-famous sloop *Shadow*, owned by Frank D. McCarthy, of East Boston.
>
> *Shadow* was built 37 years ago, in the spring of 1871, and was the only sloop able to beat the cutter *Madge* that invaded American waters in 1881.
>
> *Shadow* was laid up between the Chelsea bridges and was burned to the water. Her owner expects to raise her, not for the purpose of rebuilding, but for her lead keel.

Lead keel, indeed. Her fame had been won through the *absence* of outside ballast. But, of course, her bilge was filled with five and a half tons of lead. It had served her in good stead, and, combined with her exquisite shape and structure, had assured her a long and legendary life, during which she won (by most accounts) some 150 prizes.

She was a unique yacht; perhaps the finest American sloop ever built. She was so far ahead of her time as to be unrecognized, and when recognition came, it was too late to do more than salute her.

Mr. Herreshoff's Wonderful
Rozinante

Roger Taylor

*I*F NATHANAEL HERRESHOFF'S *yacht designs represent constructive and engineering genius, then those of his son L. Francis Herreshoff represent artistic genius. LFH's yachts possess an aesthetic balance not easily described but clearly perceived. One of his most simple and elegant designs is the Rozinante, which sails as well as it looks.*

We backed our way into this article as the result of conversations with Roger Taylor, an avid small-boat sailor with a keen interest in traditional designs. We encouraged Roger to write a two-part article on seamanship in open and decked boats, but for some reason the story wasn't falling easily into place. In one of our conversations, Roger mentioned that he had been sailing a friend's Rozinante and that she would make a great subject for the article. As the conversation progressed, we realized that he really would rather share his appreciation for the boat with our readers and save the question of seamanship for another time. We agreed, and our readers benefited from this insight into a superb boat and a later five-part series on small-boat seamanship.

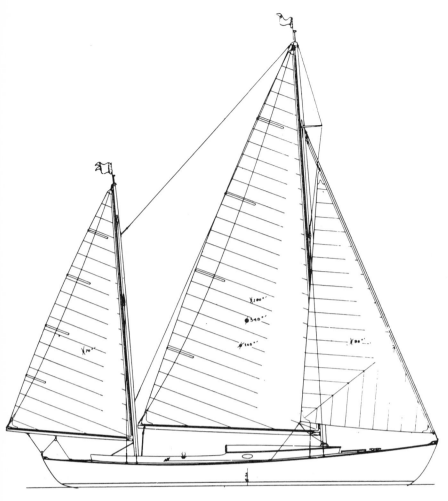

I ALWAYS WANTED to sail a Rozinante. When I learned that Ted Sprague had to be in Ohio for the summer and wouldn't be able to sail his, I offered to look after the *Arete.*

Ted is a thorough boatman and knows well that it is far better for a boat to be used, kept clean, and properly ventilated than to sit forlornly on a mooring. Fortunately for me, Ted said I could be her caretaker. That's how I got to sail a Rozinante out of Camden, Maine, all summer.

Ten years from now, when I think back on that rare sailing experience, I know very well the lasting impression that will leap to mind. It will be looking aft at that delicate, pointed stern slipping through the water. If you would have a boat, my friend, get one with a pointed stern.

As far as I am concerned, that says enough about the Rozinante to put her right into the Hall of Fame. Nothing more need be said about her, particularly since she is a heroine in that wonderful book *The Compleat Cruiser* by L. Francis Herreshoff, her designer. But you know how editors are: they always want more. All right,

Previous page — Closehauled in *Arete,* an L.F. Herreshoff-designed Rozinante type. Despite being called a canoe yawl by her designer, she is ketch rigged. *Arete* has power beyond her apparent delicacy, ability beyond her size, elegance beyond her cost.

here come more details about the great Rozinante and what she can do. But please, let's not lose sight of that lovely stern slipping along through the water. It represents peace.

Arete is a French mountaineering term meaning a sharp ridge, an appropriate name indeed for a Rozinante, for she is a very sharp vessel. She also brings to mind a violin, in a general sense, because she is so perfectly designed for her intended purpose, and in the literal sense, because of the lovely wood in her, and because of her very delicate and finely tunable rigging. Underway, I found myself tiptoeing around making gentle adjustments to things. It took me a long time to realize she wasn't going to break.

Mr. Herreshoff referred to her type as a canoe yawl, yet her rig is clearly that of a ketch. He explained all this in the first of his series of articles about the Rozinante that was published in *The Rudder* and reprinted in his book *Sensible Cruising Designs*: "This little yacht is a small double-ender of a type that used to be called canoe yawls, and in the 1890s was a very popular type in England for cruising some of their delightful waterways like the Clyde, Firth of Forth, Humber, Mersey, and of course the Solent in days gone by. This canoe yawl is sort of a descendant of some of the sailing canoes that were used in these waters for cruising during the previous decade. The name 'canoe yawl' simply means a boat with a sharp stern that is larger than the usual sailing canoe, or about the size of what was called a yawl boat in those days. Admiral Smyth in his *Dictionary of Nautical Terms*, 1867, describes a yawl as 'man-of-war's boat resembling the pinnace, but rather smaller; it is carvel-built, and generally rowed with twelve oars.' The term 'canoe yawl' in its day had nothing to do with the rigs these pretty vessels used, for among them there were sloops, ketches, yawls, luggers, and cat yawls . . . ."

Mr. Herreshoff goes on to say that a canoe yawl "should be a good sea boat and a fast sailer under a small sail plan." And those are exactly my next-most-lasting impressions (after the stern) of the Rozinante. I was amazed at her ability to cope with rough water and was always surprised that her seemingly tiny working sails could get her along so well.

One of the pleasant things about the Rozinante is that you can see and enjoy the shape of her while on board, because she's open all the way through. If you don't pile too much gear in the ends of her, not a good idea anyway, you can see from the cockpit right up into the shape of her bow and right back into the shape of her stern, as she carries you dancing along.

The boat is 28 feet long on deck, with a waterline length of 24 feet, a beam of all of 6 feet 4 inches, and a draft of 3 feet 9 inches. Her sail area is only 348 square feet. Her displacement is 6,600 pounds, and her lead keel weighs 3,360 pounds. She has very fine lines throughout, with a nice hollow at the waterline both in the bow and at the stern. Her sections are really fairly straight, especially forward, for such a shapely hull.

The sterns of the various Rozinantes I have seen look quite different from each other. The knuckle in the sternpost has to be shaped exactly as shown in the lines drawing, and the rake of the sternpost has to be set precisely as Mr. Herreshoff drew it, else the looks of the boat will be spoiled. On a couple of the Rozinantes I have seen, the knuckle is a bit too pronounced, and the sternpost doesn't have quite enough rake. These boats lack the superb grace of the design as represented by Ted Sprague's *Arete*.

She has a very nice sheerline. I didn't measure, but I have a hunch that the *Arete* has just a tiny bit less sheer in her stern than Mr. Herreshoff drew. Both from on board the boat and from alongside in a dinghy, her stern doesn't seem to spring up quite as much as expected.

I will give only the essentials of the Rozinante's construction, since the details are given by Mr. Herreshoff in *Sensible Cruising Designs*. The planking he specified is either ¾-inch mahogany or ⅞-inch pine or cedar. Frames are steam-bent white oak, 1¼ inches by 1¼ inches. The wood keel is 12 feet 4 inches long by 2 inches thick and 14 inches wide, of white oak, yellow pine, or Philippine mahogany. Stem and sternpost are 4 inches thick by 2¾ inches wide at the inner faces, of white oak or hackmatack, or could be laminated of either white oak or Philippine mahogany. Floor timbers are 1½ inches thick, varying up to 8 inches deep, of white oak. Deckbeams are 1 inch by 1½ inches, but 1½ inches by 1½ inches for three extra-strong beams, two at the forward and after ends of the forward deck hatch and one at the after end of the cockpit (the first beam abaft the mizzenmast), beams to be of oak, ash, or elm. The clamp is 1 inch by 2¼ inches, "or more," of spruce or Douglas fir, "if possible in one length." The shelf is 1 inch by 1¼ inches, of the same material as the clamp.

The deck is tongue-and-groove strips ¾ inch thick by 3 inches wide, of fir, spruce, soft pine, cypress, or California redwood, covered with canvas. Cockpit coaming and house sides are each 19 feet long and ¾ inch thick, of mahogany or oak (the former is superior for this use, in my opinion). House beams are ⅝ inch by 1⅛

inches, of oak, ash, or elm. The top of the house is tongue-and-groove ½ inch thick, of pine, spruce, or Port Orford cedar, covered with canvas. The cockpit floor is teak slats 1 inch wide by ¾ inch thick, spaced to leave an opening of ¼ inch between slats. The cabin sole is ¾ inch thick, of soft pine, cypress, California redwood, "or other suitable wood." The cockpit seats are ¾ inch thick by 12 inches wide by 6 feet 6 inches long, of soft pine (the *Arete*'s are mahogany, which is elegant).

The deck and top of the house on *Arete* are not covered with canvas. They are covered with an entirely different kind of material, one without the ancient tradition that canvas enjoys. Now it may surprise you to learn — it certainly surprised me! — that the use of this upstart replacement for canvas was condoned by L. Francis Herreshoff. In the chapter on the Rozinante in *Sensible Cruising Designs*, he wrote, "Fiberglass decks are said to be very good if painted with a non-skid paint." It says that right on page 83!

Arete was very nicely built by Smith and Rhuland down in Lunenburg, Nova Scotia, in 1969. One departure from the plans that the builders made is noticed quickly on coming aboard by true Rozinante aficionados: there is a nicely rounded cap along the top edge of the cockpit coaming. This is an improvement, for you inevitably end up walking on that edge at times, and it also gives you a nice handhold when standing up in the cockpit facing to weather with the boat well heeled over.

A glance at the Rozinante's construction plan shows what a simple boat she is. True to her canoe yawl heritage, she's really just a big, open boat partially decked over. With her stripped-out simplicity and her lack of an engine, her cost, Mr. Herreshoff estimated, would be about five-eighths that of the normal cruising auxiliary of the same size.

One of the drawbacks to the design is the narrowness of her side decks in way of the cockpit. You can see in the construction section drawing just how little boat there is outboard of the cockpit coaming. Sitting on the weather side of the cockpit, you can't see the lee rail except at the bow and stern, and this mars somewhat the very great enjoyment of watching this boat work her way through the waves. Also, if she's being pressed and you wonder if she finally may have her lee rail down, you have to get up and lean over to leeward to see. (She seldom has.)

Working around on the *Arete*'s deck in a rolly anchorage seemed a bit precarious at first. She has a quick little roll and jump at times, and it does take time to get used to her narrowness. You keep thinking there will be more deck out there on which to catch your balance than there really is. Once I actually stepped out over the coaming — onto nothing at all. Thank goodness for that cap on the coaming edge. I came to the conclusion that the most likely time to fall off the *Arete* would be at the mooring.

Her tiny, narrow stern deck is a bit precarious for working on the mizzen. A good, stout mizzen topping lift is important, because now and again you find yourself lurching against the boom when you're furling the sail and she's jumping a bit.

Then there is the problem of getting out onto that afterdeck from the cockpit. The *Arete*'s main backstay doesn't go to the mizzenmast as shown on the plans, but rather comes down to a two-legged bridle running to chainplates on the rail just abaft the mizzen shrouds. At times the mizzenmast, its shrouds, and the backstay bridle seem designed as a most effective obstacle course to keep you off the stern of the boat. I finally got pretty good at wriggling through and under, and by the end of the summer, all that rigging hardly slowed me down at all.

There is no place on board a Rozinante to stow a dinghy. On such a small, narrow vessel, you just have to put up with towing a boat. Why can't some genius design a truly easily inflatable — and deflatable — dinghy, with fine lines, that really rows well?

The big, deep cockpit of the Rozinante is fantastic. Its convenience and security more than make up for the boat's lack of deck space amidships. Just to begin with, it's a fine, secure, sheltered place in which to work at the mooring. Spread out tools and materials to your heart's content, or use the place for a sail loft down out of the wind. Mr. Herreshoff said the Rozinante's cockpit could take six comfortably for sailing. Well, I'll go four, but when I use that word "comfortably," I mean people really have room to stretch out or move around a bit without falling over one another.

The thwart across the after end of the cockpit just abaft the mizzenmast is very nice to sit on and steer when she's not heeled over too much. When Weldon described the Rozinante to his friends in *The Compleat Cruiser*, he said this thwart was placed 3 inches higher than the cockpit seats so that the helmsman could see over the heads of his crew. In the *Arete*, the thwart is only 1 inch higher than the seats, but it is surprising how much difference even that small elevation makes. In any case, it's good to have a choice of steering seats so you can sit facing forward or to leeward, just as you please.

The cockpit coaming slants outboard at an angle of 8 degrees. Mr. Herreshoff designed the cockpit seats to rise coming inboard by that same angle so that the seats and coaming would form a right angle. The *Arete*'s seats are nearer to level than that and are most comfortable, but I think they would be even better as the man from Marblehead decreed.

When not in use, the cabin doors are stowed on slides under the forward ends of the cockpit seats. There's a hook at the back to keep them from sliding back out when the boat heels; Mr. Herreshoff designed a wedge arrangement for this purpose that would be even handier than the hooks, which require a bit of kneeling down and looking and feeling back up under the seats to secure. About my biggest criticism of the *Arete* is that the lower pintles on her cabin doors should be longer than the upper ones so that when you put the doors on, you can start the lower gudgeons on their pintles first, and then line up the upper ones, rather than having to line up both at once. I got really frustrated at times doing this in the dark in the Sherman Cove surge. I tell you, it was a terrible hardship. The whole thing was probably the builder's fault rather than the designer's, for Captain Nat Herreshoff knew this trick, and I feel sure it wasn't wasted on his son.

The *Arete* has a big diaphragm pump permanently installed in the bilge at the forward end of the cockpit, discharging through a gate valve fitted at the waterline on the starboard side. This is a wonderful rig. The handle to the thing stows in clips under the after end of the starboard cockpit seat, so that if he needs to, the helmsman can be pumping the bilge in five seconds without leaving the tiller. The pump would not move as much water as a bucket, but it would certainly help and would clear the bilge below the sole quickly.

For ground tackle, the *Arete* has a pair of yachtsman's anchors, one 25 pounds and one 15 pounds. Pete Culler used to say to put down your heavy anchor and sleep peacefully, and that is just what we did. Both anchors were stowed under the seats in the cockpit with stocks folded and together with their rodes if we weren't doing a lot of anchoring. If we were, the 25-pounder was lashed on deck away forward with its stock hanging over the rail and snugged right up into the bow chock.

Mr. Herreshoff gave no companionway hatch to the Rozinante, saying it would cost $150 to build (a couple of decades ago), "and I would duck my head many times for that sum." The *Arete* has one, and I must say it's a very nice arrangement in the Rozinante. It makes a fine place to stand and watch her go.

The tops of the *Arete*'s companionway hatch

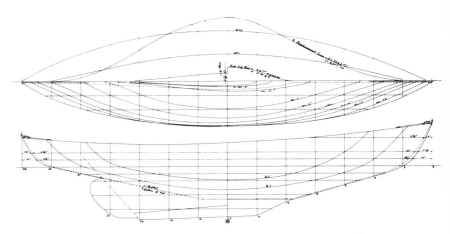

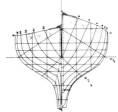

and forward deck hatch are made of thick, strong, transparent plastic. Aesthetically, these hatches leave much to be desired when compared with varnished mahogany, but they do let a tremendous amount of light below. The transparent forward hatch in particular transforms what would otherwise be a dim forepeak into a bright place where even a missing sail stop is easily found. The place where my open canvas bag of oilies and boots was stowed happened to be right under the forward hatch, and it was somehow comforting in fine weather to be able to glance down there and see foul weather gear at the ready as I walked past. I guess my preference would be to keep the transparent hatch forward but to have a nice mahogany slide aft where you need the additional light less and where you see and use the hatch more.

The glass ports in the sides of the house look nice and let you look out from below. And, sitting on the weather side of the cockpit with the boat heeled over, you can look into the cabin and down through the lee porthole to watch the foam from the bow wave flash by. This makes up a little bit for the lee rail being hidden behind house and coaming.

Below, the after end of the *Arete*'s cabin is taken up with considerable structure. At first it seemed to me that too much of the cabin was given over to this galley paraphernalia, but I later came to appreciate what is a considerable amount of good storage and work space in so small a boat. On the starboard side is a big, deep icebox that kept cubes for five days in the Maine summer. There was also a flat for the usual two-burner kerosene stove. On the port side was a nice little sink with a wobble pump drawing water from a big (maybe as much as 20 gallons) water tank beneath it. On each side were counter space, lockers, and drawers. With all the food and cooking gear stowed away for a cruise, you still had one whole big, deep drawer in which to stow ship's gear, a first-aid kit, and a few simple navigational instruments.

Mr. Herreshoff designed a comfortable chair in one after corner of the cuddy. It was made like a canvas beach chair with the canvas forming seat and back in one piece and following roughly the contour of the hull. A neat arrangement, and one that I think would be an improvement in the *Arete*, for she has no truly comfortable place to sit and read below. For use north of Cape Cod, Mr. Herreshoff said, she ought to have a small coal-burning stove in the other corner. I heartily agree, and we sorely missed such a wonderful contrivance on at least a couple of occasions.

Forward, the *Arete* has the so-called double

bunk of the Rozinante design. I never have figured out why everybody calls this a double bunk, what with the mainmast growing right up out of the middle of it. Anyway, it's most comfortable, whichever side of the mast you choose to sleep on.

The *Arete* has a W.C. under the bunkboards. It's a neat, out-of-the-way installation, but we found it so out of the way that we seldom used it, even after I cut handholds in the bunkboards (with Ted's kind permission, of course) so we could reach through to open and shut the intake and discharge valves. The bucket was far more convenient than the W.C. and, for males, even more convenient than the bucket was the lee rigging, main shrouds in moderate weather to take advantage of the mainsail as a curtain, and mizzen shrouds in heavy going because of the security of standing inside the coaming on the cockpit thwart (one advantage of the narrow side deck).

The fellow in the construction drawing smoking his pipe and doing his chores up in the fo'c's'le under the forward hatch looks more comfortable than he really is, I suspect. She's fairly cramped up in there.

It takes time, even in a small, simple boat like the Rozinante, to learn the best positions for doing things. It wasn't until near the end of the summer that I learned where to sit when getting lunch underway on a rough day. What you do is you put a cockpit cushion on the sill between cuddy and cockpit and brace your knees on the lee cabinet. You're secure, you can reach everything in the galley, and you can easily pass the results of your labors out to those eager hands.

My first impression of the *Arete*'s spars and rigging was that everything was too light, but I was thinking in terms of the length of the boat rather than in terms of her displacement and sail area. The sails are small, for she is so easily

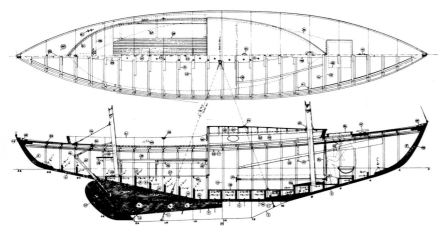

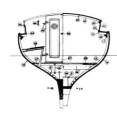

driven that little power is needed to move her. Everything on the boat is so diminutive that you find yourself handling halyards and sheets daintily between thumb and forefinger. Her mainsail has an area of 180 square feet, the jib has 98, and the mizzen, 70.

Quite complete details of spars, fittings, standing rigging, and running rigging are given by Mr. Herreshoff in *Sensible Cruising Designs*. To give an idea of the scale of things, the mainmast is 4½ inches by 3½ inches at the deck. Hardly massive. The rectangular spars are not as good looking to my eye as are round spars, but they are certainly less bulky.

The strut on the after side of the mizzenmast steadies the spar, which has no partners, since it stands in the open cockpit.

I'd be sorely tempted to raise both booms on the Rozinante by about 3 inches. The main boom does a little more head-knocking than it ought to, and raising both booms would improve visibility to leeward. When steering from the thwart, I found myself peering to leeward through the crack between the foot of the mizzen and the boom.

Mr. Herreshoff's sail plan for the Rozinante shows the springstay making to a turnbuckle aloft on the mizzenmast. On the *Arete*, the springstay led to a rope tail rove through a fairlead on the side of the mizzenmast at the same position as Mr. Herreshoff's turnbuckle and then down to a cleat near the foot of the mast. This is a great rig. It was almost as much fun to play with that springstay as it is to play with the vang on a gaff. On the wind in a breeze, if the mizzen was luffing along lazily, taking a bit more strain on the springstay would flatten the sail right out and put it to work.

The halyards and sheets are all in the cockpit — with the exception of the jibsheets, which belay awkwardly on the outside of the outward-slanting coaming. Mr. Herreshoff shows no winches on the boat, of course, but the *Arete* has a small pair of jibsheet winches mounted on the outside of the coaming, and I must say they are most handy. Perhaps a good rig would be that fancy kind of winch right on top of which you can belay the sheet. It's an awkward reach to the cleats on the outside of the coaming when she's driving along heeled over and you go to cast off the lee jibsheet to tack.

The mainsheet comes right to a cleat on the forward side of the mizzenmast which couldn't be handier. Its height on the mast produces just the right angle for the sheet so that no traveler is needed. The mizzen sheet comes in through a hole in the after end of the cockpit coaming and belays next to the tiller.

The *Arete*'s jib may have been a bit shorter on the luff than the jib Mr. Herreshoff drew on the Rozinante's sail plan. At any rate, I let the tack of the sail up about 8 inches off the deck, which made the sheet lead right, kept the sail a little drier when punching to windward, and, above all, improved visibility on the lee bow.

The *Arete*'s only light sail is a small spinnaker, but she is not rigged with spinnaker gear. We set it a couple of times tacked down to the stemhead as a ballooner, but it was more of a conversation piece than anything else. We seldom felt the need for light sails. On the wind or reaching, the working jib seems to be plenty, and she is able to get along quite well with it. Well off the wind, we found that you ought to either head up high enough to just fill the jib, or else run right off wing and wing. Running before it with the jib blanketed and main and mizzen on the same side, the mizzen just about completely kills the mainsail. A good sail for the boat would probably be a balloon jib hanked onto the stay to pole out for running. Then you'd want to take in the mizzen.

We found the *Arete* would carry full sail to windward comfortably until it was blowing perhaps 18 or 20 knots. Then we'd take in the mizzen, and with that much breeze, she'd still have just the tiniest bit of weather helm under jib and mainsail. Then, if it kept breezing up somewhere between 20 and 25 knots, depending on whether we were feeling lazy or ambitious, we'd reset the mizzen and take in the mainsail. This is a rather drastic reduction of 110 square feet. If you were racing her, you would instead reef away, say, 50 square feet of the mainsail.

But jib-and-mizzen turns the Rozinante into a wonderfully easy-to-handle cruising boat that will sail well — including going to windward — in 20 knots of breeze or more. At 40 knots if it kept breezing up, you'd want further reduction, and this could be made by reefing away, say, 25 square feet of the mizzen. For that, you'd want earings and reefing laceline all rove off, so that you could reef the sail without leaving the cockpit. (I am going on about all this because the Rozinante, I believe, is such a wonderful sea boat that it is a shame to leave her tied up in heavy weather.) Then, for that really hard chance, it would be good to have a storm jib with an area of, say, 65 square feet. Under storm jib and reefed mizzen, she would be showing only 110 square feet of sail, and I think she'd be among the last boats of her displacement to be kept from working to weather in frightful wind and sea conditions.

Yet another advantage of Mr. Herreshoff's ketch rig in his canoe yawl is that she lies head to wind very handily with mizzen sheeted flat and nothing else drawing. I don't mean this as a heavy-weather tactic. She'd be better off running under bare poles dragging most of the ropes on board. (From amidships on each side, not from that delicate stern.) But in any normal weather, if you want to stop for lunch or a nap, just take in jib and mainsail, sheet the mizzen flat, and let her lie quietly head to wind. When you come flying into a harbor singlehanded and want to catch your breath before anchoring, round up, drop the jib, let the mainsheet run, sheet the mizzen flat, and let her lie head to wind while you stow the jib below and get the anchor ready to let go. All you need is a little clear space to leeward, for of course she'll go slowly astern. When picking up the mooring, as soon as it's aboard, sheet the mizzen flat and she'll go straight astern until she takes up on the pendant instead of sailing all over the place. When getting underway from an anchor singlehanded, set the mizzen and sheet it flat, pick up the anchor and get it all washed off and stowed away while she goes slowly astern, then put on the rest of the sail and fill away. That mizzen transforms a prancing thoroughbred into a docile farm horse with the feed bag on.

The Rozinante's tiller arrangement is strange and peculiar. The tiller doesn't swing freely back and forth, but instead hits the mizzenmast. You have to lift it a few inches to get it to clear the mast. And you have to reach behind the mast even to get your hand on the thing! It all seems quite awkward — at first. But then you begin to get used to it and rather than trying to push the tiller through the mizzenmast, you get in the habit of automatically lifting it to clear. And you begin to realize that 99 percent of the time the boat is sailing along with a bit of weather helm so that the mast doesn't interfere at all!

And you get used to reaching aft for the tiller.

Then, little by little, you begin to take advantage of that mizzenmast. If you want the tiller lashed amidships (as when lying-to under the mizzen), rather than reach for a piece of line, you just wedge the end of the tiller down against the after side of the mizzenmast. And if you want her to steer herself for a couple of minutes while you go do something else, you just leave the tiller up against the weather side of the mast and go about your business. (If you have a Rozinante and want to astound friends who aren't used to her, just walk away from the helm. The tiller will fetch up against the mizzenmast and the boat will just keep right on going, but your friends, not realizing that this is going to happen, either leap for the tiller or look at each other as if to say, "Why did we come sailing with a crazy person?")

And then, unconsciously, you begin using the mast as a benchmark while steering. You find yourself reaching for it with your thumb and automatically gauging exactly the amount of helm you have on, using your thumb against the mast as a measuring stick. That thumb quickly becomes an amazingly sensitive rudder angle indicator. By now you're ready to install false mizzenmasts in way of all tillers. Such a spar might even triple as a binnacle stand and boom crotch!

The *Arete* had the 10-foot oar that Mr. Herreshoff recommended, stowed away below as shown in the construction drawing. Her oarlocks on the cockpit coaming are perhaps 18 inches farther aft than the position shown by Mr. Herreshoff. The rowing position worked fine, however; there was plenty of room to stand up and pull facing aft, of course, and you could also stand up and push, bracing your back against the mizzenmast. You can move her along at 1 or 2 knots, 1 knot being a steady pace for distance, and 2 knots being a sprint that most people couldn't maintain for more than a few hundred yards.

The tiller arrangement comes in handy for rowing, because once you get her going, you can keep her at a comfortable cruising speed with the tiller up against the mizzenmast on the opposite side to the oar, which will keep her going pretty straight. This takes some practice and doesn't really work if you're trying to maneuver the boat in close quarters around a harbor, in which case a second person to steer is almost a necessity for good control. For any serious rowing of the Rozinante, though, I think the oar should be the longest possible contraption that would stow below, namely, something like 14 feet. That would mean it ought to have plenty of weight in the handle for balance, but such an oar would be quite superior, I think, to the 10-footer, which is a bit scant for such a big boat.

But the really easy way to move the Rozinante under oars, we discovered, is by towing her with a dinghy. With any kind of a decent pulling boat, you can add a full knot to the Rozinante's speed under oar by using the dinghy as a tug and towing the mothership astern. With a short towline of about 20 or 25 feet, maneuverability in cramped quarters is excellent, for as master of the towboat, you can pull, twist, and nudge as the occasion demands. Towing a boat with a dinghy, even a boat much bigger than the Rozinante, tells you an awful lot about her: her weight, how she turns, her windage, how she carries her way. Towing the *Arete* certainly demonstrated just how easily driven a hull she has. You can't believe you're towing a 24-foot-waterline boat.

The *Arete* has a 4-h.p. Johnson long-shaft outboard that stows neatly under the port cockpit seat and mounts on a simple bracket. We didn't use the motor much, but the few times we did, it seemed very easy to put on and take off, and it shoved her along easily at about 5 knots. How much breeze it would push her into we never discovered, because if there is any wind at all, you can't resist sailing a Rozinante.

I had the *Arete* underway 30 times during the summer. Francis Herreshoff wrote of the handiness of the Rozinante for evening sailing, and that certainly proved to be true. We had a lot of afternoons of gentle to moderate to fresh southerlies on Penobscot Bay that summer, and it became a most pleasant habit to leave the office a bit after five, having picked up a crew or not, as the case might be, row out to the *Arete* on her mooring in Sherman Cove, tumble aboard, make sail, and be underway in five minutes, feeling her heel over and gather way to just fetch out through the spindles between Sherman Point and the ledges.

Once in the Bay, we'd pick out just which hole in the islands would make the best sail full and by on the starboard tack; the late afternoon breezes were so constant in direction that it almost always turned out to be "let her go about so, below East Goose Rock to miss that sunker in there, then sharpen up a bit to weather the end of Lasell Island, and then let's shoot past 10 feet off the lee side of Goose Island and see if we can surprise the seals on the other side. Then we might as well let her go for Pulpit Harbor over on North Haven."

The people in Pulpit Harbor must have thought we were nuts. We'd keep sailing in there at six-thirty or seven in the evening and, instead of anchoring, spin her around and sail right back out again. Coming back across the Bay we'd generally head up just to weather of Saddle Island and then have a nice reach for Camden. Some of the sunsets behind the Camden Hills were mighty pretty.

I expected the *Arete* to sail very well in light and moderate weather, but I did not realize how very handy, able, and dry she would be in a big breeze and sea. I would not call her an extremely fast boat, but she is certainly fast. Of course we had a few brushes with other boats. She didn't quite hold a Scheel 30 to windward in a light breeze, but she sailed even with her on a reach. She worked away from a Tartan 30 on the wind in a moderate breeze. In a faint breath and perfectly smooth water, she wouldn't quite hold an Oxford 500 on the wind. On all these occasions, the other boats had big genoa jibs.

Sailing with Bill Peterson's 28-foot schooner *Susan*, designed by his father, Murray, the *Arete* was a bit faster going to windward in a fresh breeze but was slower running in the same breeze and much slower running when the breeze eased up. But my excuse for being so badly beaten by the *Susan* running up the Damariscotta River is twofold: I should have had her wing and wing longer, as Bill rightly had his schooner, and also we were towing a dinghy, which was by then half full of water and had to be snubbed right up under the stern to keep her under control, where she was certainly making more waves than was the *Arete*.

I guess my conclusion as to the Rozinante's speed is that she is faster than most boats her length, but not faster than all. Somehow that statement doesn't seem very helpful. Let's try another comparison: the fastest boat of the Rozinante's length that I ever sailed was the *Aria*, my old Buzzards Bay 25-footer designed by Francis Herreshoff's father. There is no doubt in my mind that the *Aria* would sail around the *Arete*, but the *Aria* was designed as an out-and-out racing boat. I never thought of the *Aria* as being at all hard to handle, but by comparison, the Rozinante with her three little toy sails is absurdly easy to handle.

I guess the most instructive sail I had in the *Arete* was the day Dana and Dorothy Sheldon and I went out for a couple of hours in the afternoon when it was blowing a gale out of the north-northwest. It was calm enough in the harbor, but out on the Bay you could see little else but good-sized white breaking crests. We gave her the jib and mizzen and ventured forth. She poked her nose out around Sherman Point and began climbing over the steep head seas, still protected by the hills from the full strength of the wind. We laid her up close-hauled on the port tack and started out into the worst of it to see what she would do.

Well, she did amazingly well. A couple of crests broke maybe 6 inches over the bow, but this foamy stuff washing aft was breakwatered away by the pointed forward end of the house. There was a bit of spray flying back over the cockpit now and then, but that was far more the exception than the rule. In the hardest gusts, she put her lee rail perhaps just under, but it was clear she wasn't about to be overpowered with that amount of sail in that amount of breeze, and she was never in danger of shipping water into the cockpit to leeward. Best of all, she drove to windward at as much speed as you wanted in that sea, and she had the power to keep accelerating in the hardest gusts of all.

We all agreed it was difficult to estimate the strength of the wind that day, because it wasn't steady. It was what you think of as blowing 35 or perhaps 40 knots, but that really means that it probably never blew less than 15 or 20 knots, and gusted to 35 or 40. Probably some of the short bursts were a bit heavier. It was grand going, but my agreement with Ted had been one of caretaking, not testing to destruction, so before long we tacked and hightailed it home. Off the wind, she was as docile as a lamb and steered no harder than she ever does.

Another interesting time was beating out past Whitehead Island at the south end of the Mussel Ridge Channel on a sail from Camden to Friendship. It was blowing 25 to 30 knots, and we had her under jib and mizzen. We had just picked up a nice fair tide. Nice is probably the wrong word, because that current did a good job of heaping up the head seas as it poured out of the Mussel Ridge. The roughest water lasted only 500 yards, and Bob Howard and I were about to congratulate ourselves on getting through it in one piece when a couple of seas must have combined into one and along came a high, steep, freaky-looking thing. The *Arete* climbed it with equanimity, but then her bow fell down into the huge gaping hole on the far side of it and her stern pounded down on the back side of it with a jarring crash. As the stern dropped away from Bob, leaving him hanging onto the coaming 6 inches above the cockpit seat, he shouted "Some!" and as he caught up with the seat again, out came the word "boat!" At the same time, I was thinking, "Some wave!"

But Bob was right. The boat certainly was more remarkable than the wave. It took me a little time to realize what had happened. Usually when the bow of a boat dives into the ocean and there's a great crash, it means her bow has pounded. But the *Arete* didn't pound her bow; she dove into that hole beyond the big sea, fetched up on its bottom, pitched back the other way and whaled the backside of the receding sea with her stern.

I never had the *Arete* running in a heavy following sea. Her stern is so fine you wonder if it could always lift in time. Ted Sprague says he hasn't run her off in really rough water either, but as an experienced inlet runner, he wonders how she'd do in such conditions. My guess is she'd do just fine, but it's only a guess.

But now we come to the real crunch of thinking about this wonderful Rozinante as a boat for sailing in rough water. Francis Herreshoff wrote, "Best of all a canoe yawl can be about the safest vessel that can be had since her design is based on those most seaworthy open boats ever known — whaleboats. Rozinante is a partly decked-over whaleboat with a ballast keel that will make her non-capsizable." Clearly this statement is made in the context of coastwise cruising and daysailing, not offshore passage-making, yet still it may be a bit too strong. After all, the Rozinante is basically an open boat carrying around a big chunk of lead. If a large-enough quantity of water enters her large cockpit opening, she will sink like a stone. The question is, of course, "What is the risk of that happening on a boat that is to be sailed coastwise, not across oceans?"

That question leads to the related one, "What is the likelihood of being caught out?" Will the Rozinante ever be caught so far from shelter that she cannot escape the wrath of a rising gale before the seas get really big and dangerous? Well, I for one am willing to take that risk, because if I find myself in that situation, I will have made so many consecutive errors in judgment, not to say having lost sight of the very purpose of cruising, that I will deserve to lose the vessel and drown.

Keep the Rozinante within striking distance of somewhat protected water and she will, I believe, stand as much wind and sea as she will ever encounter.

Now, through all these words, I hope you haven't lost the feeling of the *Arete*'s lovely, pointed stern, slipping away and away through the water. When you leave her to row ashore in the dinghy, examine that stern. Get its shape really in your mind, then pull up ahead and look at the Rozinante from right forward. Can it be that that little slip of a skinny thing has carried us so far? She has.

Thanks, Ted. And thank you, Mr. Herreshoff, sir.

Moccasin — Whose Time Has Come

Stanley Woodward

S TANLEY WOODWARD, *like many readers with a new boat, wrote us to see if we had any interest in publishing something on his boat, a custom design from the rich imagination of Philip Bolger. We handle new designs in two ways in* WoodenBoat: *one is to feature them in the design section, usually with commentary by the designer himself; the other is to give the design larger play as a feature article. This one seemed to fit in the latter category, since* Moccasin *had been built and sailed successfully — it wasn't just an idea waiting for someone with enough money to make it real. Like many of Phil Bolger's creations, she represents some important design themes, both traditional and nontraditional.*

Despite her radical appearance, *Moccasin* is the picture of simplicity. There is no cabin trunk to complicate and obstruct the deck, and not a shroud or a winch on the whole boat.

JUST WHAT IS *Moccasin*? A flower? A serpent? Or an Indian slipper?

I commissioned Philip Bolger of Gloucester, Massachusetts, to design a boat for daysailing that also might serve occasionally for modest family cruises. As crew I have two small children, ages five and three, plus two very big dogs. Unfortunately, my wife dislikes sailing because she is subject to a form of vertigo when any boat heels, so a hull form that would sail fairly upright was desirable. Indeed, for a long while our project was viewed with mistrust, and it was not until the vessel was afloat in shallow water — where my wife could wade out to stand next to her before climbing on board — that confidence returned. I then proceeded with caution and sailed that boat with restraint only on her three lowers for some time, so that gradually the effect of heeling was greatly reduced.

It all started when it was difficult to find a large vacant shed for construction, but a small garage was available. I decided to build the largest possible boat that would fit the space and add the bowsprit, rudder, and centerboard after completion. The critical design dimension was a length that stopped at 36 feet 9 inches on deck, leaving only 3 feet to spare before reaching the walls; 9 feet 10 inches was selected for the beam and a hull draft of only 2 feet was chosen, relying largely on a big centerboard for windward work in deep water. With a modest lead keel of 1¼ tons, as well as the shallow draft, there was little choice for other than a sail plan of low-aspect ratio, which we made 50 feet long at the base from mizzen clew to the tip of the bowsprit.

Francisco Capilonch and Pepe Hernandes, two young and energetic Mallorquin wood fishboat builders, and I agreeably spent one year putting *Moccasin* together in that shed, knee deep in wood shavings, enjoying the scent of yellow pine, spruce, mahogany, and iroko. Fortunately, I happened to have Everdur bronze in all the necessary sizes, so we built her strong, to last, and finished her with 1-inch carvel planking in the traditional manner.

Philip Bolger seemed delighted with my specifications. I wanted an easily handled vessel whose speed would not be handicapped by any rating rule. In particular, I insisted that the boat be so well balanced sailing on the wind, or running, that no awkward self-steering apparatus should be necessary. I also wanted the boat to have sufficient sail area to eliminate the need for an auxiliary engine. Phil eventually convinced me, however, that if no provision were made to install an engine on *Moccasin*, it might be difficult to find a buyer in the event I ever considered building a larger boat for my growing family. So a slow-turning 8-h.p. Stuart Turner, two-stroke, twin cylinder, 33-cubic-inch marine gasoline engine was secured and fitted with a Luke feathering propeller. The simplicity of this little engine, which has only three moving parts, was irresistible. On trials it pushed the boat at 6.7 knots over a measured mile, and it is virtually free of vibration. I might also add that the 20-gallon fuel tank, which was filled to measure the dipstick at launching, was still half full eight months later. The engine proved no inconvenience during the first season.

During the initial stages of planning for the design, I had mentioned the possible use of certain traditional Chesapeake craft. Our thoughts turned to the pungy, the bugeye, and log canoes. We discussed Commodore Munroe's Presto concept and Philip Bolger's own successful designs for the smaller Black Gauntlet, Black Skimmer, Dovekie, and others. At any rate, encouraged by a sound historical basis for unstayed masts and sprit booms, which were very popular during the 19th century in big workboats and Virginia pilot schooners, we decided to proceed with logic and art without becoming influenced by the contemporary scene. So when Phil forwarded *Moccasin*'s surprising sail plan, it did appear rational to me. It was devastatingly contradictory to current concept. The rig was certainly less costly and quite simple. There were no shrouds or stays or any wire rigging; no need for turnbuckles and winches. However, there was no way of telling how *Moccasin*'s speed and windward ability would compare if pitted in competition against the highly developed modern ocean racer and one-ton match boats, because there had been no modern yachts around when this simpler rig was popular. Many good ideas sprang from a time when money meant more than it seems to now. Obviously everything could be mended when worn out without recourse to a yard or marina.

Phil was in favor of the cat-yawl rig, after sev-

With her unusually shallow (2-foot) draft and hard bilges, *Moccasin* is conspicuously easy to haul, store, or beach. The solid liferails and the pulpit near the mast give a tremendous feeling of security.

eral successful boats built to his design, and tried to persuade me that the absence of flogging headsails might be a real plus factor on my shorthanded boat. But I wanted something in front of the mast to play with, so the yawl was designed with a small, 117-square-foot, self-tending balanced jib. I subsequently added a three-quarter short-hoist genoa and a mizzen staysail, but that small jib proved so effective in balancing the boat on the wind or reaching that the tiller can be left entirely free, unattended for hours on passage. Short-tacking is a matter of just shoving the tiller over, with no need to adjust any sheets. Most of the driving force is in the big mainsail. Its luff remains perfectly straight on the mast and the sprit boom can be adjusted instantly to change to any desired draft in the sail. Another advantage is that the sprit does not allow the leech of the sail to twist as it does on a conventional boom. Sheeting force with the sprit boom is also greatly reduced. Reefing the loose-footed sail is surprisingly easy and the sail is fitted with lazyjacks, which keep the sail from falling in the water or messing up the deck. When lowered, it furls itself.

It was Phil who had the bright thought to add a sprit or topsail over the Bermudian mainsail, an idea probably borrowed from the racing log canoe. I suspect he got cold feet sometime during the course of the boat's gestation, because it had not been seen for several generations and there was no one left around who could remember if it worked. Nevertheless, we made the sticks according to plan and Manchester made the sail. To everyone's surprise, the first time the topsail was hoisted, it functioned without a hitch and pulled like a mule.

Both masts are cantilevered. The mainmast, which at times has to support 1,170 square feet of sail without the benefit of any shrouds or stays, is constructed hollow of thick-walled spruce. I did add some graphite fiber, supplied by Gougeon Brothers, set with WEST System epoxy to the corners of the mast, and this must stiffen the stick considerably, because the run-

ning backstays are entirely unnecessary and have been discarded. Another 200 square feet of sail area is made available on the mizzenmast so that five sails, the total measuring a little over 1,350 square feet, can be set at one time on a reach or even close-reaching in light airs. The three lowers, however, normally used when shorthanded, measure only 659 square feet and are all self-tending. *Moccasin* goes very well under these three. The boat can sail in circles without touching a line, and it takes no time at all, and no shouting or rushing about, to retrieve an object that has fallen overboard. The only sail that is not practical for a singlehander, and requires company to set and to remove gracefully, is that topsail. But once up, it needs no further attention, is self-tending when tacking or jibing, and seems to be equally as effective on a close reach as it is in a following wind. An extra hand is required to move it from the deck to the head of the mast, as it is necessarily rigged with all three spars set, and is hoisted or lowered on the windward side of the main. Once in position, it is as quiet as a lamb and balances beautifully.

The mizzen is a simple standing lugsail fitted with full-length battens, which eliminate flogging and flutter. This sail is never taken down, even when at anchor or moored, as it keeps the boat steadily pointed to windward. All summer long it remained standing when the boat was at her mooring. *Moccasin* proved ideal for daysailing. It takes less than a minute to cast off the mooring and get underway.

Her displacement is about 5 tons, although she measures 8 tons net, 9 tons gross, and 14 Thames tons. She is so easy to handle for one person that she can be considered a small boat. This may be largely due to her simplicity, her surprising lack of windage, and her extreme shallow draft. She is big on deck space, lavishly roomy in cockpit area, has generous hatches, and is very steady underfoot. Designed and built to be beached, she can even sail to windward in water a little over 2 feet deep when the board is raised, and if the tide runs out, she remains upright. *Moccasin* is also fitted with a two-point cable sling so that she can be hoisted on the deck of a steamer without removal of her masts, in the event a very long windward passage might be considered a bore. No cradle is needed for the passage as deck cargo — where one can choose to live comfortably inside her. Marinas always find room for her at their shallow end if this doubtful pleasure is required. But certainly the best asset is an infinite variety of quiet, secluded anchorages open to her.

As a beach boat with small children, *Moccasin*

Right — Though *Moccasin*'s potential for speed is not readily apparent to the modern eye, she trounced a fleet of ¾-ton and one-ton boats over a 14-mile triangular course — by more than 14 minutes.

is ideal. They can swim or stand with security and are free to go and come from the beach on their own. For cruising, the ample freeboard provided by the raised-deck profile has allowed a charming and spacious interior. Full standing headroom is limited to the companion hatch, where foul weather gear can be donned, but the saloon and fore-cabin are spacious and comfortable. *Moccasin* is the first boat I have owned without standing headroom everywhere below. It was surprising to me, therefore, that the lack of headroom has actually made the saloon appear more attractive. Proportions are certainly better, and since no attempt was made to crowd the interior, I have not lived with a better arrangement.

The prismatic decklights installed through the deck do not allow water in but provide a great deal of bright natural daylight. The small deadlights in the hull sides are adequate to allow inspection of the scene around the boat in complete privacy, and they are at eye level when one is comfortably lounging about in the saloon. The galley area, fitted with a Heritage stove, is separate to port; a large chart table is to starboard. Ample bookshelves line the forward bulkhead, where a Chelsea chiming clock and a copper charcoal stove for winter are fitted. The only door in the boat separates the forward cabin, fitted with two full-size pipe berths. There are also two large settee berths in the saloon.

All the construction details of wood (including the builder's marks on the frames, which I insisted on leaving visible in the interior) lend interest to the visual effect as well as give a pleasant touch and aroma. The total absence of wire halyards striking a metal mast or the howling of the wind through the shrouds is certainly comforting, especially when hove-to in a gale under her silent, fully battened mizzen sail. Under these conditions the shallow draft has proven an asset, and the little boat drifts quietly like a bird at rest. When the boat is being driven hard under double-reefed main, the mainsail is far enough forward that no jibs are necessary and the long main sprit boom, which moves forward of the mast when this sail is reefed, does not trip in a sea.

Our home faces a pleasant bay. Ten miles across to the other side are some seldom-frequented beaches. During the summer a solar wind takes up station around eleven each morning so, at noon, after work, we head off. Either we swim out to the mooring, or I cast off, hoist the mainsail, and ground the bow on the shore, where, standing knee-deep in the water, I can help the dogs get on board first, followed by the children, who are already learning to climb on board by themselves. My pretty wife, who turned out to be a good sport after all, carries the perishables for lunch. (There is a large icebox on board, but we prefer fresh food.) It usually takes about an hour and a quarter on a close reach to cross, sometimes a little longer. We catch a fish or two on the way and anchor for a hot lunch in less than 3 feet of water. After more swimming, shelling, and running about on the beaches, the breeze usually freshens by midafternoon to 15 or 18 knots, and we return with the children and the dogs asleep in the shade below while we lie about in the large cockpit and get browner. Generally we have a beam reach or broad reach for the return, and sometimes we make the 10 miles in one hour. All the while *Moccasin* sails herself, requiring no one at the tiller, which is left to take care of itself.

Moccasin led to a certain amount of speculation at the yacht club, and at the end of one summer I had time to satisfy their curiosity and mine.

A triangular course of 14 miles was posted in the adjacent bay, and it was decided that a proper race would settle some questions. Many bets were taken between those who speculated that the unsupported masts might fall down or break off, and opinion was divided as to whether a boat without a keel would hold up to windward against the modern fin-keelers. We started the race at 11 a.m. with over a dozen boats. Half of these were the standard modern ¾-ton and 1-ton keel racing type fitted out with winches and a very pretty assortment of star cut and extra spinnakers, large genoas, and large crews. Winds were variable but it got up to Force 3. Twenty-five percent of the race was to windward, 25 percent running, and 50 percent reaching. Results were rather unexpected, with *Moccasin* crossing the finish line 14 minutes 35 seconds ahead of the fleet. What was interesting, however, was that *Moccasin* not only went faster on a reach but she also went faster and closer on the wind and kept increasing her distance running, even though she had no spinnaker. A girl on board remarked afterward that it was the first race she had ever been in where she hadn't gotten hurt and that she had had very little to do. Everyone seemed terribly upset and puzzled.

We are still uncertain whether *Moccasin* really is a dandy flower, a sly serpent, or a silent Indian slipper. In any case, I couldn't help gilding the lily a little and added a carved seahorse covered in gold leaf for her outboard rudder cheeks, so that other yachts sailing in company with her might keep a bright memory.

The Concordia Sloop Boat

Waldo Howland

*I*T'S ALL TOO EASY *to overlook the number of conflicting ideas inherent in boat design, or the evolutionary thought processes leading to the creation of a craft that will do what it is intended to do. All too often, we look at a boat and fail to recognize that it represents a synthesis of thought from the designer, the builder, and the eventual user.*

We include the story of the development of the Concordia Sloop Boat here because it describes the creation of a boat from the perspective of one who tried to attain a perfect combination of elements drawn from a lifetime of experience in and around boats. This was adapted from a brochure by Waldo Howland, founder of the Concordia Company boatyard in South Dartmouth, Massachusetts, and catalyst behind some of the best tradition-inspired boats of the mid-20th century. The Concordia Sloop Boat was one of several good stock boats produced by Waldo's yard.

*I*N 1962, in response to the interest some of my friends showed for a little wooden day-sailing boat, I started on the rather difficult problem of listing the qualities that I thought were important for a good one. When I say good, I mean one that would be useful and appealing to a knowledgeable sailor who really enjoys sailing in small boats. Such a boat would have to sail well and be handy and able. She would have to be attractive and shipshape in appearance. She would have to be well built, with special attention to detail. For a number of reasons, wood seemed to be the best and only medium for construction, with its inherent virtues of appearance, sound, smell, feel, and flo-

The Concordia Sloop Boat is a daysailer designed for comfortable pleasure. At 17', she has room for her crew, sufficient freeboard for dryness, and length for performance.

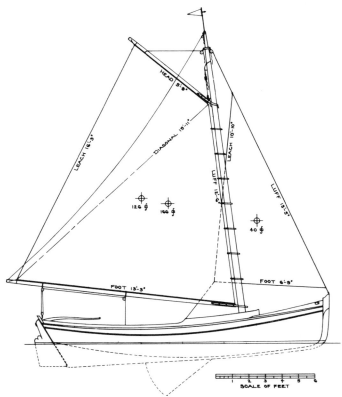

SCALE OF FEET

tation. Variation and modification by its owner are easy, and it can be painted, polished, and puttered with. In short, it can be loved.

In the search for a model, I talked mainly with "Captain Pete" Culler and my friend Major William Smyth. The former favored a boat having the general characteristics of the Scituate Lobster Boat, while the latter, who at one time ran the Dauntless Shipyard on the Connecticut River, urged me to keep in mind the Connecticut River Shad Boats. For my part, I had always liked the Bahama dinghies. We were all thinking along the same lines.

The question of size was next. Many of the daysailing boats that have stood the test of time have been in the 18-foot range. This length permits sufficient beam for comfortable seating, sufficient freeboard for dryness, and sufficient length of lines for good performance — all without requiring a large sail plan.

When properly suited to the hull, the main purpose of the rig is to be easy to handle. The

spars on a little boat like this must be light and strong, and we eventually sent up to New Hampshire for a load of small spruce trees so the mast, boom, and gaff could all be natural sticks with the center of the tree in the center of the spar. In addition to the lightness and strength of such sticks, they also have the springiness to absorb the shocks from the sudden puffs, and the boom is flexible enough to relieve the tight leech in a strong blow. The strength of the stick eliminates the need for shrouds, which both reduces wind resistance and allows the boom and gaff to go way forward. By setting the jib flying (that is, without a headstay) this sail automatically takes a taut luff as pressure is applied on the mainsheet, and bellies forward when off the wind.

The rig with a short gaff eliminates the need for a tall mast and permits a well-proportioned jib to pull opposite the peak halyard. Moreover, the gaff rig has obvious advantages over a taller and narrower rig. The cotton sails take very kindly to the gaff rig, where considerable adjustment is possible by different tensions on the peak halyard. The vertical cut of the sail is strong, and the absence of battens is a great convenience. Cotton has a quiet way of shaking in the wind, compared with the stiffer Dacron, and it is less slippery, so it is easier to furl and handle. By tanbarking the cotton sails, they become waterproof without losing their softness, and they take on the typical reddish-brown color that is so easy on the eyes.

Following the tradition, there are two halyards — one for the gaff and one for the jib. To get underway, it is necessary only to slack the mainsheet, hoist the main halyard, snap the jib tack into the stem eye, and hoist the jib halyard. The mainsail is always left bent on, and the jib, with its sheets attached, is simply stowed under the forward deck. In all, getting underway is less than a five-minute job. The mainsheet, jibsheets, and centerboard pendant all lead to the top of the centerboard trunk, within easy reach of the helmsman. All blocks are the small, rope-stropped wooden ones that are light, quiet, and of sufficient size to have free-working sheaves. In place of mast hoops, the Bahama system of lacing is followed, which is also light and quiet. Wooden cleats are used throughout.

The seating arrangement in a small boat is of great importance, since human weight is actually the ballast. The Sloop Boat has a thwart just forward of the centerboard trunk. A passenger can sit here facing aft in comfort with a good back and arm rest. When tacking, he can slide back and forth with the greatest of ease, and his

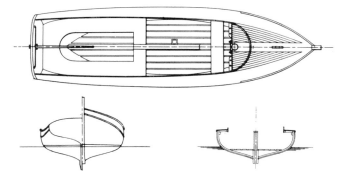

weight is far enough forward to keep the boat in good trim. (Some boats with big cuddy cabins actually force the passengers to sit so far aft that the boat sails out of balance.) The helmsman's seat is so arranged that there is support for his back while his feet just reach across to the sheathed rise of the hull.

The beam of the Sloop Boat is such that she can be rowed easily, and oars and oarlocks are provided for. The Bahamian method of sculling, however, is even more effective. The boom-crotch socket serves as a sculling hole, and a long sweep will fit out of the way in the cockpit. An outboard motor could be used, but it is contrary to the whole concept of our little daysailer.

The construction of a little boat often has a lot to do with the pleasure of sailing her. Factors of sound, temperature, feel, color, etc., all have their importance. Like most of the old-time craft, the Sloop Boat has a strong backbone: a big keel, strong stem, and a heavy, carefully shaped skeg. She can be grounded without harm and will hold her shape for many years. Oak, pine, and cedar grow together in nature and also work well together when combined in proper boat construction. Planking and decks are relatively light, the lumber locally grown, cut in the fall, and seasoned properly. Sound, hard oak for her frame and rubbing strakes, durable light cedar for her planking, soft pine for tight decks and comfortable seats — all take their right place. The construction lends itself to many finishes that are pleasing to the eye and hand. Dark topsides to show off the hull and not stain easily, light-colored sheerstrakes to show off the pretty sheer to good advantage, and bright decks and transom for those who like yacht appearance. Grey seats and floorboards give a shipshape finish inside.

She is fun for the whole family to sail. Being deep in the hull and having considerable deadrise, her performance is much like that of a good keelboat. Her sharp bow, modest beam, and long, fine run give her a lovely, easy motion and a light, responsive helm. She slips through the water fast and is remarkably dry. With centerboard up, her long, straight bottom and shoal rudder are designed for landing on a beach to picnic or explore.

Like her older sisters, the Sloop Boat is handy and maneuverable. She holds her course and does not rely on constant use of the rudder. At anchor she lies quietly, head to wind even with the mainsail set. She is sufficiently heavy and of such design that she carries her way well. Shooting a mooring or coming alongside another vessel or a float can be accomplished without haste

or confusion. Without shrouds and with both the boom and gaff fitted with jaws, it is possible to sail by the lee or lie alongside with the wind abaft the beam.

The old sailing lobsterboats had to be able, and they worked in all weather conditions. The Concordia Sloop Boat likewise is able. Handled intelligently, she will perform well in open water and strong winds. Even with a reefed main and no jib, she'll go along as nicely as a catboat.

In developing this Sloop Boat, we tried to incorporate a great many important factors into her — factors that are not even considered by many buyers today. In so doing, we felt that a few experienced lovers of small-boat sailing would understand and appreciate what we did, and that a few newcomers to the game would have an opportunity to consider and experience these same virtues that earlier generations enjoyed.

The Concordia Sloop Boat running on by. Fast, dry, and maneuverable, she has the necessary attributes to be fun for the whole family.

117

Peapods Are for Sailing

Joel White

AROUND BROOKLIN, Maine, the home of WoodenBoat, Joel White's practical wisdom is readily acknowledged and generally admired. He owns the Brooklin Boat Yard, and he is a boatbuilder, a naval architect, and an avid sailor. His sense of enjoyment on the water, combined with his need for a simple and efficient means of getting from here to there, led to the development of a suitable rig for a rowing peapod — one without a centerboard or rudder. Moreover, the rig was cleverly adapted to accommodate a topsail, adding to the versatility of the rig and the adventure it provides. Since the idea was too good to ignore — not to mention that those of us with similar rowing peapods wanted to learn how to rig and sail them — we asked Joel to tell us all about his sailing peapod.

WATER CHUCKLES under the stem, swishes along the lee rail, and leaves the pointed stern in a fascinating, ever-changing whorl similar to the one from an oar after a strong stroke. The sheet of the spritsail leads aft to the quarter, around a wooden fairlead, and forward to your hand. A 3-foot-long pennant of red bunting streams aft from the leech of the sail, curling in the afternoon sou'wester. Slight movements of your body to windward or leeward maintain the course, and your wake stretches far behind. This is peapod sailing in a steady breeze, some of the most enjoyable and challenging sailing there is.

I had used my Jim Steele-built pod for several years as a tender to *Northern Crown* (a job for which she is perfectly suited) before I ever considered the idea of sailing her. When cruising, we do a lot of exploring in the pod, and the thought of being able to sail her at least part of the time interested me. Years ago, when peapods were used for lobstering and clamming, it was common to raise a small sail when the wind favored. What I dreaded was the clutter that would result from spars, sail, centerboard, rudder, and rigging, all added to a boat only 13½ feet long. I thought it should be possible to sail off the wind without a centerboard, and perhaps steer with an oar, so a mast and sprit were made, a hole bored in the forward seat, a step fastened to the stem below, and a sail procured and bent to the mast. One day, when the wind was gentle and no one was about, I cast off, prepared to run to the far reaches of the cove, and then row back. To my surprise, the pod seemed willing and even eager to sail in any direction, from close-hauled to a run. Oh, there was some leeway when close-hauled — the wake left the stern at perhaps a 10-degree angle — but that wonderful little whirlpool danced about under the stern, distracting me from the crablike progress.

Steering with an oar soon became both cumbersome and unnecessary. To head up, move forward; to head off, slide aft. After several attempts, I found that a dive forward and to leeward would bring the boat about. Amazing! Moving way aft and letting off the sheet swings her head downwind. But no jibe. Much experimentation finally produced this sequence for jibing: weight all the way aft, sheet out, then when her head will fall off no farther, trim the sheet right in smartly, and as she turns downwind, swing the sail right across the boat and onto the other side. This maneuver is particularly fun in a good breeze, as one's weight in the

Author Joel White (left) and Maynard Bray (right) race down Vinalhaven Reach in their peapods rigged for sailing.

end of a peapod reduces stability considerably, and care must be taken if a swim is not in the plan. After jibing, move forward until the desired course results. Locate yourself at a fore-and-aft point that keeps the pod on a steady heading, then make slight course adjustments by varying the heel of the boat. More heel and you head up; less heel and she heads off.

So my experiment worked even better than I had hoped. The mast, sprit, and sail roll up into a package 11 feet long and 4 inches in diameter that rests on the cabintop of *Northern Crown* when not in use, and the pod towing astern contains no extra gear. To sail, pull the boat alongside, drop the mast in the hole, rig the snotter to extend the sprit, and in two minutes you are sailing. All the rigging is done from the deck of the mothership, which is much easier than from aboard the pod. When you return, it takes only a couple of minutes to furl the sail and have the rig out on the cabintop. A sailing peapod overcomes the objections that sailing dinghies take too long to rig and don't sail well — and you'll be surprised at her speed.

The sprit rig is the obvious choice for the boat, because of its simplicity and ease of rigging. Read Pete Culler's chapter on the sprit rig in his book *Skiffs and Schooners*. It contains a wealth of good information about the subject. His snotter arrangement, with round thimble seized into a long eyesplice, is first-rate, as it provides a two-part purchase for setting up the sprit. Maynard Bray has experimented with a brail on his rig and reports good results. With it, you can leave the mast and sprit rigged but effectively furl the sail to the mast.

Opposite — Nathanael Bray singlehands his father's peapod, without a rudder or centerboard, in the reach between Green and Vinalhaven Islands in Maine's Penobscot Bay.

There is something to be said for standardizing the size of the mast at the partners and step. This allows your neighbor's rig to fit your boat and makes rig research easier and more fun. I used a 3-inch hole saw to bore through the seat and made the mast about 2⅞ inches in diameter —just slack enough for it to rotate. The step has a round tapered hole that fits the taper at the foot of the mast — about 1½ inches in diameter. A little tallow or Vaseline at step and partners allows mast, sail, and sprit to rotate as a unit when coming about, and the sail sets more efficiently.

I used 10½-foot spars, which give me a relatively small sail that is easy to stow, and even a lightweight like me can keep her upright in 15 knots of wind. Because of the moderate area, light-air performance was not explosive, but a solution came about by chance. Jon Wilson had

loaned me a couple of sketchbooks of old Scandinavian fishing vessels, and several of the illustrations showed sprit rigs with topsails above. Why not? Another light spar about the size and length of the sprit, a couple of homemade fittings, a light sail built in Anne Bray's sail loft, and suddenly we were tough in light going. Besides, it looked terrific!

I built a peapod for a friend who is both a good sailor and a big man. She has 12-foot spars and a large topsail to boot. She is the *Intrepid* of peapods, awaiting the appearance of Jon Wilson's highly touted (but still very mythical) *Sovereign of the Seas* with her experimental rig.

Keep things simple and cheap. You don't need a halyard or reef points. Simply lace the sail to the mast and leave it. Fancy hardware isn't required — a couple of round brass thimbles are nice for snotter and topsail sheet, but you can live without them.

Spars are local spruce, with as few knots as possible. Make them down with a plane and don't sandpaper them. The finish is a couple of coats of linseed oil and turpentine. Spars should be short enough to stow inside the boat, and to allow for the lumber available. Mast, sprit, and topmast, if carried, are all about the same length. Twelve-foot spars are plenty for a 14-foot pod. For a boat this size, the foot of the sail should not be more than about 8 feet, for the sheet must lead around a wooden thumb cleat on each quarter and then forward to your hand. Don't spend a lot of time figuring centers of effort, lateral plane, and moments of your own inertia. These boats balance with plenty of weather helm, and you have to place your weight well aft of amidships to keep them on a straight course. So jam the mast as far forward as you can get it, and the balance will be all right.

Because of the low foot on most spritsails, and the consequently poor visibility to leeward, one of the hazards you face is running into things — other boats, docks, and the like. Short of making your sail of clear polyethylene, the only solution is to peek under the sail often.

When it is blowing hard, take more people with you. As the boat settles deeper in the water, leeway decreases and sail-carrying ability increases dramatically. One of our most memorable sails was beating up the length of the Washabuckt River against a 20- or 25-knot breeze with *Northern Crown*'s entire crew of five people aboard. Coordinating a five-person rush forward and to leeward while coming about takes a little practice. And that smoking run back down the river, with whitecaps almost curling over the gunwales and an oar astern to help her! Try it, you'll like it.

Sprit Topsail Rig

Two pieces of 1¼-inch copper pipe spaced ⅜ inch apart are brazed together to make the top connection between topmast and mast. The fitting is fastened to the topmast three to four feet up from the bottom with a wood screw, and should be a slip fit over the top of the mast. A lanyard through the bottom of the topmast is rove through a hole in the mast, and is then hitched around the snotter. The topsail sheet (about ⅛-inch braided line) passes through a thimble seized to the peak of the spritsail and is then hitched to the fork at the lower end of the sprit.

To get underway, reeve the topsail sheet through the thimble, set the spritsail, then fit the topmast in place and trim the topsail sheet. It is easiest to do this from a dock, a beach, or the deck of a larger boat.

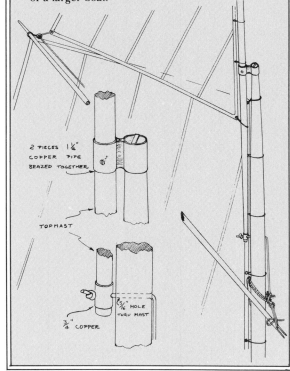

2 PIECES 1¼"
COPPER PIPE
BRAZED TOGETHER

TOPMAST

³⁄₁₆" HOLE
THRU MAST

¾" COPPER

Sam Wise:
A Skiff for All Seasons

John Erickson

A FLATIRON SKIFF floats in nearly everyone's past — the perfect kid's boat, the inshore fisherman's workhorse, the creek-crawler's transport. As we get older, we tend to graduate to more substantial craft, but there are always those who never see the need to progress or who, after they do, regress. They are the ones who tinker with flatiron skiffs and who could very well have the most fun afloat.

This revelatory article on the skiff **Sam Wise** was inspired by an earlier piece on a similar boat called Pas-

sionella, which brought all the flatiron-crazies out of the closet and into the full glare of public appreciation. For example, one response, which we published as well, came from marine artist Sam Manning, who confessed that he had, in a variation on a theme, rigged out a common aluminum canoe for rowing and sailing. It's amazing how all sorts of things are catalyzed by a simple tale. Who knows how many paint-flaking flatiron skiffs were seen in a new light because of Sam Wise.

Sam Wise with her Chinese lug rig. To further the theme, she has Chinese oculi painted on either side of her bow.

THE FLATIRON SKIFF was, and still is, the ultimate inexpensive, general-purpose small boat. A good one, rowed easily, could be made to sail quite well and could be a respectable outboard-motor boat. You could beach-cruise with it, haul potatoes, fish, and cordwood, and you could let it lie about unattended without hurting it too much.

If, in the past, you wanted to specialize in any way, you began making changes to the all-purpose boat. If sailing fast or rowing fast was an objective, you built a boat that was of narrower beam, gaining speed at the price of stability and carrying capacity. If sailing alone was the object, you might induce deadrise to the bottom to keep the quarters up when running hard; increase carrying capacity, with a loss of rowing ability, and complicate the construction of the boat. As a result, there has always been some type of boat that will do a specific job better than the flatiron skiff, but probably none that will be as good an all-around boat.

The person interested only in motoring will complain that the boat is too heavy and pounds a lot; the person interested only in sailing will generally claim she is too slow and lacks windward ability; the pure oarsman will object to her beam and weight. There is some truth to all these objections, but these things should be considered: Under power, a good flatiron skiff will be only a little slower than a pure motorboat and will pound no more than most, yet it can be rowed effectively when the motor quits. At the sacrifice of rowing ability, the flatiron skiff can be made with a flat run and heavy bottom so that it will outrun almost any other hull form.

The flatiron skiff, properly built and rigged, will sail well. It will always be a little slower than a boat designed purely for sailing, but not much slower than the usual family daysailer, and while it will not point with a deep-keel sloop or a hot racing machine, it will point well enough to get to windward in a reasonable manner. There are any number of days — this is the rule rather than the exception where I live in the southern end of Puget Sound — when a flatiron skiff using oars and sails in combination will gain her objective far sooner than the fastest pure sailboat deprived of the use of a motor.

It seemed that the flatiron skiffs would survive in the age of plastics and affluence, for they are easy and cheap to build, simple to maintain, and versatile. They were home-built as often as not, or built as a sideline by persons engaged in other endeavors. The boats were right for the amateur boatman as well, for they were stable, and there were few other design types that could be handled as well by persons of little experience.

It would seem that with such a simple hull form, there would not be much variation in the lines of the boats or in the methods of construction, but in fact, they varied tremendously in the amount of sheer and flare, the rocker of the bottom, the shape, width, and rake of the transom and the rake of the stem.

There were some very pretty boats made and some God-awful ones. There were some professional builders who specialized in the skiffs and built some fine boats. The boats of each builder had characteristics that made his boats unique and recognizable. The boats of these builders tended to be known by the builder's name; to name a few of the many, there are Leppert Boats in Portland, Oregon, Johnson Boats in Olympia, Washington, O'Neal Boats in Norfolk, Virginia, and Al Potter Boats on Narragansett Bay.

There was consistency in the size of the boats and in the ratio of length to beam. Rarely was a flatiron skiff longer than 16 feet or shorter than 12 feet. The beam-to-length ratio was between three and four to one. The height of the sides was determined by the requirement for a comfortable rowing position and varied from a foot to a foot and a half. The boats were built with broad planks (sometimes, later, with plywood) and straight frames set a foot or so apart. Most had sheer clamps but some did not. Some had chine logs and some did not. On the West Coast, most were fore-and-aft planked on the bottom, and on the East Coast most were cross-planked, but there were exceptions on both coasts.

Until very recently you could find numbers of their kind around any marina or harbor and on any beach where boats were pulled up. Like the parts of the wonderful one-hoss shay, they must have been getting old together, for it seemed that suddenly it was a rare sight to see one amid the plastic and aluminum things that clutter the harbors and beaches.

Before the coming of the outboard, skiffs of all kinds, including the flatiron ones, were sailed as well as rowed. This made sense because without much hurting the boat's ability to get about by oar, you could have a smooth and easy ride when the wind was fair. Anyone who has rowed downwind in a spanking breeze knows the "If I only had a sail" feeling. In boats used purely for getting there and back, things were naturally very practical, and it did not occur to anyone that it might not be sporting to row and sail together. It made sense to rig their boats so that the two modes of propulsion could be used together without interference.

If the boat was to be rowed and sailed at the same time, the sailing rig, when set, had to be clear of the oarsman, and it had to be out of the way when taken in. Since the boats were often used in situations where the sail was not required, it was essential that the sailing rig could be removed easily from the boat. And since the boats would normally be rowed when the wind was dead ahead, ability to tack quickly was not much concern, but ability to sail close to the wind was a sought-after attribute, since this meant that a hard row could be transformed into a close reach.

With this set of rules, the rigs used were ones that could be set and struck quickly, interfering with the rowing operations as little as possible. Loose-footed spritsails and lugsails were most often employed. The spritsail is handy, for it can be brailed up against the mast when not in use. The lugsail can be dropped in the bottom of the boat, where it is pretty much out of the way.

There seems to be some feeling among the aficionados of the modern high-aspect-ratio leg-o'-mutton rig that the older rigs were not close-winded, but it has not been borne out in my experience. It is undoubtedly true that some of the sail area of a low-aspect rig is not effective when hard on the wind, so that for a given number of square feet of sail, a boat will foot faster into the wind with a high, narrow sail, but the added area of the low-aspect rig is effective on most points of sailing and is therefore useful to the skiff. The yacht carries an assortment of jibs to produce the needed off-wind area, but the skiff sailor, particularly one of old who was simply getting there and back, could not, and cannot, be bothered with changing sails. In any case, the masts of the skiffs are limited in height, because the boats are shoal and open and because the mast must be taken down and put up frequently.

The balanced or dipping lug is a very good downwind sail, for it immediately becomes a squaresail when off the wind, avoiding the danger of a jibe inherent with fore-and-aft rigs, and overcoming completely the tendency to a strong weather helm that develops with large fore-and-aft sails when running. I suspect this

Sam Wise with lugsail set going to windward with board on the weather side.

downwind capability is one of the things that caused the boatmen of western Europe to hang onto the dipping lug until the very last days of working sail, in spite of the obvious problems encountered when tacking the boat. The standing lug can, with the use of the long tack rope, also be converted to a squaresail off the wind, and it does not have to be dipped when tacking. Why the balanced lug was often used in preference to this sail is not entirely clear to me, but it may be that the balanced lug was more effective on the wind as well as off, and this gain offset the tacking problem.

When I arrived on the shores of Puget Sound a few years ago, I found a flatiron skiff gathering moss on my friend's beach. She had a lovely upswept run and a pleasing springy sheer, a curved stem, dory-lapped sides, and a cross-planked bottom, and really seemed more typical of Narragansett Bay than of Puget Sound.

According to the bill of sale that had conveyed her to a friend's father in 1940, the boat was a "Johnson Boat" built in Olympia. To get her back in operation, I replaced a plank, part of the transom, the gunwales, and the thwarts, filled the checks in her ancient cedar planks with plastic goo, and painted her. She looked very pretty, done in light grey, with the gunwales, thwarts, and the tabernacle oiled.

First, I fitted her with a Chinese lug rig (including a Chinese tabernacle), a large dipping rudder with diamond-shaped holes in it, and Chinese Oculi. I chose the rig because I had been interested in Chinese boats and sails for some time, and I had closely observed Tom Colvin's Chinese lug-rigged vessels on the Chesapeake.

To provide more lateral plane I fitted the boat with a single deep leeboard placed over the gunwale, as Philip Bolger indicates for his Thomaston Galley. This was an ideal device and left the boat unencumbered with gear, and the thing could be simply lifted out of the boat if sailing was not the order of the day. Shifting the board across the boat on tacking takes a bit of dexterity, but it can be done.

The little junk-rigged boat sailed somewhat better than I had anticipated. Like a dog playing a piano, it was not so much how it did it, but that it did it at all. I had told a friend with a fair-sized modern plastic sloop this piano/dog story, and one day when he had trouble overhauling me on an easy reach, he called out, "That's a pretty good tune you play on that piano."

The boat did take some getting used to. If I did everything just right, she would sail beautifully, pointing up well and footing along nicely, but if I trimmed the sheets wrong, she would slide off to leeward like a tub. She had one characteristic that I thought highly admirable in a small cruiser: Once you got her settled down and sheeted properly, she would sail herself forever. You could tie the tiller with a bit of string and never have to touch it until a course change was desired. The boat was insensitive to changes of weight on board, so I was free to wander around in her wherever I liked without causing her to deviate from the course. Even in a howling gale, all it took was just the bit of string or a single finger to hold the tiller and steer her.

This boat was stable. I never feared the winds that blew, nor concerned myself with the peace of mind of my guests, for even when struck by violent winter williwaws, which come roaring down from the Puget Sound hills, the little boat merely heeled a bit and drove ahead. If the gust was particularly violent, she might slide sideways a bit to ease the strain. Never has she seriously threatened to dip her rail, and I have never been forced to reef her. There were a couple of times when I *should* have reefed, but at those moments I was too busy with other things to get to it.

A canoeist friend tells a story of me placidly reading a book in *Sam Wise* while he fought to keep his boat off before the Force-5 wind that pursued us. Actually, I was studying a tide table. (So docile and so unobtrusively useful was the boat that I named her *Sam Wise* after J.R.R. Tolkien's hobbit who was the faithful and unassuming servant in *The Fellowship of the Ring*.)

Sam Wise was sometimes a bit difficult to get through the wind and off on the other tack. As with everything in her sailing, if you knew how to handle her and did everything just right, she performed well, but frequently it was necessary to harden the foresail and back the mizzen to bring her around. The maneuvers with the sails, coupled with the requirement to shift the mainsheet to the weather quarter and to carry the leeboard across the boat, made tacking an active time.

I wondered if the boat's steadfastness was a product of her Chinese rig or of her flatiron skiff hull, and I wondered how many of her other characteristics were Chinese and how many American. When I came across a great red lugsail in the equipment of an old steel lifeboat, I had an opportunity to find out with a minimum of effort. Driven by curiosity, I fitted the boat with the lugsail. One of the great things about a boat that is simple and rough is the ease and lack of expense with which alterations may be made.

Sam retained her steadfastness and most of her other characteristics when fitted with traditional western rigs: dipping lug, standing lug, and finally a sprit mainsail with a jib. To judge all the rigs, you had to look at things beyond ability to foot, point, and tack, for there was no apparent difference in these from one to another.

The advantages of the Chinese rig lay in the ease with which the sails could be handled and the lack of skill needed to build them. Its disadvantage, at least for a small boat like *Sam*, is the fact that its complexity demands that the rig be left in place. It is not practical to drop the sails in the boat, and the rig cannot be removed and replaced easily. The sails furl with almost absurd ease and are out of the way, but they create a good bit of windage, which is a disadvantage when the boat is to be rowed or sculled into a wind.

There is little reason to choose among the western rigs. The dipping lug, to be sure, is a devil to tack, for the need to dip the yard complicates an already complicated maneuver. However, the sail in this way is more quickly converted to a squaresail and it just may be a little better on the wind than the standing lug. The sprit rig has the advantage that it is easily brailed up out of the way when not in use, but it does create some windage up there. You can go a step further and lower it into the boat. where it gives no more trouble than the lugsail. The spritsail cannot be made a squaresail and has the usual downwind disadvantages of a fore-and-aft sail.

The Chinese rudder and Chinese tabernacle were carried over to the western rigs. The rudder is the handiest of things and contributes something to the peacefulness of *Sam*'s operations, but it is not the principal factor, for the boat retains her obedient ways even when steered by an oar and no matter which rig she is flying. I tend to use the rudder only on long hauls or when trolling — times when I would like to have my hands free to do other things — and to use the steering oar for short trips, beachcombing, and the like.

The Chinese tabernacle is the greatest of inventions, for it allows the mast to be set without stays while simplifying the raising and lowering of it. That the mast can be set without stays is a feature that is essential to the proper operation of all the lug rigs. The lugsail cannot be converted to a squaresail if shrouds are in the way, and neither can the Chinese sails swing free to luff with the wind aft. The latter feature is a real advantage of a Chinese rig, for it allows Chinese landings and other maneuvers impossible with other rigs.

The tabernacle consists of a trough that holds the mast firmly on three sides for about the lower fourth of the mast's length. The trough itself is securely fastened to the hull by being bolted to a heavy thwartships bulkhead. It is the epitome of the Chinese practice of achieving strength by distribution of the loads involved. Stepped in such a tabernacle, the 3-inch-diameter Douglas-fir mast of *Sam Wise* has never broken or shown any tendency to bend excessively.

Needing some photographs of *Sam* and her rig, I talked a friend into taking some while I short-tacked the boat about the cove where she lives. There was a Force-5 wind blowing right into the cove, and I had just rerigged the boat after she had served a stint as a motorized tug. While the western lug is a simple rig, there are a number of adjustments that have to be made. Working out the bugs while short-tacking about a cove in a Force-5 wind is a wild and exciting experience. Naturally, the best shots were taken before the final adjustments were made.

The photograph shows her going to windward, and quite well, with the board on the weather side. To ease the photographer's problems, the shot of the rig set as a squaresail was taken with the boat tethered to a float. The apparent lack of strain on the gear is misleading, for the wind is fresh and the sail pulling very hard. The method of dipping the lug is illustrated.

Sam Wise is a simple boat with a variety of home-made rigs. Such "quick and dirty boats," in Pete Culler's parlance, were more common when transport by water was a necessity rather than a luxury. They crop up occasionally among the smooth, stamped-out factory products that fill the waterways and the boating magazines. Unsung, except perhaps now in *WoodenBoat*, such boats have always been around, and I can't help but hope they will not disappear entirely from the scene.

On Laying Down and Taking Off

D.C. ("Bud") McIntosh

MASTER BOATBUILDER Bud McIntosh of Dover, New Hampshire, possesses a gift for words unlike anyone else in his trade. Several years ago, he broke his ankle, and, unable to work in the shop, began to write a book on boatbuilding. We heard about Bud's project through Randy Peffer and thought it might be worthwhile to serialize the material in the magazine. Bud generously agreed. Since only a few photos and sketches accompanied the manuscript, we enlisted the aid of Sam Manning, an artist from Camden, Maine, with a precise and complete understanding of boatbuilding. Somehow he was able to translate Bud's words into illustrations that are as unique and clear as we could ever have hoped for. This happy collaboration has continued in WoodenBoat in an irregular serial form and has almost become a centerpiece of the magazine. When the serialization ends, all of the parts will be gathered together into the book Bud originally envisioned years ago.

Since laying down lines and taking them off are such mysterious processes to many, we decided to use Bud and Sam's installment on those subjects to demonstrate the style and temperament of an author and an illustrator of the highest order.

OUR TITLE would at first glance appear to suggest a confusion of bad grammar, bad taste, and the Space Age. In truth, it is an old, proper, and excellent definition of the first task in the art and craft of boatbuilding, the lofting process. Simplistically, the operation consists of drawing (laying down) an accurate, full-sized picture on the floor from which patterns are "taken off." The process is neither mysterious nor difficult, but there are some simple and essential truths. (In the learning process, there are one or two *shocking* truths as well!)

When I was very young, I held most naval architects in awe and considered myself very smart indeed to have mastered the mechanics of lofting those sacred and untouchable drawings: waterlines, buttocks, magnificent diagonals, finally the body plan — and I crawled reverent miles on hands and knees, correcting tiny (and not-so-tiny) errors committed by men who

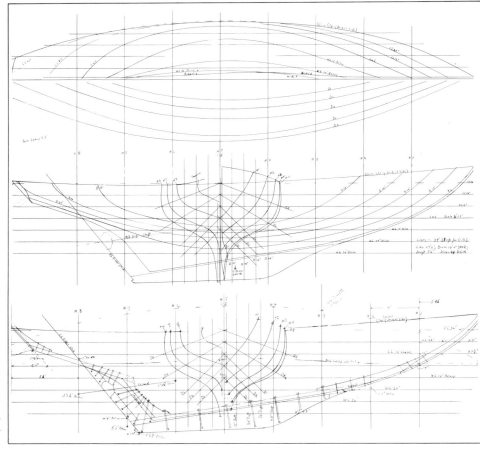

Reproduced here are the lines plan and the laid-down lines of a 39-foot sloop designed and built by the author. The drawings convey his feelings for just which lines and points should be laid down full size and which are unnecessary to the construction process.

had mastered the greatest and most thrilling of all arts — yacht design. It was an honor and a privilege to be chosen as one who would, however inadequately, bring this vision to being in wood, metal, paint, and whatever else the specifications called for (most of these items bought by the designer at one-third off and furnished to me, or our common victim, the owner, at list price, as I finally learned) — and it was wonderful.

Time passed, my work improved, my knees and my faith became worn and battered. And I discovered a shocking truth: practically anyone who can read the figures on a yardstick can lay down a body plan and a profile; and that's all you need to lay down anyway. If the designer howls betrayal for some reason, there are two suggestions you can make about that set of lines and offsets. The polite one is that he take them back to his drawing board and correct them himself. If he can't develop a curved transom, he shouldn't expect you to do it for him. If he says you can't get the angles for the stem rabbet from the scale drawing, he needs further education. And finally, if this lofting were half as difficult as you have been led to suspect, some of us old pros would still be chopping dugouts out of tree trunks and managing to make that look like quite a mystery, too.

So let's lay down what is strictly necessary, and no more; build a set of molds; make two-dimensional patterns of stem, sternpost, tail feather (the late Sam Crocker's term for the keel-of-the-counter, usually called the horn timber), and transom knee; and make the pattern for the ballast-shoe casting. This last item is the only difficult one of the four, and it will be treated separately and at length later.

For this laying-down business you need a reasonably smooth floor, slightly longer than the boat and slightly wider than the total of maximum draft plus greatest freeboard — in the case of our example, 40 feet by 10 feet. You can manage on half this length or even less, but you'll have to cope with some confusion of lines-over-lines. If the floor is good enough, and the owners don't object, give it a coat of flat white paint, and work directly on that. If it's the floor of your living room, or as rough as my shop floor, cover it with light-colored sheathing paper (40 inches wide, 500 square feet to the roll, available at any lumberyard), which you spread out and let lie for 24 hours before you stretch and tack (or tape) it in place. Don't worry if the experts tell you that this is all wrong and that you'll never be able to do accurate work on a surface that changes dimensions every time a cloud goes by. You're going to have expert trouble from now on anyway, and you might as well get used to it. (One of them used to haunt us with the threat that he'd get out his astrolabe and prolapse and show us the scientific way to figure out the shape we were seeking; and for a while we wondered that one small head could carry all he knew.)

Get yourself a 10-foot straightedge. A 4-inch strip off a half-inch plywood panel makes a good one; or you can true up the edge of a dry board with your jointer. While you're at it, make a six-footer and a long one — maybe 16 feet. Stretch a string (nylon is best) the length of your loft floor, far enough from the edge to allow for the full draft of the boat plus two or three inches. Do not chalk and snap it; instead, crawl along and mark where it lies at three- or four-foot intervals. Take up the string, mark this line with a good black #2 pencil, using your 10-foot straightedge, and you have the load waterline (LWL), from which everything else develops. Using the same technique, mark the other full-length lines (three above, four below LWL, and exactly 12 inches apart) parallel with the LWL. Now mark on the LWL the locations of all the perpendiculars shown in the lines drawing — face of stem, stations 0 through 8, intersection of sheerline projected through centerline (CL) of transom, and all the buttock lines you'll need either side of #5 station. Draw these lines in, exactly at right angles to the LWL. The safest way to do this is to erect #5 by the old high-school-geometry method of swinging intersecting arcs above and below the line, marking #5 through these intersections, and then working forward and aft (with your 50-foot steel tape) from #5 along the 36-inch load line and the 48-inch waterline. If your straightedge, joining these new marks, passes precisely through the corresponding marks on the LWL, you will know your measurements were correct. All this is dull business, and perfectly obvious, I'm sure.

The diagonals for the body plan are only a bit more complicated. Notice that in this design they all start at points where #5 station (the CL for the body plan) intersects the horizontal load line and waterlines, and they all pass through intersections of buttock lines with these same horizontal lines. Thus, D1 starts 12 inches below LWL at centerline, and passes through the intersection of 24-inch buttock and 36-inch waterline; and D5 starts 36 inches above LWL and intersects the 12-inch load line 5 feet out from the CL. Draw them all in then, forward and aft of #5, and you are ready to start working from the table of offsets. The hard work is over and the fun is about to begin.

I have known bright people to whom a lines drawing resembled a cross section through a barrel of frozen angleworms, and meant but little more; and these same people thought of a table of offsets as something you might expect to come from the maw of a mad computer that had been fed on Pictish runes, rock and all. Both these conceptions are faulty and exaggerated. If you have managed (as I did, rather late in my childhood) to master the technique of drawing a line from 1 to 2 and so on in proper sequence to 87, and got for your diligence the picture of a nice horsie, you should have no trouble with a table of offsets. Any figure in any one of the little boxes simply tells you to start from a known point, proceed along a carefully labeled line for an exact number of feet, inches, and eighths of an inch, and there put a pencil mark. For heights, you start at the LWL and measure up or down, as common sense and a glance at the scale drawing indicate. For breadths, you start at the centerline and measure out horizontally. For diagonals, you start where the diagonal starts (at the centerline of the plan) and measure along the line of the diagonal. When you've located and marked all these spots, you draw a fair curve (or sometimes a straight line) through them, and get, full size, a line that I hope looks amazingly like the corresponding line on the scale drawing. Occasionally some sadistic naval architect will take all his vertical measurements from a baseline, or something he prefers to call DWL, but he usually gives you a hint that you'd better watch out.

Now that the above is all clear in your mind, you are probably itching to get at the body plan and make the molds. For these, however, you need to know the exact height of the top of the backbone (keel, stem, stern knee, tail feather) where each mold stands, the corrected height of sheer at each station, and the half-widths of backbone, from centerline to rabbet, where the molds straddle it. So curb your impatience and lay down just enough of the construction profile to show the shape of each piece in the backbone assembly, the line of the rabbet, the exact location of shaft alley and rudder port, and the line of the sheer in profile. Indicate (and label, lest you mistake these lines for something else later) the positions of the principal fastenings in the backbone. If these are not shown in the scale drawing of the construction plan (as they certainly should be), demand them from the designer. Finally, lay off from one of the full-

length horizontal lines (assuming it, for the purpose, to be the centerline of the keel in plan view) the half-breadths of the rabbet, for each station, as given in the table of offsets. The load line 3 feet above LWL is the best one to use for this particular half-breadth, because it's in the least-cluttered section of the floor. If you want to lay down the sheerline in plan view, use the waterline 12 inches below LWL for your theoretical centerline, lest you measure yourself right off the side of the floor.

So much for the general plan of attack. Now let's choose weapons and carry it out.

Start with the rabbet line on the keel. You will observe that this is a straight line from #3 to and through #6, and that the table of offsets therefore omits height of rabbet on stations 4 and 5. This straight section of rabbet is the most important line of reference in the entire laying-down and setting-up processes, so get it right — and extend it to #2 forward and to #7 aft. Use your nylon string all the way, and be sure. Now note that the top of the wood keel is exactly parallel to, and 3½ inches above, this straight rabbet line. Mark this in, all the way from #2 to #7; repeat the performance for the *bottom* of the wood keel, exactly 1½ inches *below* the line of the rabbet. This last line is also of course the top of the ballast keel. It might be worthwhile to use a red pencil for these last two lines and all other *construction* (as distinct from *design*) details. Note, finally, that all the heights in the boat are based on the line representing the top of the wood keel: stem, stern assembly, four principal molds, and, eventually, underside of cabin sole. Check the offsets, check your measurements, check your youthful exuberance, and *get it right*.

While your straightedge is still warm, and before we get to the subject of battens, mark some more straight lines: centerline of the transom; profile of the tail feather, from its intersection with transom, across top of sternpost; lines of rabbet on tail feather; centerline of rudder stock from deck to heel of sternpost; centerline of propeller shaft; straight portion of profile of bottom of ballast keel; straight portion of rabbet line on sternpost. These straight lines, each joining two points exactly located (by measurements on the lines drawing or from the table of offsets), will precisely determine the starting points of the curves you are about to draw.

Now about battens. You'll be using these in practically infinite variety every time you turn around on this job, for a long time to come, so you'd best start your collection now. You need two immediately, at least 22 feet long, about ¾ inch by 1 inch in section. These will overlap to mark the sheerline, here on the floor, and, later, on the planked-up hull. One of them will do for marking long planks. The curve of the stem requires a limber one, ½ inch square and at least 16 feet long. The rabbet on the sternpost, and the forward end of the ballast keel, must be marked with very limber ones indeed — straight-grained oak or ash, less than ⅜ inch square. These will do also for the body plan and molds, and at least two of them must be over 8 feet long. And when you come to the outline of the curved transom, you'll be an old hand at this business and be able to judge for yourself what's needed.

If you haven't already got your ribband stock, pick it out now (2-inch by 4-inch, 6-inch, 8-inch, or 10-inch clear fir, if you can get it, at least half of it 22 feet long or better) and steal your battens out of it. Clear white pine is the best and pleasantest to use, but you'll not be likely to find a board over 16 feet long. Saw out half a dozen of them anyway, from 10 feet on up, and about ¾ inch square. Build a batten rack on the wall, out of reach of young fishermen and your own big feet.

So now you are equipped to finish laying down the construction profile. Do the face of the stem first: height at sheer from the offset table. All other points (measured horizontally on the waterlines from forward perpendicular) taken from the scale drawing. Start a five-penny box nail at each point, pull your 16-foot limber batten in against this curved line of fence posts, ease it in or out where necessary to correct for slight errors (holding it in place with nails driven against, not through, it), and mark. Move in and mark the rabbet line in the same way, with your batten flowing into and following the straight line previously marked. Now draw, on the floor, the inside face of the entire stem, the scarf joint, and the jog at the forward end of the wood keel. You will have to scale some of these dimensions from the plans. Go aft now and do the same job on the entire stem assembly — main and outer sternpost, tail feather, knee to transom, completed rabbet line, aperture for propeller, and the bolt pattern.

If you are still able to bend over, mark height of sheer at each station (dimensions, from table of offsets, up from LWL), correct with long battens until fair, and mark. Do the same for half-breadth of sheer (working from assumed CL 12 inches below LWL, remember?) and for half-breadth to rabbet. Note that this width must be exactly 2 inches at the point where the rabbet leaves the keel and goes on to the stem; and exactly 2½ inches where rabbet intersects sternpost — these figures being the half-sidings,

of course, of stem and sternpost, respectively. While you've got them fresh in mind, draw them in as they must appear in the body plan: stem siding 2 inches forward of #5 ordinate, and sternpost siding 2½ inches aft of it. Be very careful henceforth, when laying out half-breadths on the body plan, that you do not mistake one of these for your centerline. (Actually, when you get into the swing of it, you'll find that you match the 3-foot mark on your rule with the 36-inch buttock, or whatever, and ignore the centerline altogether except when laying off distances on diagonals. Thus you avoid errors and save yourself much crawling.)

Now to lay down the body plan, which gives the exact outlines of eight cross sections through the hull, and from which (after subtracting the thickness of the planking) you will derive the shapes of the eight molds.

Start with #5. Find the point where the straight line of the rabbet in profile intersects #5 ordinate. Get the half-breadth-to-rabbet distance from the line you laid off, above, from the 36-inch load line. Square out this distance, forward, from your point of intersection, and mark the spot. This one is sacred and final. Locate the uppermost (sheer) point in the same way — out, forward, from the intersection of sheer profile with #5 ordinate, to the distance shown on your plan view of the sheerline, or the breadth called for in the table of offsets, which should be the same thing. Be sure that this point is at the correct height above LWL, as taken at #5 ordinate, and *not* as it appears so attractively before you where you squat five feet forward of #5. I hate to belabor the obvious, but I have fallen into this error myself. Now, working from the table of offsets, mark distances out on all horizontals, heights above or below LWL on all buttocks, and distances from centerline on all diagonals.

Set up your row of five-penny-nail fence posts, and with trembling hand, bend your best oak batten in to the curve . . . . Take a deep breath, calm yourself, make sure that *you* haven't made any mistakes in reading or marking those offsets, and proceed to move this or that nail to get a fair curve on the batten, bearing in mind that of all the offsets, the diagonals are most likely to be correct. When you are satisfied that the curve is fair and yet as near as possible to the original offset points, draw it in and go on to the next one . . . and the next, until you've got all eight done, with no more help from me. I can do this whole body-plan job in less than three hours, which indicates not that I am a fast worker, nor even very careless, but simply that it's a quick and easy business after all.

Swampscott Dories

W E'VE ALWAYS BEEN *partial to multifaceted material, so over the years we have published a number of grouped articles on the same subject, or main stories surrounded with numerous sidebars. We generated or encouraged some of these directly, but others, like the following essays and reminiscences on the Swampscott dory, came about serendipitously. Almost simultaneously, John Carter, then of the Peabody Museum of Salem, evinced an interest in writing on these most elegant of traditional dories, the Museum's fine photo collection became available to us, Lance Lee's Apprenticeshop/Restorationshop undertook to build a Swampscott, and Evers Burtner wrote us a long letter about his involvement with Swampscotts. Our interest was piqued both by the dories and by the coincidences, so we went out of our way to publish them collectively. Like similar pieces on other subjects, this came together because of, not despite, the different aspects that were combined.*

Work or Pleasure:
On the North Shore One Boat Filled the Bill

John Carter

DURING THE WINTER of 1904–1905, while N.G. Herreshoff followed the completion of his New York Thirty class in Bristol, William Henry Chamberlain was busy in his shop behind 14 Orne Street in Marblehead working hard to put out a fleet of six or so Beachcomber dories for the newly formed Alpha Sailing Club of Salem. Unlike the Thirties, Chamberlain's boats would be modeled along the lines of the popular inshore fishing craft he had been building for some 15 years. Also unlike the New York sloops, the Alpha dories were being built for a group of people who had to think carefully about how they spent their dollars for sport. Often two or three men would pool their money to buy a fully rigged dory for less than $100. The $4,000 price tag on a New York Thirty was more than many of the Alpha-Beachcomber club members made in a year.

A brief look at these clubs and their backgrounds, the Beachcomber Sailing Club of Marblehead and the Alpha Sailing Club of Salem, provides a glimpse at small craft usage for pleasure during this period of industrialization for northeastern Massachusetts, in a society intent on the emergence of the middle class.

William Chamberlain was probably in his early twenties when he opened his small shop in Marblehead during the 1880s. He had a fine eye for line and detail and a steady hand capable of producing lightweight inshore rowing and sailing craft of strength and simplicity. The fact that he used his own boats prolifically for hunting, fishing, and pleasure no doubt strengthened and confirmed his theories concerning the design and building of small craft. He was soon building lightweight fishing and gunning dories, then the most popular type of inshore craft used in the fisheries and for pleasure on the North Shore of Massachusetts.

Dories are particularly well suited to this area for several reasons. Their shoal draft and flat bottoms make them good candidates for the region's tidal rivers. Their flat bottoms also allow an easy hitch up the beach at night, out of harm's way. Unlike Cape Cod to the south, with its easily entered landlocked harbors and estuaries close to the fishing grounds, the North Shore is bold, much like the Maine coast, with few easily entered safe harbors and few beaches. From a builder's standpoint, the craft were easily knocked together using local woods such as pine, oak, and hackmatack on standard molds that could be spaced out or brought closer together to suit the particular boat being built. Plank and other piecework patterns were common, and many of the local production shops adopted assembly-line construction techniques.

Many credit Simeon Lowell of Amesbury with the development of the dory type of boat. He founded his dory shop in 1793 on the north shore of the Merrimack River. The shop was soon shipping thousands of dories worldwide, many on dory trains out of Amesbury. Seven generations of Lowells have run the shop, which is still in operation, producing an estimated quarter of a million small craft, a number that Henry Ford might scoff at but that any boatbuilder would hold in reverence. But to give Lowell all the credit is probably like saying Fulton invented the steamboat. The process by which good workboats and such develop is one that involves many hands, each adding a subtle variation. Documented breakthroughs are few and far between. Instead, local derivations, such as a rockered bottom to ease in hauling up the beach, or more flare or round-sidedness to give stability when unloading a weir, are the rule; a steady, justified progression, with each builder adding or modifying to suit local conditions and use.

The demand for dories was tremendous at the turn of the century, and many plied the trade on the North Shore. Most builders would be forgotten if it weren't for the scraps of paper,

Opposite — A Willard Jackson photograph, taken off Marblehead Light in the harbor, at the turn of the century. This handsome dory is undoubtedly a William Chamberlain boat and is probably an early Beachcomber dory built along the lines of Charlie Smethurst's. In this good example of the early rig these racing dories carried, we can see that the crosscut mainsail is without battens and is laced on the mast and boom much like Charlie's. There are no shrouds as on the later boats, and no forestay.

a handful of half-hull models, and the marvelous examples of their handiwork they left behind. John Gardner has done the lion's share of chronicling the efforts of these men and re-drafting their lines of sensible lightweight boats for would-be builders.

The major builders we know of were the Lowell family of Amesbury, Jesse Hammond of Danversport, William Chamberlain of Marblehead, Elbridge G. Emmons, Joshua Small, and George L. Chaisson of Swampscott, and R.H. Robertson of Nahant. Of course, there were others; in all likelihood, fishermen would throw together two or three dories in a winter, selling two and keeping one for the spring run.

Derivatives were as varied as the place names that dot the North Shore: Nahant, Swampscott, Gloucester, Salisbury Point, and Amesbury, to name a few. The Swampscott type, with her rounded sides and narrow, gently rockered bottom, became a favored and copied model in the area, particularly for pleasure. The easy curving sections added seaworthiness and stability to the boat without having to incorporate several bushels of fish, which would no doubt be bothersome during a serious beat to windward in a race. Bottoms were narrow but still flat enough for easy haulage. Construction of 9/16-inch white pine lapstrake planking, four or five strakes to a side, produced a sturdy lightweight craft of handsome lines. This type of construction also had the advantage of being cheap to build, and it didn't require a great deal of time or material, important considerations that helped add to its popularity. Then as now for many of us, cash was an overriding consideration and chief compromiser in the purchase of a boat.

The dory, by virtue of its low cost and simple design, became a boat for all people, if you will. At the turn of the century, social pressures and changes had begun to thrust a working class

Willard B. Jackson, photographer and at one time a Beachcomber sailor, caught Charlie Smethurst, on the steering oar, and "Uncle Stacey" of Marblehead as they ran home after a day's fishing. Their boat is a particularly handsome round-sided dory perhaps built by William Chamberlain in the 1890s, when the photograph was taken. It is easy to see the logical development of the racing dories once the catalysts of spare time and comradeship were added. The leg-o'-mutton sail will allow Charlie's boat to heel on a tack without dragging her boom in the water; her unstayed mast can be easily shipped with main and jib rolled up; the half-round lath battens on her plank laps amidships save on the planking when the boys are hauling pots. Like *Celt* and other Alpha-Beachcombers, this boat's planking runs all the way forward without a false stem, and there appears to be just a hint of tumblehome aft in the sheer plank as on *Celt*. Simplicity, practicality, and versatility personified!

with leisure time, albeit little of it, into a position where they sought diversion. Great amusement parks and palatial excursion boats provided some distraction for the workers of the Lynn shoe factories, Lowell spinning mills, and Salem tanning mills.

Another pastime for some became the sailing and racing of dories in one of the numerous clubs that sprang up in the late 1890s or early 1900s. Men like William Chamberlain, Sam Brown, and C.D. Mower, who designed and/or built the reasonably priced craft, became talked-about heroes almost overnight. Mower designed the popular Swampscott X-Dory and Chamberlain designed and built the wonderful 21-foot Beachcomber-Alpha dory for those two clubs.

The Beachcombers are said to have been in existence as a racing club as early as the 1890s. Their Marblehead clubhouse, built in 1900, lasted until 1940, when it was turned over to the Sea Scouts. The Alpha Club of Salem got started in 1902, although the first string of dories was not delivered until the spring of 1905. At its peak, each fleet had about 25 dories. It is ironic that out of a probably 150 or 200 Beachcomber-Alpha dories, I can think of only two, possibly three, that have survived.

Races began the first Sunday in May and ran until the middle of December. They were held on Sundays because the six-day work week was still very much in vogue with mill and shop owners. Two interclub races were scheduled per year.

Both clubs reached their peaks in the early 1920s. It was at this time that the rigs had reached what has been generally considered their final stage of development. The hulls changed little over the years. Sure, Sam Brown of Marblehead knocked down the sheer on a Beachcomber, thereby supposedly decreasing windage and making a faster boat, but on the whole, the class remained pure. The rules, such

as they were, were pretty elastic and members were continually trying out new ideas: balanced rudders, sliding centerboards, or different rigs.

It is in the rig that a subtle evolution took place. Originally the rig in the early boats, between 1900 and 1905, was essentially a fisherman's rig as seen in Charlie Smethurst's boat in the accompanying photograph. In about 1914, a roach was added to a crosscut three-battened mainsail, and shrouds came in vogue. Later in 1924–25, sail track was added to the boom and mast in place of earlier lacing. On some boats, two extra battens, making five, were added to the mainsail, and on some a forestay becomes evident, as in the photograph.

The clubs were microcosms of the society that created them. Women were excluded, and no doubt card playing and similiar pastimes were a major weeknight activity, albeit in limited quantities. The clubs went with the times, and by the 1930s the outboard motor and the Depression dealt the combination punch that pretty much wiped them out. In 1964, the late E.A. Batchelder of Marblehead, then in his 80s, commented to C.L. Pattee on the longevity of the Beachcombers:

Many people have wondered why the Beachcombers lasted so long, and I believe I can explain that. We never allowed any liquor and although we played cards every night, except Sunday, no money was ever involved. I believe gambling and booze were the cause of most clubs breaking up. The Beachcombers were not a religious group, but Sunday 60 years ago in Marblehead was a special day. The cover was put on the pool table on Saturday night and no one ever thought of removing it.

There is a faint essence in those words, the sweet aroma of, well, perhaps nostalgia. But it is more than that; boats are not planked on such ephemera. A set of molds well supported on their strongback begins the process, and it occurs over and over again until it becomes a part of us, not just an essence.

The Alpha fleet of Naugus Head in Salem Harbor sometime in the early 1920s. It appears that a Sunday racing series is in full swing and boats are getting ready to leave the dock. A nifty dory-skiff, perhaps Chaisson's standard 10' model, lays alongside No. 29 at the dock.

133

A Celebration of the Traditional North Shore Dory

Lance Lee

FINE COLLECTIONS of artifacts — such as small, traditional watercraft — represent a superb opportunity to study the past. For decades they have been valued almost solely as objects retrieved from potential oblivion; this retrieval is wonderfully epitomized by the one-time curatorial observation at a testimonial banquet, "Madam, we have one of each!" Today our small craft collections are being treated as "reference libraries," but with a difference. They are the targets of more than research scholars seeking to draft lines, construction, and rig details, or prepare papers on use, handling, maintenance, and related industries or techniques. They are instead a grand route to the perpetuation of the traditions we value.

For example, the lightweight, almost delicate little 16-foot Swampscott-type dory on display in the Maine Maritime Museum's Small Craft collection served in the summer of 1980 beyond the boundaries of our past efforts at restoration. Until then, the central rationale of restoration at our Museum had been to restore boat types, older skilled practices, and the habits or tricks of a sea and seaboard heritage, instead of restoring the actual boat or artifact. This has been taking place at the Restorationshop, a specialized program of the Museum.

But in 1980 we combined efforts with another major maritime museum, The Peabody at Salem, Massachusetts, where a special photographic and model collection exhibit of the regional dory tradition was paired with a hands-on demonstration, building a reconstruction of the fine little North Shore dory shown here.

One of our intentions was to illuminate a type of small craft overshadowed for years, if not decades, by the rise of the johnboat, the runabout, and the mass-produced, often sea-questionable, and frankly ugly craft that have dominated inland waters of recent years. The joint Peabody Museum/Restorationshop celebration of a North Shore traditional type, of skills preservation, and of inter-museum cooperation was intended to kindle the broad public's fancy for all three elements of this project.

The dory selected is a superb example of her type — light, handsome, with clean lines and a long pedigree. The spareness or simplicity of her scantlings and construction suggest that she is an enticing candidate for widespread revival by amateurs and would-be builders. Accordingly, a part of the project was to record and draft her lines and make them available to the public. One of a growing series of such timely small craft plans, they are now available in two sheets by draftsman David Dillion and include lines, offsets, construction details, and a comprehensive list of the necessary building materials.

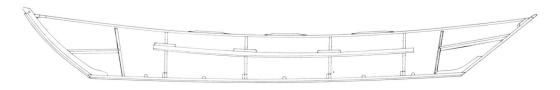

Three of My Own

Evers Burtner

I HAVE HAD three Swampscott-type sailing dories over some 45 years. The first was a 20-footer, which cost $25 secondhand and introduced me to sailing in a most excellent manner. In those days, my home waters of Lynn, Massachusetts, didn't have a dredged yacht basin, so it was easy to sell my parents on the idea of safe sailing by pointing out that with the proper choice of tide, the water was only a few feet deep and the prospects of drowning were remote.

It wasn't long before I began to understand why sailing dories were rigged as they were. Simply put, the leg-o'-mutton mainsail is easily set and furled and also stows readily. In addition, the main boom has a high rake so it cannot drag in the water when the narrow-beamed boat is heeled over.

I gained valuable experience with my first dory, but not without problems. For example, the rudder was hung on the usual pintles and gudgeons, and if the tiller was pushed aft, the rudder would slide up and the pintles would become disengaged. A better arrangement for such raked transoms was to fit the rudder with good, rugged gudgeons and hang it by them from a ½-inch diameter rod fixed at the bottom of the transom. The top of this rod was secured in a socket above the upper gudgeon.

My second dory, a Chamberlain Beachcomber racing dory, was purchased for $50 in Winthrop, about 1917. She was 20 feet 9 inches by 4 feet 11 inches, and her inventory included a jib, two mainsails with booms, a pair of oars, and some other gear. The Beachcombers were a popular racing class on the North Shore at the time.

I learned with the Beachcomber, too. During two weekends, I sailed her alone from Winthrop to Portsmouth, New Hampshire, where I was employed at the time. It was wartime, and to avoid the checkpoint cutter maintained by either the Navy or the Coast Guard near the western end of Deer Island off Winthrop, I made an "unlicensed" passage through Shirley Gut, which used to separate Deer Island from the mainland. I avoided the cutter, but Mother Nature did interfere a bit, for in the crooked Gut Channel, I accidentally jibed this new (to me) and well-loaded boat and shipped about 4 inches of water. But she was a good boat, and once through the channel, I bailed her out and carried on for Gloucester and later for Ports-

mouth. Around Portsmouth, on the Piscataqua River, the current is swift and unsuitable for good sailing. But there was one place — the shallow south channel that ran into Little Harbor — where conditions were better and sailing was more fun.

At summer's end, I set sail for the Boston area again, this time toward Marblehead. This passage, like the first one, was singlehanded save for one 9-mile stretch. At sea, I found that the dory's flat bottom forward could pound when the boat was upright, but when she was heeled over under sail, the pounding became less serious.

In calm weather, I rowed and found that the narrow waterline beam and fine stern allowed my Beachcomber to move easily with 9-foot ash oars and only one person aboard. The long waterline and flaring topsides giving good spread to the oarlocks were helpful here, too. It is true that a dory's freeboard is rather high and catches the wind, but it does provide greater confidence in a seaway. When rowing alone, I

Mildred Nason somewhat sheepishly demonstrates the stability of her brother David's Alpha dory. A strapping girl of 16 in this 1924 photograph, she is all but dwarfed by the Alpha. Here, we can pick out many of the details of the dories. Note the grown hackmatack frames, of which there were four sets, interspaced with the steam-bent frames. Also, the thwart knees are in evidence in way of the centerboard trunk in order to provide a stiffening effect. The steering yoke lies aft, its lines running to swivel blocks on the inwale just abaft the second thwart. The jibsheets lead aft to blocks on the bilge stringer abreast of the centerboard trunk. Just forward of the centerboard can be seen a galvanized rod, with a turnbuckle, running athwartships. Often older boats that were loosening up with age carried this piece of gear to help relieve the strains from the larger rigs the boats began to carry about this time.

135

found that being seated about one-third of the way from the stern seemed best.

Feeling that a dory with a little more beam, both at the rail and on the waterline, would be an improvement led me to design my third dory and have her built by George Gulliford in Saugus during 1939. Her length overall was 21 feet 6 inches, her maximum beam was 5 feet 9 inches, and she cost about $150. While the beam and waterline length were both greater than the Beachcomber's, she still proved to be as easy to row. And because she was wider and was fitted with a heavy metal centerboard and some inside ballast, she could carry more sail. She was of typical dory construction and had sawn frames located at the A, B, C, D, and F stations of the lines plan, along with one or two steam-bent frames in between. (One writer of perhaps limited experience has questioned the need for these steam-bent frames, but it has been quite clearly proven that they do act to resist local damage, as shown by the fact that in some boats they have been strained enough to crack.)

The table shows an interesting comparison.

	Beachcomber (Chamberlain)	Dory Number 3
LOA	20'9"	21'5"
LWL	16'1" (6" draft)	18'0" (5" draft)
Beam, max.	4'11"	5'9"
Beam, LWL	3'10"	4'4"
Displ.	850 lbs. approx.	870 lbs. approx.
Mainsail area	117 sq. ft.	138 sq. ft.
Mainsail cen. effort to WL	9'	10'8"

My third dory was sailed in Lynn Harbor and on Lake Quannopowitt in Wakefield, Massachusetts. On the lake, there was a mixed squadron of three Alden Indians and various smaller sailboats that were raced under handicap. The 21-foot by 6-foot 5-inch Indian class boats were of dory-type construction, but they had much wider transoms and thus could carry more sail — 240 square feet to my 138 square feet. Although my dory led downwind, the Indians' greater sail area (perhaps along with better-setting sails) proved faster overall. The Indians marked a trend toward greater beam and wider transoms in small sailing craft, which has certainly increased their speed under sail around a triangular course. However, this sailing speed has been achieved at the expense of rowing ease

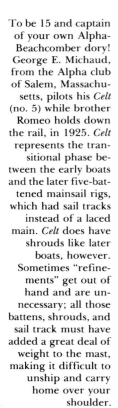

To be 15 and captain of your own Alpha-Beachcomber dory! George E. Michaud, from the Alpha club of Salem, Massachusetts, pilots his *Celt* (no. 5) while brother Romeo holds down the rail, in 1925. *Celt* represents the transitional phase between the early boats and the later five-battened mainsail rigs, which had sail tracks instead of a laced main. *Celt* does have shrouds like later boats, however. Sometimes "refinements" get out of hand and are unnecessary; all those battens, shrouds, and sail track must have added a great deal of weight to the mast, making it difficult to unship and carry home over your shoulder.

and of a more balanced and seakindly hull form.

After all my years with these craft, I have come to understand and appreciate their capabilities. The Swampscott hull lends itself well to a ketch rig, and the mizzen can be self-tending from one tack to the other. The two-masted ketch rig provides a lower center of effort than the sloop rig and allows more options when reducing sail. In place of the usual tiller at the stern, the transom-hung rudder can be controlled with a long linkage to a remote tiller near the middle of the boat where the helmsman's weight will be more effective as live ballast.

Outboard motors can be used on these hulls, too. A 4 h.p. Johnson gave my third dory a 5.9-knot speed (a $V/\sqrt{L}$ of 1.35), and a 2 h.p. Neptune produced 4.6 knots. Both outboards were mounted on the transom. Several steam-launch hobbyists have tried fitting steam propulsion units to dories, but the common high, vertical fire-tube boiler can create stability problems.

With a low, compact, one-lunger gasoline engine, these hulls made a satisfactory launch in that long-ago era when the demand for speed wasn't too great and when small gasoline engines were coming into their own. In fact, it was quite natural for the power dory to develop. One-lunger engines with make-and-break low-voltage ignition systems were not bothered much by a little spray and were less trouble than those with high-voltage spark-plug ignition. Toppan of Medford and Gerry Emmons of Swampscott were prominent as power-dory builders. Emmons had an extensive two-story plant on the site of the present Swampscott fire station and a salesroom near North Station in Boston.

There once were a number of dorybuilding shops north of Boston, not only for power dories but also for the other types as well. George Chaisson had a smaller but very active shop not far from Emmons in Swampscott, but that was during a later period. *The Rudder* magazine, in 1934, listed him as the builder of three different one-design racing classes, all designed by John Alden.

A Gardner also built dories in Swampscott; his shop was situated on the shore between the Fisherman's House and the Lincoln House Point. William Chamberlain (creator of the Beachcomber) constructed dories in a two-story barn behind the homes on Orne Street in Marblehead, and Sam Brown, although primarily a designer of larger craft, designed and built a few sailing dories of improved types near Fort Sewall in Marblehead.

The town of Amesbury, Massachusetts, was a dorybuilding center as well. In fact, Amesbury

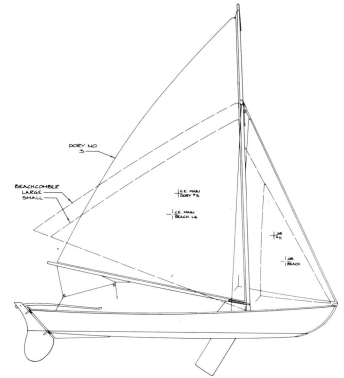

has probably given birth to more dories than any other town. Its location was a factor, since the town was near a source of good white pine for planking and oak for framing. Then, too, the fishing fleet at nearby Gloucester required hundreds of straight-sided Bank dories. Hiram Lowell started building dories in Amesbury in the late 18th century, and the company continues to build dories and skiffs there to this day.

Virtually all of the dorybuilding shops of the past are gone now, but the Swampscott type will never be forgotten. They are nice craft, with something to teach all sailors, of all levels of experience.

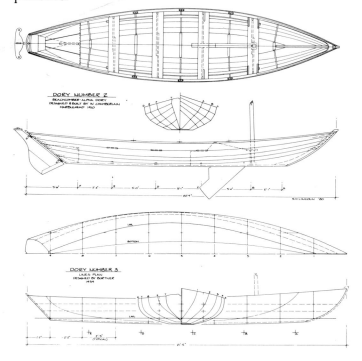

Matter of Detail: Rudders & Tillers

Maynard Bray

SOUND WOODEN BOATBUILDING techniques are, of course, the first imperative. If the boat isn't put together well, it won't stay together over the long haul. But once the primary methods have been mastered, it's time to move on to the finer details. As the interest in small wooden boatbuilding increased exponentially over the last decade, much was made over getting the boats built and little was done about the details that provide aesthetically pleasing construction. Maynard Bray, who has a fine eye for this type of thing, thought that publication of such details in Wood-enBoat *might encourage more builders to aspire to a higher standard and thus immeasurably improve the overall quality of new construction. A series of articles, one of which follows, appeared in the magazine, and all were greatly appreciated by the readers. One of the ironies of "Matter of Detail" is that the articles required Maynard to render finely detailed drawings, which he found excruciatingly difficult, hastening the temporary demise of the series. Nevertheless, Maynard has many more details left to discuss and illustrate, and we expect them to appear in the pages of* Wood-enBoat *once again.*

THERE HAS BEEN considerable interest in rudders and tillers, so this seems a good time to study their details. There are many different types and they would require much more of an analysis than can be contained in a single article, so we will start with a very familiar type.

Generally, rudders should taper in thickness toward their trailing edges, and some of them taper toward the bottom as well. Tapering is for proper distribution of strength, as well as for performance and appearance. While a taper represents extra work, the results always make it worthwhile. Wooden rudders are usually of oak or dense mahogany, with oak favored by many builders on account of its ability to hold drift iron.

Tillers that are curved are more handsome than straight ones, and, of course, they should always taper toward the working end. Ash, oak, or locust is most often used, as these woods are

strong and supple under bending pressure, and thus permit a more delicately sized tiller.

It's always more fun to sail a boat whose tiller fits tightly to the rudderhead without a lot of play. The helmsman gets an even better feel of the boat if the rudder hangers are well-fitted, although the special casting and machining sometimes needed to achieve good bearing surfaces may not always be worth it.

Cape Cod catboat rudders have to be shallow but stout, like the boats themselves — because these craft develop a tremendous weather helm when sailing downwind in a good breeze. For most catboats, the so-called barndoor rudder meets these needs well. I like it because it is so simple and beautiful, as well as very strong.

The barndoor rudder doesn't hang down below the keel, and it allows the boat to be steered in shallow water. The big weakness in a long rudder like this is its susceptibility to damage from grounding, so to minimize this risk, it is usually a bit shallower than the keel itself, while its lower edge is rounded up aft to give even more clearance back where all the leverage is in the event of a grounding.

Catboat rudders need to be big not only to combat the weather helm, but also to make up for the fact that most fat cats roll out their rudders to some extent when heeled over, leaving less area biting the water.

While I can't claim to be an expert on catboat rudders and tillers, I have been lucky enough to have looked at a good many that were products of experienced men and that have lasted well over the years. Mulling over why the good ones were laid out and put together the way they were will gradually lead to an understanding, and my approach to barndoor rudders and tillers that go with them has developed along these lines. It all begins to make sense if you have access to good examples and if you think about it long enough.

Let's look at some of the features in the drawing.

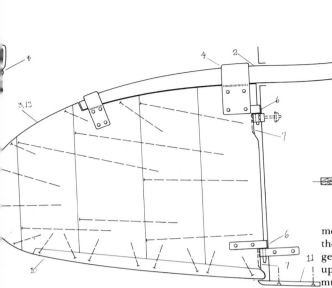

The Cape Cod Catboat

1 — A curved tiller always looks better than a straight one, but appearance wasn't the only reason catboat builders used tillers shaped like this. They wanted an unencumbered afterdeck (made possible because the tiller came into the boat under the deck through a hole in the transom) and had to have the tiller's inboard end at a convenient height for the helmsman (achieved by steam bending it upward in an S-curve where it clears the after deck). The result was a handsome and functional tiller that blended smoothly into the outline of the barndoor rudder.

2 — The tiller has to be stronger here than anywhere else along its length, and it should taper down where progressively less strength is needed on either side of this point. The taper aft enables the tiller to be wedged tightly into the two rudder straps, while at the same time it gives it a graceful appearance. Going forward, the tiller tapers to form a comfortable grip. In cross section, the tiller should be about equal in height and width, this generally being more than the thickness of the rudder at any given point.

3 — The best-looking catboat rudders are ones in which the top of the tiller and the outline of the rudder form one continuous curve, although a simpler and less expensive design omits the notch in the rudder and leaves the tiller standing proud. If built as shown, it is best to have the end of the tiller project a bit beyond the after strap so it is accessible both for initial fitting (after a rough fit, it is shortened by sawcutting here until it makes a good tight fit under the (rudder straps) and so it may be driven loose by thumping if it ever gets stuck in place.

4 — Instead of being bent to shape, straps are best if specially made up as castings — that way, they are sure to fit and can be made thick enough so as not to deform or overload their fastenings under the notoriously heavy strain of a catboat helm. Bronze is the customary material for them as well as for the fastenings (usually rivets) that hold them on. The forward strap, which should be placed as close to the leading edge as possible, has to be a good bit more rugged than the after one in order to handle the high loads at that point, and if it can be laid out to overlap the upper pintle and share its fastenings, the whole thing takes on a neat appearance.

5 — Tiller knobs always look good, and many catboats use the diamond-faced pattern shown.

6 — Standard gudgeons and pintles are the usual means of hanging a catboat rudder. The pintles are let into the rudder and riveted so as to be flush, and the lower gudgeon is likewise let into the sternpost. The flange-type upper gudgeon is bolted to the transom and can be made much more secure if let into the transom face.

7 — These cutouts allow the rudder to be lifted off its hangers, once the tiller has been removed. They are sawn to the outline indicated, then hollowed out with a gouge (as shown by the dotted lines) to match the radius of the gudgeons. The object here is to remove as little wood as possible and still have the rudder swing and lift freely.

8 — Most catboat rudders of this type were built about as shown, with the pieces running vertically, but they can be laid up the other way (horizontally) if you prefer, although it's more difficult to taper them if they are done that way. Tapering the rudder shown in the drawing from its leading to its trailing edge is made easier by using progressively thinner pieces as you work from forward to aft. Once they are carefully lined up, bored off, and drifted together, tapering is simply a matter of dressing off the "stairs" to a plane surface as indicated. (Vertical taper on such a shallow rudder is unnecessary.) To keep warpage to a minimum, the grain pattern of the individual pieces should be alternated as shown.

9 — Galvanized steel drift pins made from a round bar whose diameter is about a third the thickness of the wood are my preferred fastenings, as they are cheaply made and hold extremely well in oak. But if you're using a less tenacious wood, such as mahogany, yellow pine, or Douglas fir, you'll probably do better with through-bolts — bronze ones if you are shooting for the longest possible life.

For the rudder outline shown, the drift layout should be about as indicated, the idea being to enable progressive assembly outward from the first piece, to allow clearance between adjacent drifts, and to have enough drifts fastening each piece to its neighbor.

10 — This grounding shoe, because its grain runs fore and aft, can take more abuse than the raw ends of the main members could, and it also helps hold the entire assembly in line. Galvanized common nails, well angled, make good fastenings for a rudder drifted together with the same material.

11 — This metal plate serves to keep lines and weeds from snagging on the rudder's forward edge.

12 — The barndoor rudder's outline is a handsome continuous curve of varying radius oriented to give generous blade area below the waterline. In general, the shallower the boat, the longer the rudder must be for its height. On very shallow boats, such as the Beetle Cat, the rudders not only are quite long, but their lower edges are straight and run aft parallel to the waterline to achieve maximum underwater area.

Rudders, even the good ones, come in a variety of types, depending largely on the nature of the boat on which they are hung. With a deep-draft boat, you can get the area you need with a narrow rudder, but a shallow centerboarder or a powerboat usually calls for a short wide one. There are rudders hung entirely outside the boat in full view (outboard rudders) and there are inboard rudders whose stocks pierce the hulls of boats with overhanging sterns through a stuffing box or a rudder trunk. A book would be needed to cover them all in enough detail to be useful, but the principles used in shaping and building the specific examples described here can be applied to most other types. All of these are outboard rudders hung completely outside the boat.

Traditional New England Type

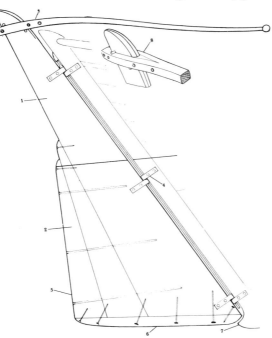

The early double-enders of New England, such as the boats of Block Island and Noman's Land, carried rudders rather like this most basic type of affair whose origins go well back in history. Tapered oak flitches, always at hand in any boat-shop, can be used to great advantage in rudders of this shape.

Taken altogether, this type of rudder is a wonderful match-up of function, aesthetics, and efficient construction.

1 — The main member is the forwardmost piece to which are attached the hangers, the tiller, and the after part of the rudder itself. In the old days, this piece was probably shaped according to the width of wood available, so it varied somewhat, even on boats of the same design. Making the most of your building stock is always good practice and was put to use more often a century ago than in our designer-oriented world. The forward edge of this piece is straight, and when hung, it parallels the sternpost. The after edge is best made straight as well — at least along its lower part — for ease in joining to the other pieces that make up the rudder blade.

2 — As many pieces as needed are used to build the after edge of the rudder and fill out the shape of it. To prevent a sliver point and get good fastening near their upper ends, and also to add a touch of class to the overall shape, the tops of these pieces are rounded off about as shown.

3 — Crudeness and woodiness are common faults of many rudders and tillers, especially back where they join together. One must pay careful attention to proportions and fastenings here if this is to be avoided and still have things strong enough. In this setup, where the tiller fits down over the rudderhead, curves, tapers, and the treatment of corners are keys to a good-looking job. By all means make the tiller out of a strong hardwood such as ash or oak so its strength comes from the nature of the material instead of from the sheer bulk of it. You can always get a more delicate appearance with hardwood because you need less of it. The tiller's curved shape is best achieved by steambending — you use less material that way and the grain runs more in line with its final shape. And while you're steaming, you might as well form the forward end of the slot by that method, too, using a wedge-shaped filler piece at the fork as shown. A second filler forms the aft end of the slot. For strength and security against splitting, rivets have to be placed horizontally close to both ends of the slot. Some kind of a knob or ball on the forward end of a tiller gives it a good look and a good feel. To me, tillers without some kind of an enlargement on their working ends look quite unfinished.

4 — If the rudder is a long one, you'll want three hangers to keep it in line. Since with its narrow blade it is inherently rugged with only slight chance of damage through grounding, and since grounding is unlikely anyway because it doesn't hang down below the bottom of the keel, there is no cause to make it easily removable. It was quite common for the old-time rudders to be attached to the boat by means of a long bronze or iron rod that passed through the hangers and locked them all together and in line. The hangers themselves would all be in the form of gudgeons rather than in pairs of gudgeons and pintles, and if you wanted a tight-fitting fancy job, you used cast gudgeons with machined surfaces. However, you could get by perfectly well with big lag-threaded screw eyes. To keep the rudder from floating up with the boat waterborne, the middle pair of hangers was oftentimes put on upside down as shown.

5 — These rudders should be tapered from front to back so that the thinnest part is at the after lower corner, where the need for strength is the least. The leading edge should be of constant thickness (as with the sternpost), so one pattern can be used for all the hangers. Some of the taper can be worked into the rudder as it is built — you simply plane the pieces to different thicknesses before assembly so there is less wood to be removed during the final tapering and fairing.

6 — A shoe at the bottom adds strength and helps keep the rudder blade from warping out of shape. It also protects the main members from damage. It is sacrificial — to be renewed as it becomes chafed or otherwise damaged.

7 — I think any aft-raking rudder should have some means of keeping rope and seaweed from snagging in the slot between it and the sternpost. Bringing the keel aft and shaping it as shown is one way of achieving this.

8 — When the rudderhead is shaped to accept a lifting and removable tiller, it takes on an appearance somewhat like that shown. The simplest arrangement for keeping the tiller in place is to use two horizontal pins through the rudderhead, one aft and above the tiller and the other forward and below it. With such a rig, the tiller can swing up to accommodate a standing helmsman but is kept from slipping off altogether by the top pin. And when let go, the pins acting together become support for the tiller, keeping it from dragging on the deck or coaming. The heads of rudders are subject to a lot of twisting, especially in boats with large rudders and strong weather helms, so it behooves the builder to make this part strong. Tenonlike shoulders, where the thickness and width have both been reduced, are weak and must be avoided in all but the smallest of boats. The strongest rudderheads are undoubtedly ones without a rapid change in cross section, i.e., ones having a smooth transition into the main part of the rudder itself. Just how big the rudderhead should be relative to the rest of the unit must be estimated based on what has worked in similar circumstances. I'm not aware of any hard-and-fast rule for doing this. Old photos and other boats are the best sources of information here.

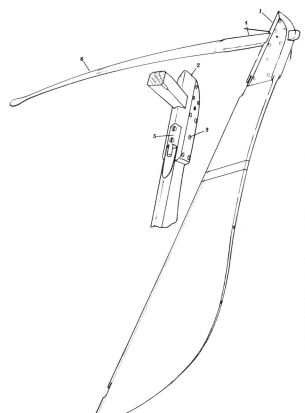

Differing from the foregoing type in the way that the tiller is attached, this rudder is from a Herreshoff 12½-footer. It is narrow enough to be made from a single piece of mahogany and to some extent is kept from warping by the three drifts that pass through it from the leading to the trailing edge. Like almost all well-built rudders, it is tapered from front to back, the leading edge being of constant width.

Herreshoff 12½-Footer

1 — Unless care is taken in proportioning the heads of these socket-type rudders, they can look mighty clunky — there is too much wood in too small a space. The cheeks should be kept just as thick and just as small as adequate strength will permit; rarely do they have to be as thick as the rudder itself. For example, the cheeks in the 12½-footer are ⁹⁄₁₆ inch, while the rudder itself at that point is nearly 1⅜ inches. The lower edges of the cheeks look good either cut off parallel with the boat's waterline or with some kind of fancy curve. The forward edge is simply a continuation of the rudder's shape, which in this instance is a 45-degree nosing to give the assembly a free swing — at least to a point. When swung to the limit, the cheeks hit the transom, the rudder fetches up, and you have what amounts to a built-in stop that, on the other end of things, keeps the tiller from banging against the coaming.

2 — For a good fit, this filler piece is best located after the tiller is in the socketed position. Grain of the filler should run parallel to that of the cheeks and the rudder blade itself.

3 — Good fastening is vital for keeping the cheeks tightly secure over the life of the boat. In this application, through fastenings are clearly called for, and they don't protrude much beyond the outside surface. Copper rivets are often used, and these old standbys would be hard to improve upon here.

4 — Tillers should be close to square in section, with their fitted ends cut to a taper that matches that of the socket, so that when inserted, they will wedge tightly into place (to be held there with a wood screw). Enough of the tiller is left projecting beyond the slot so it can be thumped loose from the rudder. This is the first step in removing the rudder, inasmuch as it's the tiller passing through a close-fitted

hole in the transom that keeps the rudder seated firmly on its hangers. Note that the aft end of the tiller is cut off to the same rake as the transom and that its corners are well rounded.

5 — As one would expect from Herreshoff, the rudder hangers on a 12½-footer are custom castings. The pintles are held in place with two big wood screws, which, after being driven in firmly until their slots are vertical, are filed off to be flush with the outside V-shape of the casting. The pintles are short, having only enough pin length to engage the gudgeon fully and no more. This limits the gouged-out areas (the pull space) on the rudder's leading edge. For extra strength and a neat appearance, the gudgeons are let into the transom and sternpost so their flanges are flush.

6 — The tiller is steam bent, and it curves and tapers just as it should. It is rectangular — a bit wider than it is high — back where it enters the rudder socket, then it goes to eight-sided, and finally to round in way of the hand grip. The egg-shaped knob on the end is something of a trademark of Herreshoff, and a practical one, too, as it's freer in form and therefore easier to make than a round one.

7 — Joel White, who has owned one of these boats for years and whose yard maintains several more of them, has found that without a guard of some kind at the heel of the rudder, lobster-pot warps occasionally get caught between it and the sternpost. Then when the slack takes up on a fast-moving boat, the lower gudgeon is sometimes pulled out. He has repaired damage from this cause enough times that he recommends strongly that a line guard of some kind be installed. I guess there wasn't much lobstering around Bristol.

John Gardner:
In His Own Words

Peter H. Spectre

*P*ETER SPECTRE HAS *always been fascinated by people who lead two lives, so after he had discovered that John Gardner, the leading exponent of traditional-boat revivalism, had interests that were generally unknown to our readers, he was determined to write about him. At first Gardner resisted the idea, perhaps in the belief that revelations about his background were irrelevant to boat aficionados, but Peter persisted and Gardner eventually gave in. Rather than a straight biographical essay, we chose the interview format because John Gardner expresses himself in a way that needs no secondhand interpretation. We included excerpts of Gardner's nonboating writing as examples of his diversity — and in the process became unwittingly the first boating magazine to publish material on such topics as nuclear power, the Rosenberg case, and Thoreau's relationship to the guaranteed income. We made a special effort to get the opening photograph of a smiling John Gardner, since, even though he is a thoroughly genial man, most published photographs of him evoke his serious, scholarly side.*

*I*F YOU ARE *a boat lover — most especially a traditional-boat lover — and you don't know John Gardner's work, then you must have spent the last 30 years or so alone on a rock in the middle of the ocean. Even if you did, you would have had to have been blind, because during those years at least one small boat inspired by his leadership must have passed by your rock. With seeing eyes you would have readily noticed, and appreciated, the boat's clean lines, sensible and quality-conscious craftsmanship, fine finish, and honest heritage.*

John Gardner's work speaks for itself. He is a boatbuilder, boat designer, small-craft historian, Associate Curator for Small Craft at Mystic Seaport, Technical Editor of the National Fisherman, *teacher, author, public speaker. Few in our field can claim such a breadth and depth of experience and expertise, and few can claim to have influenced so many people so thoroughly — though John Gardner is entirely too modest to make such claims, so I make them for him.*

Every person holds surprises, however, and John Gardner is no exception. Publicly, he comes across as a man who gets up in the morning, thinks about boats, talks about boats, builds boats, then goes back to bed at night and dreams about boats. There may be some truth to that, but there is also a private John Gardner who is at ease with larger issues, who has spent a good part of his life trying to gain a larger perspective, and who, for the most part, has been successful at it. The achievement of balance as an individual — with equal application of manual and intellectual skills — seems to have been his lifelong goal, which means that he is as comfortable talking about social theory as he is talking about the origins of the Swampscott dory. His implied message is that it is perfectly all right to become a specialist, but not to the extent that you ignore the rest of the world around you.

This interview took place in 1980 at John Gardner's home in Mystic, Connecticut, where he lives with his wife Beatrice, to whom he has been married for more than 42 years. We started in his garden, where he picked over the last of the strawberries, and ended in his living room, which is as spare and modest as his speech. I asked him questions and he answered them, but the results of the session are published here without the questions so they will not get in the way of the story. What's important here is what he said, not what I asked him. Unfortunately, the one thing this interview failed to reveal is Gardner's humor. On one level at least, he is one of the funniest men I have met, though the nature of his humor can only be understood on a person-to-person basis. He possesses the classical Yankee dry wit, which relies on understatement coupled with twinkling eyes or a wry grin, a style that cannot be conveyed by the written word. Take my word for it: he has the gift as few others do.
— PHS

M Y RECOLLECTIONS go back to very early in the century. I was born in 1905 in Calais, Maine, which is on the St. Croix River at the head of Passamaquoddy Bay, where it forms the border between Maine and New Brunswick. I come from a long line of land surveyors. My great-grandfather was one, as were my grandfather and my father.

We lived on a farm on the river about three miles below Calais. The farm ran down to the water and a mile back. As a boy I had boats on the river. There were great tides, 26 or 28 feet, and the river at that point was about a mile wide, so when the tide was out, there would be a half-mile of mud flats. Keeping a boat with tides like that took ingenuity. I had a pole about 30 feet long stuck in the mud flats and a square float — four boards nailed together — around

the pole that would go up and down with the tide. I tied my boat to that. I also had a boat similar to the one Howard Chapelle called the Farmer's Daughter with a wooden wheelbarrow wheel at the bow, which allowed it to be pushed over the mud flats.

We built boats and used boats. My grandfather, before my time, had a pinky, which he used a great deal, and even while I was small, he still went down river in the fall to catch fish for the winter. In fact, there were many boats on the river at that time. There were lumber schooners, excursion boats, and steamboats. Calais was a thriving, enterprising, prosperous place, a center for the lumber industry.

We cut our own boat lumber from our woodlot, usually at the same time we cut our firewood for the winter. We saved the good sawlogs and hauled them to a mill and brought the lumber home. My grandfather made everything. He made boats, he made hay racks and cart wheels, he built buildings and shingled roofs. He had been a carver's apprentice in Charlestown, Massachusetts, and was an accomplished woodcarver. I learned woodworking from him and my father as part of growing up.

When I was young I used to spend quite a good deal of time at a nearby boatshop owned by the Whelan boys, so called, although they were still called the Whelan boys when they were long past 70. Jim and George were their names, though they were locally known as Pete and Repeat because they always repeated each other when they talked. They were Irish, Catholic, and Democrats, which put them apart to some extent in that area. They built all types of boats up to 50 or 60 feet for commercial or pleasure use, and all by hand. The shop had no power at all. Pieces were ripped out of rough-sawn lumber with handsaws and then planed. They used adzes and broadaxes. I was influenced by these men. I was also influenced by a very skilled carpenter by the name of Tommy Webster, who lived up the road. He built my father's house with my father's assistance, without plans. The shelves and pantries were finished just like the interior of a vessel.

I never apprenticed as a carpenter or boat-builder, but I picked up the skills as I went along. My first attempt to rig my own boat came early on, when I took one of my great-grandfather's sea chests from the barn down to the brook and tried to sail it like a boat. From there I became a pretty good boatbuilder and built several craft before I got out of high school — rowboats, sailboats, nothing too difficult. Once I decided to build a dory and sent to the Maine State Library for a book with the lines of a

John Gardner, generally acknowledged to be the dean of traditional small craft, a man whose knowledge is complemented by experience.

Over the years, John Gardner has written on a number of subjects besides boats, sometimes under his own name and sometimes under the pseudonym John Clarkson. To provide a better appreciation of the "other" John Gardner, we reprint here a few excerpts from articles he has written on such diverse topics as atomic development, the guaranteed income, and chemical hazards. We wish we could publish the articles in toto, but space limitations preclude that.

The following excerpts (below, and on page 147) are from a short piece John Gardner wrote for the Summer 1965 edition of Contemporary Issues *entitled "A New England View of the Triple Revolution." The triple revolution of the title is a reference to an article written by Ralph Borsodi concerning (1) the human rights revolution, (2) the weaponry revolution, and (3) the cybernation revolution.*

"... Human society and social production has now reached a degree of complexity and interconnection, as well as an extent and mass, that requires some sort of broad planning to function. The question is not planning or rejection of planning, but rather what kind of planning do we want? I, for my part, demand an order of economic planning that frees the individual from interference with personal affairs, rather than arbitrary, dictatorial planning.

We are fast approaching a time and condition when the ancient distinction between work and play will become meaningless. It is normal and wholesome for humans to engage in *purposeful activity*, and once a universal guaranteed income has freed humanity from economic compulsions, humans will have the means and will be free, as the masses have never before been free, *to engage in purposeful activity to their liking*. My faith in human nature is such that I truly believe that under such a condition good works will be multiplied and will abound in diversity and extent as never before in history, and solely on a voluntary, amateur basis, as it were...."

pretty big dory. I scaled it down proportionally with the result that it was too tender. So to remedy the defect, I built two airtight sponsons shaped something like crescent moons and attached them to the sides. The boat became very stable and rowed nicely but looked odd. I took it down to the Whelans, who scratched their heads but admitted the arrangement worked pretty well.

I went to school in Calais, and after graduation I went to normal school in Machias. I took the standard two-year teacher-training course and then taught school for two years. I decided to become a teacher because I was encouraged to do so at home — both my aunts were teachers — and it was the most convenient thing to do, I guess. Believe it or not, I was also motivated by football. Perhaps one of the most exciting moments of my life was when I made the varsity football team in my high school sophomore year at Calais Academy. In those days you had to supply your own uniform. I sawed and split and piled four cords of hackmatack wood to buy a pair of football pants. In my freshman year at Machias Normal School I was one of the group that organized the school's first football team. But football wasn't the only thing. I had a lot of drive back then. I initiated and was editor of the *Washingtonia*, the school magazine, and was president of the student body, and did just about everything else.

During one of my teaching years, I went to summer school at Columbia University in New York, which at the time was the leading teacher-training institution in the country. I stayed on at Columbia and took the two-year course, and then went on to get my master's degree in 1932.

I got out of Columbia in the depths of the Depression. I was there in New York when they were selling apples on street corners and the financiers were jumping out of windows on Wall Street. It was a tough time to go to college and a tough time to get a job afterward, even though I achieved honor rank.

But in the meantime, in 1930, I had got a summer job as a counselor at Pine Island Camp in Belgrade Lakes, Maine. I worked there summers during the 1930s, while I was at Columbia, and afterward when I was kicking around like most others during the Depression. I was in charge of the workshop, which was one of the features of the camp. We built model boats and yachts and sailed them. I also built several full-sized boats there, such as a C.D. Mower sailing dinghy whose lines had been published in *The Rudder* magazine. I was put in charge of the shop because of my background; I had the skills and the interest. I was also qualified because I understood both inland craft, like canoes, and saltwater craft. Calais, where I grew up, was intermediate between upriver — the woods — and downriver — the ocean. I understood both worlds. I found the camp to be a delightful experience and gained much inspiration from the work I did there.

But full-time work eluded me. When I graduated from Columbia I had a first-class education. My expectations were that I would get a rather fancy job, but there weren't any. So I knocked about quite a bit and spent some time at home. I worked in the woods as a lumberman. I contracted and peeled pulpwood. I peeled a hundred cords of pulpwood one summer. I didn't teach at all — just knocked around at a lot of different things.

My life as a boatyard worker began when World War II broke out. I happened to be in Lynn, Massachusetts, at the time and signed on at the Graves yard in nearby Marblehead, because they were building Coast Guard picket boats as fast as they could and needed experienced workers. They never questioned my ability; I guess it was because I was from Maine and seemed to know what I was talking about.

The picket boats were 38 feet long and had been designed by Walter McInnis. We built 72 or 73 of them. I was on the night shift as a planker, since this was an assembly-line operation. We were building two boats at a time, and I had two men who were hanging the planks and fastening them as fast as I got them out. Another crew was getting out the keel assemblies, lowering them on the forms, and timbering them. Still another crew would finish them inside, after they were turned over. We planked the boats upside-down, and it was fast and furious work.

When the picket boats were finished and things slacked off at Graves, I went over to Reed's Shipyard in Winthrop and went to work on a big, curious Navy barge, heavily built of Oregon fir. The yard was expanding like mad. I hung plank for a while and then was assigned to build a scale model of the craft for Washington. It was a typical government mess, with constant revisions to the full-sized craft. I had to go out to the construction all the time and measure the changes and then rework the model. It was quite an elaborate job.

Soon I got a call to go back to Graves, however. I returned to work on several different types of boats, and then started in on yachts because they were still trying to carry on with their yacht business even though there was a war on. I did yacht repair and other jobs; in fact, I built the tank-test model for the Hickman Sea Sled.

It was wild over there in Marblehead at the beginning of the War. We had blackouts because the submarines were right off the coast, and a civil defense force was organized locally. We were all given guns; I had an old elephant gun that belonged to Graves's father-in-law. The foreman turned out billy clubs for blackout wardens in the joiner shop. We stopped work on several afternoons to go to the gravel pit and practice with our guns. We were given posts behind various rocks on the beach in case the submarines should land. It was completely wild.

By then I had given up on being a teacher. I was doing what I wanted to do, and the job was over at four o'clock on Friday. I had a great many intellectual interests that occupied me when I wasn't working. That was more or less the pattern until I went to work at Mystic Seaport in 1969. For example, I began to measure boats and take off lines. Some of those lines I put away until much later when I began to write. I then drew upon those resources that I gathered in Marblehead.

I started taking off lines because I was interested in boats and their shapes, and I was interested in drawing them. I was also influenced by the people I worked with. I was working with a very fine boatbuilder, Charles Lawton, who was then considered to be the dean of his craft north of Boston. He was almost 90 at that time, still building boats at Graves. He had come down from St. John as a young man and had begun building boats in Boston as early as 1880. He worked at the Navy Yard before coming to Graves.

World War II was the last hurrah of the old-time boatbuilders, many of whom came out of retirement for the duration. We had one boat joiner at Graves by the name of Dan Grant. He was a Nova Scotia Scotsman, an extraordinarily talented woodworker, sparmaker, carpenter. He could do anything. He made violins to pay the hospital expenses for one of his sons who had polio. He made very fine violins. He claimed he ruined his eyes working nights making them. He was a very ingenious man, and I count myself lucky for being able to work with people like that.

I stayed at Graves until the end of the war, then I went to work for Simms Brothers in Dorchester, where they were building fine yachts for Sparkman & Stephens. Simms had formerly worked for Lawley, and his yard was sort of a home for old Lawley hands. We were double planking yachts 50 to 60 feet long. The outside layer was 7/8-inch African mahogany and the inside was 3/8-inch white cedar with white lead between. The outside planking was so smooth and

Gardner is an expert with hand wood-working tools. Here he hews a log in the old style — with an axe after sawing to the line.

tight you couldn't see where the seams were. I finally left Simms in the 1940s, because it was too far from my home and the pay wasn't too good. I went to work at Dion's Boatyard in Salem. Relations there were very good. If you could do the work and you were reliable, Fred Dion didn't bother you. In fact, he gave me his youngest son so I could train him. I did all repair work, no new construction.

From the late 1940s until 1969 I worked at Dion's, with the exception of two years during the Korean War when I worked at General Electric in the template room. I was essentially a patternmaker in the turbine division, though when business was slow, I went out on the floor and tried my hand at welding and boilermaking. It was interesting work, but not too hard. I was generally done with my task in three or four hours, and for the rest of my shift I used to make things for myself or write.

You have to understand that I was leading two lives. I was a manual worker to make a living but was engaged in intellectual pursuits the rest of the time. In the 1930s I had been doing a lot of reading in many fields, including boat design and building. I read the very fine articles in *Yachting* written by Howard Chapelle in the 1930s; they were quite definitely the foundation of all his work — those are the articles he contributed on the Friendship sloop and a series of other traditional American craft. I had Chapelle's book on boatbuilding, for example, which came out in 1941. I brought a copy in to work and showed it to Dan Grant. He said not to pay too much attention to it, because he had given most of the information to Chapelle, and it was old-fashioned.

During this period I used to go to the Associates meetings at Peabody Museum of Salem, which was a very loosely constituted group. We used to meet more or less regularly, and different people would talk and present papers — people like Samuel Eliot Morison and William Avery Baker. It was also during this time that I started to write about boats for publication. I wrote my first article for the *Maine Coast Fisherman* (which later became the *National Fisherman*) in 1951, and after my piece on the Hammond dory appeared, I became acquainted with Howard Chapelle. We met and established a very close relationship, working together and exchanging information. For example, in the late 1950s I spent a week at his home in Maryland, where I learned much about Chesapeake Bay boat construction.

Howard Chapelle was an extremely interesting man and had much influence on me and others. You hear occasional revisionist talk about him now, but I must say that he was an extraordinarily gifted man who made an enormous contribution. When I say gifted, I mean he could turn out prodigious amounts of work. He could draw boat lines, intricate boat lines, and carry on an animated conversation on an entirely different subject at the same time. He was the first man in our field, a completely virgin field. There was an abundance of material scattered around just to be had for the asking, and he attempted to gather in so much that quite naturally he sometimes missed things. Sometimes he arrived at conclusions intuitively rather than from laborious digging. Sometimes his intuitions were not accurate, although they could be enormously brilliant. He read extensively but kept few notes. Occasionally his references are not to be trusted completely. Yet you have to give the man credit; he did a tremendous amount of work when no one else was paying any attention to it. He got the thing started, but some of what he did has to be refined.

Marion Brewington, another pioneer, was a meticulous researcher, extremely fussy about the most minute details. He and Chapelle in the beginning were quite close friends, and I knew them both. Some of the slips that Chapelle made, Brewington couldn't take. On the other hand, Chapelle said he just couldn't understand Brewington. Yet Chapelle was an extremely generous person, was always sharing his information. He was also argumentative and his politics were quite conservative. You have to give Chapelle credit for what he did, and you need to be cautious about what you accept without checking. Incidentally, I believe that goes for all of us.

But boats weren't my only interest. I was very much involved in Freudian psychology at that time and still have a whole Freudian library, which I don't read anymore. I almost wrote a book on the Oneida Community. I still have the copious notes. I researched the obscure literature in the Widener Library at Harvard after getting special entree through a friend. I spent hours in the Boston Athenaeum, the Hart Nautical Library, and the Boston Medical Library.

At the same time I was a contributing editor of *Contemporary Issues* magazine, which was published in England and has since gone out of existence. I wrote under the pseudonym of Clarkson. I did a long study of the Rosenberg case, one of the first analyses of what was going on. I did a very long analysis of the early background of atomic energy, with the mistaken notion that it was going to solve all our energy problems. Some of the others connected with the magazine thought otherwise. But I was wrong, and I know it now. I contributed to other publications as well, including *Balanced Living*, published by The School for Living. This was on ecology — back to the land, organic gardening — long before the present interest in that sort of thing. All this took quite a bit of time and research. I received no money at all; I did it just for the interest. I was making enough at the boatyard to get by on, but you might say it wasn't a life of luxury.

Very early on in my writing for the *Maine Coast Fisherman* I did a series of articles on the Whitehall boat, which marked the beginning of the Whitehall revival. Prior to that, the boat was pretty much forgotten except for a short article Captain Charlton Smith had done for *Rudder* back in 1943. About 1958 or 1959 Kenneth Durant, after retiring from journalism, became interested in Adirondack guideboat history. He started out with the idea that the guideboat might have developed from the Whitehall, and got in touch with me. From then until his death in 1972, we had a very productive working relationship. We shared research and boatbuilding knowledge. He was researching in Hanover, New Hampshire, Cambridge, New York, and he had contacts abroad. We were together accumulating a great deal of boatbuilding background, both history and development. Durant was working in conjunction with the Adirondack Museum, and it was through him that I began to work on and off with that museum as a consultant. And it was because of Ed Lynch, whom I worked with at the museum, that I came to Mystic Seaport in 1969.

When Ed Lynch went to Mystic as curator, he decided he wanted to start a small craft pro-

"... Let us not be sentimental about country living. In the 'good old days' the farmer's life was a hard one, and often a degrading one. Thoreau has some observations about Concord farmers, how some of them plowed themselves as compost into their fields, and how they crept painfully down the road of life pushing their great barns before them. It was a pity, they deserved more than scorn. And Thoreau, what right had he to point them out? To start with, someone paid his way through Harvard College. He never married or had a family to support. He died in his early forties, before infirmities of old age had overtaken him. During his sojourn at Walden he was a squatter on Emerson's farm and when he wanted a good meal he could visit friends in Concord. Besides, his stay at Walden was only for a short time — a brief episode in his life. As I recall, James Russell Lowell did not think too highly of Thoreau and said something to the effect that if a man wanted to live like a woodchuck, that was his business. Well, if one has no more responsibilities than a woodchuck, he can play at that game for a short while, as Thoreau did, but for a family man and for keeps, it takes more resources.

But with the resources, country life can be beautiful, and why shouldn't the Government provide such resources in the way of a Guaranteed Income if the productive capacity of the country is capable of it, as seems quite well established. Argue, if you can, that the national economy is not equal to this and if you can make your point, we shall have to bow. But don't say that a Guaranteed Income would lessen freedom, for it would do just the opposite. Or that it would be bad for character, for it would actually be the best thing for character that ever happened. Nothing brings out meanness worse than carking financial worries. A man tied for life to a routine job is just as much a slave as if he had a chain on his leg.

What I implied above, but did not say specifically, was that without those Concord farmers composting themselves into their fields and wearily dragging their great barns down the road of life, there would not have been, and could not have been, any Thoreau or any Walden, a fact that Thoreau, I believe, never recognized. Without a vast industrial complex subject to centralized planning there will not be, and cannot be, any 'modern appliances' to take the 'drudgery' out of homesteading. But how to get those 'modern appliances' down on the farm? They cannot be 'bought' in the old sense, for the farmer, *by himself and by farming*, can get nothing to buy them with. He can receive them only through free distribution of some sort. But he need not be ashamed to receive a gift, for it is no gift. It is his own to begin with; his own share of the social inheritance...."

147

The following excerpts are from an article by John Gardner entitled "Chemical Hazards in the Boatyard," published in the April 1955 edition of Yachting *magazine. It was based on an article that originally appeared a few months previously in* Maine Coast Fisherman *and could very well be the first article in a boating publication directing attention to chemical hazards in the boating industry. Like much of Gardner's work, it broke considerable ground.*

❝. . . Chemicals in bewildering profusion are moving into the boatyard and the backyard, bringing hazards undreamed of in the old days when tar, pitch, and turpentine held sway and paints were standard compounds of lead and copper. Of course lead and copper are poisonous when taken into the body in sufficient quantity. Lead poisoning or 'painter's colic' is the classic type of *cumulative poisoning* to be met with in the boatyard. Lead poisoning rarely occurs today because experience has made it second nature with painters to guard against it. Lead is not eliminated from the body, and when ingested over extended periods, even in minute amounts, can build up to pathological and even fatal accumulations. But, unlike some of the newer 'industrial poisons,' standard lead compounds are not absorbed through the skin, so it was mainly a matter of guarding against entry through the mouth. Professional painters generally were safe if they followed simple precautions like washing before eating and keeping the fingernails clean.

Such limited precautions no longer suffice. There are products today that affect the skin or are absorbed through it to injure internal organs. Harmful vapors may be breathed into the lungs. And with the uncontrolled use of power sanders, chemical dust has become a real hazard. . . .❞

❝. . . With the coming into universal use of power sanders and fast cutting abrasive papers, one of the hazards from paint is from its dust. Paint dust was always bad. For years hardy souls at fitting-out time have crawled from beneath low-lying bottoms, spitting and blowing red or green for days after. But old methods involving scraper, remover, and the hand sanding block did not raise the whirling clouds of fine dust thrown into the air by fast-spinning disc sanders. It is so easy to grab the handle, flick the switch — and how the dust does fly! Perhaps the bottom was painted last spring 1500 miles away. Boats move around a lot. Who knows what it was painted with? Meantime the dust clouds are swirling red, green, or brown. Chances are the enthusiastic operator is not wearing a respirator, nor even dampened handkerchief tied across his nose to filter out the coarser particles . . . .❞

gram. He arranged to have me hired. At the time I was still living in Lynn and working at Dion's in Salem, and it would be necessary for me to move to Connecticut. But it was a very promising job in many ways. I was getting older, and I could look ahead and see that the type of work that I was doing in the boatyard would be getting harder and harder for me. Although I liked the work at Dion's, it was fairly difficult, particularly in the wintertime, as we worked in unheated sheds. I was almost at retirement age. I came to Mystic for more money than I was getting in the boatyard, and it was a very interesting type of work, more or less a continuation, a culmination, of something that had been building up and growing for a long time.

When I came to Mystic there was no small craft program at all. I hunted around for a place and found an unoccupied corner of a storage shed where they had wagons and sleighs. I took that space and built a bench from materials I picked up around the Seaport and started building a boat. I also started traveling around New England for the Museum, buying up tools. There were many holes in the Museum's collection. Tool collecting at that time had not quite reached the dramatic proportions that it has reached today, and I got a lot of good buys.

That first year, 1969, I was invited to go to the Thousand Islands as a judge at the antique boat show, which was then in its fourth or fifth year. But there were no small craft. I saw St. Lawrence skiffs, which I had been interested in since I first went to work in Marblehead, and I suggested that they enlarge the program from one to two days and include small craft. The next year they did. I got the idea from there that we should have some sort of small craft meet at Mystic, with the result that in the summer of 1970, the following year, we had our first rowing workshop. That was the first meet of recreational small craft in this country, and it was the beginning of a continuing movement.

That winter I decided to institute instruction in boatbuilding at Mystic Seaport, but not vocational boatbuilding. Ed Lynch had been toying with the idea of vocational instruction, but had discovered that there are all sorts of state regulations we would have to meet, which didn't seem feasible. It didn't seem to me that the regulations would prevent us from having instruction in recreational boat building. We started our program in the winter of 1970-71. It was the first of its kind, to be followed later by Lance Lee's establishment of the Apprenticeshop in Bath, Maine, where he felt that boatbuilding could be used to mold character. He, too, succeeded, and many other similar programs followed from those beginnings.

As you can see, I have concentrated on small craft all of my life — unlike Howard Chapelle, for example, who studied the larger boats and ships as well — perhaps because that was what I was interested in as a boy, and in a certain way I am reliving my boyhood. I have always stressed practical experience in addition to theoretical study, perhaps because my father placed a high value on manual skills with woodworking tools. When I did a good job, I was praised for it. Maybe that's part of the reason I get satisfaction from using hand tools now. There is probably a psychological connection.

Sure, I could have turned my efforts to recording the lines and details of larger vessels and luxury yachts, but my deeper interests lay with the smaller, simpler craft of my boyhood on the St. Croix River. And there were good examples of such craft still conveniently at hand in Salem and Marblehead 30 and 40 years ago. I was drawn to them, as I was not to the larger craft, and it was easier, too. As it turned out, there are many people now interested in building boats, and they do well to turn to the simpler, smaller craft of traditional design in making a start. My interests coincide with theirs.

Traditional small craft are the field of my study and practical experience, but I have always been experimenting in new techniques within that framework. There are those who see this as something of a paradox — but innovation is traditional. If you go back in the development of boatbuilding, you will find that builders were innovative and always ready to adopt anything that came along that was good. In fact, boatbuilders seem to be more innovative than sailors, who tend to stick with what is tried and proven. There's a good reason for that. Sailors don't want to go out to sea in an experiment and drown.

Boatbuilders, on the other hand, want to do the job as quickly as they can. One of the bywords of the trade is: "Hurry up. The man wants his boat." You hear that a dozen times a day around a professional boatshop. Sometimes it is said in earnest and sometimes it is said satirically, but either way, the emphasis among boatbuilders is to use techniques and materials that will get the job done quickly, yet produce a satisfactory boat.

Innovation has always made the difference. Without the type of wood screw with a point on it that we have today, a great many traditional boats would not have been built. We all consider the Adirondack guideboat to be traditional. Yet

The following excerpts are from a long exposé of early atomic politics and economics published in the October-November 1954 edition of Contemporary Issues. *The article was written by Gardner under the pseudonym John Clarkson and is the product of considerable research. It was a spinoff from Gardner's research into the Rosenberg case, and though the conclusions have been dated by subsequent events, it is an indication of the author's thoroughness even at a time when most information on atomic technology was difficult to locate.*

"...Some claim that the interest evinced by the chemical industry (including oil companies) in atomic power is largely pretended and cloaks 'a desire to get into the fissionable material production business — with the Government as an exclusive customer which could easily be pressured into an infinite procurement program similar to Federal purchases of silver. One chemical company executive, indeed, made it plain that his company is more interested in producing plutonium than power if there came a choice between the two; and another company executive has expressed a similar view.' This may well be a substantial part of the reason why billions have gone into plants run by duPont and Union Carbide for the production of plutonium and enriched uranium, while millions, and only a few at that, have been made available for power. Be that as it may, nuclear research has opened up a new frontier for the chemical industry, and such giants as duPont, Monsanto, Dow, and Union Carbide and Carbon, like their opposite numbers in the electrical equipment industry, have gone into the 'forefront of that change' to control it. To what extent they are sitting on the lid of that change, is more difficult to gauge than the open sabotage of atomic power. It is probable, even now, that discoveries of the first order, in this field, are being cozily kept under wraps until the provisions in the law governing atomic patents are changed...."

"... It is probably not the fear of Russian competition, primarily, that sparks the American turn toward atomic power. More likely it is a belated realization in business circles that atomic power is coming and coming fast in numerous countries outside both the U.S. and the U.S.S.R., and that in spite of America's head start and great industrial resources, including her hoard of enriched uranium, she is in danger of being left behind in the atomic power race. Much against its retrogressive conservatism, the American business oligopoly is being pushed into the atomic age by energy-hungry smaller nations, to date notably those in Western Europe, who see in the atom the only way out of the impasse of their power shortage...."

it could not have been built until self-tapping wood screws and small copper tacks came along. Those fastenings were just as much an innovation a hundred years ago as epoxy resins are today.

There is misunderstanding of the meaning I give to traditional boats. I have explained the concept a number of times, but it still doesn't seem to sink in for many people. To me, traditional boatbuilding means the type of boat construction that blossomed toward the end of the 19th century. That period was one of immense technical progress in every area, and it was the culmination of refined and perfected boatbuilding techniques extending back over a period of centuries. There was a proliferation of small-craft types for sail and oar perfected to the ultimate for speed and convenience. The boats were quite different in the Chesapeake from what they were in the Gulf of Maine or the swamps of Louisiana or San Francisco Bay or Boston Harbor. Boatbuilding was to some extent an ethnic melting pot, and this all came to a head — blossomed, so to speak — toward the end of the 19th century before the advent of the gasoline engine.

Yet the end came very quickly. In 10 years, between 1900 and 1910, all the Hampton boats in Casco Bay, Maine, were converted to gasoline engines, because they would no longer have to depend on the wind. Americans are prone to adopt new things even when it's not advisable to do so. They might be sorry afterward but it doesn't stop them from doing it. Given this climate, then, all the refinements, all these diverse boat types, were no longer in demand because you could stick a gasoline engine in any old tub. Such craft didn't have to be hydrodynamically perfect any more.

Everything changed. The old boatbuilders were no longer needed, they died off, and boatbuilding to the standards of the late 19th century died with them. Such boatbuilding had never been recorded, as it had been carried on by rule-of-thumb methods. It was almost an illiterate trade until fairly recently. So with the advent of the gasoline engine, plus many other changes in American life brought on by the automobile, the bicycle, and the canvas canoe, we came to the end of an era.

When I talk about traditional boats, I mean that perfection of design and technique for boats of oar and sail that came into predominance in the last decade of the 19th century. Yet I also believe that if the boatbuilding of that time had been allowed to progress naturally as it had before then, it would have evolved gradually, picking up new methods and techniques as it went. Therefore, I see no contradiction when plywood and epoxy are applied to the perfected designs of the late 19th century. Not at all. It's a mistake to think that all progress came to an end at a certain juncture, and that there was no chance for improvement after that. We must not restrict ourselves only to what was done in the past. Definitely not.

What do I think about the future of wooden boatbuilding? It seems to me at the present time in some areas it is taking on the characteristics of a fad, and I don't like it. A lot of people are jumping on a bandwagon. Some are doing it because they think it is a way to attract tourists or get some easy money from a foundation, and I wish it were not developing as fast, or along some of the lines that it is.

I am also concerned about its vocational aspect. I have been making a certain amount of restrained comment concerning vocational programs, considering that there is little prospect that all who graduate will get jobs building wooden boats at wages they can live on. As you no doubt recall, I wrote a short piece for the fourth *Mariner's Catalog* advising young people interested in learning to build boats that perhaps the best way would be for them to teach themselves, while they held down a stopgap job of some sort to put bread on the table. Find a place to set up a bench, hang around boatshops and watch, read the books, start collecting hand tools, and begin with a simple boat with the idea of selling it. After a couple of years, they will know if they want to build boats for a living, and should have enough equipment to start out in business in a small way, if they do. They will have supported themselves in the meantime, won't be out any tuition, and will have learned much of value on their own.

I don't want to sound negative about this. That is farthest from my intention. I think I see a better future for wooden boatbuilding than what we have today, even though it will be primarily in the recreational field. I have felt that way all along. There will always be people who will want wooden boats for recreation, and many won't want to build them themselves. Consequently, there will always be a place for a few commercial shops building a limited number of wooden boats. I hope that in the process, the best that was developed in the past will be preserved and passed on, but I should expect this heritage to be reworked and even improved to some extent to meet the needs and preferences of future times. Our obligation is to make sure that the richness of our small-craft heritage is passed on intact to the generations that will come after us.

The Dutch Boeier

E.H. Bon

DUTCH GEOLOGIST E. H. Bon came to this country several years ago. An avid sailor and amateur designer, he was much involved in the traditional boating scene in the Netherlands. Distance from his country must have put his knowledge and experience into perspective, for he wrote down his thoughts on the Dutch boeier — a shallow, bluff-bowed leeboarder — and submitted them to Wooden-Boat. The result, we think, provides a solid perspective on such beautiful craft.

IN THE NETHERLANDS, as in the United States, there has been a renewal of interest in traditional wooden craft. This interest, which began in the 1950s, has been manifested in the building of new boats to old models, and the renovation and restoration of original craft whenever possible. As can be expected in a country with the diverse maritime heritage of the Netherlands, there are many different

Ancient landscape, shallow water, quiet breeze, clear skies — the *Phoenix* is in her natural habitat.

types of craft that could be classified as "traditional." Unfortunately, there are few restorable original boats of any type to be found. Take the *boeier*, for instance.

The boeier is a type of yacht intended for pleasure sailing, and in the past it was built in several parts of the Netherlands. It was developed from a family of freight-carrying double-ended sailing barges fitted with leeboards that, until a few decades ago, could be seen on all the numerous inland waterways of the Low Countries. Boeiers were built until the early years of the present century, when most yachtsmen lost interest in them in favor of keel yachts introduced from other countries. Only a few of the original boats still exist, mainly in the province of Friesland, where traditions lingered longer than elsewhere in the Netherlands. Boeiers were not built from drafted plans, so, for someone interested in building an authentic new one, the only way of obtaining lines has been to take them off an existing model, and since the 1950s, a number of boeiers have been so measured.

In 1973 I became the owner of *Phoenix*, one of the last surviving wooden boeiers from the province of Holland. She was originally named the *Piet Hein*, after the popular 17th-century admiral of that name, and she was built at the Het Jacht (the yacht) shipyard in Amsterdam in 1898. The owner and master shipbuilder of this yard was Nicolaas Adrianus Bernhard, a member of a family with a long shipbuilding tradi-

tion. Of the many boeiers built at Het Jacht (at first of wood, later also of steel), only one wooden specimen besides *Phoenix* is known to exist — the *Ludana*, built as the *Olga* in 1898. This boeier is in England, in a state of neglect.

Other than having a list of successive owners, I know little of *Phoenix*'s long yachting career. Her original name was changed in 1923, for reasons unknown, to *Miami*. Under this name she was a frequent entry in the yearly regattas held in the yachting centers of the Netherlands. After World War II her name was changed, once more, to *Phoenix*. When I bought her in 1973, her age was showing through her brightwork. After her state was compared with old photographs, it was apparent that her original rig had been cut down and that much of her original woodcarving had disappeared. But she was still fit enough to sail, and her accommodations were cozy and livable. So we decided to sail and cruise her during the sailing season and to restore her gradually during the winter months. Each spring she was a little fresher, stronger, and brighter than the preceding one.

Phoenix's restoration was straightforward but time-consuming. A tentative five-year plan was drawn up, and I was fortunate to be able to hire Willem Strofberg of Leimuiden, a veteran shipwright of great experience and ability, to work on her. Most of the boatstock in *Phoenix* is oak, and supplies for her restoration were obtained from France, where quantities of ancient and completely seasoned inland oak are sometimes available from salvaged buildings. (I might add here that while oak is a wonderful material for shipbuilding, its resistance to rot is low, especially in fresh water, where *Phoenix* spends much of her time.) Constant care is required to prevent fungi from starting their destruction.

During five successive winters at Strofberg's yard, the following items in *Phoenix* were renewed: bow planking, stem, keel, breasthooks in the bow, a few frames, one floor timber, the mast thwart and the tabernacle. Part of the *boeisel* — the planking above the wale — was also replaced. Since the seam between the boeisel and the wale was worn beyond caulking, a stealer plank was inserted all around. After all that work, *Phoenix* is now in fine condition.

The day-to-day maintenance of a vessel like *Phoenix* is relatively easy, contrary to what one might expect. The exterior woodwork only needs a single coat of good-quality varnish each year after the old varnish has been given a light rubbing down with fine sandpaper. We take a yearly trip to the tidal flats in the north of Holland and Germany, and the change from fresh to salt water helps to combat rot and marine

The wide, shoal bottom of the boeier is ideal for a craft that will spend much of her time on a mudflat when the tide goes out. *Phoenix* lies almost upright when the other yachts could be lying on their ears.

growth, and the salt bleaches the teak deck. For the rest of the maintenance, it is a question of keeping the interior well ventilated and dry, and the bilges clean. Frequent sailing keeps a wooden boat alive; the motion refreshes both the air and the bilgewater inside.

The boeier, though similar in concept to the Dutch working craft, was designed and built exclusively for pleasure sailing, so the requirement to carry loads obviously did not exist. Length and draft were the only limiting factors. That the boeier did not evolve to the extreme "skimming dish" forms of the 19th-century American centerboarders is perhaps due to Dutch common sense, which held that a yacht, next to being able to sail well and win races, should also be easy to handle and pleasant and comfortable to live in.

Sailing a Boeier

Phoenix is quite stiff in a breeze despite the complete lack of ballast, except for the mast counterweight and the engine. But you can't delay reefing and must take care handling the sheets in a strong, gusty wind. When she was raced under her original rig, a certain amount of inside ballast would have been carried.

Under her present cruising rig, *Phoenix* is somewhat sluggish in light airs, though it is remarkable how well she ghosts along in a breath of wind.

Tacking up a 100-foot-wide channel is no problem, although the helmsman must know the boat's habits well. The secret is to keep the ship moving and to drop the leeboards at exactly the right moment, which is just when she starts gathering leeway. If the board is let go earlier, it will float up again; if too late, it won't go all the way down. I have to admit that I learned much of this only during the season when the engine was ashore for an overhaul. The experience very much increased my admiration for a boeier's sailing ability.

The order "ready to go about" not only warns the cook to look out for the crockery, but also alerts the *fokkemaat* to go forward to tend the foresail and another crewmember to watch the leeboards. At the command "ree," the helm is put down while the man on the foredeck takes a turn around the weather shroud with a short lanyard attached to the clew of the foresail. As the vessel shoots up into the wind and the pressure on the foresail eases, this lanyard is tautened as much as possible and held fast. When the ship is head to wind, the foresail is thus held aback, which helps the turning movement. At the same time, the crewmember looking after the leeboards loosens the hauling part

of the weather leeboard tackle, keeping a turn around the cleat, ready to let go. The fokkemaat has to judge the exact moment to let go the foresail clew. This must happen just before the vessel has reached the heading of the new tack, so that the sheet will slam fully across the deck along the horse and not remain stuck somewhere amidships. Letting go too early means that the sail will keep slatting about, loosening the hitch of the hauling part of the sheet, which means everything will have to be set and trimmed again on the new tack. If it is done right, coming about requires no effort at all. It is a joy to see a little girl of 10 perform as an expert fokkemaat on a large boeier of Lemsteraak!

On board *Phoenix*, the hauling part of the leeboard tackles leads aft to the cockpit, enabling the helmsman to drop the board if need be. On busy canals, however, he leaves this task to a member of the crew, as the helmsman has enough to do calculating his new course in the midst of other shipping. When handling Dutch-type boats, maneuvers must proceed slowly and inexorably. They have to be anticipated well beforehand. It simply doesn't work to find out, when halfway through a turn, that the new tack will bring you right across the bows of an approaching tow of heavily laden barges.

When cruising, going to windward requires only the attention of the helmsman, but during races, the fokkemaat is on the foredeck, holding the foresheet in his hands with a turn on the block, constantly trimming the sail according to each shift in the strength or direction of the wind. With the wind aft, the foresail is boomed out to windward in the usual manner. When the wind is not too strong, a loosely cut spinnaker

A fleet of boeiers rafted up for a traditional Dutch watercraft rendezvous.

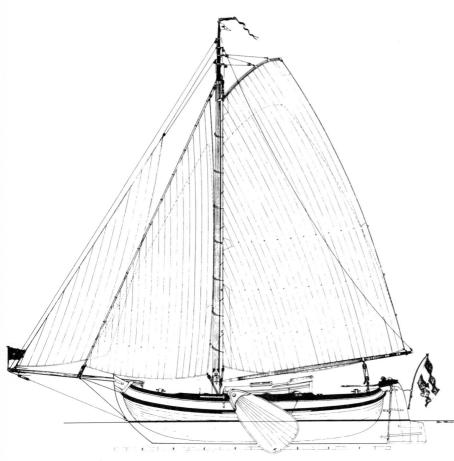

accomplished by wearing the ship around. With only the reefed foresail set, the leeboards raised, and the helm lashed to leeward, *Phoenix* drifts downwind easily, making an enormous wake to windward. However, a lee shore is never far away in the Netherlands, so it is wise to carry an oversize anchor ready for use.

It appears from several timed passages that *Phoenix*'s maximum speed is a little over 7 knots. At 7.2 knots, the speed factor (maximum speed divided by the square root of the waterline length) would be 1.4, which most people would not consider her capable of when they first looked her over.

Under her present cruising rig, *Phoenix* handles quite well in a Force-7 wind, with a double reef in the mainsail and a single reef in the foresail. Racing under these conditions requires a seasoned crew and careful handling of the sheets. Going to windward really becomes exhilarating then, with the mast bending, the lee rail under, and spray flying sky-high. Under these circumstances, it is sometimes easy to forget that you are sailing in a museum piece — especially when you are just inching through a competitor's lee!

Measuring Phoenix

One of the first things I did after acquiring the *Phoenix* was to take off her lines. I did this so others could build a new ship from the plans if they so desired and also because in the back of my mind I was thinking about building a model of her. I took off her lines in the winter of 1973-74, when she was hauled out for her first period of restoration, and the resulting plans are reproduced here.

Sections were marked on the keel at intervals of 50 cm, measured from the after perpendicular. Horizontal battens were fixed at these points in the baseplane, perpendicular to the centerline. On these battens, distances of 10 cm were marked starting from the centerline. The vertical distances between these points and the outside of the hull planking were measured on the port and starboard sides, averaged, and then plotted on a scale of 1:10. From these sections, waterlines parallel to the baseplane were derived. These were faired with verticals (buttock lines) and diagonals in the usual manner. The slight angles between adjacent planks, as indicated in the construction plan, were smoothed in the process. Other items of the hull and the construction details were measured with a measuring tape and bevel, and they were fitted into the framework of the lines drawing.

or *jager* is then set on the jibboom and boomed out with a longer spar. The sail can also be used when reaching. The clew may reach from the end of the jibboom to well aft of the mast, so jibing may be risky when it occurs inadvertently.

The leeboards are hoisted up on a broad reach. In *Phoenix* it may even pay to pull up the board with the wind on the beam in order to reduce water resistance, but I would not recommend this in a ship with a bottom that is really flat, like a *botter* or a *schouw*. As was mentioned before, the tack of the mainsail can be triced up. This can be especially helpful if the ship carries weather helm when running or reaching in a strong wind.

Other sail-reducing tricks may be attempted during such circumstances: Either the peak may be dropped or the sail may be "scandalized" by letting go the throat halyard; the reef tackle may be set up (without tying in a reef); or the topping lift may be hauled in, spilling wind from the sail. If the wind really starts to blow, the mainsheet must be hauled in to tie in a reef or two. When a double-reefed main and a reefed foresail are still too much, the lowering of the foresail brings great relief. Thus the vessel will hold her own in a Force-8 wind, although going about will normally only be

The lines are drawn to the outside of the planking. Sections and waterlines are at intervals of 50 and 20 cm, respectively; the verticals are at 40-cm intervals from the centerplane. The section numbers represent each section's distance in meters from the after perpendicular. The actual waterline of the vessel, as she floats in fresh water, fully equipped but without crew, is given in the plan as a dashed line. The displacement curve refers to this waterline.

The sailplan, drawn on a scale of 1:20, was derived from an original drawing of a 9-meter-long boeier from the old Bernhard yard. The placement of the mast and the lengths of the boom and gaff correspond exactly with those of *Phoenix*, although the present mast is 1.5 m (about 5 feet) shorter than the original one. I am sure that this drawing represents the *Phoenix* as originally rigged. The present "cruising" rig is indicated in the plan as a dashed line.

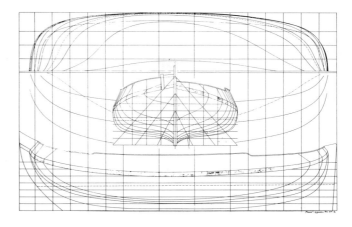

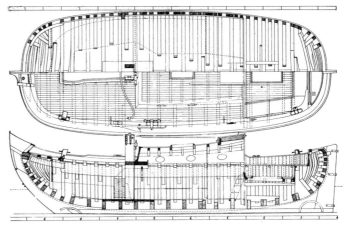

Details

The traditional model of the working sailing ships of the Netherlands is broad and shallow, with full ends. Surprisingly enough, this model was the result of the search for speed. The great beam was necessary to obtain stability to carry a large rig, which also had to be lofty to catch the wind on rivers and canals lined with trees and buildings. The draft was limited by the shallowness of inland waterways and offshore tidal flats. Length and beam were also limited by the extensive system of locks in the Netherlands.

To obtain the displacement needed to carry maximum load, the bow and the stern were built with very full lines. Ease of handling was an additional requirement born from the economic necessity of having a small crew. It is interesting to study the various ship types of the Netherlands and note how the complex requirements were provided for. To me it is evident that, given the building material existing at the time these craft were developed, modern nautical theory could not have come up with better solutions.

The lines of the *Phoenix* show the characteristics of the boeier in the latest stage of its natural development and are based exclusively on tradition and the lessons taught by practice. Nautical theory, hydrodynamics, strength calculations, and the like, although at the time already highly advanced in big shipbuilding, were not applied. Most boeiers were in fact built without a model or molds, the frames being set up and faired by eye. It is said of Nicolaas Bernhard that he was the first boeier builder to make drawings of his projects.

The lines show a hull of extreme width in relation to depth and length. The great beam is carried forward and aft well into the ends of the vessel, so the upper planks of the sides converge at the stem and the sternpost at an angle of nearly 90 degrees. A heavy *berghout*, or wale, makes the sheer and is the line of extreme width of the hull. Below the wale, the hull shape quickly loses its stubbiness, as can be seen in the easy-flowing curves of the buttock lines. The displacement curve (projected jointly with the diagonals) is especially instructive in this respect: It shows a remarkably fine entry and a smooth run aft. As can be imagined from the lines, the fullness of the ends above the waterline results in an enormous increase in stability when the hull is heeling.

The S-shape of the frames near the keel is a refinement of the hull model introduced in the boeier during the latest stage of its development. Undoubtedly it eases the flow of the water and increases windward ability. However, it also increase the draft by some 8 inches. In my view, this indicates that at the time when the latest boeiers were built, draft was not felt to be as crucial a constraint as it was earlier, before mechanical dredging of the waterways.

The great amount of external deadwood at

the base of the stem and sternpost is another typical feature meant to increase lateral resistance. In fact, *Phoenix* is not as extreme in this respect as other yachts of her type, where the forward end of the keel is carried forward for some distance outside the curve of the stem. Modern research into the sailing qualities of the Dutch-type yacht has confirmed that this *loefbijter* (literally, luff-biter) considerably improves windward performance.

All major construction features are given in the plans, so the following remarks may suffice. The keel is an oak beam, 10 cm (4 inches) thick, about 14 cm (5½ inches) wide and 7.20 m (23 feet 7 inches) long, extending 8 cm (3⅛ inches) outside the rabbet at the main section (no. 5). It is fastened to the deadwood, stem, and sternpost with semicircular bands of wrought iron, which are sunk into the wood and fastened with iron rivets. This is a very old method of fastening timbers that can be seen in antique ship models. The keel, stem, and stern pieces taper out to a thickness of about 3 inches.

The hull planking and the boeisel are of oak, 30 mm (about 1¼ inches) thick. The frames and floor timbers are sawn from crooks of 8 and 10 cm (3⅛ inches and 4 inches) oak. The heads of the frames are either bolted to the wale or are continued to the underside of the deck. The space between the frames (in general, about 35 cm or 1 foot 2 inches) is occupied by intermediate frames, which are not connected to the keel. Below the waterline, the frames and floor timbers are connected with treenails to the planks; the floor timbers are bolted to the keel with long iron drift bolts. The deckbeams are supported by a wide clamp, which is bolted to the heads of the frames. The clamp is interrupted by the heavy hanging knees that support the mast thwart. The boeisel or upper planking consists of a wide plank, which is doubled above the deck. The deck planking, the cabin trunk, and the roof are teak, which is a departure from the traditional oak, indicating that when the vessel was built, money was no constraint. The sides of the cabin trunk are shaped from massive teak logs of at least 10 by 50 by 300 cm (4 inches by 20 inches by 10 feet).

The mast is stepped in a tabernacle, where it can pivot on a bolt for lowering. It is counterbalanced by a weight consisting of a number of 1-inch steel plates bolted to the mast heel. A long hatch in the foredeck called the *uitwip* allows this weight to swing upward when the mast is lowered. This system, invented early in the 18th century, makes child's play of lowering the massive 9-inch spar. The mast was originally unstayed. It is made of a type of fir that was for-

merly imported from the Baltic port of Riga. Nowadays, this tough and flexible wood cannot be obtained, and new masts are therefore usually made with laminated spruce planks. Such laminated masts cannot be bent without starting the glue seams, so shrouds and stays have become indispensable.

It is clear that the lofty rig, combined with the great stiffness of the hull, puts enormous strains on the mast step. Its construction is therefore a marvel of solidity. The tabernacle consists of oak planks of 9 by 23 cm (3½ inches by 9 inches), the lower ends of which are let into a step that is bolted to three floor timbers. Lateral support is provided by a thwart 10 by 60 cm (4 inches by 23½ inches) running across the full width of the vessel. This plank is connected to the heads of a set of closely spaced frames with two pairs of heavy hanging knees (one pair is made of wrought iron). The thwart was originally a massive oak timber, but to avoid dismantling the deck and the forward part of the cabin trunk during restoration, it was replaced by an assembly of six 4-inch by 4-inch oak beams bolted together.

The leeboards (*zwaarden*) are 5 cm (2 inches) thick. They are built of edge-bolted oak planks. The outer surface is flat; the edges on the inner side are rounded. Around the edges, a wrought iron stave of triangular section is fastened with galvanized iron nails. The boards pivot around a bolt let in the head piece. This bolt carries an eye at its inboard end that fits over a hook connected to an iron bar bolted to the deck. The position of the leeboard can be adjusted by moving the hook fore and aft along the bar. As can be seen in the drawing, the whole leeboard is free to swing outward from the side of the ship. When sailing close-hauled, the board on the lee side is lowered. Since it is parallel to the tumblehome of the boeisel, its position in the water becomes almost vertical when the vessel heels, thereby increasing the board's depth and efficiency. The leeward component of the ship's movement presses the board against a rubbing strake fitted to the underside of the wale. The outer edge of this strake is not quite parallel to the ship's centerline, but toed in slightly toward the bow. This improves the effectiveness of the leeboard by increasing the hydrodynamic lift.

The cockpit is watertight; the sole slopes aft, where a pair of lead scuppers can drain out the water. The companionway is covered by a teak sliding hatch that conforms in shape very neatly with the smooth, S-shaped curve of the after part of the cabin roof.

The rudder is 6 cm (2¼ inches) thick. Below

the waterline this thickness is reduced aft to 3 cm (1⅛ inches). A wrought iron tiller is let into the head of the rudder. The tiller's section measures 45 by 45 mm (1¾ inches square), with beveled corners. It tapers forward to 30 mm (1⅛ inches), where a wooden hand grip is fitted to it with brass rings. A traditional gilded wooden lion ornaments the rudderhead.

Phoenix's interior arrangement was not original when I bought her. It appears that formerly a galley with a coal stove was fitted in the forward part of the fo'c's'le. At present there are two sofa bunks in the main cabin, an enclosed head on the after starboard side next to the companionway, and a galley with butane stove and sink on the opposite side. In the fo'c's'le there are two fore-and-aft bunks and

one athwartships bunk. The great beam makes the accommodation very spacious, although the headroom, especially forward, is rather low. The interior woodwork is mostly teak and mahogany, all varnished except for the cabin roof and the underside of the deck, which are painted white.

Outside, the wood is all varnished except for wooden moldings fitted to the boeisel and following the sheer, which are painted white. The upper part of the boeisel is black. The berghout is also black, except for a pair of parallel lengthwise grooves, which are white. The rudderhead is black. The Friesian boeiers are brighter in appearance, with red or green stripes, gilded scrolls offsetting the raised central part of the boeisel, and gilded stars ornamenting the

A tribute to Dutch common sense, the boeier is able to sail well and win races, yet is easy to handle and is pleasant and comfortable to live in.

hawseholes. All of these color schemes and ornamentations are strictly traditional and may not be modified at will, if you wish your craft to remain authentic. There is much brasswork that has to be polished constantly. In the old days the iron fittings, such as the tiller and sheet horses, were rubbed down every day with water and sand until the metal shone like silver. Nowadays, since paid hands are extinct, the iron is painted with aluminum paint.

Sometime in her career *Phoenix* was fitted with an engine. The existing Gray Marine 4-cylinder gasoline engine was probably fitted shortly after World War II. It is bolted down on two fore-and-aft engine beds fixed to three floor timbers below the cockpit sole, as indicated in the drawings. An ugly hole, not shown in the drawings, is cut in the sternpost, and the leading edge of the rudder houses the propeller. There is a 50-liter copper fuel tank in the space below the tiny afterdeck, which seems to have been created for this purpose. Two 100-liter water tanks are fitted below the cockpit sole alongside the engine.

Compared with the rigs of modern yachts, the rig of a boeier has several peculiarities, some of which may seem truly atavistic. A closer look, however, will reveal that the overall scheme reflects simplicity, strength, and ease of handling. Although new materials have been adopted in the rigging of traditional boats, boeier sails are still cut in the antique manner with a full belly, panels parallel to the leech, and a loose foot. The curved gaff of the mainsail is another typical feature. The reason for this shape is not purely one of aesthetics, as is commonly thought, but essentially one of practicality: The sail was originally made of flax, which stretches a lot when new. If such a sail, with its full, round cut, were laced to a straight spar, stretching would produce pronounced wrinkles at the throat and peak.

The tack of the jib is set up on a short iron bowsprit, called the *botteloef*, bolted to the stemhead and stayed with iron straps to the wales. A wooden jibboom can be carried alongside the botteloef, and a jib is set flying on it. Before you enter a lock or a busy harbor, this boom is topped up with a topping lift to the masthead. As the boom's heel is set up on a removable fitting, it is easy to unship the boom completely. The forestay — originally a wrought iron bar, nowadays more likely a steel wire — is set up on the botteloef with a three-sheave luff tackle. The foresail is sheeted to an iron horse crossing the foredeck just forward of the mast. Thus, the foresheet does not have to be reset after going about. The loose-footed mainsail is fitted to the mast with short lengths of rope and wooden parrels called *kloten*. The tack is set up with a four-sheave (one double and two single blocks) tackle, which is slackened when reaching in order to give a nice belly to the sail. The clew can be "catted up" with a light tackle alongside the mast, which is a quick and easy way to reduce sail area. The boom can be topped by means of a topping lift or *dirk*, which leads via a masthead block to a tackle set up on the tabernacle. Since the masthead block is higher than the main halyard blocks, the sail can be hoisted on either side of the dirk. The absence of backstays and aft-leading shrouds makes the setting and lowering of the sail easy, even when the wind is aft.

The top of the mast is adorned with a permanent pennant, a 5-inch red or blue ribbon, serving as a wind indicator. It can be from 5 to 10 feet long, and it is boomed out with a small stick revolving on a pin in the masthead. The national flag is flown from a flagstaff on the rudder. Don't ask a Dutchman why this stick is curved! He could only say that a straight pole would look simply awful. A small regional flag is often carried on the tip of the jibboom. In the sailplan I drew the flag of Amsterdam to honor the hometown of both *Phoenix* and her owner.

Traditional Yachting in the Netherlands

The revival of interest in traditional Dutch sailing that began during the 1950s has led to the institution of an association of boat owners and the establishment of a register in which existing traditional yachts are entered. Newly built yachts have to meet certain qualifications in order to be eligible. These qualifications embrace hull form, rig, equipment, and materials; for instance, fiberglass, balloon spinnakers, and colored sails (except white or brown) are out. Many new *platbodems* are of the *lemsteraak* type, which is higher in the bow than the boeier, with the mast stepped farther aft. The old model, with its round ends and U-shaped sections, is faithfully copied in steel at many inland shipyards.

The association, the Stichting Stamboek Ronde-en Platbodemjachten, organizes a yearly meeting, usually in a yachting center where a celebration is taking place — it could be a centennial, a celebration of a naval victory, or a club's jubilee. An important event is the so-called *admiraalzeilen*, or sailing in fleets, with mock battles and a salute to the admiral. The annual meeting is an unforgettable spectacle that is still little known outside the Netherlands.

Boadicea

Roger Taylor

*T**HE FINE PROSE** of boating writer Roger Taylor suggests the extent of his boating experience. Unlike many whose major sailing is done in an easy chair, Roger gets out on the water as much as possible and makes it a point to use the widest variety of craft imaginable. He has sailed in boats of every type, from flat-bottomed skiffs to Navy submarines, from cruising yawls to Chesapeake skipjacks, from sailing Whitehalls to Maine lobsterboats. When Roger travels, which he does often as President of International Marine Publishing Company, he seeks out unique craft to sail. One year, after a business trip to England, he called to say he had sailed on a great old boat and wanted to write about her. Not too many people today can claim they went sailing on a boat built in 1808, and we thought anyone who had done that would have something worthwhile to say about it.*

T HE *Boadicea*, an "unobtrusive" — her owner's word — little gaff-rigger lying moored off Bussand Creek at West Mersea, was pointed out to me by Maurice Griffiths, the cruising boat designer and former long-time editor of *Yachting Monthly*. I had taken time out during a business trip to England to pay my respects to Maurice at his lovely waterfront home on Mersea Island, a ways north of the Thames Estuary. He was kindly driving me around and didn't want me to miss the little green fishing smack.

I was excited to see her, remembering reading about her rebuilding in an English book we had published in the United States, *Restoring*

Boadicea hauled up on the hard for painting.

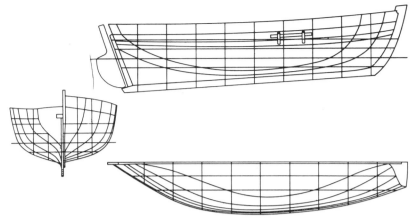

Vintage Boats by John Lewis. "She's the oldest one we have, you know," said Maurice. "Built in 1808." I had forgotten she was quite that old and made some appropriate exclamation. Yet her great age didn't really sink in at the time. Mr. Griffiths might as well have told me that a light year is 5,865,696,000,000 miles.

When was 1808, anyway? Well, on this side of the Atlantic, Thomas Jefferson was the president of our country, in his second term. (In his first term, he made the Louisiana Purchase, extending the western boundary all the way to the Rockies.) In England, from whom we had declared independence over 30 years earlier, George III was still king. (Not until 1811 would he be declared insane and replaced by a regent.)

The year before 1808, the *Clermont* had made her famous run from New York to Albany. The three-masted schooner had recently been "invented," but Chebacco boats had not yet evolved into pinkies, and the development of such new, specialized types as the Cape Cod catboat and the Friendship sloop were still decades in the future. That's when 1808 was.

I spent the next couple of days not far from the *Boadicea*'s mooring with my friend John Leather, the marine surveyor, writer, sailor, and designer. About the first thing John told me after I arrived at his Ballast Quay Farm was, "Michael Frost is going to take us out for a day's trawling in the *Boadicea* tomorrow." Now I really was excited. Trawling under sail in a 170-year-old smack! Talk about your lessons in maritime history!

John filled me in a bit on Mike Frost and his *Boadicea*. "You know," he said, "he's had her more than 40 years." Michael Frost bought the *Boadicea* in 1938. Except for World War II and the major rebuilding, he's been sailing her year-round since 1938. Another mind-boggler.

The *Boadicea* was built by James Williamson at Malden, a few miles up the Blackwater River from her present mooring. She worked out of Malden, dredging oysters, and was owned by

Bradwell and Burnham until 1825. From that year until 1871, she was owned and fished by John Pewter out of nearby Tollesbury. From 1871 until 1917, she was owned and fished by a man named Binks and then by his son, Isaiah Binks. The elder Mr. Binks rebuilt the boat extensively in 1890. From 1917 until 1938, she was owned and fished by E.W. French of West Mersea. Michael Frost gave the *Boadicea* a complete rebuild, which took from 1963 until 1972. The *Boadicea*'s five owners each had her an average of about 34½ years.

One thing about a wooden boat: she can be rebuilt as necessary to withstand the ravages of time. The *Boadicea* now has just one bit of wood in her deadwood that is perhaps original. So, is she still the *Boadicea*? I won't attempt to argue "the *Constellation* question" here, but my simple answer to it is a resounding and unequivocal "Yes!" (My reasoning doesn't depend on that possibly original chunk of deadwood.)

The *Boadicea* is named for the East Anglian queen who fought a losing battle against the Roman occupiers of Britain in 61 A.D. Scholars say her name should be spelled Boudiccea. Anyway, *Boadicea* has a soft C and the accent is on the next-to-last of her five syllables. Those who know her well get away with calling her the Bodasher, or, more affectionately, the Bodie.

She's a normal English fishing smack (in England, the word "smack" indicates neither a carry-boat nor a boat with a wet well, as it does in America) of her time, but, as I have emphasized, that time was long ago. She has an old hull form.

The lines drawing reproduced from *Restoring Vintage Boats* by the kind permission of John Lewis was drawn by Peter Brown in 1974. The drawing doesn't show great detail but certainly gives a general idea of the hull shape. My impression is that the boat presently sits deeper in the water than this drawing shows — the actual load waterline is perhaps halfway between the one shown and the next waterline above.

There is great balance in this set of lines. The bow is short and curved, and the flat transom and sternpost are moderately raked. She is at least as fine aft as she is forward. She has generous beam amidships. Her sections are gentle, with an easy turn to the bilge. She has a long run and a long, straight keel.

The *Boadicea* is 30 feet long on deck, with a waterline length of 24 feet, a beam of 10 feet 3 inches, and a draft of 4 feet 6 inches. Her displacement is about 11 tons, and she now has about 4 tons of inside lead ballast.

The day we were to go trawling with Michael Frost in the *Boadicea* was warm and sunny, par-

Thomas Jefferson was President of the United States when *Boadicea* was originally built. Though rebuilt many times thereafter, she remains an authentic sail-powered oyster dredger.

ticularly warm for October. I always think of English sailing weather as being abominable, but this day was absolutely lovely.

When you go sailing on the east coast of England, the first thing you contend with and the last thing you contend with are the same: mud. Lifelong East Anglian sailors, like Maurice Griffiths, can write eloquently about the beauties of mud, but they are usually referring to sitting in the cockpit at sunset watching the tide creep back in over the stuff. As we made our way toward "the Hard" (that's a gravelly place along the shore where you don't sink in above your ankles), John Leather warned that there might be slippery patches here and there. In his three-sizes-too-big boots, I approached

the foreshore as if I were crossing Niagara Falls on a tightrope. Speechless with concentration, I didn't dare nod acknowledgment of his message for fear of losing my balance. We made it to the water's edge without mishap.

Mike Frost had seen us coming and, with his little daughter and the ship's dog, had tumbled into his dinghy and sculled along so that he arrived at the Hard just as we did. We boarded the tiny craft, and Mike pushed her off with his oar and quietly sculled us out to the *Boadicea*. The dinghy was burdensome, heavily built, nicely balanced fore and aft, beamy amidships, and rather low all along the gunwale. Mike admitted he had designed and built her himself. Looking down at her shape as he sculled her along, he shook his head and said, "I am afraid that unwittingly I made her a small *Boadicea*."

Mike's wife, who had been keeping ship while the rest of the *Boadicea*'s company had gone to fetch us off, greeted us as we came over the rail. Then she went forward and was ready to cast off the mooring by the time Mike had the Sabb two-cylinder diesel turning over. Mike said he regretted running the engine, but otherwise we'd have a long, slow beat in a head tide. No doubt of that, for the wind was light, she wouldn't quite lay out the creek, and the flood was running hard. The *Boadicea* has a solid, off-center wheel. Driven smoothly by the Sabb, it shoved us out over the flood.

As soon as we were underway, we started making sail to help her along. It was immediately apparent that the Frosts had worked out just the nicest ways to handle the *Boadicea*'s traditional cutter rig. John and I pitched in to help, and the Frosts explained the ship's ways to keep us from doing things out of order or according to — in my case — some strange foreign custom. Soon we had the sail and staysail up and sheeted flat to draw a little, and then we bent on and set a tiny spitfire jib. All these sails are very heavy canvas, tanned and thoroughly waterproofed.

The tack of the loose-footed mainsail is left free rather than being bowsed down. Mike said he only lashed down the tack if the main was double reefed and it was blowing really hard or if he had the third reef tied in. The sail is heavy enough so that the luff stands well without being stretched taut.

There is no parrel line on the boom jaws, but evidently she's never jumped her boom off the mast. I suppose after 170 years you can trust it.

The bitter ends of all the halyards are made fast, not only so they can't get aloft by accident, but also to keep the rope from unlaying.

The sheet of the loose-footed staysail is made fast back on itself and works on a horse running across the deck. To flatten the sail, there is a bowline on each forward shroud to go right 'round the sheet and bowse it aft and outboard.

The spitfire is set flying on a ring around the bowsprit held forward by an outhaul, and a two-part halyard. The sheet is trimmed in through a hole in the bulwarks and is belayed right forward. There's no inhaul on the ring — a pull on the sheet is sufficient to bring the whole sail inboard after the outhaul has been let go. The little sail sets well back from the bowsprit end.

Like many traditional boats, the old English smacks are rigged according to a series of rules of thumb, based on the length of the boom.

Mike explained that the formula for the *Boadicea*'s boom length was two-thirds of the length of the smack (two-thirds of 30 equals 20) plus 4 feet for overhang. Then her 24-foot boom determined all the other dimensions of her rig according to set proportions.

Once clear of the creek, we laid her off a little to a close reach and headed out along the edge of Mersea Flats, already well covered by the flood. We were to trawl in company with another smack in sight to seaward of us. She turned out to be a pretty young thing. She wasn't even 100 years old yet, and her relatively recent design, by comparison to that of the Bodie, had been influenced by turn-of-the-century racing yachts.

We got the trawl ready to go overboard. The net was maybe 15 feet across its mouth and twice that from head to cod end. We hoisted it aloft on a single-part whip just to be sure it was clear and then faked it down on the quarter. The buoy on its rope was made fast to the cod end, and the cod end was tied shut with a fancy knot that wove back and forth in such a way that its bulk plugged the cod end, yet it could be released completely with one pull when the time came. A pair of otter boards, maybe 2 x 1s and quite heavy, were rigged to the sides of the trawl. Then the warp was taken down from the place where it hung in the shrouds and was faked down to run clear. It was led from the stern through a single block on a fairly long bridle leading to the otter boards, then forward outside everything to the big, heavy wooden windlass around which turns were taken and the warp then belayed. In the bitter end of the warp back aft, a stopper knot was tied so that if that end of the warp should somehow be lost overboard, it couldn't run out through the block on the bridle and cause the net to be lost.

Not long after the trawl was ready to go overboard, we had gained enough offing and were ready to let her go back toward Mersea Island, towing her gear in toward the flats with the tide. Our companion smack had done this; we went out a ways beyond her, shut down the engine, and were ready to follow suit.

The operation of shooting the net has been well described by Michael Frost in his book, *Boadicea: CK 213*, published in England by Angus & Robertson in 1974. He wrote, "A sailing trawler works with the tide and only exceptionally does she tow her gear behind her. Almost always she works broadside on to the wind and tide and is usually more or less hove-to while working. I say more or less because there are any number of variant combinations of sail areas which can be employed and altered at will to adjust the amount of pull the vessel is exerting.

"When the vessel is in this broad-side-on working attitude she is referred to as being 'put-to,' and the term goes back beyond memory. It is an apt term and means simply that she has been put to work.

"A distinction should be drawn between the act of putting-to and the steady state of being put-to which results. The one is a complex evolution, while the other is a state of moving equilibrium relatively easy to maintain.

"The evolution took us years to learn and, even when learned, practice allows it to be polished until it becomes one of the most graceful maneuvers in the whole of seamanship. In contrast the steady state can be maintained by simple rule of thumb.

"It would be out of place to describe the act of putting-to in detail when talking about our trawling of that first winter, but in broad outline, the trawl is made ready in the lee scuppers. At the time of putting-to the vessel is wended [tacked] to come round hove-to on the other tack and while she does so the net is cleared over the side. After she is round, the vessel will be making more leeway than forward way, so the net streams clear on the weather quarter. When it has steamed to its full length it opens out rather like a parachute and at that moment the beam [in our case that day, otter doors] is pushed over the side and the warp is lowered away until the trawl reaches the bottom."

We put-to in the *Boadicea*, and as Mike checked away the bridle to the otter doors, one part in each hand, he looked like a sorcerer imploring spirits of the deep to open his trawl doors.

Once the warp was slacked away and belayed, we began to experience "the steady state of being put-to." It was my first time, and I enjoyed it hugely.

Being put-to is, if anything, more peaceful than being hove-to. Wind and sea are abaft the beam, rather than on the bow, so that the vessel gives more readily to the seas. The trawl tethers her enough so that she moves very slowly through the water. Being off the wind, she pitches only a little. She is even quieter than when hove-to. And, as you sit along the weather rail, the wind is at your back. Who wouldn't sell his farm and go to sea?

Maybe putting-to should be studied as a heavy-weather tactic. In a discussion of this sort of thing with Melbourne Smith some years ago, I remember he opined that perhaps a good way to take care of a vessel in a heavy breaking sea would be to run off with the wind and sea on the quarter, and slow her down, control her head-

ing, and even give her a bit of a lee by towing one or more heavy warps made fast on the weather side, one end forward and the other aft to form a big bight to windward of the vessel. Such a maneuver would approximate being put-to.

As Mike wrote in his book, it was very easy to keep the *Boadicea* put-to nicely. We controlled her heading by shifting the lead of either the forward or the after part of the warp by leading it 'round tholepins stuck in a number of holes along the rail. Speed through the water was controlled with the staysail; we let it draw for maximum power, hauled it aback for medium power, or dropped it for low power.

Once she was put-to, Mike took the tiller out, since the rudder wouldn't be used. With his vessel happily put-to, Michael Frost really relaxed. So did we all, lounging around on deck in the sun watching the little vessel do her work and drinking Mrs. Frost's good coffee.

While the tide carried us back toward Mersea Island, Mike told us about a few of his experiences with the *Boadicea*. It seemed that on occasion he had done a bit of what he called "playing about" with the little vessel. He told about being out in a gale one time when he and his crew got to talking about whether or not she could be driven under. Mike didn't think she could be, and, to prove his point, instead of luffing in a heavy gust, he pulled the helm up to drive her off. He managed to drive her bow under, and she went right over, mast in the water. He thought she was gone, but up she came slowly to right herself. Once she had pitched off the water trapped on her deck by her bulwarks, she popped up like a cork. Mike said he doesn't play about with her now as much as he used to.

Mike was quick to point out that he still has much to learn about handling the *Boadicea*, things he says that any smacksman used to know. You can take Michael Frost at his word on this, rather than putting such a statement down to undue modesty, because you can sense from sailing with him and from reading his book how deeply involved he is with the minute details of handling his vessel under all conditions. He is talking here about fine points, let me assure you, though his argument is that they weren't so much fine points to the fishermen as practical necessities of everyday life.

As we talked, the wind increased to a moderate breeze. It was fun to watch the little Bodie going quietly about her trawling untended except for some occasional attention to the staysail, or the moving of one or the other parts of the warp forward or aft one hole to a different tholepin. How many and many a time must she have been put-to just this way to let the tide drag her trawl over this same bottom! Had her log been kept every day, it might now run to 32,000 pages!

We made an hour's tow and hauled back all too easily. These waters are overfished. We pulled the trawl on board over the weather rail, and it was a "water haul." There were a half-dozen plaice too small to keep, lots of little crabs, a bit of seaweed, surprisingly little sand, mud, or stones, one good-sized starfish, and some tiny shrimp. The haul was barren of edible fish, but of course no haul is barren of the excitement of dumping it out on deck and sorting through it to see what was on the bottom.

Mike had been experimenting recently with the otter trawl. He normally uses a beam trawl, which is what the smack accompanying us had over. She got one big plaice and a stone crab big enough to keep.

A couple of us now went below into the cabin. The smack has no cabinhouse, just a slightly raised hatch in the deck. So all the time you are on deck there is no evidence or any suggestion that the boat has a cabin; and once you have dropped below, you are absolutely removed from the deck and there is no suggestion that the boat is anything but a cabin. On the *Boadicea*, deck and cabin are two totally separate worlds. You can pass easily from one world to the other through the hatch, but as you enter one world, you leave the other completely behind.

That's a nice feeling that I had never experienced so completely before in any boat. The arrangement enables you to have the best of both worlds, actually. You have your choice of remembering or forgetting the world you are not in, depending on circumstances. If it's rough and cold and you've just come below, you can forget all about the world of the deck. If it's rough and cold, and you've just come on deck, you can remember and look forward to re-entering the other warm, dry, quiet world that you know must still exist below.

The *Boadicea* is arranged very simply below deck. Forward, there are two wide, comfortable transoms for sleeping or sitting on, leaning back against the curve of the frames. At the after end of the cabin are lockers and stoves. A gimbaled Primus enabled Mrs. Frost to produce hot coffee and tea all day long. The cabin was warm and cozy. Aft, under the rest of the deck, is a steerage where the engine lives and where there is lots of stowage for all sorts of odds and ends of ship's gear.

We beat up into the River Blackwater a ways, and I thoroughly enjoyed sailing the *Boadicea*. She has no cockpit, and her tiller is relatively short and stout. Because of the smack's heavy displacement and the extremely hefty appearance of her tiller, I expected she would be a brute to steer. When Mike turned her over to me, I sprawled on deck to weather of the great helm, grasped it firmly with both hands, and gritted my teeth, determined not to let her luff too much. Ten seconds later I relaxed and grinned. There was simply nothing to pull against; she had no will of her own except to forge steadily ahead, responding quickly to the slightest whim mentioned to her rudder by her tree trunk of a tiller. She's some actress! She has the soul of a lively dinghy and has been masquerading about the seas all these years hiding it behind her heavy timbers and planks.

Mike said diplomatically, "I think she'll go a little higher." Indeed she would. She was the nicest boat to sail, somehow at once very serene and very lively.

Mike Frost has written that the fishermen steered standing to leeward of the tiller, hands on knees, nudging the tiller as necessary with the inboard leg. In such a position they were certainly more ready for action than I was spread out on deck, and they certainly would have kept warmer in cold weather, but that day I would not willingly have given over the subtle feel of the *Boadicea*'s tiller to a mere knee.

For a while we were able to keep our younger cousin smack tucked away astern and to leeward, but then I began reaching off a tiny bit, assuming it was Mike's intention to head back for his mooring in Bussand Creek, whereas both smacks were to continue beating up into the River Blackwater. By the time I came to, the new smack had worked up well to weather of us.

But Mike seemed pleased we had held her for a while. He said the *Boadicea* always sails at her best when there is no regatta on. He suspects it may be because on regatta days he finds it necessary to replace his beloved little spitfire with a much bigger headsail, which gives her a slight lee helm and kills her responsiveness.

A funny thing happened while I was sailing the *Boadicea*. I began to like the angle of her bowsprit! It's parallel to the water, thus spoiling her gentle sheerline, which it fails to carry out, and looks generally droopy when you view her from the side when she's at rest. But there was something very purposeful about the long, straight spar pointing right at the horizon instead of at some point above it. I am not converted, mind you, but for the first time, I saw the possibilities of the level, English bowsprit.

Later, we ran off back down toward Mersea Island, jibed, and headed up the creek for the mooring. By now the tide was ebbing strongly.

We took in the jib and eased up over the tide. Fifty yards from the mooring, Mike signaled to drop the peak. Then, when he was sure he had way enough to come up to the mooring and carry it up against the tide a little before she lost way over the ground, we dropped the staysail and mainsail. Mike had a kedge anchor all ready to let go forward in case he had found his mooring buoy towed under by the tide.

We folded the mainsail down atop the boom, tied its stops 'round the gaff only, and then hoisted the throat up out of the way. Mike bowsed the bobstay up under the bowsprit so it would clear the mooring pendant.

While we were forward after straightening her up, Mike explained how a skipper, mate, and boy would position themselves to handle the smack. The skipper would be aft, steering and handling the mainsheet. The mate was at the mast to starboard. Here he could reach all the important running rigging: the peak halyard, the main topping lift, the jib halyard, the staysail bowline, and, a step or two forward, the jibsheet. The boy would be at the mast to port with the throat halyard and staysail halyard — far less used and less critical than the mate's lines — and the staysail bowline and jib-sheet on that side. Little needed to be said among these three to carry out the most precise maneuvers.

We all now settled down on the bow, got out our sandwiches, and enjoyed a four o'clock lunch in the last of the glorious sun. It had been a good day with good people, Mike enjoying sailing his smack as always, his most competent wife equally enjoying the day's sail, their precocious daughter wheedling very poor jokes indeed out of "the American one," and John Leather increasing his already great familiarity with the Bodie. The ship's dog seemed to have been on board forever. I was just trying to drink in as much as possible of the whole new experience and was certainly enjoying every minute of it.

At length, as it got cool, we went below to that other world and leaned back at ease. It took a while to absorb the massiveness of the smack's construction and the massiveness of the task and accomplishment of Michael Frost's renewal of it.

The *Boadicea* was originally clinker-built, but when she was rebuilt in 1890, her planking was changed to carvel. Old Isaiah Binks had told Mike Frost that he "thought that the change had not improved the hull. The water did not flow as smoothly past the new skin as it had done with the old one and, although the change had made the vessel stronger, it had also made her pitch more in a seaway, so that she became

Boadicea moves to windward, providing a fine view of her deck layout.

heavier and rather wetter. She had never been quite as fast with the new skin."

This business keeps coming up. How many times have you read that such and such a type of indigenous boat originally had overlapping planks but gradually evolved into a smooth-skinned craft? And that the change was no improvement? Will the *America*'s Cup eventually be lifted by a clinker-built racer? Maybe we'd best feed in one lapstrake defender each time, just to be safe. You see what imaginings can take place in a cabin like the *Boadicea*'s?

Michael's herculean rebuilding of the *Boadicea* involved a greenheart keel, frames of English oak, bottom planking of greenheart, 1½-inch larch for topside planking, a teak transom, and many a pound of Monel nails. John Lewis gives a very complete description of the rebuilding in *Restoring Vintage Boats*.

Michael Frost's perseverance, skill, and workmanship appear to have ensured that the *Boadicea*'s long life will continue far into the future. How could her owners in future centuries fail to respond to the way he has cared for his vessel with their own care of her? Could it be that this little smack is just getting started?

The Venetian Gondola

Leslie Bruning

IF EVER THERE was a boat whose design and construction was shaped directly by the purposes to which it is used, the gondola is it. An evolutionary craft — one that has developed over a long period of time in response to the demands put upon it — it is functional, beautiful, artistic, finely tuned. No magazine that takes boats seriously as a reflection of culture can fail to celebrate the gondola. The only regret about the following treatment is that there isn't more information on design and construction. That must wait for another time.

Gondolas awaiting gondoliers and passengers.

THE VENETIAN GONDOLA has evolved for a thousand years. As Horatio Brown said in 1900, "It is in no sense an invention; it is a growth directed by the needs of its native place, bearing on its structure of today the impress of Venetian life and history. Through centuries of experience the boat has been fashioned and modified, until at length it has achieved the union of beauty, ease, and usefulness."

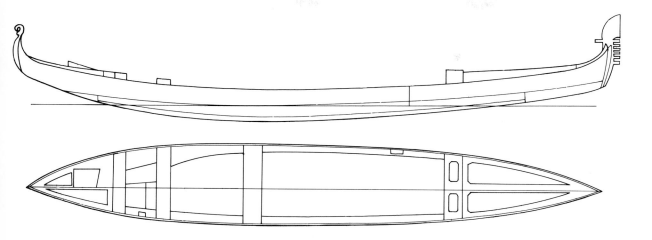

These words still apply to the gondola. Originally flat-bottomed boats, *barchette*, were used for transportation among Venice's lagoon islands, which were just becoming populated by those fleeing the barbarian invasion on the mainland. Sometimes manned by as many as 10 oarsmen, these craft were the taxis and trucks of the era.

As Venice became a major sea power, boats began to evolve into shapes adapted to different functions. The stubbier, wider, and slower boats were, and still are, used primarily for the conveyance of all produce that arrives daily in the city. For human transport, the gondola developed.

It became increasingly longer and slimmer (which in turn, increased speed) and was made of thinner, finer woods. By the end of the 15th century, there were as many as 10,000 gondolas in Venice.

A covering, called a *felze*, was added to protect the passenger from the sun or rain. This piece, once cloth stretched over poles, became a complex wooden structure complete with doors, windows, gilded carvings, and inlays of ebony, ivory, or jewels.

"Keeping up with the Joneses" took on such elaborate proportions that the city council voted various laws in the 16th and 17th centuries to abolish such displays of wealth. Gondolas owned by the citizenry had to be painted black to denote simplicity.

With the decline of Venice's power and the final fall of the Republic in 1797, a certain austerity developed, and it was at this time that the gondola began to take on its current form. The skill of such craftsmen as the Fassi brothers, Giuseppe Canal da Perarolo, and Domenico Tramontin, a century later, gave the unmistakable lines their definitive refinements.

The grandson of Domenico Tramontin, Nedis Tramontin, is today considered Venice's finest gondola-maker.

The sense of tradition and long training that go with the skills necessary to build such a complex structure is uniquely Venetian. There are no schools to teach the art of building a gondola, nor are there any formal apprenticeship programs. Some may try for decades and never master the art. Others start by carrying wood, watching, asking questions, and learning — until they finally produce a gondola of their own.

In the *squero*, or gondola yard, of Tramontin, wood is stacked outside under an awning to season, usually for a year, depending on its thickness. Most woods are local, but the oak is from France and the fir from Russia.

Sloping up from the canal are boards on which finished, drying, or repaired boats wait to be launched. Inside the large shed are boats under construction. Past and present merge, where an electric saw may be next to a hundred-year-old angle iron. There are no drawings or designs; these are in Tramontin's head, and he still uses the old Venetian system of *piede* (about one foot) and hand spans as guides.

The only immovable and immutable aid to the gondola's construction is a very old wooden form having the length and curve of the gondo-

Two gondoliers returning from work.

la as seen from the side. Spaced along this long structure are metal struts, which indicate the placement of the ribs. With this as a guide, his son as apprentice, and one other full-time worker, Tramontin can build a gondola in a month.

Traditional gondola construction begins by placing two poles (*aste*) roughly 36 feet apart. Three master ribs (*maestri*) are sited — two near the ends and one near the middle. The latter master rib determines the gondola's width, which averages about 4½ feet. A belt (*cinta* or *cerchio*) about ½ inch thick is set along the length of the gondola and nailed to the poles and the master rib.

Thirty-three ribs in all will be fastened with galvanized nails between these long planks. Most have two curving side pieces (*sanconi*) and one flat bottom piece (*piana*). Those near the bow and stern have only side pieces and no bottom piece, to avoid undue thickness. Nearest the bow, a 34th rib (*cuore di prora*) is inserted. This solid triangular piece of elm resembles a heart, hence its name of *cuore*.

After the ribs are set, work that requires all three men, two cherrywood bands run across the frame where the bow and stern deckings will form. These serve to counter the pressure of the belt on the ribs. At this point, the structure, measurements, and stress points of the gondola's construction are complete.

The gondola begins to take on its characteristic form with the addition of various pieces of wood (*corboli, sottocorboli, nerve,* etc.). Large pyramidal hunks of larch, lime, or walnut (*zochetti*) form the bow and stern sections nearest the poles. The only screws on the gondola are used here, and since repairs are more frequent to this area, brass screws are used to facilitate removal of the parts. These blocks are in turn covered with long, thin curving planks (*fiubone*), which are roughly triangular, and upon which carvings are done.

Corboli and *sottocorboli* run along the ribs to aid in keeping them in place. The oak *nerve* are placed on top of the ribs to serve the same function as well as to encase the rib tops.

To bend these pieces, swamp cane from the lagoon is set afire and run along the damp board. A long pole attached to the ceiling of the building shed is pushed farther and farther toward the middle of the piece, which is resting on a sawhorse. This sets the bend while the flaming cane is passed over and under the wood. Cane is used here because it is always accessible and cheap; the fire is gentler and easier to control and can be moved more easily. Steam, though, has come into occasional use for the bending of the thicker cherrywood pieces (*trasti*), which are about 1 inch thick. There are four main crosspieces on the gondola (*catenella, grande, di mezzo,* and *a spigolo*). The *trasto a spigolo* may be made of walnut.

The bow and stern sections have by now taken on shape. The gondola is turned over and work is begun on the sides and bottom. Triangular pieces (*cimonelle*) curve in from the two poles. They are the only pieces to be glued on the entire gondola. Their juncture with the belt is held with Swiss marine glue, as this area of the craft is prone to spreading and catches the brunt of the waves' force. Fir sidewall planks (*nomboli*) are positioned below the belt. A piece of larch (*spigolo* or *coppo*) forms the angle between the sidewall planks and the bottom of the gondola. Fir planks (*fondi*) cover the bottom.

The gondola is returned to its upright position for some final fittings. Elm strips are nailed to the outside of the belt again as a protective device. Two steps (*trastolini*) are placed both to aid the embarkation of passengers, and to serve as an extra seat. The client will walk on the *paiuoli* in order to be seated. These fir planks rest on top of the ribs and are removable to allow bailing. They protect the ribs, while also keeping the customer's feet dry in the event of a leak or recent rain.

The stern is a sloping, multileveled, many-pieced structure built to support the gondolier's weight. The gondolier's right foot rests on a fir board (*puntapiede*) from which he gains leverage, while his other foot rests on a larch plank (*sopralai-puntapiede*). Thin beech strips (*filetti*) form designs on the stern planks, which are also sometimes carved and sculpted. Under the crosspieces, there is room for bailing equipment and oar and rope storage.

Return for a moment to the bow section. A pentagonal door, which slides in and out (the *travola a spigolo*) closes off the bow and allows that space to be used for storage. These doors are carved or painted, and since they are interchangeable, one supposes each gondolier might have several he can use according to mood, weather, or prestige of clients.

At this point, some 280 pieces of wood, plus nails, brass screws, elbow grease, and sweat have been expended. The exact measurements of each wooden part depend on the skill of the worker, the stress the wood must endure, the type of wood, and lastly, on which side of the gondola the piece is placed. The gondola, as if it were not complicated enough, is asymmetrical. (The starboard side is about 9½ inches closer to the centerline than the port side.) This gives the gondola its characteristic inclination, which serves to keep the oarlock on the starboard side closer to the water level, which in turn increases maneuverability. The imbalance also serves to anticipate the weight of the gondolier. Mainly, though, since the gondola is usually rowed by one man, the curvature keeps the craft from constantly going toward the left.

The gondola is now a formed wooden boat weighing about 1,100 pounds. Before it becomes what one sees in visits or photos, several things are done. First (and not visible), pitch is mixed with a petroleum-based oil and painted along the pieces of wood under the bow and stern that will likely receive moisture indirectly and could eventually begin to rot. The rest is painted with a black oil-based varnish, the composition of which was once a secret of the older men. It is now common to mix two or three readily available commercial brands. The bottom seams are sealed with pitch and usually finished in green.

For the passengers (the capacity is six) leather-covered cushions are built into the front of the stern structure. Three cushioned black wooden chairs are added. Removable black armrests are placed on the sides of the fixed seats. At the end of each armrest is a brass seahorse.

The stern has a small, curling aluminum decoration (the *pinzo di poppa*) which at one time was similar in size and shape to what now adorns the bow — the *ferro*. This is one of the few parts of the gondola that is not wooden. (Except for the boat's nails, which were originally wooden.) The highly decorative *ferro* allows the gondolier to judge whether he can make it under a bridge at high tide and also serves as a small protection during collisions with other boats or walls. Formerly made of iron and weighing about 26 pounds, virtually all *ferros* in use now are of aluminum and weigh about 13 pounds.

The larger flat blade on top of the *ferro* represents the Doge's hat. The six teeth facing forward stand for Venice's six sections, while the long tooth pointing toward the stern is symbolic of the island alongside Venice, Giudecca. Three ornate pins are placed among the teeth and once held the *ferro* to the gondola. The long metal strip curving along the bow helps hold the whole in place as well as protect the lower section of the wooden *aste di prora*.

The oars are about 10½ feet long, weighing 11 pounds, and are made of beech. Those who manufacture the oars also make the oarlock. They, too, are a diminishing breed. Giuseppe Carli is the most famous and respected of such craftsmen in Venice. His walnut oarlocks (*forcole*) are often now bought as works of art, such is the beauty of their form. For the gondolier, though, the oarlock is essential; without it, his oar is virtually useless.

The oarlock probably evolved from a Y-shaped stick. Whatever the origin, the result is now one of the most specialized gearshifts in existence. On the lower part is a sort of ledge (the *sottomorso*) from which the gondolier starts the rowing motion. Once moving, he switches the oar to the bite, the distinctive C-shaped depression on the top of the oarlock. The remaining curves on the elbow have five placements. One side serves mainly for forward motion, while the other side controls halting or backing. When the gondolier is not using it, he is likely to take it with him, much as one takes the keys from an automobile. A smaller version of the oarlock is used near the steps when there are two oarsmen (such as for weddings).

Venice's traditional taxis are an expensive investment. In the late 1970s, a simple gondola cost $3,000, while an ornate version could run to $4,750. The aluminum *ferro* could set the gondolier back $150, the oars cost $50, and the oarlocks cost between $107 and $120.

Once the gondola lasted a gondolier's lifetime. Now, he can count on 15 years or so, depending on how much of the time his gondola is buffeted by the waves that are particularly severe near the city's center, San Marco. There are only 450 gondolas left in Venice. As the waves worsen due to increased motor traffic, expenses rise, the gondola's endurance lessens, and the number of men plying the trade shrinks, the city of Venice will soon have to take steps if it is to ensure that the gondola will survive.

Gino Macropodio uses his gondola for weddings. Different from his everyday 'working' gondola, this craft has an incised *ferro*, finely sculpted *fiubone* and *trasto a spigolo* as well as carved chairs. As a final touch there is a gilded and carved *forcola*.

Gauntlet: A Cautionary Tale

George Cadwalader

ONE WAY to help pay for the restoration of a wooden boat is to write about the process, and we have received our share of manuscripts written and submitted with that in mind. We couldn't possibly publish all of them; we limit ourselves by accepting only those that will be particularly instructive, such as the following piece by George Cadwalader. George began his project with high hopes, but the deeper he went, the more complex the restoration became. We discussed the possibility of doing a series on the restoration, although nobody was certain how long it would take. But we wanted at least to emphasize the depth of involvement when it comes to old wooden boats, so we published George's first report as a cautionary tale to present the frightening, as opposed to the romantic, side of resurrecting an old boat.

I SUPPOSE that just about everyone who goes sailing dreams from time to time of long cruises to foreign waters. The event that set me thinking along those lines was the arrival in Woods Hole several years ago of a strongly built double-ended sloop named *Gauntlet*.

She bears little resemblance to the Tahiti-ketch-type designs that have captured the popular imagination, so she may not appeal to many as the ideal blue-water cruiser. However, much reading and somewhat less practical experience have convinced me that deep, narrow, close-winded boats are in one critical respect

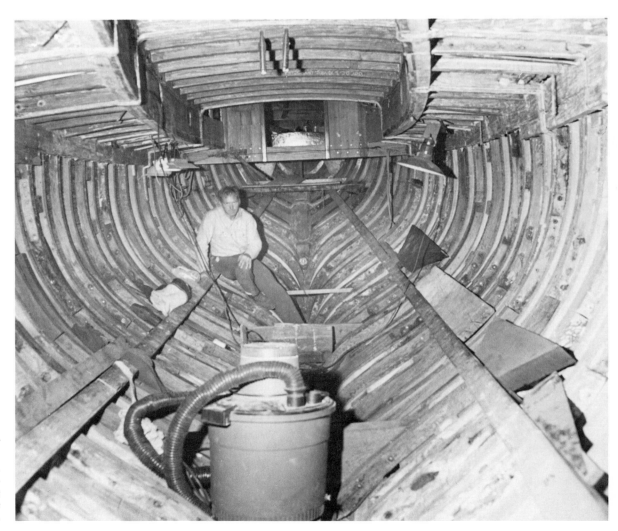

Gauntlet's interior. The gentleman taking his ease in the main salon is the author.

170

preferable to broad shallow ones for offshore sailing. This preference, which is well argued by Bob Griffith in his book *Blue Water*, was proven to my satisfaction by the superb performance in hard weather of another English-built double-ender named *Josephine* that I have owned for the past 10 years. *Josephine*, sister of Adlard Coles's famous *Cohoe*, will go to weather in just about any condition, and although I hope never to have to claw off a lee shore in a storm, I think the ability to do so is a necessary attribute in any cruising boat.

Gauntlet measures 41 feet 6 inches overall and 32 feet 6 inches on the waterline, with a beam of 9 feet 6 inches, a draft of 5 feet 8 inches, and a mast that towers 50 feet above the deck. *Gauntlet* and *Josephine* have much in common. Both have fine entries, balanced ends, and roughly the same beam-to-waterline ratio. *Josephine* has a somewhat more cutaway forefoot, but both are long enough on the keel for good directional stability. Of the two, *Josephine* is the prettier boat, but *Gauntlet* has a certain air of invincibility about her that I find appealing. Even more appealing is that she has room enough for our family of four to live in with more privacy and less tension than sometimes exists in *Josephine* on long rainy cruises.

In the years that followed *Gauntlet*'s arrival in Woods Hole, I seldom saw her without succumbing to dreams of sailing once again to Ireland and thence on to Portugal to visit my Brazilian-born wife's ancestral home. Such thoughts invariably were put to rout by more practical considerations: our children were too small; Yara and I were tied to our jobs; what would we do with the dog; etc., etc., etc. Another deterrent was the realization that buying a boat suited to such an undertaking would involve the unthinkable necessity of selling *Josephine*.

By chance the winter of 1978–79 found *Gauntlet* and *Josephine* rafted side by side in Eel Pond. I was rebuilding *Josephine*'s galley at the time, and in the process I must have climbed across *Gauntlet* a hundred times going to and from my shop to our boat. Close up, *Gauntlet* looked pretty rough. Her teak cabin trunk had been butchered by some overzealous scraping. Rotten sections of both sheerstrakes were patched with body putty. Below, teak, mahogany, oak, and elm were all indiscriminately covered with thick layers of peeling paint. There were signs of numerous deck leaks and evidence that the mad scraper had carried on his destruction here as well. These defects, however, could not hide the fact that *Gauntlet*'s construction was enormously strong.

She is planked with 1¼-inch African mahogany over alternating sawn oak and bent elm frames on roughly 9-inch centers. Each pair of frames is tied together across the keel timber by massive wrought-iron floors. The clamps and stringers are huge oak timbers, and the entire structure is solidly tied together with iron and bronze straps. She is fastened with copper rivets on the bent frames and naval brass screws on the sawn ones. An interesting feature I have never seen elsewhere is the laminated stem piece that extends aft over the keel timber to form the mast step, thus providing 16 inches of timber beneath the mast and spreading the compression load over a large area of the keel.

Despite enough dissimilar metals in her construction to build a pretty good battery, I could see little evidence of electrolysis on any of the iron. The floors were largely intact where they were copper-riveted to the frame ends, their worst corrosion occurring lower in the bilge where they had lain in salt water. *Gauntlet* had problems, but she had been built so strongly in the first place that despite many years of indifferent care, there appeared to be plenty of strength left in her. All in all, she seemed the best "go-anywhere boat" large enough for a family of four that we could hope to afford. If ever we were going to make a long cruise, it seemed that we had better get on with it. So one night, as we sat looking out over Eel Pond, we decided to buy *Gauntlet* and go.

Gauntlet's owner turned out to be an engineer and marine architect whose varied talents pulled him in so many different directions that he found little time for his boat. What time he did have, he had wisely decided was better spent on sailing than on cosmetics, which accounted for the boat's somewhat down-at-the-heels appearance. He was enthusiastic about our intended use for *Gauntlet*, since some years back he, too, had taken a year off to cruise with his family in the Caribbean.

He was kind enough to lend us *Gauntlet* for a weekend, and we had a wonderful overnight sail in her. Due to the boat's weight and large wetted surface, she was no racehorse in the relatively light air we encountered, but once she got going, she was by no means slow. Compared with *Josephine*, which will turn on a dime, *Gauntlet* answers her helm in a rather leisurely way, but once used to this, I found she handled quite easily under both sail and power. Yara reveled in the unaccustomed luxury of three separate living compartments, a proper galley, and an enclosed head. The children delighted in having their "own room" with space enough to accommodate the giant stuffed animals that had always been banned from *Josephine*. By the time

Gauntlet, then *Gay Gauntlet,* as she looked shortly after she was built in 1948.

we got back to Woods Hole, any doubts we might have had about living on *Gauntlet* were pretty well put to rest.

The following week the boat was hauled for survey. Surveys are generally depressing for both buyer and seller, and this one was no exception. The most serious defect noted was the almost complete deterioration of the naval brass fastenings throughout the boat. Some evidence of electrolytic rot was found around a few fastenings below the waterline, but this was judged "not serious at this time." Electrolytic rot had also softened several bent frame ends behind the iron floors, but all visible sawn frames appeared intact. The gate valves, which had been used instead of seacocks, were all found to be frozen, and the electrical system was declared "a patched-up mess." The surveyor estimated the yard cost of making the necessary repairs to be around $10,000, but on the whole, he found *Gauntlet* to be "a well-built craft of heavy scantlings — and a good risk."

The seller and I then sat down to what could no longer be described as a strictly businesslike negotiation, since we had in the course of our association become good friends. What resulted was a document setting forth an "agreement made on this date of the Autumnal Equinox, in which the owner agrees to sell and the buyer agrees to buy . . . etc." Suffice it to say of this arrangement that the owner agreed to defer payment until I could sell *Josephine*, in exchange for which I ended up offering somewhat more than I felt the boat was worth in her condition.

The next step was to figure out how to accomplish all that would have to be done if, as we hoped, we were to get away the following spring. The first necessity was the saddest, since this required putting *Josephine* on the market. I then set about making the recommended repairs to *Gauntlet*. There was no possibility of my doing everything in the time available, so I turned to my friend Steve Ballentine for help. Steve had started a small yard in Cataumet, specializing in the building, restoration, and repair of traditional wooden boats. He and his assistant, Bob Williams, set such high standards for the work they do that they simply will not do any job less than perfectly, no matter how much of their own time is required to see it through properly. This is not a policy that is likely to make them rich, but, I suspect, they find a measure of compensation in the pride they take in their work.

Steve agreed to take the job, and I attempted to arrange my affairs so I could devote two days a week to the boat throughout the winter. On a flat calm day in early October, I motored *Gauntlet* around to Parkers Yard in Cataumet, where I spent several days removing the engine, the fuel tanks, and the two giant water tanks that filled the bilge below the main cabin (an advantage of composite construction is the elimination of wooden floors, leaving a more open bilge). This done, I set about ripping out the largely delaminated plywood ceiling that covered the frames from the clamp to the floorboards.

With the boat opened up, it became more apparent than ever how much filth had accumulated in *Gauntlet* over the years. The cleanup that followed resembled an archaeological dig. From beneath the wet muck that lay in previously inaccessible places, I unearthed a variety of cutlery, assorted medicine bottles from foreign lands, and quantities of small change from England, France, and several Mediterranean and Caribbean countries. After a week or so of these excavations, I summoned my friends to a glue-sniffing party. Fortified with beer and armed with gallons of paint remover, we descended into the cabin and began stripping the many layers of paint that some barbarian had coated over the teak and mahogany. Fifteen minutes later, we staggered back on deck, victims of the apparently synergistic effects of alcohol and paint remover fumes. After a series of increasingly short sorties back into the boat, and longer periods recuperating around the jug, my guests departed, mumbling incoherently about brain damage and leaving me with what was now a truly gargantuan mess. I finished the job with a torch, which seemed a less hazardous way of removing paint and, if done carefully, does less damage to the wood than the caustic chemicals in paint removers.

We trucked the boat around to Ballentine's and set to work carrying out the surveyor's recommendations. While I continued the endless task of scraping and cleaning, Steve removed the bad section of the sheerstrake and Bob began lifting the floors behind which the frame ends had gone soft. Those friends not permanently alienated by the glue-sniffing party volunteered time, and the job moved along steadily.

All the while the boat was drying out. Then one ill-fated day, while working deep in the bilge, Bob noticed behind one of the sawn frames a plank seam that for a length of a foot or so was opening up noticeably wider than had the adjacent areas of the same seam. As time went by, this gap continued to widen and the adjoining planking visibly began to break down. Apart from its color, which was light grey, the wood in the infected area looked as if it had been charred, leaving the fibers shrunken and dehydrated. We chopped out the bad planking from the outside and discovered that the frame beneath, although apparently sound from without, had been literally hollowed out by the same mysterious process of dehydration.

Other areas of planking now began opening up in the same way, and it became clear that the problem was widespread. I lifted a few more floors at random, and behind each one, I found that the wood surrounding the copper rivets that held the floors to the frames was gone. In some places the rot was so far advanced that the floors could be pried up, drawing the rivets right through the oak frame ends. I could no longer ignore what all of us already knew. With the floors adrift from the frame ends and the planking behind cut across in places by the same rot, *Gauntlet* came close to being beyond

Between two new sawn frames lies an original iron floor. Note the open seam behind the bent frame.

my ability to salvage. What happened to *Gauntlet* is well explained in an article titled "Corrosion Process Shows Why Bonded Fittings Are a Bad Idea," by Robert L. Kocher in the September 1979 issue of the *National Fisherman*. Kocher describes an experiment showing that the introduction of an electric current through wood by electrolysis or any other means will set in motion a chemical reaction producing concentrations of lye that will dehydrate and ultimately break down the wood fibers. I later tested an infested section from one of the frames with litmus paper and got a Ph reading of 11, proving that Kocher's experiment had been duplicated on a much larger scale in *Gauntlet*.

We stopped work and, in an atmosphere appropriate to a funeral, considered the options. Apart from scrapping the boat, there appeared to be only two. Either we could patch things up as much as possible by saturating the infected areas with epoxy, or we could remove every

floor in the boat, scarf in new frame ends, replace the bad planking, and fix her properly. *Gauntlet* sat forlornly in her shed while I debated whether it made sense, both financially and structurally, to try to save her.

Neither question was clear cut. *Gauntlet* was built in 1948 to Lloyd's highest standards, and at the time we bought her, the surveyor who looked her over for us estimated her replacement cost at $125,000, her market value at $25,000, and her potential value if properly restored at between $60,000 and $75,000. This appraisal, which was made before the extent of the electrolysis problem came to light, assumed the boat needed only partial refastening to be once again structurally sound. The total cost of this and all the other repairs recommended by the surveyor to make *Gauntlet* ready for sea had been estimated to be $10,000 at yard rates.

So these figures had made her look like a rather good buy. She was one of a class of famous offshore cruising boats, very strongly built, and with ample room for our family of four to live on while sailing the west coast of Europe. We had found few other boats possessing similar attributes available for a comparable price, and the proposition was made doubly attractive by the thought that our own work in rectifying the results of many years of indifferent maintenance might contribute sufficiently to the boat's market value to enable us to realize a modest profit on our investment at the end of the trip.

We had taken a $10,000 second mortgage on our house to cover the cost of putting her right. Several hundred hours of my own time and nearly half of the money intended for repairs had been spent before we discovered the extent of the damage. I was thus left with the fact that with approximately $30,000 already committed to the project, the value of our investment now stood at little more than the scrap value of the boat.

Selling the rig, engine, lead, and other equipment would probably net about $5,000, for a loss of about $25,000. Alternatively, we could spend the remaining $5,000 of the second mortgage to put her back together and attempt to sell her as-is in the hopes that someone looking for a floating home capable of light-weather sailing might pay $15,000 for her, thus reducing our loss to $20,000 if she in fact sold.

Neither prospect was appealing. On the other hand, it was hard to muster up much enthusiasm for continuing with a project that had lost its original purpose and that, with the money and time available, would be of at least several years' duration. I had spent 10 years restoring *Josephine* and had little heart for starting all over again on an even larger undertaking. Financially, however, there seemed to be little choice.

I have found that a good guide to evaluating the feasibility of any contemplated restoration project, be it a boat or a house, is that the purchase price plus the cost of the rebuilding should not exceed the ultimate market value of the restored item. Judged against this standard, *Gauntlet* seemed marginally worth saving. Although predicting what a one-of-a-kind wooden boat will bring on the market is an exercise fraught with peril, I think the surveyor's estimate of $60,000 for a boat such as *Gauntlet* in first-rate condition and fitted out for living aboard is a reasonable one. Theoretically, then, if the job could be completed for an additional $30,000, equity would equal investment — or, more simply put, we would stand a reasonable chance of breaking even. The hooker, of course, was that we didn't have $30,000 more, and it was going to take some time to come up with this sum either in cash or in the equivalent amount of my own labor. However, with the alternative being the certain loss of almost everything already invested, I was already in too far to back out. Initial mistakes, warned Thomas Paine in *The Age of Reason*, "beget a calamitous necessity of going on."

How to go on now became the question. My original intention had been to replace the seven iron floors rotted through by corrosion, chip and paint the sound floors, scarf new ends on the few bad frames noted in the survey, and stop there. Accordingly, we had only removed enough of the machinery and interior to gain access to these areas and had spent some time scraping down the remaining joinerwork and the areas behind it. The rotten iron floors had been taken up, faired back to their original shape with Bondo, and used as patterns for fabricating replacements from mild steel. The new floors, although far less durable than the original Swedish wrought-iron ones, were intended to be galvanized and coated with epoxy before installation. I had borrowed an air-driven needle gun with which we chipped the floors still in place before treating them with Ospho, a fine product consisting of an acid that interacts with the iron to form a protective coating that both inhibits rust and improves paint adhesion.

By now you no doubt will be wondering how all this could have been done before anyone noticed the rot in the rest of the frame ends. The answer lies in the nature of the particular rot afflicting the boat. Electrolytic rot is caused when an electric current through a metal fastening causes a buildup of highly caustic sodium hydroxide (lye) in the adjacent wood. The first indication of the presence of this problem is the appearance of whitish "halos" in the wood around the electrically active fastenings. As the lye continues to build up, the impregnated wood becomes rock-hard, thus defying both the icepick and the hammer with which fungus-induced rot is usually detected. Finally, the wood begins to dehydrate and shrink, leaving an area that, except for its light-grey color, looks exactly as if it had been charred with a torch.

It seems that as long as the infected area is kept wet, some residual strength remains in the wood, perhaps because dehydration is retarded. As *Gauntlet* dried out, however, floors that initially had felt solid to the chipping hammer began to come adrift as the wood literally shrank from around the fastenings and turned

With the iron floor removed, a sawn frame reveals considerable disintegration of wood around the rivets.

to powder. Even then, however, the problem remained invisible from without, since the whitish deposits were hidden behind the floors, and the frames were so large that in only a few of them had the telltale hardening spread to the surface. Everywhere else the wood appeared intact, as in fact it was. The accompanying photographs tell the story.

Our discovery that the entire boat was infected meant that she would have to be gutted completely to expose the remainder of the frames. Out came the cockpit, the cabin sole, and the rest of the interior. This was a major setback, although it must be said that little of what was lost was really first-class joinery, since the layout below had been modified rather crudely at some point in *Gauntlet*'s past. The saddest thing of all was to look down at the length of the now-spotless bilge and realize that the impression of vast strength created by the row of massive frames and newly primed wrought-iron floors was only an illusion. Were it not for the still-intact bolts holding the floors to the keel, a good heave with a prybar could yank almost any one of those floors free from the frame ends it was secured to.

At that point I had still planned to restore the boat as she had first been built by replacing the original iron floors after renewing the frames. This seemed to be the simplest way to proceed, and I had already made a considerable investment in fabricating new floors and cleaning up the still-sound old ones. The more I thought about it, however, the more convinced I became that if I put iron back in the boat, we would run the risk of having the same type of problem occur all over again. Granted, there are many composite boats far older than *Gauntlet* that are still going strong, but there can be no denying that the presence of iron structural members adds a whole new range of potential rot, corrosion, and electrolysis problems to those that

New sawn frames lie adjacent to where a pair of bent frames will be boxed into the keel and fastened.

conventionally built wooden boats are already subject to. I suspect that the increasing use of steel bulkheading and the near-inevitability of electricity "leaking" into the waters of busy harbors increases the risk of electrolytic damage to composite (wood and iron) boats.

Another risk in replacing *Gauntlet*'s iron floors was that I wanted to strap her up with 1/8-inch by 1 1/2-inch Monel let in flush to the outside of the lead keel and the planking on every other midship station, and riveted through to the frames and floors behind. This is a simply done modification that had added greatly to the strength and stiffness of our old boat, and I expected that it would do the same for *Gauntlet*. However, in her case the rivets would serve to connect the Monel on the outside to the iron on the inside and, even if insulated with the Lexan bushings I intended to use, would still provide a potential conductor from the lead via the Monel and copper and iron — an unsettling prospect!

All of these considerations convinced me to eliminate as much iron from *Gauntlet*'s construction as possible by using wooden floors in all but the extreme ends of the boat. Although this may seem an obvious-enough decision, it was not an easy one to make. The consequences have been to increase both the time and the cost of the project. It has meant forfeiting a lot of usable space in the bilge, since the wood floors occupy much more space than the iron ones they replaced. Finally, it will require making new tanks to replace the ones that will no longer fit beneath the cabin sole. In compensation for all this will be the peace of mind that comes from knowing that the "new" *Gauntlet* will be less likely to self-destruct than the old one.

With the wisdom of hindsight, I believe there were some clues to *Gauntlet*'s deterioration that the buyer of another composite-built boat might do well to be on the lookout for. The English have successfully combined copper and wrought iron in boat construction for many years. *Josephine*, for example, has copper-riveted iron floors in the area of the mast step, and the wood and metal here remained intact. However, *Josephine* has always lived in relatively cold water, and *Gauntlet* spent many years in the Caribbean. I suspect that warm water may promote increased electrical activity, and I would advise viewing any composite-built boats from the tropics with particular suspicion.

Gauntlet's poor wiring and the lack of fuses in many of her electrical circuits should also have put us on the alert, since with dissimilar metals below the waterline, she is particularly vulnerable if a stray current finds its way into the bilge.

The amount of wet muck that lay so long in the boat no doubt also contributed to the problem by serving as an electrical conductor. Dirty, damp interiors should sound an alarm about the probable condition of any boat, but particularly one of composite construction.

Finally, I think we should have attached more importance to the evidence of electrolytic rot that was found. Much of the boat was inaccessible to view due to the ceiling and the tanks in the bilge. In the relatively small area of the bilge that could be seen, three bent frames were noted "with serious electrolytic rot" during the survey. While I assumed that this was a localized problem, I suspect that someone with more experience with composite construction would have inferred the probability that the condition was general throughout the boat. In the future, if I find evidence of electrolytic rot anywhere in a boat, I will assume it exists everywhere else in her where conditions are roughly similar to the infected area. I would advise others to do likewise.

The earliest survey of *Gauntlet* of which I have a copy was made in St. Thomas in December 1969, shortly after she passed from her last English owner to her first American one. At that time she was found "to be suffering from severe electrolysis." It was "noted that the iron floors are secured to the wooden keel with bolts — some of which are wasted clean through." The surveyor recommended removing all these iron bolts and replacing them with bronze ones of the next larger size. He further suggested that "while the boat is opened up, it would be desirable to electrically bond all metal with a suitable copper bus to one of the keelbolts and provide an external zinc on the lead keel."

Gauntlet must then have been in pretty sorry shape, since the same surveyor returned a month later at the request of an insurance company to pass judgment on whether she "was sufficiently seaworthy to make the passage to Martinique for further repairs." He opined that "with due caution" the trip could be made, concluding his report with the observation that although "the vessel is well and strongly built," she had been "neglected for a long time." The next survey was done in Marblehead in May 1971 at the request of a potential buyer who apparently was scared off by the results. The hull was still "neglected and poorly maintained," although some of the work recommended in St. Thomas evidently had been done. "Some floor bolts appear new and . . . there is bonding for a common ground." Nonetheless, "cathodic protection for the hull [was] only by way of one completely eroded zinc on lead keel."

During the next year, *Gauntlet* underwent extensive repairs, and in August 1972, she was again surveyed, this time in Vineyard Haven. "Topsides were found to be smooth and fair... engine (Westerbeke 4-107) and keelbolts new... varnished teak in excellent condition . . . and mast newly refinished. No obvious signs of deterioration were seen in the bilge [where] the wooden frames and iron strappings all appear sound." The only major flaw noted was in the electrical system, which was "substandard throughout . . . with no master switch and no fuse panel."

A sales brochure put out shortly after this survey describes *Gauntlet* in predictably glowing terms, rhapsodizing about "a unique copper bus which carries any electrical current . . . through a keelbolt to the lead and thence to two zincs."

From the 1969 survey, it would appear that

at least for the 10 or so years *Gauntlet* was in the hands of her last English owner, few or no active measures were taken to combat galvanic corrosion. No electrical bonding system was in the boat at that time, nor is it likely that there ever was one earlier.

Despite this apparent negligence, the only evidence of "severe electrolysis" cited in the 1969 survey was the wasting of the iron lags holding the floors to the keel. Wood and iron elsewhere were declared sound. Now, even without electrolysis, 21 years (which was then the age of the boat) is a long time for $\frac{1}{2}$-inch bolts to hold up in a saltwater-filled bilge. This makes me wonder if the surveyor's diagnosis was correct. My guess is that electrolysis was not a serious problem during the first 21 years of *Gauntlet*'s life and that those bolts simply rusted away naturally. The "unique copper bus" later added in Martinique to bond all metal to a sacri-

Where an entire frame was not damaged, the author was able to scarf in a section of new wood.

ficial zinc may have helped preserve the iron in the boat during the next 10 years, but I suspect it did so at the expense of the adjacent wood.

So there it is. It will be a while before we see Portugal from our own boat. Worse yet, *Josephine* must still be sold to pay for a replacement that is unlikely to be sailing again in the next couple of years. It would be nice if there were someone besides myself to blame for all this, but there are no villains in this story. *Gauntlet*'s previous owner was painstaking in his efforts to point out everything he knew that was wrong about the boat. The surveyor cannot be faulted for failing to find a problem that defied detection until the boat was opened up and dried out.

We will continue to rebuild *Gauntlet* as money and time permit. In the meantime, as I sit here feeding the chunks we have had to rip out of her into the woodstove, I take satisfaction in the thought that ours is probably the only house in Woods Hole, or anywhere else for that matter, that is heated by burning teak!

Giffy's Hammer: Surveying Wooden Boats

Jerry Kirschenbaum

W HEN WOODEN BOATS change hands, one of the most important steps for the buyer to take is to survey the boat — that is, the condition of the craft must, in every respect, be checked over by a professional who knows what to look for. But what is it that a surveyor looks for? For that matter, how does one judge the capabilities of a surveyor and the results of his work? Just about the time we were asking ourselves these questions, Jerry Kirschenbaum, then a regular writer for WoodenBoat, was having direct experience as a boat buyer with Giffy Full, judged by many to be the best surveyor in the business on the East Coast. Jerry proposed to follow Giffy around on a typical survey and put together a multilayered article on all aspects of the business. The result couldn't have been better unless it were written by Giffy himself, and even then we would have missed a profile of an artist in a technician's trade.

"Giffy's Hammer" represents a synthesis of all we have labored to express — the article looks at the technical side as well as the human side of a subject with considerable allure that is usually discussed in one dimension only.

GIFFY FULL has velocity. He operates in one straight line . . . no doglegs . . . one speed . . . flank. A human being with the metabolism of a hummingbird. His body is built for surveying boats. It is small, engine-room small. Giffy's voice is high, hear-me-upside-down-in-the-bilges high. I have never seen him sit quietly. He does sleep, though. I saw him do it once.

Survey morning. The waning darkness of 5:30 a.m. in the early spring. Breakfast is a foggy memory of muffins and eggs somewhere in Marblehead. Back to sleep as Giffy drives his cranberry-colored elderly Mercedes to Rhode Island. The yard . . . by the time I roll out of the back seat, Giff has his white coveralls on, tool chest on the fender, and a clean inspection sheet on the clipboard. He goes off somewhere to scrounge a ladder.

Smoke hangs in the blue TraveLift. Her bottom is scrubbed, light green, still damp, waiting for Giffy's hammer.

Propping the ladder to one side, Giffy starts a general walk around the boat to get a feel for the job, and a look for fairness in the hull. The survey begins. It is 8:30.

"She'll be a good boat." (We've been there for maybe 10 minutes.) "Knutson built a good boat and he used the right stuff to do it. I've done eight or nine of these little yawls . . . usually people who know something about boats buy them and take care of them. I'll be surprised if she's bad.

I asked Giff if any of the principals in the *Smoke* sale would be here.

"Probably the buyer; and I'm supposed to call Dick Sciuto [the broker] as the day gets on. You know I usually like to have the prospective owner on the job. It can make a lot of difference. You see, we're not just surveying a wooden yawl, we're looking over a people situation. I always ask first off what a fellow's going to do with a boat. If this man tells me he has sailed for two years and now wants to take *Smoke* off to the Canary Islands, that's quite a different thing than weekends on the Cape. Doesn't mean I will allow things — just different approach to the problem. Hope he comes."

Giff starts on the bottom. As he works his way around the hull, he keeps cocking his head from one side to another to catch different angles of light on the hull, looking for some stray line that will signal a problem. Then, he takes out a small brass hammer and begins a steady, bouncing tap on the hull. Not timid strokes, steady firm blows, letting the hammer bounce back off the surface, all wrist and forearm. Continuous concussions, roaming. After a time you

With the boat hauled out, the first step is a careful look at the hull from all angles as a means of checking for general fairness. Hard spots, hogging, and sagging butt joints will show up here, and indicate the need to check out obvious trouble spots.

can tell when he moves across a frame or an internal tank.

The hammer is the key tool. Bad wood, wood that is rotted or split, will have a soft, dead sound. The hammer hits and stays with the wood. Good wood bounces the hammer back with a clear, hard ring. Of course, each type of wood has its own characteristic tone. It is this set of sharp or dull notes that plays to the surveyor's ear.

Giffy takes a couple of hard strikes at the flange on the head outlet seacock. Good and solid, no telltale powdery residue showing metal decay. As he moves on with the hammer, shifting from hand to hand, Giff marks certain areas with white chalk where he will later pull fastenings. Either they are his normal sampling areas or something in the hammer's response asks for a closer look.

"I always take a minimum of three to four fastenings per side. One or two forward, one in the heavy section of the hull near the engine, and another at the stern. You know, a lot of surveyors won't pull fastenings unless they are specifically requested to do so, and even then, they will have the yard do the actual work. I don't understand that — you want to get into a boat, not just do a tap dance on it. You can tell a lot just from how the fastening backs out, that first turn of the brace."

Giff moves to the propeller and gives a hefty pull on each of the blades to check for play in the stern bearing. He nods approval. Then, he pulls out a large magnifying glass and goes over the prop, inch by inch, checking for hairline fractures, nicks, or cavitation erosion. A sharp blow with the hammer makes a bell-like ring that is the sign of a healthy, live prop.

Opposite — Giffy wields his hammer.

Rudder hardware is checked for excessive wear and freedom of movement.

A tiny baby eel wriggles out of the rudder channel, disturbed by the commotion.

A close look at the rudder channel to check protection, taps on the rudder mounting hardware, a check for rudder play, and that completes the stern end of things.

Working in the shadows near *Smoke*'s deadwood, Giffy pays close attention to the straps connecting zinc anodes to bronze hardware. As he taps the anodes, some crusty grey zinc flakes off — they are about 20 percent gone, but still good for a while.

"With a good, light hammer like this, you can differentiate resonances on either side of the butt, but it is going to take a couple of hundred boats until you can really hear it." (Giffy Full does not, repeat not, like overnight mail-order surveyors.)

As we pass the depth-finder transducer, he notes that it has been painted.

Giff rummages in his box for a bit brace to go after his first fastening. He digs out the bung carefully with his knife and then leans into the brace. The fastening is at a butt and comes out fairly easily. It is just starting to deteriorate seriously.

With magnifying glass, Giffy checks the prop and hardware for corrosion and cavitation damage.

"I don't care about the age of the fastenings. It's all in the maintenance. Once water gets in the butt, it moves to the fastenings like a magnet and they start to go. Let's take a look at a few more.

The next fastening (plank section only) is a lot better.

"One indication you get is whether the screw will back right out (bad) or you have to bear down and nudge the brace for those first few turns (good and tight). That's why I do my own pulling. Just did a schooner the other day down to Vineyard Haven. All the fastenings were gone and she had just been completely refastened 10 years earlier. The rot was so bad in her frames and planks that the moisture went right after the metal. Called a halt to the survey right at the beginning and told the man not to waste his money on me or the boat."

The third screw was just fine. When Giff started on the fourth fastening, he felt the brace hitting something hard as the bit turned. As the screw came out, the plank moved. This made the other fastenings at the butt suspicious, with the possibility of some older or badly driven fastenings being buried somewhere in the butt area.

Giff completes the bottom by thoroughly checking the external lead ballast for any signs of loosening or breaking away. He also looks for any telltale gouges or fill areas in the lead that will signal a past grounding.

At 9:30, Giff begins to sound the topsides. There are several areas that obviously need attention — mostly at the stern.

Planks, meeting at the starboard quarter, have opened and started to deteriorate. You can see an open seam about ⅛ inch wide in the uppermost corner. Weather and water are doing their work. Giff probes with an icepick, feeling each bit of wood debris he picks out of the seam. "Wood's OK . . . no rot . . . has to be reefed out, treated, caulked, and refinished . . . it's a vulnerable spot.

"I'm telling you," he continues, hammering, "I'm amazed at how many owners really do not know the *real* condition of their boats. They dabble around with a lot of superficial stuff and just turn away from fixing basic things before they get serious.

"Look at us. It's 10 a.m., two hours gone by and we've only got started. Some guys who call themselves surveyors would be finished by now and on to the next job, probably got the bill all made out. Well, that's a lot of junk, not a survey. It's like getting your annual physical in the waiting room with all your clothes on. You just can't do it. Any guy who comes out and spends an hour or so in his suit and tie is not doing a job on a real survey. Sure, I can tell whether a boat is going to be basically OK after the first hour, but that doesn't mean anything. There could be a real problem lurking somewhere. Like I think this one is going to be basically a sound, good boat. Knutson did a good job on them. And she looks fair and healthy, but we'll keep going and see what we can pop out of her."

And after that speech, Giff drags out his magnifying glass to inspect the bobstay plate and tang. Paint is blistering off in the area. Certainly not right.

"Look here," Giff mutters, "looks kinda bad, don't it? It's not. Just needs some good reefing out and proper care. Some guys would really jump on this, fill in the blanks on their checklist. That's really all good wood in there, but it does have to be looked to.

"A lot of surveyors think they are only doing a good job if they really tear a boat down. They think that's how they earn their fee. I don't. There really is no such thing as the perfect boat, and any survey, even on a new boat, will show something worthwhile. There are lots of good boats, lots, and one of the best things a survey produces is a list of things that should be done to keep them that way."

We have been working for 2½ hours. We have not been aboard, on deck, or below yet. The day has warmed and we leave our sweaters in the car before going on deck.

Smoke seems orderly, clean, and well laid out. The last of the morning damp has disappeared from the canvas covering the decking.

"That first glance tells you a lot," Giffy says as he unlatches his varnished box and ties off the extension cord on a stanchion. "Very rare that you see fairly good maintenance on deck and not in the rest of the boat. I think generally this is an excellent boat, unless there is something here in the shadows that even the present owner knows nothing about."

At this point we decide to take a guess at the price. "Well, I would say, without anything bad coming up as we keep going, she should be going somewhere in the low 30s." We check the agreed-upon price on the specification sheet. It is in the middle 20s.

"If she's OK, this guy has himself a good deal, but we'll see."

There are some cracked and flaked sections in the canvas deck covering. Giff picks away at them, working amidships just forward of the cabin trunk on the starboard side.

"Boy, here's some overmaintenance. Just kept putting paint on without enough takedown first. Too much buildup. The deck

needs stripping now, and it can be saved with a minimum of work."

Giff turns and starts digging away at the cornerpost of the cabin. There's a small seam opening there. "No big thing. Just needs some looking to. My problem is that I love too many boats. When I get around a nice little boat like this, I'd like to own her. Take Charlotte out on a nice fall day. You'd think I'd have seen enough boats, but I always like a good one."

We're in the cockpit now. Giff is working in the lockers under the seats. The propane storage locker is empty so we will not be able to test the stove. It is a good little installation, though, on-deck, well ventilated (just missing the cover gasket). Giff gives both sheet winches a spin as he leaves to get his clipboard. The ratchets click smoothly.

Just before sitting down to his morning notes, Giffy goes over each stanchion and its base with his glass. He throws his full weight on each upright, looking for weakness.

It's almost lunchtime and the prospective

With two fastenings backed out, Giffy leans into the bit brace to remove another one along the sternpost rabbet.

Left — This one's in good shape, and the wood was sound enough to get good holding.

Right — This one's not so good, but the threads are probably gone at the end because they were turned alongside some other fastening. Another will be pulled nearby to get a better indication.

Below left — He produces this zinc pencil, which has been totally eaten away.

buyer has still not shown up. "He's missing a lot. The buyers only come about half the time. It's a real shame. They could learn a lot about the boat they have selected — and a lot just gets said as we go, doesn't make the official report. I really don't understand it; they are going to sea in these boats. I've even had people in other parts of the country put deposits down on boats, have me do a survey, close the deal, and take delivery without ever actually seeing the boat themselves. Anyway, I like having them around to empty out lockers."

As I finish re-stowing the port locker, I turn to see Giff's coveralled legs disappearing down the tiny lazarette hatch behind the helm. Giff's small . . . he needs to be. All I can see are his ankles and boots bobbing as he wriggles about. Then a hand reaches out, fingers groping.

"Light . . . ."

The stuff starts coming out of the hatch. Four Type I life jackets (OK, but a little musty), a green horn, two cushions, spare line, a flat fender, and a bunch of moldy green flares.

"Getting into the minor stuff, but if the new owner was taking this boat somewhere right after the sale, he would want to know about those flares. The engine looks some kind of all right from here. Should be. Jim Archer down to Concordia just put this little Westerbeke in here. Finestkind."

He would have kept going, but I dragged him off to lunch. Giff told the yard to put *Smoke* overboard since he would be doing the engine

checks in the water and finishing the survey afloat.

We are 3½ hours into the job. While Giff picks his way through his bay scallops and potatoes, he talks about how he got started surveying.

"Remember now, a surveyor is just a guy who has been around boats for a long time, loves them, keeps his eyes open, and learns. When I was a kid in Marblehead, we lived in a house just across the road from Graves's Yacht Yard there in town. They couldn't keep me out of that yard. I'd close it each day. They did great work then. Great boats. Building and maintaining them. Just terrific. The standards were very high. I just absorbed that place and ran through a couple of small boats as a kid. Then I went out as a crew on a very big yacht, over 100 feet long, and we worked some. Traveled, too. Those days you managed a yacht like a business. You did it all. Supervised all of her yard work and maintenance. Did all the correspondence. A regular business. Then I went out as a professional yacht captain myself. Worked for these people, the Fords, for a long time. Ran a boat for them, and also supervised getting their new motorsailer, the *Canterbury Belle*, built. And then I ran her.

"Throughout all that time people kept asking me to come and look at boats they had or wanted to buy. Called me all the time. So after a while, besides skippering, a portion of what I was doing was surveying. Then I went at it full time — but I had already been at the work for years by then.

"I was lucky. I was brought up in boats when the quality of the yachts, the people, and the yards was really high and you could learn a lot all the time. I don't really know how a young fellow could go about learning to be a surveyor today. I do know you are not going to make it with some sort of flimsy mail-in course or just by reading a bit. I guess the best thing you could do would be to attach yourself to a really good surveyor as an apprentice and just follow him around, working under him for a couple of years. But I don't know that you could really get someone to take you on like that today. There is no motive for a man to do that. It's a real problem. I don't know where the surveyors of eight to 12 years from now are going to come from.

"Sure, there are a lot of guys with business cards and newspaper ads saying they are surveyors — licensed surveyors — that's a lot of air. I know of only one good young man in the business today. The rest of the good ones are older guys like me. There's plenty of business around for good surveyors, the business is growing.

"It's a tough life, though — tough on the family. Boy, do I hate motels. Even when you're at home, the phone doesn't stop. There's always somebody who wants you to just sort of 'drop over and take a look for a minute or two.' Now what do you say to that? How do you charge for it? My problem is that I can't say 'no' often enough. Right now I'm booked solid months on end. I get sort of crazy by the time June comes around. This year, no matter what, I'm taking Charlotte and *Caribou* to Maine and just disappearing. I'm also going to try to cut back to a four-day outside work week. The paperwork itself and the scheduling need tending to. My survey reports run eight pages. Add to that the billing and the correspondence and it's a lot of administrative time.

"It's a good profession, though. I see a lot of boats, a lot of people, most of whom are good types; and, to a great extent, my time is my own. Another thing, I do my work my way. If a guy just wants a real light survey, I can refuse it. And, if I get into the job and see that the boat is a disaster, I will call the guy who authorized the work and tell him to call a halt right there. Sure, I could let the time run, but no use spending the money and effort.

"Most of the boats I see are in the 25- to 40-foot range . . . about evenly divided between sail and power with some commercial fishing boats thrown in. I've done big boats, some of them up to 100 feet, but that is some kind of job. Remember yours? *Endeavour* was 63 feet and we did a full sea trial and complete survey on her. That ran three full days — and we had Jimmy Archer there for two of those days just working on the mechanical end of things. But she was unusual . . . gives you an idea, though. Most of the time I do one boat per day — a full eight- or 10-hour day. It takes all of that to do it properly. Maybe if I am doing insurance work, I'll get two boats in, but not too often.

"I try to group boats geographically and spread the travel expense over several owners. I guess I easily do a couple of hundred boats a year, which means I surveyed almost 3,000 boats. Damn, I never thought about that number.

"I do a lot of wood. I want to, and I have a reputation for it. But about 30 to 40 percent of my boats are glass. I've done steel and aluminum, and usually bring in special equipment for that, like audio-gauging gear. I've never done any cement boats, though, thank you. Three-thousand boats . . . good Lord!"

Smoke was back in the water when we returned. As we stepped aboard, we could hear water running. Seawater was overflowing the

Along with the obvious bobstay fitting problems, the surveyor uses the magnifying glass to check for fatigue and failure.

head — no anti-siphon valve on the discharge and it had back-pumped. Giff shuts the seacocks and the flow stops.

Giffy heads forward. The boat is neat and clean inside. All personal gear is gone and the lockers are clear. She smells good, aired out. He crawls into the circular opening of the chain locker to look at the stem area and the frames forward where there is no sheathing. All OK.

When Giff lifts the forward berths, he frowns a bit. "The ballast needs some air and washing. There's moisture collecting in some of the bilge debris here. Needs cleaning."

Giffy's hammer is back. He sounds the mast partners and mast step, the bronze hammer

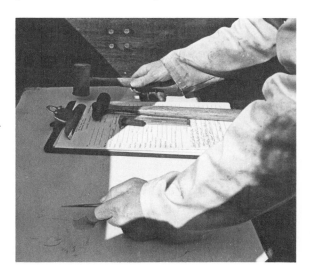

The canvas on the bridge deck has too much of a paint buildup, and the paint has been cracking. The canvas, however, is all right. If done soon, stripping and repainting will solve the problem.

You've got to be agile to survey boats well. The surveyor is checking the engine's water-jacketed exhaust.

ringing back from the oak. Then he reaches into the bilges, striking each accessible keelbolt and frame bolt — no mushy thud signaling bad wood. *Smoke* is sound deep inside.

We move aft to the galley, checking drawers and lockers, making an inventory. The marine AM radio is noted (for what it's worth). The fireplace heater is clean. No drawer, shelf, bin, pullout compartment or niche is left uninspected. Giff makes notes on the fire extinguishers. One is badly mounted, another has a safety pull pin missing.

After the galley, Giff pulls the electrical panel. Not much to it. *Smoke* is a basic, small 12-volt sailboat. There is a 110 VAC shoreside connection that is a bit too basic, no overload protection fuse or breaker, no ground and no cover on the outlet. The back of the panel is an average installation, a rat's-nest of tangled wiring, but all in sound condition.

At the engine panel you cannot tell what does what to whom. The switches need labels. Giff points to the battery boxes. "Now that's a poor job. They're badly built, no liners, and you can already see some of the acid damage in the starboard box. Dangerous."

The engine installation is just fine. The diesel squats like a shiny red Buddha, sitting squarely behind the companionway ladder. "No problem here, got less than 10 hours on it since Concordia put that plant in . . . ." He notes some rust streaking on the sheathing near the exhaust. "Must have been the prior installation done that. This exhaust is tight."

He reaches down with a crescent wrench and works at the heat exchanger. "Look at that, though, there's a zinc electrode that's completely gone. Just because the engine is new doesn't mean you can ignore it. They better get on this right away or they'll have a big problem."

Giff starts on the frame inspection. *Smoke* has strip-laid ceiling that sheathes the entire interior of the cabins. Giffy takes out all the drawers above and behind the starboard settee. He fetches a spotlight and presses his face up against the drawer frame, angling the light in at the exposed frames. A grunt and then a sigh. "Well, there's the first really serious problem on her. She's got some cracked frames. They don't look very bad, but they're definitely busted. About four of them I can see from here with cracks running about a third of the way through. There is also some moisture marking the planks at the frame sections."

The cracks are all hairline, at the turn of the bilge. Tough to see or probe. Giff takes a small mirror from his box. His pick probes both sides of the frame.

"They're sound enough from a hardness point of view, but they are definitely stress-cracked. About eight frames are involved."

The prospective buyer arrives. He is a young doctor from South Dartmouth; tall, well set up, calm. He likes *Smoke* very much.

Giffy shows him the frame problem right away. "Now this is not a problem that will kill the sale. Least it shouldn't. But it is there and it is material. You've got them in a classic strain point in the hull, at the turn of the bilge. They're very fine, but they do go through at least a third of the way in several frames. The hull's fairness has not been affected, though."

One thing is clear. There is no way that anyone except a thoroughgoing, highly experienced surveyor could have detected the cracks. The doctor says as much. (He's very right. A friend of mine bought a New York 32 several years ago and had what he believed to be a professional survey job done on her. A few years later, during a major renovation, he discovered *65 broken frames*. They weren't merely cracked, either. The frames were massively fractured clean through, for the entire length of the boat. Most had been broken for many years. So much for casually acquired surveyors.)

Giff goes over the port side. There are no drawers here — just the ceiling. He digs a bit with his knife and then slowly pries off three of the strips. Peering in with his light, he can barely see a few frames — they have similar hairline cracks at the same level.

"Now some surveyors would let this go, but this is a good boat and basically well cared for. I know the owner has no knowledge of this situation. She should be fixed properly no matter who is going to own her."

Giffy and the doctor discuss sistering the frames and the cost involved. They discuss yards and the possibility of Giff's getting some quotes. He feels that a competent yard would charge a minimum of $1,000 and the job should not exceed $1,600 at the very outside. The frames will definitely be the subject for a re-negotiation of the selling price.

Giffy starts up the diesel and runs it for 30 minutes in gear. Oil pressure and water temperature are noted on the sheet; they are within good limits. The controls work well.

"You know, somewhere I heard that 80 percent of the marine insurance claims are for fire and theft. Well, the fire part means problems in the galley or the engine room. When I look at the engine installation, no matter what the size, I look for two major things. First and foremost, I want to see a good fuel system. Is the system in good condition, secure, tight, and leak-free? Can I smell fuel? Are there fuel stains on the bottom planking where leaks have traveled through? I check to make sure the lines are well supported and protected from chafe.

"People still don't get fuel venting right . . . or fill pipes. I was down to Derecktor's the other day and saw a boat with fuel tanks under the berths in the main cabin — and their fill pipes were there, too. Just terrible. Imagine snaking a big, dirty fuel hose down there, near the galley and all. Think about what is going on below those bunks. You want fill pipes entering on the top of the tank, with vents going outboard so that the fumes won't blow back. And you want Kerotest packless valves like the one here on *Smoke* on all the connections leading out of the tank.

"Next, I look at ventilation. *Smoke* does not have enough. Most boats don't. Did a boat a week or so back where the poor little diesel aspirated whatever it could steal from the bilges or the cabin. No ventilation provided at all. You want a good natural flow of air into the engine compartment *and* a proper blower. The exhaust for the blower should be overboard, and the blower pickup in the bilge. It has got to

be below the level of the carburetor, too, since gas fumes are heavy and sink down.

"There's a lot more I look at — wiring, engine beds, exhausts, cooling system, but those first two, fuel and ventilation, are the real dangers."

While the engine rumbles, Giffy checks out every light and switch on board. He notes that there is a radio direction finder on the spec sheets, but he cannot find the unit aboard.

All of the floorboards come up. Giff checks the tanks for material, soundness, and proper connections. Then, he goes to find out where the spars, sails, and missing RDF can be found. There is also a dinghy to locate and inspect.

He returns after calling Dick Sciuto and then the owner. "He's got the rest of the stuff at his place in Little Compton, about 30 minutes or so from here. We'll go down there in a bit."

Giff sits down with the doctor to find out more about his plans for the boat. *Smoke* will be the doctor's second cruising boat. His first was a slightly smaller Alden design. He has sailed for about 10 years, and he plans to use *Smoke* for day and weekend sailing in southern New England waters. He has three children. By now, he is very glad he came to the survey.

Checking the structure thoroughly requires some very tight fits. In the chain locker forward, Giffy is checking frames, beams, clamps, and the underside of the deck for problems ranging from broken structural members to those resulting from poor ventilation.

The inspection reveals hairline fractures (see arrow) in six to eight frames along a line a few inches above the bilge stringer.

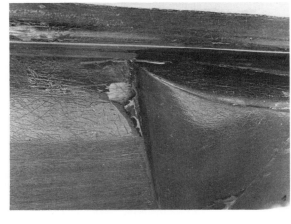

There's an adhesion problem with the varnish where the cockpit coaming joins the trunk cabin side. Looks like too little varnish for too long a period.

As he moves through each area of the boat, the surveyor fills out his checklist and makes notes for elaborating upon later, when the full report is sent to the owner.

Giffy completes his on-board worklist. Then, he closes all switches, checks the seacocks, closes all lockers, and collects his tools.

We leave for Little Compton. Total time on the survey to this point has been 6½ hours (and we're not finished). We're chilled and tired, and the heater in the Mercedes helps as we head to Little Compton.

"This was a fine boat to do a sample survey on," Giff remarks. ". . . it would be easy to just pick a really bad one, a disaster, and build a long list of problems. But that's not typical. Most of the time, the boats I survey are sold. Not always at the agreed price, though. This one's good, frames and all. Sure, there are things to be done, and now that young doctor behind us knows where his work lies. And the survey popped up something serious, too — but not bad enough to kill the sale.

"You know, since I really specialize in wooden boats, I get to see a higher percentage of bad boats than most. It's the age factor. Since they're not really building a lot of wood now, although it's coming back, I get to see the older boats — and sooner or later, time or a bad owner catches up to a boat. One thing, though, boat for boat, wood holds up better.

"Take the two boats we've done in the past days . . . both the same size just about . . . one fiberglass, one wood. The glass boat we did yes-

A Surveyor's

"I've been at this business long enough so that I really care about opinions. There are serious and dangerous problems in surveying today.

"First, there are more and more people getting into boating (many with little experience and a lot of misconceptions). And, there are more boats. There are all the fiberglass production boats with questionable layup schedules. What wood boats are being built are coming from smaller shops, many of which are gaining their experience as they build. Desire does not replace competence. The used wood boats have been out there for a while, and age is catching up with a lot of them. Finally, there are a lot of very good boats around today of wood, glass, and steel, but they have important maintenance to be done on them if they are going to stay that way.

terday down to Graves's [a Bristol 38] was roughly the same size, she slept the same number of people, the accommodation was identical in every way, she was averagely maintained, and she was 12 years old. On the plus side, she had wheel steering. On the negative, she had a gasoline engine. Now *Smoke* is older by a few years — but she's 10 times the boat. What's really incredible is that *Smoke* sold in the middle 20s — and the glass boat sold in the middle 40s — almost double. And there's no reason for it except for the way people's brains have been trained.

"*Smoke* has most of her active sailing years ahead of her if she is cared for. The glass boat is on the decline. She had real problems, too — and they were caused more by the way she was built than anything else. She was an average glass boat. Her steering stops are poor and are causing strain in the hull. And her water tank and forward bulkhead are adrift because the retaining tabs in the layup schedule just did not have enough strength. So, when that boat hit something (and she did) like a float or low dock, it all broke loose. All that's wrong with *Smoke* is a few hairline cracks, and they can be easily tended to. I don't understand the dollar difference, double for a lot less, but people have been conditioned."

Smoke's owner lives in a large, open field in

When the boat itself is finished, the spars are checked thoroughly. Here the masthead fittings undergo close scrutiny.

the middle of good farm land. The afternoon is gone and the day is golden with a smoky wind coming across the peninsula. The owner lives in a California kind of house. There is a big hot tub lying on its side in the yard, pipes disconnected. There are large, nonobjective sculpture forms in the field. They do things with the light

Thoughts on Surveyors

"*Standing at the center of the entire boat buying, selling, insurance, and maintenance scene is the surveyor — and that is no overstatement. He is the only one who must be expert and objective — free from the desire for profit, the need to keep on manufacturing, or the owner's blind love for a particular boat. And yet, in this country at least, that surveyor is governed by no regulations or standards except the ones he sets for himself.*
"*Standards is the key word.*
"*I certainly think we are overregulated, over governed, overburdened, and underprotected by a lot of governmental bureaucracy — but there has to be something done about a man who gets to call himself a surveyor and gives opinions that will determine if people go out to sea in a particular boat.*

"*In England they have recognized the need to protect the boating public ... and they do not use the government to do it either. Virtually every English surveyor is a member of the Yacht Brokers, Designers, and Surveyors Association. Rules for membership are extremely strict. First, a candidate must work for five years as an apprentice surveyor before a committee passes him for an associate membership. Then, he has to spend another five years as a surveyor working in his profession before he can become a full member. The surveyors have to carry full indemnity insurance and follow a published scale of fees. The real teeth in this system comes from the fact that the British insurance companies will only give coverage on a boat surveyed by an Association member. If you are a boat owner in the U.K., you can go to the Association for a man, and you can*

make some fundamental assumptions about his competence.
"*Not so here in the United States — and that has got to change. When you step into a doctor's office, or sit down in an airplane seat, or buy a container of milk, there are certain assumptions you can make. You have been protected. There are standards. And yet, it is possible to make a major investment in a boat and then place yourself and your family in that boat out on open water with virtually no possible assumptions about the standards of the people and their performance that protected you along the way.*
"*These standards could come from the government, but I don't think that would work well at all. They will have to come from the boating community itself if they are going to mean anything.*"

as the day darkens. The owner leads us down the dirt road to a long shed. The spars are there. They are spruce of hollow box-type construction.

Giffy takes his magnifying glass to each fitting on the sticks. He checks the diameter of the standing rigging with calipers. Each plate, clevis, swage fitting, terminal, and tang gets a careful inspection. The spars are bright finish, but bare wood shows through the peeled varnish. It's all cosmetics, the spars are good, but they will have to be completely wooded and brought back up. Giffy's hammer ranges the length of the main, the mizzen, and both booms. They're sound.

Back at the house now, coffee is the final fix for the last hour of work. Giff and the doctor hunker down and help the owner spread sails and covers on the living room floor. There are six sails in all: a new working suit by Hood, a Hild spinnaker and spinnaker staysail (both fine), and an elderly Ratsey #2 genoa, which has a couple of seasons left in it. There are three sail covers and bags for all the sails.

The RDF comes out of its box to be counted. The owner realizes he knows Giff. They met on a float in Maine when Giff and Charlotte brought *Caribou* in for water. He remembers the frequency level of Giffy's voice.

On the second cup of coffee, the frame problem also gets on the table. A rare discussion (the kind that gives brokers the night terrors): the owner, the buyer, and the surveyor dealing with a negotiable problem. The owners wants to know more about the frame cracks . . . it's all new to him.

He wants to know how the repair can be done. He's got some construction experience, and obviously he cares about the boat. She will be fixed, sale or not. What is also obvious is that the doctor will still buy *Smoke* after some final price movement.

After everyone understands the problem and the ways to cure it, Giffy steers the subject out the door, to be taken up by phone with Sciuto Yacht Sales.

It's 6:30 p.m. now; the light's almost gone. Giff goes outside to take a look at the small glass dink that goes with *Smoke*. There are sheep in a pen behind the house. He catches a small lamb and scratches the grey wool at its neck.

Elapsed time on the survey is 10 hours.

EPILOGUE

Within a week, the final survey report was done and sent to the buyer. It was eight pages: a 450-word summary, a note sheet of 21 priority items needing correction, and six pages of detailed inventory and survey findings.

Smoke was sold to the doctor with a $1,000 adjustment in the price to be used to correct the frame problem.

SURVEY FACTS

Why Get One in the First Place.
What It Costs
What You Get. What You Don't Get.

Why use a surveyor in the first place? if you are looking at a 14-foot catboat or a small motor launch costing less than two or three thousand dollars, you probably don't need a surveyor. But, if you are about to get adopted by any sort of a seagoing boat, one that you will place yourself and family in and go out on big water, you need a survey. If you are looking at a boat with the potential for restoration, you need a survey that will tell you to put down the varnish and plug in the bandsaw (or walk away).

There are many kinds of surveys. The classic "purchase survey," of course. But there is also the survey ordered by the *seller*. This is done so that he can find out what items to correct to get the very best possible price for his boat. There is the insurance survey, which is relatively light, superficial, mostly concerned with safety, evaluating actual risk, and setting market value (the basis for your quoted premium rates). There is the periodic maintenance survey, to monitor the condition of a boat continually and set the priorities for work. This is a tremendous use of a surveyor's talents, and one of the least used. Then there are damage surveys, where the insurance carrier assigns a surveyor to assess and evaluate damage in a particular incident. Here the surveyor takes on the additional role of insurance adjustor. He verifies reported damage, explores the real extent of the damage (perhaps unreported or unseen to the amateur eye), and establishes what will be done to correct the problem. His job is not to minimize damage and reduce the claim, but to find *all* of the damage that is appropriate. He actually sets up the financial boundaries of the claim (called the "reserve") against which the final bills are compared.

All of these surveys affect the value of the boat as it changes ownership. But there is also a more subtle aspect to the survey that has a direct effect on the new owner. This is when the survey sets the basis for the costs of new insurance. When the surveyor sets the "market value" or "replacement value" of your boat, he is giving the insurance company the basic building block of their rating structure.

Put briefly, the survey report has many lives and will live with the boat throughout her ownership. The report should be a full one.

Almost any wooden cruising boat with an overall length of 25 feet and up should take most of a day to survey. No one-sheet survey report will do the job (there are far too many of those). A proper survey report is much more than a simple inventory. The fact that you have three instead of two bilge pumps to handle all the leaks is of secondary interest. *The survey must be a detailed statement of condition.*

The best survey reports consist of a one-page narrative summary, followed by a very specific listing of the surveyor's notes and comments. This, in turn, is followed by several pages of a checklist giving details on every aspect of the boat.

If all you get is an inventory of the boat's construction features and gear, coupled with a bunch of disclaimers on why this or that could not be run or inspected, you have been shortchanged. Be warned.

Just as the survey itself is the professional "service" that you buy — and you should attend that even to take full advantage of the experience — the survey report is the all-important "product" you purchase. The report, when done correctly, is the *only* objective opinion you will get.

The broker is definitely unobjective. So are you. When you have put a deposit down on a boat and signed that contract (conditional on the survey, of course), then you have already cast a preliminary vote. When all the hammering, probing, rhetoric, and anguish are over — and you sit there in the wee hours talking to yourself and about to take that last step — that survey will either reaffirm what everyone has been shouting at you, or it will be the single truthful voice in the night giving you a ticket out of the confusing and discouraging mess. Best dollar you ever spent.

The report can also be the light that guides you through the tunnel of wood shavings, canvas, caulking, and paint, of the first years of ownership, as you make the boat your own by setting your work schedule. Find out what kind of survey and survey report will be done, *in advance.*

What should a good survey cost? About $250-$300, assuming it's a fairly basic boat of about 28 to 40 feet that can be properly and thoroughly done in a single long working day. Travel expenses are extra. Rates do vary somewhat. Some surveyors charge by the foot, some by the hour, some with a flat day rate. Some have distance charges as well. There are even some surveys (done on very large yachts) where the fee is a percentage of the selling price (rare).

You can get so-called cheaper surveys (you can also put brass screws in a saltwater boat, so what is "cheap?") Many buyers try to shop for lower rates, or downgrade the work done in the survey, hoping to lower the cost as the first step in their frugal approach to owning a boat (is *that* a paradox in terms!). They would be better advised to spend their time shopping for the very best surveyor they can find. The "best buy" in surveying is measured in competence, not cost.

When you commission a survey, you own that survey. The surveyor is ethically bound *not* to transmit that information to anyone else without your specific permission. Sometimes, though, a boat has been recently surveyed, and you can purchase the existing survey report. That is no substitute. All sorts of things could have happened to the boat starting the minute she came off the railway. Purchasing a *recent* existing survey can be of value if you get another surveyor (perhaps the same one, if he was good) to update the report. This means another haulout anyway, but perhaps a shorter job overall. You can reduce some costs this way, but there are negative aspects to the concept, such as missing attendance at the original work.

Usually a good survey on an average boat will more than pay for itself in the renegotiation based upon survey findings — or by properly allocating, ordering, and scheduling corrective work. The value is obvious.

So much for what you get and what it costs. Here is what you *don't* get:

You get no guarantee that you have bought a good boat. A survey is a professional *opinion* — no more than that. All the signs may point to a fine boat, and the surveyor may give an upcheck to everything he inspects. He cannot pull out every keelbolt and do a test boring on each plank. There are parts of every boat that are totally inaccessible. He gives his opinion based upon what he *can* see, the rest is inference, and you can expect no more.

Many do, however. Recently, our society has gone a little lawsuit-crazy. And, for the first time, surveyors are coming more and more under fire as the obviously available victim when a boat turns out to be less than the owner expected. While virtually none of these suits against good surveyors are won, they have to be defended. The cost of that defense as well as professional liability insurance sooner or later will show up in the fee schedule.

This does not mean that surveyors should be beyond the law. After all, the surveyor does hold himself out to be an objective expert. If he does an inadequate job, is sloppy, negligent, or just plain ignorant, and you base a buying decision on his bad performance, a buying decision that causes you material damage, then you should avail yourself of every legal means to recover your position.

Not long ago, a man fell in love with a Colin Archer double-ender. He casually hired a surveyor he found in the Yellow Pages, who did a perfunctory job and filed a report saying that the boat was in fine shape, just the best thing going. The sale went through, and the erstwhile owner set out to take his prize from the Jersey shore to Long Island Sound to start their beautiful life together. Within an hour or so, the ketch was in deep trouble, water coming in everywhere, all sorts of things letting go. The man's life was in danger. The Coast Guard managed to get boat and owner in to City Island, barely afloat.

Once dry, the owner's fear turned to outrage. In preparation for the holocaust to come, he ordered another survey. When Giffy Full looked at the boat, she was rotten clean through, stem to sternpost, a totally unseaworthy hulk. There was no possible way that this condition could have been missed. The first surveyor is currently named in a lawsuit — as he should be.

But there are also side effects to this general tendency to rush to legal judgment. The threat of legal action (however unfounded) may eventually cause the good surveyors to keep their heads down and withhold that all-important, instinctive, look-me-in-the-eye-and-say-OK oral opinion that never reaches the written report but is the thing you clasp to your life jacket when the going gets rough. He is human.

The surveyor is not all things. He does not cause the damage. He does not repair it. He is the umpire (they have been known to get tackled).

Here is Giffy Full's legal phraseology on that subject — a paragraph that appears on all reports bearing his signature. Read it carefully; each word tells you the limits of the product and service you purchase.

"This report is submitted in good faith and constitutes a description of the condition as then found. The surveyor assumes no responsibility for any defects and is to be held harmless for conditions subsequently arising. This report does not warrant (expressly or implied) or guarantee the condition of the above yacht."

The best defense is to take extreme care in selecting your surveyor — and attend the survey yourself.

Selecting a Surveyor

Selection of the surveyor is the most difficult, badly done, neglected, and confused aspect of the surveying process. Paradoxically, the most inexperienced boat owner (or owner-to-be) is the fellow who needs a good surveyor more than anyone else — he is also ill informed, least equipped, and least able to find one.

Most of the time, brokers recommend a surveyor on a sale. This often works out fine (although the broker does have some minor fish to fry). A good broker will get a good surveyor, though. The broker depends on repeat business for his real trade — and he will usually have a group of good surveyors he knows well. He also will be able to match a surveyor's particular specialty to the boat under consideration. However, to the uninitiated, it is a vague business at best.

Standing at the core of the problem is the fact that anyone, absolutely anyone, can get some business cards printed up, buy a hammer and an icepick, take out an ad in the phone book or local newspaper, and proclaim himself a surveyor. The title "licensed surveyor" is an empty one, since the only license needed is a commercial business license, the same type used by your local grocer or TV repairman. Compound this problem by the fact that there are absolutely no standards, controls, review procedures, or sanctions regarding the performance of surveyors today. It is sort of like going up to the cockpit of a Boeing 747 and finding Chuckles the Clown at the controls.

There is a certain selection process caused by the marketplace itself. Surveyors who do turn in poor performances usually don't get rehired. Insurance carriers, sooner or later, will drop a bad surveyor. The *word* will get out. However, this Darwinian winnowing away of incompetents is not very comforting if you happen to be the victim of a surveyor who is in the learning or going-out-of-business process. That is the equivalent of being operated on by a surgeon who got a C+ in your particular disease when he was in medical school.

There is no formal training process, no diploma or degree, no school tie, no badge of office.

The picture is not all that bleak, though — there are some great surveyors working today. Here are some of the people you can talk to about locating one of them.

- Banks specializing in marine financing (ask for the loan officer specializing in that category)
- Insurance carriers or agents
- Brokers, not only the one selling the boat
- Boatbuilders
- Other owners
- The National Association of Marine Surveyors

This last group sounds like a good source, but it is of limited use. There are virtually no rigorous standards for membership — only a set period of time during which a candidate member has offered himself to the public as a surveyor. There are no standards for continual performance, and no method of monitoring or sanctioning the membership. While many fine surveyors are members of this group, many of the best are not.

Here is a possible path out of this unfortunate situation — a path to a good surveyor.

1. Locate a respected boatyard or boatbuilder in (a) your area (preferred); or (b) the area where the boat is located. Do not contact a yard that merely stores boats and pumps gas.

2. Go to see the foreman, chief rigger, head joiner, or head of the mechanical department of the yard. Ask them about a good surveyor for the

type of boat you want inspected. Try to see as many of these older, more skilled men as you can with your questions. You probably will get several recommendations.

3. Now, check out these names with your bank, insurance company, or broker. However, value their opinion on a lessened basis than that of the yard people. Use it as a cross reference.

4. Call each surveyor and talk over the project. Ask about the type of boats he generally works on. Surveyors have specialties. Ask if he will be comfortable in all phases of the work (electronics, mechanical, electrical, steel, etc.). Ask him for references (and plan to call each one of them). Also,

be fair, let him know as much as you can about the boat, what you plan to do with it, and what level of work you expect from him.

5. Ask him to send you a blank copy of his survey report form.

6. If you find several men you like and feel comfortable with, select one that does most of his work in your home waters, and in the area where the boat will be maintained. Do not merely use a local man in the area where the boat is, or will be hauled, just to keep costs down. It is false economy.

This is a word-of-mouth selection process — but that's the true way that reputations are made and known.

Preparing a Boat for Survey

Surveyors are skilled professionals. They get paid as such. It is foolish and expensive to expect a surveyor to spend his time waiting for a boat to be hauled, lugging ballast, cleaning out lockers, or tracking down bits and pieces of a boat's gear. Most of the time, boats are not properly prepared, adding needless hours and expense to the survey process. Surveyors make very expensive manual laborers.

The party ordering the survey has the basic responsibility not only to pay for the survey but also to get the boat prepared properly. So, for the prospective buyer (who foots the bill) and the boatyard (which must live through the process) and the seller (who wants to keep the parting painless and profitable), here is how to prepare a small cruising sailboat for a thorough survey.

1. The present owner should remove all personal and boat gear not included in the sale.

2. The owner should unlock all hatches and lockers. Keys should be left with the yard (including the engine ignition key).

3. The broker should make sure that the surveyor has a copy of the specification sheet. He should also ensure that all items included in the sale are available at the yard.

4. If the owner wants any work done for him during haulout, he should make this clear at the outset, and separate billing records should be kept at the yard.

5. The buyer should take the following steps to prepare the boat (or instruct the yard to do them):

• Try to obtain plans of the vessel — particularly a profile construction plan to aid in blocking during haulout.

• The boat should be hauled and securely blocked in an upright and level position. If the boat is permitted to incline seaward, her sheer and fairness will be hard to evaluate, and there will be an unnatural flow of water on deck.

• Have all inspection panels and ports removed.

• Request that a good portion of the movable bal-

last be removed. At least two or three bays in the bilge should be cleared, particularly in the keelbolt areas.

• Remove chain, rode, and anchors, but keep them available.

• Make sure the surveyor has a list of any items or conditions you particularly want checked out based upon your self-survey. Try to be present at the survey. It is a rare opportunity to gain truthful insights into the boat. Do not continually question; observe.

• Remove the contents of all lockers but have this material available for inventory.

• Lift rugs, if any.

• Have bilges drained or pumped out.

• Make sure a battery (preferably the boat's own) is available for engine starting.

• Locate all sails and running rigging.

• Ask to have propane bottles available for stove test (or alcohol if that is the fuel used).

• Request the yard to have ladders or staging on the job site.

• Verify that the spars are at the yard, properly tagged for identification, unwrapped, and complete with all fittings.

• If yard labor will be required (for example, in removing keelbolts), make sure it is ordered in advance.

• Know how to reach the broker and owner during the survey.

• If the boat is already hauled and covered, have the cover removed.

• Verify with the broker that there is insurance in force, either with the owner or yard to protect you from damage that might occur.

• Make sure the surveyor will have what he needs to work efficiently:

— Electrical power and extension cords
— Lights
— An area to unfold sails
— Bosun's chair

From the Surveyor's Final Report

Smoke: Auxiliary Yawl
Year Built: 1961
L.O.A.: 35'
Beam: 9'10"
Designer: Thomas Knutson
Builder: Thomas Knutson
L.W.L. 25'
Draft: 5'
Type of Construction: Carvel planked on oak frames
Topsides: Planked with Philippine mahogany

Bottom: Philippine mahogany
Stem: Mahogany, minor repairs required
Fastenings: 2" x No. 12 Everdur bronze
Keel: Oak
Worm Shoe: None
Propeller: 2 Blade 14" D x 8" P
Shaft: One, 1" bronze
Bearing: Rubber type; Cutless
Rudder: Wood, in good order
Stuffing Box: Self-aligning type

Notes:
1. Vessel requires refastening of butt in sixth plank up from keel (first butt forward on starboard side.)
2. Refasten butt in third plank below waterline port side/forward, approximately 4'6" aft of waterline at stem.
3. Depth finder transducer painted. Clean off. Neither of the butts is seriously bad, but it would be wise to refasten.
4. Both top corners of the transom need prompt attention to open seams at the corner; fresh water has begun to get into the planking; starboard also has a small soft area on the end; some on port end but not so critical.
5. Stem rabbet seam needs to be recaulked, both sides in the area of the bobstay plate. Reef out and rebed the bobstay plate.

Decks: Canvas-covered marine ply
Superstructure: Mahogany trunk cabin and cockpit
Deck Hardware: All bronze castings
Ground Tackle: One 18-lb. Danforth anchor, one 20-lb. Yachtsman anchor, two 150' half-inch nylon rodes
Winches: Two #3 Merriman sheet winches
Horn: Freon canister type
Flares: Obsolete and unusable
Life Jackets: Four, Type I jackets
Stove Tanks: Two separate stainless steel lined and sealed compartments in cockpit, tanks removed.
Notes:
1. After stanchion (starboard side) needs pin in base.
2. Second stanchion aft (starboard), base is loose, requires refastening.
3. Cap missing from port chock on taffrail.
4. Gate missing from port chock on taffrail.
5. Paint should be stripped from decks before further damage from buildup.
6. Install gasket in top of propane gas bottle locker.
7. Flares should be replaced before operating the boat.
Tanks (Fuel): Diesel, one Monel, under cockpit. 25-gallon capacity, square with tapered bottom. Framed in place. Filling lines and vents made of 1½" pipe with ¼" copper vent line. Bonded. Overflow runs outboard properly. One Kerotest shutoff valve at bottom. All fuels lines ⅞" copper tube.
Tanks (Water): Two tanks. Oblong. Under cabin berths. Stainless steel. In good condition.
Frames: Oak 1½" x 1¾" spaced 7¼"
Deckbeams: Oak 1¼" x 1¾"
Accommodation: Main cabin with three berths, two V-berths in forward cabin. Separate head port side forward. Painted interior with bright mahogany trim.
Bulkheads: Partitions only.
Ventilation: 10 opening ports and one forward hatch.
Electronics: Apelco RDF-40 Radio Direction Finder, Apelco Marine AM Radio (obsolete), Apelco MS-10C Depth Finder
Compass: Ritchie bulkhead, Kelvin White spherical 12 volt. All OK.
Galley: Heritage propane stove fed from two separate

bottles on deck. Bottles not aboard, and stove could not be tested. Stove shutoff is a proper master packless valve. Stack is 3" galvanized pipe. Refrigeration is a stainless steel lined icebox. Three opening ports ventilate galley. Two B-1 Fire extinguishers present. Insufficient.

Main Engine: Westerbeke, Model 4-108 diesel, 4 cylinders. R.P.M. 3,000 max. Horsepower 37
Reduction Gear: None
Year of Engine: 1976
Approx. Speed: 6.5 knots
Condition: As new
Engine Bed: Good
Cooling: Freshwater
Ventilation: Insufficient, one vent only
Blower: None
Fuel Pump: Mechanical, metal bowl, filter ATC-T-60. All OK.
Exhaust Line: 2" I.D. hose, copper-water-jacketed section
Exhaust Silencer: Elasto Rubber type
Generator: 35-amp alternator/engine
Shaft Log: Tube through sternpost
Bearings: Cutless rubber type
Bilge Pump: Bronze, manual
Toilet: Wilcox-Crittenden Imperial
Seacocks: Five, bronze
Wiring: #14-1 copper stranded PVC/jack
Storage Batteries: Two, 12-volt, Surette of approximately 70 amp/hour cap.
Switchboard: Vapor Proof master switch
Lightning Arrestor: Yes, one
Aerials: Obsolete AM type
Ground: On engine
Charger: Engine alternator only
Notes:
1. Battery boxes are not lined, and the bottom of the starboard box is partially deteriorated. They should be replaced with containers of proper construction (lined with sheet lead or fiberglass).
2. Zinc electrode in engine heat exchanger deteriorated to zero. Requires prompt replacement.
3. Lead ballast should be removed from under the forward berths and cleaned. The bilge area should be treated with Cuprinol.
4. No circuit breaker or other overload protection on 110 VAC outlet. Outlet also not grounded and missing cover.
5. Toilet has no anti-siphon valve on head discharge line, head is flooding back.
6. No proper labels on engine start panel.
7. Two B-1 Fire extinguishers not properly mounted. Boat should have three B-1 types.
8. Approximately eight frames are partially cracked at outside turn of the bilge under the starboard berth.
9. Partially cracked frames on port side under locker. Unable to determine full extent due to permanent sheathing in place.

Dudley Davidson's Secrets

Michael Broom

ONE DAY we received an inquiry out of the blue: "Hi. My name is Michael Broom." Michael wanted to know if we were interested in reading his profile of Dudley Davidson, "a master with a disc sander." The story line's originality intrigued us, but we were cautious, very cautious. After all, what can you say about a guy who sands boats for a living? But Michael produced the goods — a manuscript that brought Dudley to life and photographs that captured it all. Nevertheless, there were doubters. Dick Gorski in the WoodenBoat art department thought those waterheads in the editorial department had finally lost it. Only upon reading the piece did he change his mind.

ON A CRISP, sunny morning in March 1978, I let *Tenderfoot*'s lines go, crossed Puget Sound, and was hauled out in Shilshoal Bay. I planned to strip her of all the aging, peeling layers of bottom paint she had acquired over the years, make some repairs, and give her a fresh coat of paint before putting her back into the water.

I had considered several methods of paint removal and figured two would be efficient: disc sanding or burning. I thought disc sanding

Dudley Davidson's keen eye and deft touch yield quick and flawless results with his powered disc sander.

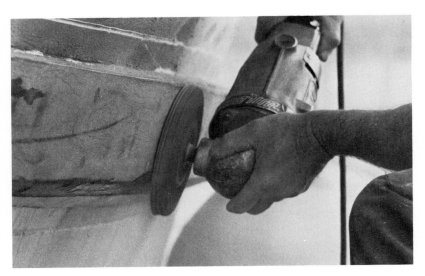

With the right touch, the paint strips quickly from the wood.

would be the quickest way to get the paint off, but I had tried that on another boat and ended up spending countless hours fairing out all the waves I had created. Not wanting to alter *Tenderfoot*'s lines, I called a rental center to get a torch. The fellow who answered had just stripped his kitchen with an "electric paint remover" and said it took paint off in no time. The tool didn't amount to much — just a wood handle stuck on a covered electric coil — but I thought it was worth the reduced fire risk and decided to try it.

It was spring break at school, so I armed as many friends and relatives as I could with electric paint removers. We went to work, anxious to get down to bare wood. Our enthusiasm waned rapidly, however, as we discovered our "tools" made better hand warmers than paint removers. There had to be a better way!

Throughout this time, I had been aware of a whining disc sander across the yard. It came from somewhere within a thick cloud of bottom paint that billowed out under a 34-foot cruiser. As everyone looked at me for an answer, I looked at the cruiser. The cloud was still billowing, but this time it came from the opposite side of the boat. Could whoever was creating the cloud have sanded half the bottom in the time it had taken us to clear about 20 square feet? I headed over to find out.

Sure enough, the entire bottom on one side was free of paint. Rubbing the planking gently with my hand, I walked toward the stern, amazed at how smooth she was. I checked her thoroughly. There was hardly a flaw. Scattered around the ground were spent discs that looked as if they had been made by gluing fine gravel on paper. I'd been around people who were "good" with a sander, but this was something else.

I rounded the stern. There, huddled in a most uncomfortable position, sat the phantom sander, gently rocking his screaming sander overhead, sending paint flying in all directions. He was wearing a hood shaped much like a bee keeper's, but it had an air hose running into it. He was engulfed by the copper paint dust; it covered him and clung to the sweat on his muscular arms. What was most singular, though, was that amid all this apparent adversity he was singing. Singing! His words were muffled, but the melody was strong, buoyant, and refreshing.

Intrigued, I watch and listened as he moved along steadily, leaving a trail of bare wood behind him. He would finish an area, move ahead a few feet, and sand off a long, even line. Then, with short, rhythmic strokes, he would sand back and forth between the bare spaces, taking the paint off from top to bottom, with a fluid motion that was similar to shaking a piggy bank gently up and down. After the paint was removed, he would come back with a finer paper and employ longer, smoother strokes as he moved along to fair the hull.

He finished a section, and the screaming sander stopped. The cloud dispersed. He turned to grab a new disc, saw me, and nodded. As I introduced myself, he pulled off his hood, dropped his respirator, cocked his glasses, and, with a quick smile, said, "Hi, I'm Dudley Davidson."

Dudley eventually sanded my entire hull. I was lucky to have found him. *Tenderfoot* is 37 feet overall, with a full keel. It took him two hours to sand her bottom and just over three hours for her topsides. He did a beautiful job, leaving her ready to paint and fairer than she'd been in years. The $140 for the entire job was more than worth the time saved and satisfaction delivered.

I didn't see Dudley again for two years, but I heard his name mentioned numerous times. The big guy with a disc sander was known in virtually every boatshop and major harbor I visited in that time. Then I had the pleasure of seeing him once more. He was still the same: a jovial master with a feathery touch. I spent a day with him while he sanded the topsides of a 58-foot purse seiner, and I later spent an evening with him in his Seattle home.

He is a fascinating man who has enjoyed an active life. He hiked, climbed, and fished all over the Northwest before most of it was ever charted. He began skiing with a group of friends in the days of homemade lifts and strapped-on skis. When the snow melted, they helped pioneer the first water-ski club in the area and put on shows, with Dudley usually the comedian. He belongs to an outboard-motor club, having gathered one of the largest collections of outboard motors in existence. His main interest, though, is inboards, and he may have *the* largest collection of those. Together they're a wonderful timeline of engine development going back to the turn of the century. He's a trapshooting enthusiast with a fine collection of old shotguns, and he's also in a motorcycle club and makes an annual ride to Mexico. He was born and raised in Seattle, has worked hard over the years, and has now retired. He was a boatbuilder before he began sanding. But I've talked too long. He collected these stories, so I'll let him share them with you as he did with me.

"I can't recall just exactly what possessed me to go into boatbuilding. I went to work for an old Swede who was a real butcher. Boy, how he built 'em. When the war came along, boatbuilding really slowed down, but I stayed at it. It was during the war that I got started sanding. I was working with a guy who had worked for Chris-Craft back East. He was quite a guy. H. Carver Gherling: international sportsman, big game hunter, and world-renowned trapshot. He was as full of it as a Christmas goose, too. He was a lot of fun to work with. He's the guy who got me started trapshooting. He also taught me a heck of a lot about boatbuilding, although he wasn't well rounded in all phases of it. But he was a darn good craftsman, and of course, that's all they needed at Chris-Craft, where you just do one job over and over again.

"One day I was watching a guy at work sand a little Chris-Craft with a disc sander. It looked like hell. I'd always heard you couldn't do a decent job with a disc sander, so I told Gherling about it. He said, 'All new Chris-Crafts are sanded with a disc sander before they leave the shop. The trouble with these guys is they don't keep it flat.' Well, the next time I tried it, and it came out a lot nicer. That's how I got started.

"The next job I went to was at Blanchard's. We were building little Navy picket boats. We'd get a few planks on them that day, and I'd stay and sand them that night. Then we'd build some more on the next day, and I'd sand some more the next night. When we got the darn thing finished, it was all sanded. We wouldn't hold up production, plus I'd get time-and-a-half.

"At the next boatshop I went to I told them I could sand but objected to doing it for regular pay. The owner wouldn't give me time-and-a-half, but the foreman told me to work two days and take one off. He'd punch me in and out, so in effect, I got time-and-a-half again.

"I was married at the time and got to thinking: 'If I could make that kind of money at it,

The tools of Dudley's trade include various grits of abrasive.

why not do it for myself?' I had a hundred bucks saved up from sanding water skis nights and weekends; I was going to buy a bandsaw for my home shop. Instead, I bought a sander, a respirator, and an extension cord, and went into business.

"That was 1946, and for the first six or seven years it didn't amount to much — too seasonal. Spring's the biggest, and I'm usually snowed under for three or four months. Then there's a spurt in the fall. Summer and winter are generally pretty slow. It took a long time before I could stretch it out over the year, but there was a lot of boatbuilding going on then, and there were two or three shops I could work in any time I wanted. Gradually I got the business built up enough so I could make a living at just that. I quit all the other jobs and have been boat-sanding ever since."

"Did you enjoy it more than boatbuilding?" I asked.

"Well, it's dirty, miserable work. It's harder work than boatbuilding, but it's a little more rewarding, in that you're working for yourself. You can come and go as you please. I set my own hours and my own wages — that sort of thing. If I want to take time off to get a haircut, I just shut 'er down and go get a haircut. You don't do that when you're working 40 hours a week for the other guy. On the other hand, when there's four or five guys screaming at you, all to do their boats at the same time, you work. Everyone wants his boat done yesterday, and they don't call you until tomorrow.

"I took a job a lot of these local boatbuilders said couldn't be done — that you couldn't do a good job with a disc sander. But Gherling had said they were doing it at Chris-Craft, so I knew damn well it could be done. It was just a matter of learning how. Of course, he told me how to do it. He said, 'The secret of sanding with a disc can be summed up in about 30 seconds. You just have a flat pad and hold it flat.' That's the basis of it. Learning to do it is something else again, but there's really no great secret to it.

"He was saying that the Chris-Crafts were all sanded with flexible-shaft sanders. There were quite a few around before the portable ones came out. They had a thick steel cable that spun around in a long flexible shaft. One end was connected to the power source, while the other was connected to a light spinning gearhead you worked with. I tried one once. There wasn't as much weight in your hands, but wrestling that damn heavy cable around was awfully awkward. The portable ones are much easier to use. Over the years I think I've tried just about every brand on the market. Black and Decker has always been the best for my type of work. It has the most power and the brushes seem to last longer than any of the others."

"Did it take you long to get the hang of using one?" I asked.

"No, it didn't. I think I got it right away. The problem was getting pads that were flat. Most of the other people using the machines tipped the thing way up on edge. That broke down the pad so it wasn't perfectly flat anymore. Finally, when I went to work at the place where I got a day off for every two, I told them to buy a new pad. Then I worked it over to suit me, and I've had my own pads every since.

"The pads in those days were made out of short strands of sisal fiber, a rope fiber, held together by a brown plastic bonding material. That material was what made up the hub, too. It was a heck of a good pad for the way I handle a sander. Now the pads are made of rubber. I don't like them at all. I had to buy one recently because the last of my old ones are wearing out, and I can't get them anymore. Those pads were stiff, but they gave a little bit. You didn't have to tip them much, and you were putting a lot of pressure on that outside edge. You could tear the paint off easily. And to get that paint off, you've got to put pressure on it! A rubber pad isn't flat in the first place, so you can't hold it flat. In the second place, you can't get the same pressure on it, so it's slower cutting. When you tip it up on edge to tear paint off, the edge folds back, so you have to tip it some more. By the time you get any pressure at all, it's *way* up on edge. Now, you can't control a pad nearly as well when it's up on edge, plus when it is on edge, it's cutting a very small area, comparatively very fast. The farther up you go, the worse it gets. So, if you don't have a perfectly uniform rate, if you hesitate just a little bit, you'll take off a little more. Then if you happen to hit a soft spot or go through the paint somewhere, the more you're on edge, the more you'll take off there, too. That's how you get your digs and gouges. No, it's nearly impossible to do good work with a machine on edge. But everyone uses them on edge and that's where they screw up."

"Can you feel when you've gone through the paint layer?"

"You can see and feel both. Early in the game I took a big piece of plywood that had been cut out of an old Navy boat. It still had all the coats of Navy paint on it. I sanded the paint off and finished it all up. It takes four operations. First you tear the paint off. Then you go back over it with a fine paper and cut off all your digs and gouges. Then you go over it with a finer paper still and smooth it up. Then you go over it with a vibrating sander and take off all the little ripples. You see, every time you stop and go the other way with a disc sander flat, there's a little semicircle you've cut. Those show up in high-gloss paint, but a vibrator takes them right out. Well, anyway, I measured the thing before and after, and I took off $1/64$ of an inch — that's paint, wood, and everything in a normal removal.

"So you take off the minimum. When you take the paint off, you *just* take it off. No more! Quite often you leave a little paint here and there because you're going over it three more times. Each time you do, you're going to take off a little more. You don't want to take too much. And you want to keep that sander moving; if you stay in one place too long, you'll dig in. It takes a lot of practice and the right touch, I guess.

"Well, as I say, the business as a whole was pretty slow at first. I had a lot of convincing to do. Before I started, a really fine boat was hand planed. When you get done planking a boat, it's rougher than heck. A series of flat planks on a round hull leaves you a series of flats. You have to knock the edges off, so they'd hand plane them diagonally with big wooden planes. First one way, then the other. It was just a hell of a job. They'd get everything fair that way. Then they'd hand sand them with half a sheet of sandpaper on a big block. They'd sand and sand. They could do a beautiful job that way, but gosh, it was hard work. Time consuming, too. I could do in one day what it took a whole crew of men a week to do — hand planing and hand sanding.

"When I first started, they used to hand plane them for me, too. Gradually I gained their confidence, and they started leaving more and more for me. Man, they left some mighty rough ones, too. Some of the old fishing boats had quite a bit of flare in the bow. They'd have a lot of twist in those heavy planks as they narrowed to the stem. Lots of times they couldn't pull the lower ends all the way in and they'd leave the bow looking like a Venetian blind. Boy, I'd have to wear them all down....

"Back then, most of my work was on new boats. I'd say 75 percent was new boats and 25 percent was refinishing. There was an awful lot of wood boatbuilding going on. About 10 years ago things really slowed down. Now almost 100 percent of my work is refinishing. I think I've sanded four or five new boats in the last five years. Those were boats built by a private owner in his backyard — that type of thing.

"I charge $30 per hour for bottom sanding and $24 per hour for topsides. My charge has always been just a little below what the regular boatyards charge. I charge a little more for bottom sanding because of the difficulty and risk involved. Copper paint dust isn't any good for you. That's why I always wear a *good* respirator and my hood. It works pretty well. The air hose is to keep the glass shield from fogging up."

"You must have sanded quite a variety of boats over the years," I said.

"I've sanded small boats, big boats, fishing boats, sailboats, runabouts — just about every kind. I think the smallest was about 6 feet and the largest was around 175 feet. That was an old Army minesweeper. I sanded the biggest wooden pleasure boat built in the United States after the war. That was a 104-footer built for a wealthy eastern man by Vic Frank's yard: the *Kakki M*. She was a nice one, too. Nobody knew how much she cost, but at that time (1967), around a million bucks."

"Who's going to take over now that you've retired?"

"I don't know. Some other big dumb Irishman, I guess. The only requirement is to fit a size 46 coat and a size 5½ hat!

"I ran across a kid a while ago who wanted to try it. I don't know if he's got it, though. It takes a certain touch with your hands. I don't know what it is. It's a touch. You have to know what that damn machine is doing. When it hits a hump, you've got to know it's hit a hump — give it a little more, you see. I seem to have a talent at that; I can feel what a power tool is doing. But with hand tools I'm relatively no good, just a so-so mechanic. I don't have the same touch. With a power screwdriver, I can drive more damn screws than anyone else in the shop. With a hand screwdriver, there's plenty who are better.

"There's a talent to disc sanding. It's not something everyone could do, but there's a lot

of other people around who could if they wanted to. Most of them just don't want to. It's a dirty, miserable, hard job. Hell, a lot of guys wouldn't do it for the same wage they'd get in a boatshop drilling holes and putting in plugs; you simply couldn't get the guys to do it. That's probably why I've been so busy — nobody else wants it.

"You know, I was lucky. Everyone has a talent — something they're especially good at. Some people just fall into it. The majority, however, have to spend a lot of time looking for it, usually well into their 30s. One reason for so much mediocrity today is that people stop looking before they find it. A person may have to try many things, but he owes it to himself to try. Our failures and drifting are part of the journey, necessary to send us onward. Finding and exercising the talent is an essential step toward attaining true health, happiness, and fulfillment. I never would have been anything more than a so-so boatbuilder; fortunately, I landed on sanding at 26."

I, too, was fortunate. Dudley's presence on that crisp spring morning — laughing, singing, creating clouds — and the sharing of his knowledge has been an inspiration.

Handling a 14½-pound disc sander is enough of a job on a small boat in the best of conditions. Dudley handles it hour after hour on all sorts of craft, and from top to bottom. His work is thorough and fast, and he equips himself with respirators appropriate to the task.

Looking Good Again:
A Refinishing Story

Maynard Bray

THAT A MAGAZINE'S staff should get out of the office as much as possible is made all the more obvious by the following article. One day Maynard Bray stopped by Paul Bryant's boatyard in Newcastle, Maine, and was reminded of the tremendous efficiency and quality work underway at this small place. Maynard felt that both professionals and amateurs could learn a thing or two from Bryant's yard, especially regarding the refinishing of small boats. When we discussed an article, we realized we should cover Bryant's methods using a specific boat with common problems as an example. Maynard found an owner with a boat that needed refinishing and made the necessary arrangements with Paul, and we called in our trusty photographer, Benjie Mendlowitz. Judging from the response, the resulting article was one of our most successful efforts.

THE SCENE is Riverside Boat Company in Newcastle, Maine; the time is January 12, 1981; the temperature is 12 degrees at 12 noon. Paul Bryant, who runs the yard, is beginning to sand the Herreshoff 12½-footer *White Cap,** which is scheduled for a thorough refurbishing. He's doing this outdoors, where at the end of the working day the temperature will have dropped to 7 degrees.

Working with the weather, and in spite of it when he has to, is something Paul has grown up with. The yard was started by his father, and Paul has worked there since he was in the sixth grade. With only two other men besides Paul,

the yard maintains about 70 of the 90-odd boats it stores and does as good a job of it as you're likely to see anywhere. With few exceptions, the boats are stored outside under canvas covers during the winter, and the smaller ones are cycled through one of the two heated shops a few at a time until the weather breaks and the others can be worked on outside.

Riverside faces conditions similar to those familiar to many do-it-yourself owners: outside storage, limited time for each job, a schedule to meet, and the return of the same boat season after season. Presented here is only part of that story — the approach to a single refinishing job from beginning to end.

Power Sanding

Heavy-duty disc-type machines, held flat and kept moving, are used for sanding whenever possible, because they're the fastest way to fair and smooth a surface.

For fairing and shaping and for stripping off paint and varnish, the coarser grits of a very abrasive heavy paper called Greenbak (like that used in floor-sanding edgers) on a firm pad in a medium-speed (5,000 r.p.m.) grinder work best. A slower machine can be used, but it takes longer.

The finer sanding for smoothing up painted surfaces and feathering off flaked paint is best done with a low-speed (2,000 r.p.m.) disc-type sander/polisher with a soft foam pad. A higher-speed machine heats up the paint, making it so gummy that it clogs up the grit of the finer papers. Neither a vibrator nor a belt sander is used much, since they don't do as good a job and work more slowly.

The two machines favored by Paul are the Black & Decker model 4046 grinder (4,800 r.p.m.) with a very firm phenolic pad and 7-inch Norton "Bear" brand Greenbak metalite abrasive discs (#16-80), and the Rockwell model 661 (2,000 r.p.m.) with a Norton 8SR-K sanding-pad kit and 8-inch-diameter aluminum-oxide production-paper sanding discs (#36-220). Norton No. 10 disc adhesive, a type of contact cement, holds the discs to the foam pad.

The initial hull sanding and fairing, which in-

*White Cap is one of the so-called 12½-foot (waterline) class built by the Herreshoff Manufacturing Company of Bristol, Rhode Island. She is gaff-rigged and her overall length is about 16 feet. The class was designed by Nathanael G. Herreshoff, and the first boats, which were used on Buzzards Bay, were introduced in 1914. White Cap dates from 1929 and carries HMCo hull number 1107. It was with the cooperation of her new owner, H.W. Detert of Norway, Maine, that these photographs were possible.

cluded the bottom, took about five hours and consumed about 25 discs from #36 to #120 grit. Generally, the topsides were sanded with #100 and #120, the boot-top (which was taken more or less down to the wood for rescribing) with #80 and #100, and the bottom with #36.

Getting rid of old paint and varnish and fairing off *White Cap*'s transom is a snap with this grinder. The coarse #36 disc makes a quick job of it, and the firm pad enables one to build up more pressure for grinding off troublesome spots, aids in fairing the surface, and leaves crisp corners at the plank ends. Some further smoothing with #50, #60, and #80 grits is then done before changing machines.

The rest of the transom smoothing is done with a foam pad on the low-speed machine, starting with #80 grit and going to #100 and #120. Care must be taken at the sharp corners to avoid rounding them over. The entire process of stripping and sanding this transom took only about half an hour, and when it was finished, there were absolutely no sanding marks, and the surface was ready for refinishing. A dutchman, however, was later fitted in way of the upper rudder gudgeon where the wood had gone bad.

A foam-backed disc is the most effective way to smooth up a hull for painting. Used with #60, #80, or #100 paper, it does a beautiful job of knocking down the high spots and feathering out the transition between painted and unpainted surfaces — provided the paper is sharp, that is. It's a waste of time to use dull discs; they only polish the surface without fairing or feathering it. When feathering by hand, a coarse grit, say, #60, will do the work faster and better — just as with the machine. Final sanding (power or hand) at this stage will be with #120 grit paper.

Scribing the Waterline

A crisply painted level waterline goes a long way toward making a paint job look right. There are a number of ways to mark it so it's level, but one of the simplest and most direct was employed on *White Cap*. (Her existing line, like the waterlines on so many older boats, was neither straight nor decisively marked.) First, the boat is leveled athwartships and two straightedges running in that direction are set up — one forward and one aft, as shown in the photograph. These, of course, must also be made level. From there on, it's a case of one person "sighting in" on the imaginary plane between the two straightedges while another person adjusts the pencil until it corresponds with that plane. Gordon and Jason are doing that in the photo, making marks on the hull about a foot apart.

The individual marks are then connected with a continuous pencil line by means of a stiff batten held on edge, that is, held square with the waterplane. This batten is hand held as shown and need not be very long.

A full-length batten, flexible enough to conform to the marked line when temporarily nailed against the hull, is placed so its top edge is on that line.

Scribing tools can be adapted from worn-out hacksaw blades or files, or whatever else is handy and can be used to cut a good scribe line — one that is sharp enough to look good and deep enough to last for a few years. Scribe lines are a great aid in painting the waterline or boot-top but they all fill up with paint eventually and have to be battened off and cleaned out occasionally. The tool shown here was made from a piece of 1/16-inch brass, filed so it will scrape out a shaving when pulled along the batten.

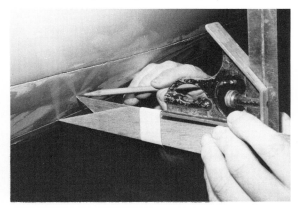

For each width of boot-top, a set of these sliding wooden pointers has been made up, a 1¼-inch-wide pair being used here. The assembly is kept level (by means of the spirit level built into the try square), while the lower pointer is placed in the scribe line representing the waterline, and the top pointer is slid into contact with the hull and marked with a pencil where it touches. From there on, the process of getting a scribed line at the top of the boot-top is exactly the same as for the waterline. No seam compound has yet been applied to the topsides, so the open hull seams are much in evidence.

Stripping the Brightwork

Using only scrapers, always kept sharp with a file, most of the varnish is stripped off. (A single application of chemical paint remover on the coamings speeded up the work a bit by softening the surface coats.) All the wood is oak and was weathered and stained in places. Careful scraping gets rid of most of the discoloration — bleach has been found ineffective and is not used at all. Almost all the scrapers have at least a slight crown to their blades so sufficient pressure can be brought to bear on a flat surface and peel off a good shaving. Grinding and filing can shape them to fit almost any surface. A fair amount of strength is needed for good control, however; otherwise, the tool is inclined to chatter, or the corners, even if filed off a bit, tend to dig in.

It's often easier to remove all the metal fittings than it is to scrape, sand, and varnish around them. *White Cap*'s were all taken off before any scraping began. The entire stripping and scraping job on this boat took about four hours.

If you've never wooded down a round spar by dry scraping, by all means try it. It's the quickest method by far, and you don't need a great deal of strength. Just keep the scraper sharp by frequent filing (use a flat mill file). The small and convenient wooden handle is yard built — only the hardened steel blade came from the store. It was simply screwed to the handle.

A fairly wide and slightly crowned blade is best for flat surfaces. Here, with the varnish removed, the weathered wood is scraped away to expose the oak's real beauty. The big-handled commercial scraper is OK here where two-handed force is needed.

A small scraper, guided by the left hand and drawn along with the right, does a fine job of getting into the corner between the sheerstrake and the covering board and cleaning out all the old varnish and discoloration. Some of the other scrapers and the ever-present sharpening file are lying on the deck, along with a putty knife. A chisel or sharpened putty knife is sometimes useful in getting into corners where a scraper won't fit.

A convex scraper mates well with the concave

shape of the Herreshoff molded sheerstrake. A deft touch is needed, but it's not difficult to develop such a "feel" after a bit of practice.

Sanding the Brightwork

Sanding is the most tiring of all jobs, and more than a man-day of hand sanding alone was done on this boat — and that just on brightwork. Coarse #40 and #60 paper makes the work go faster, but it's still a big task to recover from a period of neglect (this is *White Cap*'s first year at Riverside). Sanding is done with the grain and a backing block is used on uneven surfaces to make them fair. Six sheets of #40, a couple of #50, one of #60, and two of #80 were used before the brightwork was ready for final sanding with #100 and refinishing. The feathering of peeling brightwork that has not been stripped is best done with coarse (about #60 grit) paper, after which the scratches can be sanded out by going "through the numbers" to #120.

The basic sanding technique is to go back and forth with the grain of the piece being sanded. A sanding block sometimes helps cut down the high places or even cut away the scraper marks, but much of the work is done with the folded piece of paper itself. Gloves keep the skin from being abraded.

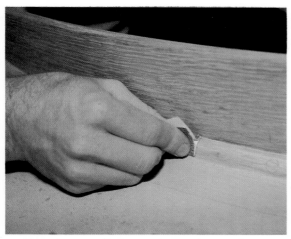

Torn into small pieces, the sandpaper fits into tight places.

The sheerstrake is sanded fair with the aid of this drum made from a short length of plastic drain pipe around which a sheet of sandpaper has been taped.

The rest of the sheerstrake is done barehanded in order to feel any unfairness.

A sanding block held like this evens out the edge of the newly installed covering board. Loose or blackened bungs in the sheerstrake and coaming were popped out and renewed, and the new ones were glued in with quick-setting epoxy. Great care must be taken during all hand sanding to keep from rounding off any corners that should stay crisp.

A strip of sandpaper wrapped around a putty knife gets into tight corners.

Moisture leaking in behind unbedded woodwork or joints is the greatest cause of lifted and discolored varnishwork. Rebedding is an effective solution, and that's what is being done here with these trim pieces. The opened joint between the top of the stern knee and the transom will be filled with a fitted wedge, since a warped transom plank prevents the joint from being drawn up tightly by refastening.

Filling and Surfacing

White Cap's hull has dried out, and her seams, particularly topside, have opened up. She'll swell again after a time overboard, so what is called for here is a soft, nondrying seam compound that will squeeze out. Paul chose Interlux No. 31, planning to resand and repaint the hull again in midseason once the seams have come together. In the future such excessive drying out will be prevented by a good buildup of paint and by keeping the boat out of the hot sun or heated sheds while ashore (except for a brief annual visit to the marginally heated paint shop). Trowel cement, Interlux No. 93, is used on nicks and scrapes; in subsequent years it will be used in the topside seams also, as long as they haven't opened up.

A wide, flexible putty knife ensures an even application of seam compound and trowel cement (no sanding is planned afterward), and masking tape keeps the compound from getting into the grain of the yet-to-be-varnished sheerstrake. A good vacuuming and priming are needed before the seams are filled with compound and before the hull planking is faced up with trowel cement; neither substance sticks well over dust or bare wood.

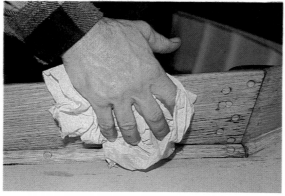

Paul uses a combination filler and stain as a base for all brightwork. He used Interlux No.

1643, a natural color, on this oak and thins it out to a brushing consistency with turpentine, brushing liquid (Interlux No. 333), or special thinner (Interlux No. 216), depending on the drying conditions. The excess is rubbed off after a few minutes and the remainder is allowed to dry overnight, just as with a fresh coat of paint or varnish. The filler-stain's purpose is twofold: (1) it fills the open grain and enables a glasslike varnish job, and the protection of the surface that goes with it, with fewer coats, and (2) it gives a more uniform appearance to the wood — some of which is old, some new, and some a bit weather stained.

Buildup

From this point on, it's a case of building up enough coats of varnish and topside paint to give good protection and appearance. This amounts to three coats of topside paint over the first thinned-down coat (for best adhesion, Paul used Interlux No. 220 semigloss right over the bare wood and for the subsequent coats as well) and five coats of varnish (Interlux No. 90) — the first one cut about 25 percent with turpentine. Sanding is needed between all coats; #120 grit is used with a fairly light touch on both the varnish and the paint. Each sanding is followed by vacuuming and wiping down with a tack rag to eliminate dust, and each new coat of paint is preceded by facing up with either trowel cement or seam compound, as appropriate, in order to have the hull virtually flawless when the buildup is complete. Trowel cement, if used after the buildup (i.e., just before the final painting) will cause flatting out of the gloss by "flashing through" the finish coats.

Final Sanding

Final sanding consists of hand sanding the varnish with #150 grit paper and machine sanding the paint with #220. As always, the varnish should be sanded insofar as possible with the grain of the wood, and care must be taken to go very lightly, if at all, on the sharp corners, such as on the toerail. Once the buildup is complete, Paul never sands the sharp corners, feeling that they are vulnerable to wear in service and need all the varnish they can get. Yet inside corners, such as those at the base of the coaming, often don't get enough sanding, so for good adhesion, it's important to be thorough there.

Final Varnishing

Since it's easier to cut paint into varnish than the other way around, the final coats of varnish are done before the final painting. Paul has found it best to apply the last two coats of varnish *without any sanding between them.*

Interlux No. 90 varnish, always strained before use, is what Riverside uses. Rarely are additives used — only a bit of Interlux No. 333 to keep the varnish from setting up too fast in unusually good drying conditions, or some turpentine to thin it in cold weather.

A very thorough vacuuming and wipe down (with a painter's tack rag) precedes all the varnishing, but these steps are particularly important before the final coats.

The 1½-inch brush used by Jason Burns, one of Paul's crew, is of badger hair, and those fine bristles will spread about as uniform a coat as it's possible to get. That's the whole secret to good varnishing: getting a coat that is nowhere thick enough to sag or run yet is sufficiently heavy everywhere to protect the surface and make it shine. Varnish has to be "flowed on," as the books all say, but flowed on evenly. Considerable brushing with the right technique is needed to achieve this end, no matter what kind of varnishing brush is used. Paul himself never bothers with fancy badger-hair brushes. The success of his varnishing depends more on the application techniques, an important one being speed. Paul advises that you go fast so the stuff is all brushed evenly before it starts to set up and then there's no need of an expensive brush.

Vertical or near-vertical surfaces are where the runs develop, so the varnish must be brushed out a bit more on them than on horizontal surfaces.

Final Cleaning

Dust and dirt are the enemies of high-gloss finishes, and they are most commonly produced by a dirty surface to begin with, dust in the air (which settles on the surface while it is still wet), dirt in the paint or varnish, and dirt in the brush. A thorough vacuuming — even on parts of the boat that aren't being worked on — and subsequent dusting off with a painter's tack rag (paint stores and auto body shops have them) will take care of any dust on the surface itself. But a clean shop that has been well swept down and vacuumed out beforehand is also a must. (If you're working outside, then get the boat far away from sources of dust, such as busy dirt roads, and do your work on a day when there is little or no wind.) Paul religiously strains all his paint and varnish before use; he is careful to keep his brushes cleaned out so that paint won't dry on their bristles, and he stores them where they won't get dusty. His consistently dust-free jobs make all this extra fussing worthwhile.

Getting enough varnish on the top of the coaming is ensured by applying it in this manner.

The varnish is then smoothed out with a light stroke along the top edge.

Any runs off the top edges must be picked up and blended into the coating now being applied to the sides, such as on this outside face. Every brushful of newly laid-on varnish is brushed out until it feels and looks smooth and even. Jason is doing only the vertical side of the coaming, stopping at the covering board, which will be done separately afterward.

Now the same treatment is given to the inside face of the coaming, always stroking back into the already-varnished area with the final smoothing.

For better control of the film thickness on top of the toerail, a small brush was used. That brush also comes in handy for varnishing in tight places where the bigger brush won't fit.

It's very necessary to sight frequently for runs,

sags, and bare spots while the varnish is still wet enough to make corrections. These imperfections show up better, of course, in good light. Note the graving piece or dutchman set into the transom in way of the rudder gudgeon, and the newly painted name — applied just before the final coats.

Final Coats of Paint

Getting a good gloss job is more than simply having a good surface to start with. Other things to consider are: good paint, with the right additives to make it flow well; a good brush that will lay on a paint film of uniform thickness in a reasonable amount of time; and the correct technique for laying it on. In regard to additives, Paul has this to say: "Painting is something that requires adjusting to the prevailing conditions. When painting outside in the wind or on a hot day, or in a shed where a hot-air furnace is running, there is always a need for adding a retarder (Interlux Brushing Liquid No. 333) to the paint. If the weather is cold, some thinning (with Interlux Special Thinner No. 216) is a must to achieve the right viscosity. And if the wind is blowing, it will probably need some retarder also." If drying conditions are really poor, certain solvents such as Japan dryer can speed up drying. For painting, Paul generally uses good-quality natural-bristle brushes, ones that are big enough to spread paint fast and fine enough to spread it evenly. *White Cap*'s topsides, however, were painted with a 2½-inch synthetic-bristle brush, which Paul admits doesn't stay as firm — and therefore is not as good for cutting in — once it has had some use.

One has to keep moving to avoid lap marks and the runs that sometimes go with them

(retarder helps here), and at the same time cut in accurately against other colors (such as the sheerstrake on *White Cap*). Paint put on too thin (brushed out too much) won't flow enough while drying to develop a good shine, and paint that is too thick (not brushed out enough) is almost certain to sag and run. The objective is to get a job that is between these two extremes while still cutting in accurately and leaving no bare spots. Brushing back into, rather than away from, the fresh paint, as Paul is doing here, tends to give a smoother coat.

The fastest and easiest way of cutting in is with a bigger brush than you'd imagine, turned on edge. Small brushes are of little use here — they just don't hold enough paint. When cutting in around the transom, Paul not only uses the brush on edge but also forces the bristles to separate into two groups, only one of which is actually being used for cutting in. Thus, only the needed amount of paint is being applied to the plank ends, where any excess would be difficult to get rid of.

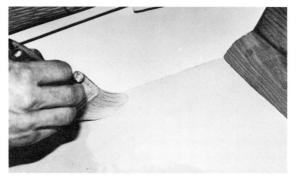

This is the proper way to hold a brush when cutting in against other paintwork or varnish. Cutting in, or lining off, as it's sometimes called, is done before the adjacent body of paint is applied. Care must be taken all the while to keep the brush moving in order to maintain a "wet edge" where the next brushful will be worked out.

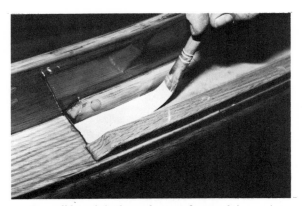

A small brush is the only type for applying paint with good control in tight places like this one. Paul usually has two or three sizes of brush at hand, for example, when painting a deck, and he uses the one most appropriate for the job.

With a good scribe line, painting a boot-top or waterline is quite easy. Again, the way to do it is with a brush that's big enough and turned on edge. Paint up into the scribe line; don't stop at its lower edge or you'll never have a good-looking job. At the lower edge, the masking tape keeps the red paint from being spread over the green, but the final line there, as at the top, will be done "with only a sure eye and a steady hand."

Bottoms are hidden from view once the boat is overboard and needn't be fussed with as

much. A big brush is called for here to get this nasty job done quickly. Cutting in can be done with a slightly smaller brush if you want, and it is done just as for the top of the boot-top — that is, the paint is run up into the scribe line, not stopped short of it. Unless the owner requests otherwise, Paul prepares boat bottoms for painting with only a serrated scraper — sandpaper is not used at all. He sticks with oil-based paint, which lends itself to scraping, unlike some of the vinyl bottom paints now on the market.

Completion

How much time did the refurbishing of *White Cap* take while at Riverside? The refinishing of the hull and spars, described here, consumed about 110 man-hours. Beyond that, about 40 additional man-hours were spent on repair (new toerails, covering boards, seat supports, transom repair, etc.).

A variety of materials were used, including 38 sanding discs, 46 sheets of sandpaper, 60 oak bungs, 2 ounces copper tacks, 72 screws, 1 pint varnish remover, 3½ pints wood filler stain, wood dough, ½ pint trowel cement, ½ pint seam compound, ½ pint bedding compound, masking tape, 8 pints paint, 5¼ pints varnish, 2 pints red lead, 1½ pints bottom paint, ¾ pint turpentine, ¼ pint thinner, ¼ pint brushing liquid, tack rag, and gold leaf.

Many elements combine to make up Riverside's efficiency, but one of its keys is good organization. As Benjie Mendlowitz, who took all the photographs and who has seen a lot of this type of work go on in other yards, observes, "Each step here is done in its proper order to completion and perfection before and in preparation for the next step. This is probably obvious, but it is the cornerstone of the whole operation. They don't work on 'areas' of the boat; they do *all* the scraping, then *all* the sanding, then *all* the filling, prime everything, varnish everything coat by coat, then paint in the same way."

It is doubtful that one who wasn't doing this type of thing every day and was without the experience of Paul Bryant and his crew at Riverside could get the same results in the same amount of time, but by utilizing these techniques, we feel certain that your spring outfitting will go faster and look better.

Paint on the hull interior and floorboards, and installation of the newly varnished seats just about completes the job on *White Cap*, except for reinstallation of the hardware.

Bedding compound, along with the good build-up of varnish over the wood, will keep moisture from behind fittings — like the mast partner bale — for a long time. While the metal fittings were off, they were cleaned of old paint and varnish and buffed up a bit, both jobs being made easier because the fittings weren't left on the boat. The Herreshoff nameplate lies on the deck — the next item to be put back in place.

Before arriving at Riverside, *White Cap* had been reframed and repaired in a mediocre way, so considerable time was devoted to making her look good in spite of this history. She had somehow developed a noticeable hump in the sheerline on both sides forward. New toerails, made higher where they join the stem, and lower in way of the hump, helped make her sheer look presentable, as did a faired-out and somewhat higher paint line at the bottom of the sheerstrake forward. The new garboards, however, which were apparently installed at the same time, aren't completely fair with the rest of the bottom planking, as can be seen in the photo.

Annie

Art Brendze

Annie was built on speculation by Brendze and Wester (now Arundel Shipyard, Inc.). Her construction is cedar on oak. The Honduras mahogany sheerstrakes provide a more solid base than cedar for anchoring the fastenings from the covering board. Below the ribbands on the port side lies a spiling batten clamped in place.

I N THE EARLY 1970s, while going over
some old issues of *Rudder* with my late friend
Capt. Francis Herreshoff, we came across the
plans of a small, rugged, double-ended yawl designed by Fenwick Williams in 1932. The Skipper, whose sentiments against yachts of fishboat
descent are well known, surprised me by making an exception here. He explained with enthusiasm that this was a remarkable little yacht,
that he had liked it ever since Fenwick had
drawn it, and that it had inspired him to draw
his Wagon Box design some 24 years later.
Needless to say, I was more than just a little impressed by this unusual endorsement of
another designer's work!

Several years later, Fenwick handed me a set
of rolled-up plans and said he thought that I
might "enjoy looking them over." To my great
pleasure, these turned out to be the very same
double-ender. As the photographs here will at-
test, I ended up doing a bit more with them
than either of us would have suspected at the
time!

Profit is not what motivated us at Arundel
Shipyard, Inc., to build this little gem. Instead,
this challenge was undertaken as a kind of "rite
of passage," for to succeed in living up to the
high degree of excellence implied by this design
would determine whether we were to be a special yard or just another plastic parking lot.

The decade between the end of World War
I and the beginning of the Great Depression en-
compassed the last years of America's Golden
Age of yachting. All over the country, designers
whose names now conjure up a quasi-religious
sense of awe and admiration were getting up

Above — At the stern-
post, a hood end of
plank is clamped and
fastened home. The
pencil lines scribed
along plank edges
form guides for
setting the plank
fastenings.

Left — With her
deck framing com-
plete, the port cov-
ering board is fitted
and clamped in place
for fastening. Along-
side the hull is Art
Wester's Francis
Herreshoff-designed
double-paddle
canoe.

Below — The view
from within the hull
provides a sense of
the amount of room
the boat has. The C-
clamps at right hold
the covering board in
place.

Annie was an impressive sight when she was planked and caulked. Her seams were painted after caulking to prevent the cotton from creeping.

Opposite — Annie's sweet lines are proudly revealed as she awaits the TraveLift which will lower her gently into the water.

designs that with hindsight we now call classics.

Marblehead, Massachusetts, during this period was a Mecca for many of the most gifted and creative of these men. W. Starling Burgess, B.B. Crowninshield, and L. Francis Herreshoff are only a few of the well-known designers who lived in this inspiring, yacht-oriented New England town. One could almost say that the very dynamics of the age were at home here, and examples of its excellence were commonplace.

Early each weekday morning, men such as Fenwick Williams, Murray Peterson, Aage Nielsen, and John Leavitt could be seen making their way to the Marblehead Depot to catch a Boston-bound train into work. Work for this group of young men was at the office of the John G. Alden Company on State Street, then perhaps the most successful and prolific yacht design and sales office in the world.

The yachts that this busy office turned out during those years represent some of the best and most popular of the period. Alden's small schooner-yachts, descendants of the much larger Gloucester fishing schooners, are perhaps the best known of these designs.

A few words about the relative size of the words "large" and "small" as pertaining to these boats are in order here. Although the average size of Alden's schooners could be set at around 50 feet on deck, they were considered small in their day and were absolutely small in relation to the Gloucestermen or the yachts of the generation before. *Annie* would have been considered tiny then.

The myriad of design problems associated with transforming a huge, heavy workhorse into a much smaller pleasure craft were a daily challenge to Alden's young draftsmen. Fenwick Williams and the rest of this Alden crew were responsible for more than 400 designs that were built and successfully sailed during those years! Stop for a moment and consider the depth of this unusual experience. How many of today's designers would gladly sell their souls to Sinbad for a similar opportunity?

With the coming of the Depression, the social

and economic standards of the world changed abruptly, and the average size of the American yacht had to shrink or face a dinosaur's death. Some of the Alden boys found themselves out of work during this period, as yachting was not very high on the country's priority list. Fenwick found himself with plenty of time to draw "on speculation." He speculated that perhaps someone might go for a small, more affordable yacht of big-boat proportion and character. *Annie*'s design was the result. Her specifications are as follows:

LOA	34'0"
LOD	24'0"
LWL	21'4"
Beam on deck	8'8"
Beam at waterline	7'10"
Draft	3'10"
Displacement	9,100 lbs
Sail area	333 sq ft
Cedar on oak construction	

The heritage that Fenwick drew upon to achieve his big-boat proportion and character is, of course, deeply rooted in 18th- and 19th-century workboat tradition on both sides of the North Atlantic. The Westray Yole of the Orkney Islands, the Scarborough Mule of the east coast of Scotland, the pink-sterned Bawley of Kent and Essex, the Manx fore and mizzen yawl, and the Falmouth Quay punt are all reminders of *Annie*'s Norse and British roots. On this side of the ocean, such old New England standbys as the Block Island cowhorn, the Eastport pinky, the Isles of Shoals boat, and the Hampton whaler join their European cousins in forming *Annie*'s husky workaday family tree.

While all of the above-mentioned craft were highly successful at hauling and fishing, none of them would be acceptable today as yachts. These boats, in spite of their fine seakeeping and other desirable abilities, would be considered to be too slow and cumbersome by a modern yachtsman, and the first mate would find little, if any, space below for comfortable accommodations. In *Annie*'s design, Williams accomplishes a successful transition from workboat to yacht, and it is this accomplishment that Skipper Herreshoff graciously recognized and appreciated.

Very soon after we started building *Annie*, an uncanny combination of large and small began to reveal itself — a harbinger of things to come. Most boats seem to shrink as the building process progresses. Not so with *Annie*! Every time we endeavored to fill her up with timbers, bulkheads, or deckbeams, she just seemed to get larger. This took some getting used to, and many a visitor to the yard would guess her length to be between 32 feet and 36 feet instead of 24 feet. At the float after launching, *Annie*

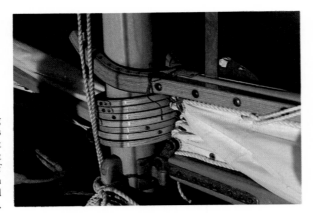

Opposite — Under sail *Annie* is comfortable and dry. Her rig is simple, powerful, and forgiving.

The traditional rig includes roped sails and bent oak mast hoops. Bar stock at the throat of the gaff lies in the slot when the gaff is peaked up.

steadfastly refused to look her size, and at sea her big act continues.

When sailing in a hard chance, *Annie* remains well mannered even if left grossly overcanvased. Her sensible, seakindly shape keeps her crew warm and dry at all times, while her rugged, experienced proportions instill a sense of safety and well-being even in extreme condi-

Vertical staving and paneled companionway doors lend an elegant traditional touch.

tions. In light air, she moves easily through the water, her sensation of speed a strange contrast to the lack of turbulence aft. And how many 24-footers have you seen lately that have plenty of room for a dandy little tender on deck? *Annie*'s handsome, varnished-mahogany tender was designed and built for us by Bill Peterson, Murray's son. His interest and commitment to this

The name *Annie* was chosen because at the time of her launch she did not have an owner; she was an orphan. To carry the parallel further, the tender that stows on deck or tows astern was named *Sandy*, after Annie's little dog.

project, as well as his family's close ties with Williams, added greatly to that all-important "strength of spirit" mentioned earlier.

Annie's handy, well-proportioned yawl rig is worthy of some special attention. The unusually long, light gaff is equal in length to the main boom, and when set, it is peaked up quite a bit higher than most. This is one of Fenwick Williams' trademarks, and it seems to impart to *Annie*'s hull an uncanny will to go to weather. All in all, *Annie* is contrary in every way to what most folks want to believe today. One latter-day doubter observed tersely that, "*Annie* seems to sail better than she has any right to."

When the sails are furled and everything is secured on deck, *Annie*'s size continues to hold out below. The visitor is astonished to find a large, comfortable cabin, not at all cramped by amenities usually found only on larger yachts. There are two extra-large settee berths and a huge, comfortable double. A two-burner Skippy coal stove lends a cozy warmth to the cabin and is fed through a separate, deck-loading coal bin. This bin can also be loaded with charcoal if desired, and it does away with most of the mess associated with having either of these two fuels in the cabin. There is 6 feet of headroom under the house and 6 feet 4 inches at the galley under the closed companionway hatch. Here one finds a good-sized sink and a two-burner cookstove for anyone too fastidious to cook with coal. *Annie*'s engine compartment is light and airy, and all sides of her husky little Sabb diesel are easily accessible.

Experience aboard *Annie* proves Fenwick Williams to be as innovative a designer as any of his younger plastic-oriented colleagues. Williams differs from these men through unequaled experience and an almost unique traditional memory. His ability to create a small, handy, timeless yacht of time-proven heritage will be his legacy to the history of American yacht design.

Whenever it comes time to commit to a course, the most desirable goals always seem to lie to weather. Fenwick Williams' old friend and colleague, Murray Peterson, often used to say, "Start only as you can hold out." Those of us who have reached the weather mark with *Annie* have held out well in spite of some heavy weather and occasional poor visibility. Our original goal of living up to the standards implied by this design has been achieved with a minimum of compromise. Now there is a warm feeling of satisfaction that comes when thinking of the *Annie* off on some future cruise, for her crew will reach their goals in safety and comfort — even if they should lie well to weather.

The Issues of Maritime Preservation

Peter H. Spectre

THE IMPETUS to publish a special section on maritime preservation stemmed from a series of conversations between Maynard Bray and Peter Spectre. Peter had read a lot of material on the subject, and Maynard had worked in the field for years, at Mystic Seaport full time and then later as an independent consultant. They were struck by the vast number of preservation projects underway and the sizable amount of money being spent, yet the issues — Why is this done? How much is too much? What are the goals? etc. — had stirred very little public debate. With Maynard's assistance, Peter began to gather as much material as he could on the subject and interviewed some of the key people in the preservation movement. In the meantime, we asked Lance Lee and Peter Stanford, two sincere preservationists with conflicting views, to state their cases for publication. The two Peters and Lance wrote the following articles that, when taken together, went a long way toward acquainting our readers with the "business" of maritime preservation and prompted them to take a more active role in the field by being aware and involved. Since maritime preservation is an emotional subject, we published many of the responses to this section in a follow-up forum in a later issue of the magazine. Not long afterwards, the British and Argentinians went to war over the Falklands . . . .

The repair of ships [in the Falkland Islands] was a fitful business, but it continued for years — sometimes weak, sometimes strong, depending on the moods of Cape Stiff and how many ships were hurt there.

Some of these vessels were so badly damaged that though they reached the Falklands, they were not worth repairing or, alternately, their owners or insurers did not want to make a further investment in them. These craft were condemned and put to use in a useful way as floating — or beached — storehouses.

— Karl Kortum, Chief Curator of the
National Maritime Museum at San Francisco

The relic-rich Falkland Islands together with the Straits of Magellan, account for almost everything left to collect: their extreme isolation, constantly fierce drying winds, coldness of water, and benign and vandal-free sparse population have combined to save what remains of America's Cape Horn trade.

— Eric Berryman, in "Scope of Collections
for Ships and Boats, National Maritime
Museum at San Francisco"

THE FALKLAND ISLANDS lie off the tip of South America, downwind from Cape Horn, and though they are a desolate place, they have been and continue to be the focus of attention for shipping interests and historic maritime preservationists. The Falkland Islands are a graveyard of remarkable ships; in fact, in Port Stanley alone there are enough recognizable hulks left over from the age of sail to keep the most demanding ship buff happy for weeks. They are a museum, a global treasure chest of structures and artifacts — the home of the 1856 wooden packet ship *Charles Cooper*, the 1851 wooden clipper *Snow Squall*, the wooden immigrant ship *Vicar of Bray*, said to be the last of the '49ers, and a number of other craft great and small, abundant with examples of unsurpassed excellence in the art of shipbuilding.

For more than a century the hulks in the Falklands received scant attention except from wool merchants and coal dealers, who used them as storage bins. Preservationists weren't interested until fairly recently, because there were more accessible ships in better condition to consider — the *Charles W. Morgan*, the *Cutty Sark*, the *Balclutha*, the *Star of India*, the *Falls of Clyde*, and many more. But when the more obvious ships to save had been dealt with, or so it seemed, the focus of the Karl Kortums, the Peter Stanfords, the Norman Brouwers, and the Peter Throckmortons — historic maritime preservationists all — turned to Port Stanley and became a virtual fixation, not only on the ships' availability, but on their uniqueness as well.

They weren't alone. I can't remember when I first heard about the treasures of Port Stanley, but when I did, I developed a strange fantasy. I imagined myself packing a small travel bag and saying quiet good-byes to my friends and relatives. I would get on the road, hitching rides south, traveling by car and truck, steamer and mailboat, until I somehow made my way to the Falklands. I would roam the gale-blasted shores

Opposite — The derelict schooners *Hesper* and *Luther Little* at Wiscasset, Maine. There is a move afoot to stabilize these ships.

217

The lumber schooner *C.A. Thayer* with a tug alongside off San Francisco's Hyde Street Pier. The steam schooner *Wapama* is moored beside the pier.

exploring wrecks, and somehow live happily ever after in the presence of artifacts from an era I was so unfortunate to miss.

I haven't left yet, but I better go soon, because if the preservationists have their way, the hulks of the Falklands will be the museum displays of New York, San Francisco, and who knows where else. Those Holy Grails will be waterfront attractions to be interpreted by curators and poked at by graduate students and used as scenic backdrops by office workers on their lunch hours.

A shame? Yes, it is, especially when you consider that these ships are part of our heritage and deserve considerably more than the type of slipshod preservation or restoration and maintenance so many others of their type have been accorded to date. If they are to be treated this way, they should remain in the Falklands until they turn to dust or for eternity, whichever comes first. It would be better for them and better for us.

In true archaeology, when they find a ruin, they call in the boys with the camel's-hair brushes. In ship restoration, they call in anybody and start mucking around indiscriminately. They say, 'Look at this, a ship. Let's make her whole again.' But they don't have the training or the skills for the job.
— Richard Fewtrell, Ship Restorationist

There are a number of experienced restorationists who will wholeheartedly agree, but there are many vessels that are notable exceptions. You can travel around the country and see some ships that have been excellently restored and meticulously maintained — the lumber schooner *C.A. Thayer* in San Francisco, the frigate *Constitution* in Boston, the whaler *Charles W. Morgan* in Mystic come immediately to mind. Yet these ships are from what Fewtrell calls "The Golden Age of Restoration," a period

when the ships to be saved were in reasonably good shape to begin with and the people who did the work, or at least directed the work, were experts who learned their trades on working ships similar to those being restored. A ship that has been out of service for a short time with a shipkeeping crew aboard is a far cry from a hulk on a beach that has gone unattended for decades. A restoration gang that has worked together for years and learned the maritime trades in the old manner — through apprenticeship — is a far cry from a well-intentioned crew of greenhorns cadged together at the last minute as meager funds would allow.

Ironically, as the number of restorable historic ships and the skilled people who work on them declines, the desire to restore ships increases, and the assumption is that where experience fails, money — lots of it — triumphs. The few projects of the past have become the many of the present, so much so that ship restoration could be termed a growth industry. It seems as if nearly every port worthy of the name has a project going or an exhibit planned or the hope to get something together in the near future. According to a report for the National Maritime Museum at San Francisco prepared by Eric Berryman, "There are 128 historic ships preserved in the United States. . . . Many are in private hands and serve as props to foster commercial or some other independent enterprise. They include restaurants, stationary schools, and a showboat. Others are still actively at work. . . . Still others are in various stages of uneasy restoration. . . ." Any reasonable person who spends even a short time looking and listening must come to the conclusion that there's a lot of activity around the country, and it seems to be picking up rather than slowing down.

Disregarding the whys of the preservation boomlet, let's consider the diminishing number of "subjects" to be saved and the historical value of some of the projects that are being promoted — two vital matters that have led the critics of ship restoration to charge that any old ship is fair game for the preservationists.

I think the idea that there are people who want to restore everything is a bogeyman that has been raised by the people who don't want to restore anything. The real problem is the amazing misapplication of resources. They seem to be trying to save any ship that is lying around handy, not with any real philosophy behind them. They figure their waterfront needs a ship as a tourist attraction and they grab the first thing available.

Norman Brouwer, Ship Historian, South Street Seaport, New York City

Norman Brouwer ought to know. He has gained some measure of fame for his annotated lists of ships and wrecks extant around the world that can in some way be termed "historic." He has found, for example, that there are 15 lightships being preserved in the United States, 14 of them built since 1900, and there are about as many World War II submarines being saved. No one can argue successfully that lightships and submarines aren't historic vessels, but in an age of finite resources, one can certainly argue that a few representative lightships — perhaps one on each coast — should be enough for the most steadfast preservationist. But the lightships and submarines were available and the government was giving them away. They would make nice tourist attractions, would they not? And they may very well go a long way in revitalizing aging waterfronts.

Lightships and submarines are not in short supply, but American-built and owned deepwater sailing ships are. There can be no argument that the ocean traders, especially the Downeasters, have a firm hold on our romantic imagination, and any museum or historical society that could count one in its collection would be in an enviable position. But there are none available for restoration. The last reasonable possibility, the 1899 Maine-built steel bark *Kaiulani*, was in restorable condition in the Philippines in the 1960s, was acquired by the National Maritime Historical Society in trust for the people of the United States, was subsequently unsatisfactorily managed and maintained, and as a result was taken to the San Francisco Maritime Museum on a barge in unrestorable pieces. All that remains of this once-proud ship, acclaimed by Peter Stanford of the National Maritime Historical Society as "the last of the square-riggers that built the United States and made the Republic's flag famous at sea," are some rusting plates on a San Francisco pier.

There are a few unreasonable possibilities left in the Falkland Islands, specifically the wooden ships *Vicar of Bray, Charles Cooper*, and *Snow Squall*, but they are relics whose restoration to floating condition is unanimously considered to be virtually impossible without building new ships around them at enormous expense. The best to be hoped for them is that they could be moved to this country and exhibited as-is under cover, still at substantial expense. Norman Brouwer estimates just the stabilization and moving expenses to New York of the *Charles Cooper* to be on the order of $1,000,000 to $2,500,000, not including housing and exhibition of the ship in an as-found

condition. Even so, he feels the expense would be worth it: "When you see the remains of the *Cooper*, you can walk around on the original decks, you can see beams, knees that are 8 feet in height, cut out of trees that were in our forests 120 to 130 years ago. You can see fine workmanship, something people who build replicas today don't understand."

Norman Brouwer, like other levelheaded preservationists, is in a quandary, however. He, more than most, recognizes the value of the *Charles Cooper*, which he calls "the best-preserved wooden-hulled square-rigger built in this country left in the world as far as we know." He speaks with awe of a ship that symbolizes the craftsmanship of mid-19th-century shipwrights, of beading even on timbers that are normally out of sight, of his hours crawling around inside her with a flashlight to record as much about her structure as possible. Yet he knows that unless the *Cooper* is handled with skill and the utmost of care, her utility as an artifact for scholarly study will be destroyed. He would love to see her moved from the Falklands to the United States and placed under cover as an educational exhibit, complete with interpretive displays. "I would treat the *Cooper* as an artifact — something that has never been tampered with, unlike the *Constitution*, which has been rebuilt over and over again and nobody knows what she looked like originally."

This is the essential "why" of ship preservation — to demonstrate with a physical object the way things were and to allow us to learn something of our past without having to resort to models, photographs, and manuscripts — which, while worthwhile in themselves, cannot equal the real thing. As Brouwer says, "To acquire a ship to add spectacle to your waterfront is not to me pure maritime preservation."

C.A. Thayer in a gale off Cape Cabrillo, California, in 1957.

The hulk of the *Vicar of Bray* in the Falkland Islands. The plan is to move this ship's remains to San Francisco, to be put on permanent display there.

We believe that in a seaport-waterfront experience, you have to have a big ship. She has to be a monument, really, that attracts people. We also feel she has to interpret man's ocean experience.

— Peter Stanford, President of the
National Maritime Historical Association

That's the rub, of course. Many ship preservationists equate the size of an exhibit with pulling power at the gate and the ability of the spectator to appreciate what he is seeing. For them, photographs won't do it; models won't do it; interpretive multimedia displays won't do it. So recent acquisitions to demonstrate America's deep-water maritime heritage include South Street's *Peking*, a 347-foot four-masted bark built in Hamburg, Germany, and the *Wavertree*, a 274-foot iron ship built in Southampton, England; and the Galveston (Texas) Historical Foundation's 149-foot iron bark *Elissa*, built in Aberdeen, Scotland. The tenuous connection of those ships to the cities where they are preserved is glossed over. They're splendid ships, aren't they? As Harry Allendorfer of the National Trust for Historic Preservation says, "The connection of the *Elissa* with Galveston is not tenuous at all. The *Elissa* did visit Galveston twice. She is typical of the hundreds of ships that visited Galveston, and she is the only one around. If you had a ship that was homeported in Galveston, that would be fine. But you don't."

This is the only-game-in-town theory of ship preservation, brought about in some part by economics. Maritime museums, historic seaports, and ship preservation in general are expensive propositions, and like too much else in our society, there is a feeling that money will flow toward spectacular projects, those that can recoup their expenditures through gate receipts and grants from private and public benefactors. Historical groups don't like to admit it — after all, they are dealing with Culture — but to draw people and money, you need an attraction. Signs and billboards are tacky, of course, but big ships with their masts scraping the sky aren't: they are the perfect way to capture the errant passerby, who thinks to himself, "H'mmm. Look at those masts scraping the sky. I think I'll drop down there and have a look."

So, too, the ships serve as a base of substantiality to attract large contributions. Like college alumni who have a habit of donating to their alma mater when the football team enjoys a winning season, private and public donors have a habit of contributing to maritime projects that have a big, visible ship. How else can one explain the fact that huge sums of money are granted for ship preservation and small sums for research, data collection, small craft, and training?

I'm convinced that government money is required for ship preservation, because the size of the projects is beyond the resources of private groups.

— Karl Kortum, Chief Curator of the
National Maritime Museum at
San Francisco

The overwhelming bulk of the funds for large-ship preservation is going to come from the private sector. . . . The money is going to come from corporations, foundations, and individual citizens who see value in this heritage.

— Peter Stanford, President of the
National Maritime Historical Association

Kortum and Stanford are fast friends who, although they see the world of resources differently, are at the core of the large-ship preservation movement. In fact, they *are* the large-ship preservation movement, in the sense that they are the visionaries who have crusaded for years to save countless ships. Through their writings and speechmaking and lobbying, they have kept the maritime community's nose to the save-the-ships grindstone, and the tonnage they have managed to acquire over the years would make Stavros Niarchos envious. Kortum, especially, has been a powerful force. Almost singlehandedly he brought to San Francisco the *Balclutha* (256 feet WL), the *C.A. Thayer* (156 feet WL), the ferryboat *Eureka* (300 feet), the tug *Hercules* (139 feet WL), the paddlewheel tug *Eppleton Hall* (100 feet), the steam schooner *Wapama* (204 feet), and the hay scow *Alma* (59 feet). In addition, he has acted almost as a broker to get ships placed in other locations, among them the *Elissa* in Galveston and the *Polly Woodside* in Australia. His latest project is to rally the forces to move the wrecked *Jenny S. Barker* from South Georgia Island off Cape Horn to Portsmouth, New Hampshire.

Peter Stanford, who is based in New York, has fewer ships to his credit but has been amazingly successful in marshaling public opinion and getting organizations off the ground — significantly, the National Maritime Historical Society and its magazine *Sea History*, and the South Street Seaport Museum, of which he was director. Unlike Kortum, who tends to be colorless, he is a vibrant personality who makes compelling arguments for his cause.

Both men have come to their points of view on the sources of preservation funding through success with their favored methods. Stanford has raised millions of dollars by appealing to corporations and wealthy individuals in support of the South Street Seaport, the *Wavertree*, and such unsuccessful projects as the *Kaiulani*, the *Alice Wentworth*, and the *Alexander Hamilton*. Kortum, on the other hand, has managed to turn a small, privately funded local effort into a Congress-mandated and funded National Maritime Museum by skilled and quiet, but effective, political maneuvering. (In fact, he had his National Park Service-administered museum named the National Maritime Museum at San Francisco so quietly that other museums who might have considered themselves worthy of the appellation were caught standing still.)

The source of funding is an important matter because of the huge expenses involved in acquiring, restoring, and maintaining historic ships, particularly wooden ones. For example, the restoration of the 88-foot schooner *Bowdoin* is estimated to be $300,000 to $385,000; that of the U.S.S. *Constellation* to be $2,500,000. With scores of projects around the country competing for the same dollars, how one goes about raising money can mean the difference between success and failure. No wonder that Karl Kortum thinks the federal government is the answer.

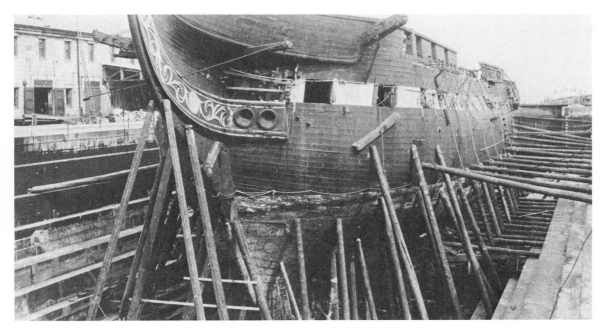

The *USS Constitution* undergoing restoration in the Charlestown (Boston) Navy Yard's drydock number 1 in 1927. Contributions from thousands of schoolchildren helped pay for the ship's extensive rebuilding.

Restoring the upper-works of the passenger steamer *Sabino* at the Mystic Seaport's shipyard. Being able to work on her under cover is a significant advantage.

Recently, a third source of funds has come on the scene — the National Trust for Historic Preservation. The organization's Maritime Division, headed by retired Navy Captain Harry Allendorfer, has created a controversy of sorts because of the large amount of grant money it has disbursed in the last few years.

The National Trust is a foundation, chartered by Congress, and part of its funding comes from the private sector and part from the federal government, giving it a quasi-governmental or quasi-private aura, depending on your point of view. The Trust was organized in the late 1940s to look after this country's landbound heritage, but in the 1970s, after intense lobbying on the part of the ship preservationists, it redefined its charter and included maritime preservation as part of its work. As a result, it has granted more than $5,400,000 in matching funds in the last few years and has gained substantial leverage in the maritime preservation community in a very short time. Most of that money — $5,000,000 in fact — was granted in one year, 1979, as a result of a special appropriation from Congress. That amount was a one-time grant of funds to make up for many years of emphasis on landbound projects. Nobody expects such a large appropriation in the future years — 1980 and 1981 federal budgets for NTHP grants made no express provision for maritime preservation, but the National Trust made available $100,000 in each of those years for maritime projects.

Such a large sum from a single source is enough to get a group of money-strapped maritime preservationists quite agitated, to say the least. Everyone has an opinion about how this grant money should be administered, with the result that few people are satisfied with the division of money. For example, the large-ship preservationists suggest that not enough money has been allocated fast enough to hand the difficult projects they have on hand and contemplate in the future, while the proponents of skills training and data collection feel they have been neglected in favor of the more visible, larger-than-life projects. In actuality, the large-ship restoration and preservation projects have been winning out — approximately 60 percent of the National Trust funds has gone to them. The largest grants went to three ships: $436,532 to San Francisco's liberty ship *Jeremiah O'Brien*, $600,000 to Baltimore's U.S.S. *Constellation*, and $500,000 to Galveston's *Elissa*.

Money isn't the problem. In fact, the influx of large sums of money is not a good thing at all. What is required — given that a restoration project by its nature is going to be a long, drawn-out affair — is a steady, modest income. Once that restoration starts to roll, it's imperative to have regular income and a commitment from the parent body to make sure you have the income. You can't do a proper job on a stop-go basis.

—Richard Fewtrell, Ship Restorationist

Richard Fewtrell is a bitter man. He spent seven years at South Street Seaport training a yard crew and laying the groundwork for the restoration of the *Wavertree*, but the funds ran out and he and his crew were laid off. During that period, large sums were raised for acquisitions — most spectacularly to purchase the *Peking*, a vessel similar to the *Wavertree* but in better condition — which is all well and good, but if you put all your money into acquisitions, you don't have much left for restoration and maintenance. Caught between the proverbial rock and a hard place, the overextended Seaport found itself lacking the money and other resources to maintain the ships it had, never mind restore them to their original, historic condition. Now the original purpose of the Seaport — to preserve ships in an environment that is representative of the late 1800s when South Street was truly "the street of ships" — has been temporarily set aside while the museum locates more funds for the preservation projects. In the meantime, the shoreside part of the Seaport is being commercially developed by the Rouse Corporation, which was the developer of Boston's Quincy Marketplace, and we are likely to see the creation of a fashionable area of food shops and boutiques. Presumably money realized by commercial development will go into the eventual restoration of the ships, but by then Richard Fewtrell and his trained crew will be using their talents elsewhere, and the preservation effort will be back to square one.

A sailing ship built for ocean voyaging is an artifact of compelling power. She is an expression of purpose, will and work in which men invested more than we generally invest in the furniture of our lives — how much more! That is what hits and staggers the bored suburbanite, or the child of the urban slum who comes to one of the ships of our long story. It doesn't hit people with words, it comes with the mute testimony of the thing itself.

— Peter Stanford, in *The Ships that Brought Us So Far*

Her deck, once red with heroes' blood,
Where knelt the vanquished foe,
When winds were hurrying o'er the flood,
And waves were white below,
No more shall feel the victor's tread,
Or know the conquered knee; —
The harpies of the shore shall pluck
The eagle of the sea!

— from "Old Ironsides" (September 14, 1830) by Oliver Wendell Holmes

Both Holmes and Stanford, though separated in time by more than one hundred years, are trying to do the same thing — galvanize support for ship preservation projects. Holmes was outraged by the Navy's decision to dispose of the frigate *Constitution*, and his poem was instrumental in swaying the public opinion toward the expenditure of funds for the repair of the ship. Stanford is saddened by the lack of commitment in this country to the preservation of historic ships, and through his National Maritime Historical Society, has been at the forefront of the preservation effort here and abroad. Like Holmes, Stanford uses his considerable power of persuasion to create desire, garner resources, and make things happen. Like Holmes, he leaves the actual work — the restoration and maintenance — to the experts.

But Oliver Wendell Holmes was lucky. He lived in an era when, if you had the desire and money to restore a ship, you also had the resources, both skilled tradesmen and authentic materials, to do the job correctly. You had the lumber, the fittings, the goops, and the gunks that could put your ship back into the condition of her original build. What's more, you could be sure that the use of those materials was authentic, because the men you employed knew what they were about. Peter Stanford isn't so lucky. He lives in an era when, even if you are long on desire and money (which, alas, is not true anyway), you are short on both skilled tradesmen and authentic materials, particularly large timbers for wooden ships. Practically all gear used on today's ship restorations must be custom made to be authentic, and this fabrication must

be done by people who know what they're doing. Unfortunately, these people are few — in fact, there aren't enough of them to go around. You can raise sea chests full of money and fill our ports and museums with newly acquired historic ships, but if you don't have the people to take care of them and the *desire* to do the job right, you will wind up with ships that are caricatures, not floating symbols of our proud heritage.

Some ship restoration work today is well done. A lot isn't.

—Norman Brouwer, Ship Historian
South Street Seaport

The main reason why many ship-restoration projects are poorly done is the lack of standards, helped along by such other factors as the dearth of proper funding, the lack of understanding about what constitutes accurate restoration, the poor ordering of priorities that puts tourist attraction ahead of proper preservation, and the institutional hamstringing or whatever that prevents the leaders of the preservation movement from insisting on historical accuracy. On the latter point, Harry Allendorfer of the National Trust for Historic Preservation said this when asked about the poor quality of the work to date on South Street Seaport's *Peking*: "We have great respect for the autonomy of the owner. Who are we to criticize the very prestigious board of directors? There are reasons. One of the reasons that I know of from talking to people there is that they wanted, with the little bit of money they had, to get the *Peking* to look like a ship at least. Granted, for the super sailor, it's not doing the trick. But to the little kid and his mother and the people coming down there and taking a look, it's giving them a feel for a square-rigger."

John Carter, director of the Maine Maritime Museum, sees this as a common perception of ship restoration, that of serving up "the spirit, the essence, the nostalgia. This is what many ships in museum atmospheres have been relegated to — the capturing of an essence of the past. This is what many in the ship-preservation movement allude to about 'saving ships.' We're not saving ships, we're hoodwinking tourists — often at the vessels' expense."

Indeed, the ships suffer. Not everywhere, however. At Mystic Seaport they did suffer for many years, but in the last decade or so, the administration there saw the light and reexamined both the purposes of the museum and the methods used to see that those purposes were carried out. Standards were set in all areas — restoration, preservation, and, most important, maintenance — and the result has been a continued upgrading of the museum's ship collection. Nowhere is this more obvious than in the restoration of the passenger steamer *Sabino*, which is a working display and a model for other restorations of the type. The project took careful research, a dedicated yard crew, and an iron-fisted leadership that would settle for nothing less than a proper job. It also took the willingness of the museum's board of trustees to forgo future acquisitions of ships, at least until the present collection is put into proper order. But to view the collection at Mystic is not always to understand the commitment behind the scene, which reflects the emphasis on preservation, as opposed to promotion.

Standards have worked for Mystic and can work for other museums and historical societies as well, but surprisingly, they don't seem to exist on a broad basis. Again, John Carter: "I would like to see restoration projects reflect: (1) a percentage for research, (2) a percentage for approved consultation throughout the project, (3) monies for materials and personnel to carry out restoration, (4) a percentage for documentation, (5) a percentage for development of an ongoing maintenance program once restoration is finished, and perhaps a visit after a year by another approved consultant to gauge the success of the maintenance program." Such broad-based standards do not presently exist (most of the money goes for item no. 3 alone); the closest thing to them are the National Trust standards, drawn up for house and building restorations, not ships, and the National Park Service standards, which apply only to work done by that organization. Surely, they should be given serious consideration before any future acquisitions are made by any organization.

In San Francisco the extraordinary opportunity exists to create a Mount Rushmore of the Sea reasonably easily and at relatively modest cost by acquiring two additional square-riggers which would, in company with the Balclutha, *re-create the "forest of masts" described with wonder by visitors in 1849 and 1850.*

— Eric Berryman, in "Scope of Collections
for Ships and Boats, National Maritime
Museum at San Francisco"

Look at this [the Berryman Report]! It's a shopping list for new acquisitions, and we are having difficulty enough taking care of the ships we already have.

— Harry Dring, Foreman,
National Park Service, San Francisco

Harry Dring is a man of strong opinions. He's also the man who is most responsible for the excellent restoration and ongoing maintenance of the amazing collection of large vessels brought to San Francisco by Karl Kortum. It's safe to say, in fact, that if it weren't for Dring, the ships at San Francisco would be in sorry shape. And the National Maritime Museum at San Francisco, like Mystic Seaport, is respected around the world for its accomplishments.

No matter how organized the San Francisco museum is, however, taking care of the present collection is a struggle. The restoration of three of the ships — the *Jeremiah O'Brien*, the steam schooner *Wapama*, and the tug *Hercules* — has not been completed yet, the remains of the *Kaiulani*, which are supposedly to be displayed, are tucked away out of sight and mind, and much maintenance is required for the other ships. One has to wonder, then, about the wisdom of following the recommendations of the Berryman Report, which contemplates the creation of a "forest of masts" by acquiring "square-rigged former merchant vessels (1) that are still afloat, (2) those that are hulks but whose physical condition is sound enough to justify restoration, and (3) those already in museum collections that may have become available."

Harry Dring is a man of strong opinions because he, and a precious few other people like him, has to deal with the realities of the visions of the Berrymans, the Kortums, the Stanfords, and the Throckmortons. He has to organize the workforces, locate the materials, keep the ships afloat, maintain the exhibits, and perform all the myriad tasks required to keep large wooden, steel, and iron ships in a museum environment. One must wonder what he thinks about Berryman's statement that "Maintenance is not a major factor because deterioration can be brought almost to a halt by modern preservation methods." Perhaps Dring and his overworked compatriots should be making the decisions about what ships should be left in their graves at the ends of the earth.

[The Falkland Islands are] the most incredible, accessible ship graveyard in the world: a unique repository of American, British, and Canadian nautical antiquity.

— Peter Throckmorton, Curator-at-Large
National Maritime Historical Society

So we're back to the Falklands. While a huge amount of work remains to be done in this country, another group is trying to figure out a way to "save" the *Charles Cooper*, the *Vicar of Bray*, the *Lady Elizabeth*, and a host of others. I encourage them to think about the consequences of their plans. I suggest that those activist preservationists who remain consider a rational policy for selecting historic ships for preservation and a set of restoration and maintenance standards for the ships we already have on hand.

The Testimony of the Thing Itself
Peter Sanford

FOR THREE THOUSAND years, man voyaged across deep water under sail. We have come to the end of that chapter of our story in our lifetimes. In it, we invented our languages, our laws, the trades we live by — and much of what we learned came to us through our experience sailing on the wind across wide oceans.

The last of the deep-sea merchant sailing ships that carried our story for so long are scattered about the globe, rusting and rotting away in quiet corners of the world ocean. In another generation, they will all be gone, except for the few we have been forehanded enough to save.

We save odd things in our passage through the generations: an Egyptian temple, a Chinese vase, a Flemish painting. It is, of course, the glory and part of the purpose of man that his work lives across the turning generations, that he knows and acts on what other men lived through and learned before his time.

Have we nothing, then, to learn from our ships? Each of these ships was a little world, a planet traveling in the divided universe of sea and sky, fashioned with the learning of millennia to battle waves and catch the winds of distant skies. We have inherited a great body of song and story from the men who sailed in these ships, and we have not lost Solomon's wonder at "the way of a ship in the sea."

Our sailing ships commanded men's admiration and loyalty in their time, and men come back to them, today, to learn, to extend their understanding of how man got where he is in the world, and what it was really like along the way.

The citizens of London knew that a remarkable thing had been done, a thing that changed their world, when Francis Drake brought his *Golden Hind* back from a freebooting voyage around the world in 1580. Accordingly, they saved the little ship; years later, the Venetian ambassador reported her lying in a dock in the lower reaches of the Thames. But time and decay caught up with her; after that she vanishes from our records.

Other ships have seized men's imaginations and so have been preserved. Nelson's *Victory* of 1765 was saved and carried the Admiral's flag in Portsmouth in World War II while Nazi bombers shook her frame in dry dock. Our frigate *Constitution* of 1797 was saved by public outcry and public contribution and is maintained afloat by the U.S. Navy in Boston today, where the public may visit her. The *Constellation* of 1797, rebuilt as a corvette in the 1850s, is undergoing restoration afloat in Baltimore, after many vicissitudes. The *Vasa*, a great Swedish warship sunk in 1628, has been raised and is being preserved by a major national effort.

Viking ships have been recovered from funeral mounds in Scandinavia, and remains of

The *Vicar of Bray*.

medieval ships are being recovered from the drained fields of Holland today. In New York, we saved the stem of the Dutch *Tijgre*, burnt here in 1613, when it appeared as the Seventh Avenue subway was being dug in 1916; we failed to locate the rest of the hull when the foundations of the World Trade Center were dug in 1968–69.

But the "general traders" or "merchantmen" or "deep-watermen," the merchant sailing ships that did the world's ocean carting a century ago, and well into the lifetimes of men now living, have vanished with few exceptions. What of those exceptions — what makes a ship live on, supported past her sailing life?

The instinct to save our ships runs deep. When William Webb, the designer of the *Young America*, saw her off on her maiden voyage in 1853, he said to her captain: "Take good care of her, Mister. When she's gone, there'll be no more like her."

That was more than 120 years ago, when big clippers like the *Young America* raced the steamship and the clock of technological change, and, making the fastest passages ever recorded under sail, did indeed seem to make the sun stand still in the sky.

Time has passed since then, and countless ships that should have been saved, weren't. Despite great effort on the part of dedicated preservationists, a number of important ships, like the *Glory of the Seas*, *Tusitala*, and *Benjamin F. Packard*, were not saved. But is it so much to save an old hulk? You have to see the ships, and walk their decks, to know the answer to this question. These old ships gain power past their time when they are, in fact, preserved and men come to walk their decks as other men walked them in another time.

It is partly the world the ships come out of that draws us, a world of half-forgotten ideas, and of real winds that blew in vanished sunlight. It is a grey dawn making up over a smoking sea, with the ship's whole fabric straining in moving air and water, in a world wider, stranger, tougher, and often more lovely than the world we know, a world in which, if you look at it carefully, you see that time itself is different, more diffused across experience, less crackling in its passage, more taken up in rhythms not of our own making. Events in such a world come not in a nervous string, but in a broad tapestry of experience.

And it is also the ships themselves. A sailing ship built for ocean voyaging is an artifact of compelling power. She is an expression of purpose, will, and work in which men invested more than we generally invest in the furniture of our lives — how much more! That is what hits and staggers the bored suburbanite, or the child of the urban slum who comes to one of the ships of our long story. It doesn't hit people with words, it comes with the mute testimony of the thing itself.

The matter of old ships, in fact, is a bit beyond our verbal reach. A hundred years from now, men will say very clearly why they were important, in dimensions we still grope after. They will not think well of us for what we overlooked and lost in our time, that we could have saved out of this experience of man.

Yet we can sense the importance of what we do at certain times as we struggle to save a bit of our past. I remember the extraordinary jubilation all of us in South Street felt while the *Wavertree* was at sea under tow from Buenos Aires. One watched the sky anxiously in the mornings, though the ship sailed under quite different skies. The *Wavertree* came in under tow of the little tug *Titan*, of the redoubtable Dutch firm Wijsmuller. The men did not fully understand what they had in tow, until they saw the men of McAllister Brothers, the Sandy Hook Pilots, and the National Maritime Union donating harbor tugs, pilotage, and line-han-

The stern of the *Charles Cooper* as she appeared in the Falkland Islands in 1966. The hulk is covered with a corrugated steel roof, which protects her from the weather.

dling without fee, and grown men standing on the old ship's deck with tears on their cheeks; then they understood, they told me, what their long ocean haul had been for.

We saved the *Wavertree* from shipbreakers, but unfortunately we have lost all too many other ships that should have been preserved. Allow me one case history as an example:

More than 50 years ago, the great French bark *Champigny* put into the Falkland Islands to leeward of Cape Horn, dismasted. The sea had dealt harshly with her. There she was condemned and used as a hulk. Slated for destruction 40 years later, she was found by Karl Kortum of the San Francisco Maritime Museum, who persuaded the Pacific Bridge Company to buy her. She was then towed to Montevideo and taken for restoration to a port up the River Plate — where she languished. Despite desperate efforts to pull her out to complete her voyage to San Francisco, she was scrapped.

She was the last of ten thousand sailing ships to round Cape Horn and bring cargo into San Francisco. She was, after the earlier loss of the *Ville de Mulhouse*, the last of the famous French "bounty" ships that trained international crews while they carried cargo. A German cadet who sailed in her wrote of her that she was one of the "most beautiful on earth." Did people care? Those who knew her did. Could she have been saved? Of course.

The German bark *Moshulu* flourishes in Philadelphia today — and plans were well advanced for *Champigny*'s installation in San Francisco, where her masts, 17 stories tall, would have made her mistress of the waterfront.

Karl Kortum has on this ship, as on others, a bunch of notebooks, photos, records, filling out a foot or two of bookshelf. . . materials going back to the life stuff of the ship, the men who sailed in her, her owners, the Societe des Longs-Courriers Francais. Well, this long course she did not make. Her voyage of 1927 will not be completed. We have lost her. What was lacking? Perhaps $25,000 on loan to secure her, pay her debts pending the working-out of her placement in San Francisco. A little staff time, to help put all things together. That is all.

"There was no place to call to get help for her," says Karl Kortum. There still isn't. But she would have rewarded the city that saved her. She would have brought us cargo now lost forever in the seas of time.

The Case for the Restoration of Skillfulness

Lance Lee

MELVILLE'S GREAT and memorable opening to *Moby Dick* — in which Ishmael finds himself in the mood to knock off gentlemen's top hats because of the grey November of the soul — is again central to maritime history. Ishmael had an alternative to the despair he found ashore, and he took it. He shipped on a whaler and doused his social rage in the timeless waters of experience and skill.

Those who analyze our times philosophically have identified an "existential vacuum" (that's the grey November of the soul) and a "hunger for effect" (that means kids want to do something). Let's provide an alternative of value equal to Ishmael's.

The small coastal town of Bath, Maine, where I live, provides a rather perfect platform from which to consider the issue of placing major national emphasis on the restoration of skillfulness. In the south end of the city, the 100-year-old wooden tug *Seguin*, a handsome monument to the design skill of William Pattee and the construction competence of the Morse yard, lies waiting, if an abundance of funds can be found, to be restored to steaming condition as either a towboat or a passenger-carrying adjunct to the Maine Maritime Museum. Astern of the tug, on the same slipway, lies the 88-foot schooner *Bow-*

doin, symbol of great skill and experience transfer gained through some 300,000 miles of exploration, much of it in the Arctic. A Maine Maritime Museum pilot restoration program, involving seven shipwright-trainees, is at work on both of these vessels. Also in the south end is an apprentice shipbuilding program, perhaps as intensive and modern as any other that the nation possesses. In a "very stringent selection process," the Bath Iron Works not long ago took 39 apprentices from 750 applicants. Prior work experience, a math background, work in the shipyard, or a combination of some or all are prerequisites.

And in the north end, the place I work, is a small-craft apprenticing effort that seeks to pair hands-on wood building and seamanship experience with increasing research in the field. The program seeks to track down and "bank" traditional methods before older practitioners die, and to set these methods in motion in the lives of youths and in print in the publications of a Technology Bank.

Today there is a strong movement toward restoring artifacts — at almost whatever cost — rather than establishing programs in which new working vessels may be built. What about building another *Alice Wentworth* at Mystic Seaport, a

Sea Witch in New York, or perhaps a Maine pinky in Bath? Such maritime projects, while restoring the skills and attitudes that are primary, would restore types of historic vessels for operation rather than display alone.

The argument in favor of restoring the old artifact instead is that the government will expend very considerable sums to erect shrines to the greatness of our past. A good example is Fort Concho in Texas, ground well worked over by *Time* magazine in an October 1980 issue. Another is the reconstruction of the Civil War northern gunboat *Cairo*, which is costing in excess of $5,000,000. Is a monument or shrine to the very divisive Civil War a sensible way to spend millions of dollars today, simply because the vagaries of Mississippi mud allow us to retrieve the fragments of a wreck? We mustn't ignore where such precedents lead us. Comparable efforts are now afoot to retrieve and preserve the underwater wrecks of the *Monitor* and the *Titanic* and the *Bonhomme Richard*. Who's in charge here?

It is true that little of such restoration money, if left unspent, might otherwise go into training youth. But if such illustrations of what we as a nation value continue to reach the media spotlight and funding sources in place of programs to train youth, then how will we avoid becoming a culture marked by symbols of past greatness instead of skilled continuity?

Mine is a reasonably vehement prejudice: Train youth. Snag older artisans and learn anything you possibly can about how the skilled workaday maritime world worked yesterday and works today — how, for instance, four turn-of-the-century apprentices, a couple of ABs, the bosun, and the officers pulled the 10-ton steel lower masts of a nitrate vessel after they had been sprung rounding Cape Horn and the crew had abandoned hope of fixing them. That handful of seamen and boys pulled — without cranes, without travel lifts, without hydraulics — two 10-ton spars, reriveted and restepped them, and were on their way again after the insurance company had written them off. The book from which I learned about this, however, didn't tell us *how* they did it. We must learn and pass on such methods, not to get a job done by either cheap or cussed means, but for the sake of sustaining the quotient of capability and verve in the next generation.

The quiet remark of Neils Jannasch, who worked alongside a Finnish first mate fixing a steel topgallant yard after it had been bent in the Roaring Forties, has led me for years: "That man gave me enough inspiration for a lifetime."

Inspiration. We are in need of living causes, not reminders of past greatness. A man who put in long years of fine work restoring a vessel for an excellent maritime museum moved on when he perceived too clearly the difference between dockside restorations and seagoing vessels. "I want to put my work into something that will wear out, not rot out," he said.

We are quite removed from the $5.00-wage-for-a-$50.00-effort world immortalized by Melville, Conrad, McFee, and Riesenberg. Fascination for that world appears to have led us to believe that the *Kaiulani*'s presence, berthed along a dock in Washington, DC, or a rebuilt steam schooner or a Gold Rush vessel's reflection in the oily waters of a 1980s San Francisco Bay will usher in the same old values that characterized that period — the two-fisted arrogance, the capable cussedness, the willful perseverance, or the awesome personal strength that Jack London and much later Farley Mowat wrote of in the sealing trade.

Whether to restore ships or restore skillfulness breaks down into an issue of money, as most things do. To get funds you must offer assurance. The assurance that a tangible monument will result has more appeal still than the promise that a guy with a 5-inch beard who may drive around in a 1952 GMC will become capable and useful to our future if given increased experience and skills. This is the crux of the issue. We must take a chance on the proposition that the bearded trainee will drive keelbolts at a respectable number of feet per hour or a Skilsaw fast enough to rough out a plank in time to keep future yards, projects, or private dreams off the financial mudflats.

The best projects have a financial life of their own. They are not based on fishing for grants but fishing for oysters, or cargoes, or training through which certain income is derived. A grant, it seems to me, ought to represent seed corn — the leg up to get something in motion that will be tied into the economic and educational life of a community or nation. It would be wonderful to see communities or institutions or little clots of boat nuts begin to put together a series of living and moving projects. Rather than being static *community symbols* (and the *Constitution*, the *Fram*, and the *Star of India* are fine ones), we might call these efforts *symbolic actions*.

Let's say four Massachusetts towns — Nantucket, Fairhaven, Manchester, and Monument Beach — agree to build or have some educational organization build a Race Point surfboat. There are several boatbuilding schools in Massachusetts struggling to survive; let some community cash flow into them if a town group isn't ready to undertake the construction itself.

Those four communities could compete with each other in their surfboats, not just in rowing races from Provincetown to Minot's Light but also in boat maintenance, in the building and the upkeep of a launching carriage, and in a special competition launching in surf. The challenge, the skills, the experience, and the fun of the whole affair could generate community pride, great spirit, and funds for similar projects to fire up the kids of those towns. Such a concept is not revolutionary; the New England firemen's musters operate in a similar vein.

Then Massachusetts could start pushing Rhode Island, which also has a struggling boat-building school, and New Hampshire and Maine, which have five schools. After the surfboat competitions become a drag, the towns and states could get out a series of working catboats and compete by volume of fish captured between Friday and Monday dawn. Then they could institute interstate catfish fries. Then fish and chips stands to breed income for maintenance. And when the chips are down and the wallets still out, each of those communities could start on a series of little fishing schooners. Symbolic action, not symbols.

William James pleaded with us some 80 years ago in *The Moral Equivalent of War* to start sending our kids to "fishing fleets in December." He's still right. The problem of greyness in November, the existential vacuum, is still as real as any we have in the nation. And the antidote remains the same. Restored monuments just do not reach kids, youths, or even the antiques over 30.

I'm for putting out money toward making kids capable. I'm for valuing the act, rather than the artifact. I'm for an all-out, caring effort to marshal our remaining talent, treasure, and time to encourage and enable the next generation to carry on. Perhaps it is too late for symbols alone, even though they have stirred me, greatly, in the past. I first went on board the *Charles W. Morgan* more than 30 years ago, and today I'm still moved by that memory — one of romance, amazement, fear, and little-boy awe. The romance came from imagining life on board in the cramped quarters and the hazards of trying-out the whale blubber. The fear was from a glance aloft. And I still absolutely value the little-kid awe. Would I have been moved to do what I do today, think what I do, and be motivated to sustain what I do had I not stepped aboard the then-rotting hulk of the *Morgan*? I can't answer that; I ask it here to be objective, for I am no enemy of the ships of the past.

But I am an enemy of wasted talent and treasure. If we train the 18- to 32-year-olds who are highly motivated to learn the old skills today, we'll have a pool of competent "mechanics" 10 and 20 years from now. We must tap the competence of those most experienced today to train these people — not wait until the old-timers are gone and then expect our apprentices to relearn those skills from the older texts and back issues of *WoodenBoat* alone.

The difference between restoring a vessel and restoring skills — by training a pool of competent mechanics — is this: In 20 years' time the maritime world will still require senior journeymen and master builders. By training young people, we protect our ability to restore old vessels as well as build new ones. Yet the blocks of money needed to set up workable training programs are significant. Unfortunately, these programs lack the fascination of the old hulks. Ringing rhetoric about the structural glories of the past seems to work. Appeals to train youth, many of whose motives are constantly questioned and whose future performance cannot be guaranteed, do not cast a comparable spell.

But this is all theory, and I much prefer very definite examples. In seeking old "tricks" to teach our apprentices, we at the Apprenticeshop learned the following from a man of rare and widespread competence: In cutting a block of granite for a mooring, after sinking a series of holes with a two-point star drill, you set your wedges in the resultant holes, tunk them in along the line of intended breakage, and then stand aside and smoke a cigarette while you let the stone "worry." When your smoke is over, you gently tap the wedges again and the stone drops apart. This isn't simply technique; it's a very distinctive respect for the material elements, which are "personalized." Let the stone "worry." I have come to revere *attitude* toward what is done, not simply the "how to" involved.

I believe we must concentrate on attitudes and skills. We are being blinded by the grand old monuments — which are, after all, only *objects* — to the importance of learning all the little intricate tricks of self-sufficiency, through which we might train a new generation in how to live by common sense.

Can such learning be effected through the rebuilding of the old? Again and again this becomes a key question. My answer lies with the former ship restorer's response: "I'd rather build one to wear out than to rot out." Youths crave meaningful exposure. What I hear them saying, in voices spanning 150 years, is "Let me be of my times, and fashion or execute something useful and beautiful that works and helps me gain stature and a living."

Ancient Masterpiece: The Royal Ship of Cheops

Nancy Jenkins

THROUGH NEWSPAPER reports, we knew that considerable concern existed among preservationists over the condition of the Royal Ship of Cheops, which had been found entombed at the base of the Great Pyramid in Egypt. We wanted to publish something on the vessel as a measure of our own interest, but Egypt is over there and we're here . . . . Then Jon Wilson had the good fortune to meet John Ross, whose exclusive photographs of the vessel were an inspiring resource. As it happened, John was working in cooperation with Nancy Jenkins, who was writing a book on the subject.

Working with contacts in New York, London, and Rome, we were able to put enough of the pieces together with these two professionals to publish the following. Fortuitous circumstances and unadorned detail work produced what we consider to be one of our finest efforts.

MARINE ARCHAEOLOGISTS are all too often hampered by the fact that most ancient ships are wrecks, lying at the bottom of a sea, a harbor, or, more usually, in inaccessible storm-wracked reefs. The combination of initial damage plus centuries of attack by water, worms, coral, and other sea parasites may mean, as in the wreck of a 12th-century B.C. Phoenician trader at Cape Gelidonya off the south coast of Turkey, that we know a great deal about the ship's contents (her captain was a Syrian, and she was probably bound for the western Mediterranean with a cargo of copper ingots) and nothing whatsoever about her structure or construction, so thoroughly has the ship herself been destroyed.

It is comforting, then, to report that the oldest boat ever known to marine archaeology is magnificently preserved (or at least she has been, until now), intact and entire, an elegant sweep of still-aromatic Lebanese cedar, nearly 143 feet long and some 45 centuries old.

The Royal Ship of King Cheops, as she is known to Egyptologists and archaeologists, is the unique exhibit in a singular rhomboid-shaped museum with glass walls that has been built over the pit in which the ship was found, next to the Great Pyramid on the desert plateau west of the modern Egyptian capital of Cairo. But don't rush to Cairo to see the Royal Ship, for although the museum was completed and the boat was installed in 1970, it has never been open to the public, and only a few scholars have ever been given permission to examine the ship. For a couple of piasters, the guard who sits outside the museum will let you scramble up a scaffolding from which, by brushing the desert grit from the windowpane, you can get a glimpse of the Royal Ship; but that is as close as most people can come. I happened to be one of the fortunate few, and because I was writing a book about the Royal Ship, I was allowed to spend a few hours examining her in the spring of 1978.

The Royal Ship was part of the burial equipment of King Cheops, the great Fourth Dynasty leader who reigned over Egypt around the middle of the third millennium, that is, circa 2500 B.C. She may well have been the funerary barge that bore the mummified body of the king in a stately procession down the Nile from Memphis, the Old Kingdom capital of Egypt, to the king's final resting place inside the Great Pyramid, which had been built as his funerary monument on the lonely, wind-swept plateau overlooking the valley of the Nile.

Once the royal mummy had been sealed inside its pyramid tomb, the ship was carefully dismantled into 651 constituent parts, which were then buried in a separate grave, a large pit hewn into the bedrock of the plateau next to the south face of the pyramid. The pit was covered with 41 enormous limestone blocks, each one the size of a small pickup truck and weighing between 15 and 20 tons. Then a liquid plaster of pure white gypsum was poured around the blocks, effectively sealing the pit and creating an airtight and perfectly stable environment in which the cedar timbers lay undisturbed for 4,600 years.

Like many great archaeological finds, the discovery of the Royal Ship was fortuitous. In the early 1950s Kamal al-Mallakh, a young Egyptian archaeologist, had been assigned by the Department of Antiquities to supervise the clearing of a huge mound of rubble dozens of meters high that had accumulated against the south face of the Great Pyramid. Beneath this debris, Mallakh's workmen came across a wall, part of the *temenos*, or boundary wall, that had originally enclosed the sacred precinct of the pyramid. It was a fairly routine discovery, for the wall had been documented already in the 19th century. Of greater interest to Mallakh was a layer of beaten earth that had been spread over a large area of ground beneath the wall. When this layer was removed, there were revealed two sets of limestone blocks, 41 to the east and 40 to the west. (The westernmost set of blocks, presumably covering a second boat pit, have never been removed.) Instantly, as Mallakh retells the story, he recognized "the huge and confident stonework of the Fourth Dynasty."

In hindsight Mallakh claims that he had suspected the existence of a boat pit, that he had in fact been looking for a boat pit all along, though on the evidence it is difficult to accept this. Still, clearly something lay beneath the stones, something that the ancients had gone to great pains to conceal, and in May 1954, Mallakh was granted permission to make a small opening in one of the blocks of the easternmost group to find out what that something was. It was late in the archaeological season, he recalls, and tremendously hot, with the desert sun beating fiercely on the white pyramids, when he took the stonecutting tools from his workmen to make the final cut himself. "The last bit of stone fell away," he said, "but in the glare I

could see nothing. So, like a cat I closed my eyes. And then I smelt a very holy, holy, holy smell. I smelt time...I smelt history...I smelt centuries. And I knew the boat was there."

Until the discovery of the Royal Ship, we knew a great deal about the shapes of ancient Egyptian boats but almost nothing about their construction. Hundreds of little model boats have been found as part of the burial equipment in Egyptian tombs, and the walls of these same tombs, brightly painted or carved in relief with scenes from Egyptian daily life, would often include a boating scene. So we knew what Egyptian boats looked like in all their variety — fishing punts, ritual vessels, pleasure and work boats, great barges that transported incredibly heavy loads of stone downriver from the granite quarries at Aswan, sailboats that beat up the Mediterranean coast to Byblos and returned with a load of the same Lebanese cedar that went to build the Royal Ship — but we knew almost nothing about how these boats were built, or what their internal structure was like.

There was a clue, however, from Herodotus, who wrote about Egyptian boatbuilding in the 5th century B.C.: "They cut planks 3 feet long which they put together like courses of brick, building up the hull as follows: they join these 3-foot lengths together with close-set dowels (and) stretch crossbeams over them. They use no ribs...." This description was discounted as a completely unreliable fabrication until late in the 19th century, when three small craft were found near the burial place of an important Twelfth Dynasty king at Dashur. These little boats were primitively built, but they confirmed what Herodotus said, for they are made of short, uneven lengths of wood, joined at the ends and along the edges with little dovetail clamps. Furthermore, they have no ribs or frames. (One of these boats is on display at the Field Museum in Chicago.) But they are so poorly constructed that it is inconceivable that they could have been part of the burial equipment of a great king and hard to believe they would have been viable craft in the swift current of the Nile.

The engineering works of the ancient Egyptians are nothing short of miraculous. Without the wheel, without any lifting device more sophisticated than the lever, without heavy draft animals, they were still able to quarry, cut, and transport over hundreds of miles enormous blocks of stone, and with this stone to erect huge monuments as well as to carve statues and reliefs of impressively fine detail. How then, on the evidence of the Dashur boats, could they have been so inept at shipbuilding?

Opposite — The Royal Ship of Cheops is set up in a special glass-walled museum building next to the Great Pyramid. Designed to protect her, the building instead could lead to her disintegration.

The topmost layer of the dismantled ship, from the eastern end of the pit, after the enormous limestone blocks had been removed. The oars can be seen clearly, and in the center and background are parts of what was later found to be the cabin assembly.

The discovery of the Royal Ship provided the answer. Whatever the Dashur boats were meant to be, we now know that the ancient Egyptians were as skilled as shipwrights as they were at handling stone.

The whole ship, 142.4 feet long and 19.4 feet wide, with a displacement of about 45 tons, had been planned from the beginning and down to the last detail to be taken apart and stored and then put together again when necessary. The parts of the ship had been laid in the excavated pit in an orderly, rational fashion, almost as if the ancient shipwrights had known that some day, thousands of years later, someone would put her back together again. It was a giant do-it-yourself boat kit that lay in the pit when the stones covering it were finally removed, but it was a do-it-yourself kit that came without a set of instructions on the lid.

A detail of the bottom and side planking at the forward end of the boat, with the original temporary lashing still in place.

The task of lifting and conserving the parts and reconstructing the ship was given to Ahmed Youssef Moustafa, Chief Restorer in the Antiquities Department and a man who is almost legendary for his skill and perspicacity in the demanding craft of restoration. Of course, restoring a Ramesside gold necklace or an ivory box from the time of Tutankhamun is quite different from reconstructing a giant ship; in the beginning, moreover, Hag Ahmed (the title indicates he has made the pilgrimage to Mecca) knew nothing at all about boatbuilding. Before he did anything else, therefore, he apprenticed himself to the shipwrights in the small yards along the river in Cairo to learn their craft. It was a useful experience, although, as it turned out, the Royal Ship was different, in ways that were totally unforeseeable, from anything that is built in modern Egyptian boatyards.

All told, it was to take Hag Ahmed more than 10 years from the day he approached the first piece in the boat pit until he had finished the job to his own meticulous satisfaction. There were a number of false starts, and in the end he was to put the ship together five times before she came to a final rest in the museum in 1970. When all the components of the ship were disassembled (the deckhouse paneling, for instance, stripped down), there were 1,224 pieces to the puzzle. The legend, which Hag Ahmed refuses to confirm or deny, is that 1,223 of them were put back together.

The Royal Ship is built almost entirely of Lebanese cedar. No tall trees grow in Egypt; it was only in the mountains of Lebanon that the ancient shipwrights could find the long, broad timbers they needed for the Royal Ship. The hull planks are between 4.7 inches and 5.5 inches in thickness, and the longest of them, the central sections of the sheerstrakes, were more than 72 feet in length. Some local Egyptian woods, acacia and sycamore, were used for minor details in the woodwork, such as the pegs that help to hold the planks in place. No metal is used in the ship except for a few almost pure copper brads used, in one instance, as part of a door latch, and in another as curtain loops.

The ship is what the maritime historian Bjorn Landstrom, who has studied this and other ancient Egyptian boats calls a "papyriform" vessel; that is, a boat built of wood to emulate the rafts made of bundles of papyrus reeds (like Thor Heyerdahl's *Ra*) that were the earliest form of transport in Egypt. By 2500 B.C., however, this simulated raft had already become a sophisticated structure, bearing only a slight resemblance to the primitive rafts that were still very much in use in the marshes. (The papyrus raft also had a strong religious connotation in Egypt, for it was said to be the means by which the all-powerful sun god traveled across the heavens.) The high stem piece and the steeply raked stern of the Royal Ship, carved to represent tightly bound papyrus reeds and capped with a highly stylized representation of a half-open papyrus bud, are all that remain to suggest a reed raft, unless the broad, shallow draft of the ship is also meant to recall a raftlike construction.

I have to stress, however, that this papyriform type of craft only *emulates* reed rafts; it is not an imitation, and it is most certainly not a raft itself, nor a development of a raft. The true antecedents of King Cheops' Royal Ship are elsewhere, in a long and highly evolved tradition of wooden boatbuilding. How these boats developed we don't really know, but that it was a long line we can say with certainty, for the sophisticated technology exhibited in the Royal Ship could only have come from hundreds of years of experimentation and development. Until contrary evidence is presented, we must assume that most Egyptian wooden boats were part of this same tradition.

This was a tradition of shell-built, edge-joined, sewn hulls, mostly flat bottomed and without keels. (The keel did not come into use until about a thousand years later.) Instead of a keel, the Royal Ship has a long central plank that is made up of eight timbers joined together in three sections: forward, amidships, and aft. The angles at which these three sections of the central plank join or butt together determine the fore-and-aft rocker of the ship. It was the most difficult problem that faced Hag Ahmed in reconstructing the ship, for on the rocker of the ship's bottom obviously depended the profile of the vessel. And there was no indication of how to solve this problem except through trial and error, putting the sections together over and over again until they looked and felt right, and worked together with the other parts of the hull.

The hull of the Royal Ship is made up of 22 planks, 11 to a side. The broadstrakes and the sheerstrakes each have three planks; the binding strakes have two; and between the garboard and binding strakes on either side of the ship, three extra stealers have been fitted to fill out the hull curvature. The hull planks are joined at the ends with big hook scarfs to form a continuous strake, and smaller knuckle hooks along the edge ensure a snug fit between strakes.

The hull planks are pegged together with

mortise-and-tenon joints, but what holds the ship together is a system of rope lashings that weaves through V-shaped seam holes let into the inside of the hull planking. The strakes are literally sewn together, with an over-and-under stitch like that of a fine tailor — and, like the work of a fine tailor, it is all concealed on the inside. From the outside, the hull presents a smooth, flush, streamlined appearance. From the inside, a continuous strand of rope can be threaded through the entire transverse girth of the ship from sheerstrake to sheerstrake, adding immeasurably to the strength and flexibility of the hull.

This was a startling and totally unexpected

In the restoration shed, the parts of the Royal Ship were laid out as closely as possible to the order followed by the ancient workmen when they buried the ship. Here, two sections of the floor beams have been temporarily pegged together, with the bow section in the foreground; the starboard timbers are stacked on the left and the port timbers on the right in the picture.

Ahmed Youssef Moustafa at work on the precise scale model of the boat. Pieces were tried on the model before reconstruction began.

235

A trial assembly that was to prove erroneous. Note that the long, slender, notched timber is lying in the bottom of the ship, since it was still felt at this point that it functioned rather like a keel into which the frames or ribs would fit. Only later did it transpire that this "stringer" was in fact a central shelf that ran the length of the ship and supported the thwarts or deckbeams, giving the structure its necessary rigidity.

discovery. Sewn boats have a long history, particularly around the Indian Ocean, but it is a tradition that has almost completely died out in modern times. In boats with sewn hulls, Arab merchantmen traded regularly with China as early as the 7th century A.D. along a difficult and dangerous route around India and Ceylon and through the Strait of Malacca into the South China Sea, testifying to the seaworthiness of these strange craft. When wet, the rope bindings shrink, the hull planks expand, and the result is strong, flexible, and watertight — more or less. Now it appears that this may have been a much older and more widespread tradition.

Coils of hemp rope were part of the equipment found in the Royal Ship's pit, sometimes lying in tangled disorder, but often enough knotted intricately so that many of the knots Hag Ahmed would use in restoring the boat were derived from techniques laid down some four and a half millennia earlier. Lionel Casson has suggested that stitched hulls may have been a tradition throughout the Mediterranean at least until medieval times. Certainly it seems likely that wooden boats of any size in ancient

Egypt were always made with sewn hulls. When and where and why the changeover took place is an interesting question, and one that marine archaeologists in the future should address themselves to.

Inside the hull there was no evidence of caulking between the seams, nor had any caulking material been found in the boat pit. Instead, long thin battens, hemispherical in section, were lashed over the seams on the inside of the ship's hull between the strakes. These battens not only helped to keep the vessel watertight, they also took up some of the stress of the rope bindings on the hull planks themselves.

Inserted in the hull are 16 curved frames, each carved from a single piece of cedar, with runnels cut across their outside faces through which the battens pass. On the frames rest forked stanchions that, in their turn, support a central shelf or stringer that runs the length of the ship. The 46 deckbeams or thwarts are set into notches in the stringer and rest on other notches carved into the topmost edges of the sheerstrakes. A "side shelf" runs down each side of the ship, resting on the thwarts, and between the side shelves the deck flooring is laid over the thwarts in a series of removable hatches. The combination of frames and thwarts, and side shelves and stringer, gives strength and rigidity, both latitudinally and longitudinally, to the flexible shell of the boat.

A curious aspect of the ship's construction is the way the papyriform stem and stern pieces were attached to the boat. The Viking ships also had separate stem and stern pieces that were scarfed onto the ship's keel. But the Royal Ship has no keel, and the papyriform stem and stern were socketed onto the actual hull planks by means of a pair of long, blunt-ended blades at each end of the ship. The decorative papyriform prow, for instance, is made up of six closely interlocked pieces that are bound together and then slide over the forward blades like a gauntlet over a sleeve. They are enormously heavy, these stem and stern posts, but the ingenious manner in which they have been socketed on prevents them from breaking off, and indeed adds to the overall strength of the boat's structure. The only part of the ship's construction where it was necessary to bring the lashing to the outside of the hull is in the joining of these stem and stern pieces onto the ship. In order to maintain her streamlined appearance, the ancient builders designed two big curved battens forward and aft whose only function is to conceal this lashing on the outside.

For much of the year it was extremely hot traveling on the Nile. The ancient river boats

that we see in reliefs and paintings have a light lattice-work deck housing over which woven mats were thrown for protection from the sun but that still let the river breezes pass through. With this in mind, the deckhouse on the Royal Ship looks strange indeed, for it is a completely enclosed two-room cabin, about 29.5 feet long, its sides and roof made of removable screens of cedar paneling. The cabin covers the whole afterdeck area between the two longitudinal side shelves, and it is surrounded by a framework of slender columns with papyrus-bud finials that support thin beams arching over the cabin roof. This canopy extends forward of the cabin over the deck space. Hag Ahmed believes it was meant to support reed mats, which, when wet down with buckets of river water, would provide a primitive kind of air conditioning. Even so, the dark and airless cabin space would have been extremely uncomfortable. I suspect the cabin was built like this to conceal the royal mummy, which was considered sacred and probably kept hidden from the sight of everyone but important high priests. The cedar panels are easily removed and were probably put in place only when there was something sacred to be concealed.

On the forward deck a smaller canopy, just the right size for one short person, provided protection from the sun — but who stood there? The watch looking for obstacles on the river? The captain or coxswain facing aft to direct the five pairs of oarsmen? A high priest, given the sacred nature of the cargo, whose job was to prevent evil spirits from boarding the ship?

There were six pairs of oars in the boat pit, including a pair of steering oars in lieu of a rudder, but they do not seem adequate to propel a ship of this size. No evidence of any sailing rig was found. The prevailing wind on the Nile is northerly, and most boats were therefore provided with a detachable mast and sail for the upriver journey before the wind, as well as oars for the downriver trip floating in the strong current. Some Egyptologists, ignoring the fact that what goes up must come down, have cleverly suggested that every Egyptian of substance had two boats, one for each direction on the river!

As a ritual vessel, the Royal Ship was probably towed by other, smaller craft. The oars would then have been used simply to help keep her on course, or they may have been manned, symbolically, by priests and court officials. There are some, however, who state flatly that the Royal Ship was never used on the Nile at all, that it was built and dismantled and laid in the pit all at the same time, the intention being

purely for the pharaoh's use for any voyages or pilgrimages he might have to make in the afterlife. Those who agree with this viewpoint believe that the second pit, if it is ever opened, will reveal a boat with sails rather than oars, intended for the upstream Nile journey, sailing with the prevailing north wind, while the present Royal Ship, with her oars, is intended for proceeding downstream.

The discovery and reconstruction of the Royal Ship has raised almost as many questions as it has answered about ancient Egyptian history as well as the history and development of ships and shipbuilding. The problems of why and where the tradition of sewn hulls developed, and when, where, and why it died out are only one of the many areas where further research is needed.

The only thing certain in all this speculation is that many questions will be answered when (and if) the second pit is opened. But the Egyptians have wisely decided to leave the second boat in the pit until the vexing question of the preservation of the first boat is settled. Certainly

One of the most interesting aspects of the ship's construction is the way in which the bow and stern pieces fit like sleeves over the fore and aft sections of the hull to produce the magnificent papyriform shape.

View along the port side of the reconstructed Royal Ship, looking forward. The internal ropes stitching the ship together are just visible between the hull timbers, though originally none would have been seen from the outside.

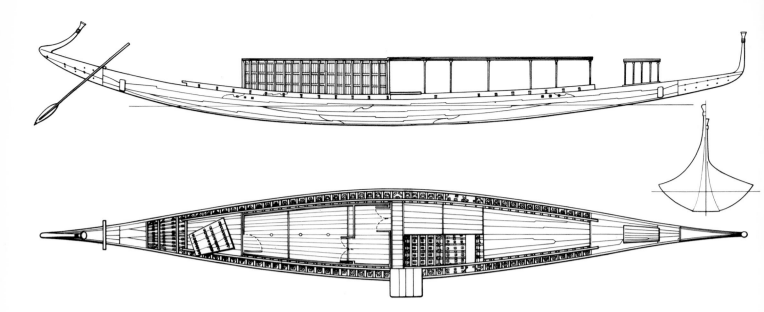

if the second pit is as well sealed with gypsum plaster as the first one was, the boat is safer there than it would be if exposed to the vicissitudes that the first boat has been forced to suffer.

A glass-walled structure in the middle of the desert is hardly an appropriate shelter, but a glass-walled museum without any temperature or humidity control is sheer madness. Though the glass museum was completed 10 years ago, the massive air conditioning that was meant to provide a controlled environment for a 4,600-year-old artifact has never been put into service (lack of power being the usual excuse given), and today it sits in a rusting heap beside the museum. The temperature in this desert greenhouse can vary by more than 50 degrees C. within a 24-hour period, subjecting the ancient timbers to unbearable stresses and strains. Although Hag Ahmed has so far been able to keep a fairly constant vigil over the ship, there is little, under the circumstances, that he can do to correct the situation.

The Egyptian Department of Antiquities is apparently unable to cope with the problem, partly for lack of funds (though the funds would be immediately available were a feasible solution to be presented), and partly because,

with the remains of 5,000 years of human history to oversee, it is difficult to overcome a certain apathy. At the risk of sounding frivolous, however, I must point out that while there are several dozen pyramids, and several thousand tombs, there is only one boat.

Why can't the ship be moved to a more appropriate location? (The best suggestion so far is an underground museum approximating the conditions of the boat pit before it was opened.) At the very least, why can't air conditioning be installed in the present location? These are questions to which the Antiquities Department has failed to address itself.

But the fact remains that the Cheops boat is unique — one is tempted to say it is *absolutely* unique — a survival from Egypt's lustrous past, a thing of beauty as well as a reminder of the common history of all mankind that has been brilliantly and faithfully restored by the man who is probably the only person in the world qualified to do it. If help comes quickly enough, the boat can be saved. It would be a shabby commentary on our times if, having survived intact through 4,600 years of history, Cheops' boat were to disappear, through our own mismanagement, in our lifetime.

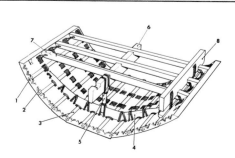

The internal structure of the Royal Ship: the hull planks are held together partly by pegs (1), but more importantly by a system of ropes stitched through seam holes (2) that do not penetrate to the outside surface of the boat. Long, thin, hemispherical battens (3) are lashed over each seam, making caulking unnecessary. Frames (4) inserted into the hull to strengthen it support a series of stanchions (5), which in turn carry the weight of the central shelf or stringer (6) that runs the length of the ship. The thwarts or deck beams (7) are let into the notches of the stringer. Side shelves (8) similar to the central stringer rest on the thwarts and give further rigidity to the hull structure.

Gathering the Finest:

The Herreshoff Rendezvous
The Classic Yacht Regatta

Peggy C. Nicholson and L.E. Nicholson

O NE OF THE FINEST aspects of the wooden boat revival has been the development of meets and gatherings around the country that celebrate the best our heritage has to offer. Among these events, the Classic Yacht Regatta and the Herreshoff Rendezvous are perhaps the finest examples of the current enthusiasm existing for the exemplary wooden yachts of this century. We would be remiss in our *responsibilities if we did not celebrate their existence in print. To do so was easy, since our photographer Benjie Mendlowitz attended both gatherings in 1981 and came back with hundreds of photographs, while the Nicholsons sent in their reports on the goings-on. The only difficult part was choosing which images to use, those we didn't are just as stunning.*

The great Fife ketches *Belle Aventure* and *Isabelle* (nearest camera) race to the first mark of the Classic Yacht Regatta.

Above — Prelude rounding just ahead of the Concordia yawl *Paramour*.

Below — Nirvana and *Bill of Rights* at the start.

The Classic Yacht Regatta

DESPITE A WEEK of strong easterly winds and a series of offshore hurricanes, 90 yachts ranging from just over 30 feet to over 100 feet made the trek to Newport, Rhode Island, for the Classic Yacht Regatta over Labor Day Weekend, 1981 — four days of racing, yarning, and first-class ogling. No one was disappointed at having made the effort.

Saturday was race day, centerpiece of the event. Northly winds of 18 knots provided most of the boats with enough wind to border on a reefing breeze.

More than 80 boats in five classes crossed the starting line. Only 2½ hours later, the hometown favorite, *Gleam*, crossed the finish line, sailing the 17½-mile course at an average speed of over seven knots and winning the newly donated *Atlantic* Cup for her efforts. Second boat over the line was the 72-foot Rhodes yawl *Escapade*, followed five minutes later by the 64-foot Sparkman & Stephens yawl *Refanut*, Class A winner on corrected time.

The most incredible racing performance was undoubtedly that of *Bambino*, a 41-foot Herreshoff sloop built in 1904. Now owned by the Herreshoff Marine Museum and skippered by Halsey Herreshoff, the Class D sloop was fifth around the course on elapsed time but on corrected time was the winner by three minutes over the Herreshoff Newport 29s *Dolphin* and *Mischief*. Halsey Herreshoff was awarded the *Sappho* Trophy for *Bambino*'s performance.

The Leiter Cup, for best corrected time by a gaff-rigged yacht, was won for the second consecutive year by the Buzzards Bay 25 *Aria*, sailed by Paul Bates of Noank, Connecticut. The schooner prize went to the Concordia-designed *Mya*, the Concordia yawl prize to *Moonfleet*, and the Rhodes 27 trophy to *Tiny Teal*.

Boats designed by N.G. Herreshoff and built by the Herreshoff Manufacturing Company put on an unbelievable performance. The eight N.G. Herreshoff designs racing won three class firsts, one class second place, two third places, the Leiter Cup, and the *Sappho* Trophy. Herreshoff boats were first, second, and third overall and occupied four of the top nine fleet positions.

Four nonracing prizes were awarded this year. The Alden schooner *Tar Baby*, the English cutter *Shiris*, and *Dolphin* were recognized for their superior condition. The 85-foot Fife ketch *Belle Aventure*, by any standard one of the world's most beautiful, flawlessly maintained yachts, was recognized as the finest yacht in the Regatta. A special award for accuracy and excellence of restoration was given to the 53-foot

Herreshoff sloop *Neith*, whose hull has been magnificently rebuilt over the last two years.

Through the Classic Yacht Regatta, the Museum of Yachting draws attention to the form and function of antique sailboats. For the owner of a classic wooden yacht, it provides a once-a-year chance to commune with the kindred souls who share the private madness of owning large wooden sailboats. For the spectator, the Classic Yacht Regatta is a wonderful reminder of a past still very much alive and a future full of growing interest in the beautiful, long-lived creations of the great yacht designers and builders.

L. E. Nicholson

Above — In formation (*left to right*) are *Refanut*, *Nirvana*, and *Escapade*.

Left — *Gleam*'s crew enjoying the beat to the finish line.

Below — *Bambino* was overall winner.

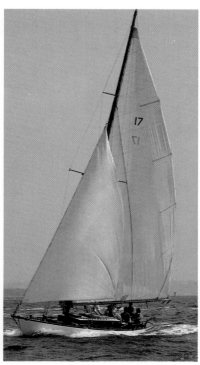

The Herreshoff Rendezvous

Above — A couple of winners from the year 1914. *Aria* (foreground), a Buzzards Bay 25 (32 feet overall), took Class B while *Dolphin*, a Newport 29 (35 feet overall) won Class A.

Below — *Mashnee*, a 1902 Buzzards Bay 30 (47 feet overall), to windward of the 56-foot yawl *Belisarius*. *Mashnee* tied with another boat of her class, *Catspaw*, for the oldest yacht in the Herreshoff Regatta. *Belisarius* of 1935 vintage is the last big yacht designed by N.G. Herreshoff.

H ERRESHOFF — a name of near mythic proportions around Narragansett Bay. Herreshoff — a reputation for speed, elegance, quality, ingenuity. Herreshoffs — subtle sheers, hollow entries, wide sterns, responsive helms. Three generations of American yacht design history: Nathanael G., L. Francis, A. Sidney, and Halsey Herreshoff — their reputation grows and endures, and so do many of the yachts on which it was built.

At the Herreshoff Marine Museum Rendezvous '81, August 21-23, 78 sailboats, each designed by a Herreshoff and most of them built at the Herreshoff Manufacturing Co., returned to Bristol, Rhode Island, to celebrate the 10th anniversary of the Herreshoff Museum and to find out who was fleetest of the fleet.

On Saturday, five classes raced in a brisk

A couple of nicely executed major restorations were represented by *Neith* of 1907 (*above*), whose hull and deck have been completed, the remaining work to take place next winter, and by *Aquila* (ex-*Anemone II*, of 1905), a New York Thirty finished just in time for this event.

sou'westerly under damp grey skies, with the big Class A yachts starting first. New York Thirties, Newport 29s, Buzzards Bay 30s, Fishers Island 31s, several big racer-cruisers —— Class A was pure Nathanael Herreshoff. The largest yacht to race was the 56-foot yawl *Belisarius*, N.G.'s last large boat, built in 1935.

Of special note were the 53-foot sloop *Neith*, a husky but graceful custom design built in 1907, and the gaff-rigged New York Thirty *Aquila*. Both boats were almost basket cases three years ago. Each has since been rescued by a new owner committed to an extensive and thoughtful restoration.

Winner of Class A was John Lockwood's

Newport 29, *Dolphin. Kestrel,* a Fishers Island 31, took second.

Class B consisted of smaller Herreshoff designs — Fish class and Buzzards Bay 15s, with Paul Bates's *Aria*, a Buzzards Bay 25, finishing first, and *Hornet*, a Sidney Herreshoff-designed Fishers Island 23, second.

The Open Class was for all boats designed by a Herreshoff, but built elsewhere. Michael Jackson's *Rogue*, a Newport 29 replica, took first place.

In the S class, 26 boats raced, with John Migliaccio's recently sunk, raised, and repaired *Wistful* coming in ahead of the pack.

Peggy E. Nicholson

Coronet: Whither Away?

Timothy E. Murray

WHEN MAYNARD BRAY, who has crossed the decks of more wooden boats than anyone we know, went aboard the almost-100-year-old schooner-yacht Coronet *in Gloucester, Massachusetts, he found the details of her construction overwhelming. He encouraged Tim Murray, who grew up aboard* Coronet *(Tim's father is skipper), to write an excellent article on her which further confirmed her importance to yachting's history. This was all we needed to cause us to pull out all the stops. Jon Wilson immersed himself in digging up old photographs, Benjie Mendlowitz went to Gloucester for several hours of shooting detail photographs, Spencer Lincoln, a Brooklin yacht designer, redrew* Coronet's *old lines and arrangement plans, and Maynard helped Spencer work up detail views. We put an inordinate amount of effort into this piece, but it was worth it. For a lot of people who tended to look at* Coronet *as an old hulk, the article served to change their perspective considerably. What's more, this appreciation of the vessel was something of a catalyst in the development of Newport's new Museum of Yachting.*

SOME TIME in the early 1880s Rufus T. Bush had a brainstorm. Why not build a yacht? And why not make it a big yacht? Rufus T. Bush was a New York millionaire; with that thought was born a vessel that has probably seen more newsprint devoted to her, felt more salt water under her keel, and known more of the vagaries of the world's weather than any other yacht afloat today. And she has earned a reputation or two: one for sea ability (in the language of the day, she was "able" enough), and one for mystery.

But in 1885, still on the stocks in Poillon's yard at Brooklyn, New York, *Coronet* was a brand-new and untried schooner. Bush suspected she would be a good sailer. Built on the New York Pilot Boat model, she ought to be fast, and she ought to be able. But one thing he

was sure of: she was sound. Chris Crosby had seen to that. Captain Crosby had had a fair share in her design, collaborating with Smith & Terry, her architects. And Chris Crosby had combed the timber racks in Poillon's yard, inspecting every stick that went into her. A native of Nova Scotia, he was no stranger to the demands of heavy weather on a vessel. He was later to remark somewhat laconically that he had "left two ships" off Cape Hatteras himself. But he never left *Coronet* until she was sold out from under him. And that was not to happen for another 20 years.

Coronet's design called for a plumb stem, structural strength, and speed. As she lay on the ways in August of 1885, her wineglass counter stood 133 feet from her stem, her steep floors fell to a flat keel 12 feet in draft, and her beam was 27 feet. Under a coat of gleaming black (soon to be permanently changed to white), her great frame combined massive strength with some of the sweetest lines on the New York waterfront. She was generally considered (by the press, at least) to be the finest product of Poillon's yard up to her time. Keel, keelson, frames, and planks were all white oak from Maine. Three-inch planking was mated on the inside with a 4-inch hard-pine ceiling, through-fastened in the good old-fashioned way with treenails. Great naturally grown knees secured her deck timbers both laterally and vertically.

As he strolled about the white pine deck on her launching day, Rufus Bush must have been pleased. Varnished teak stanchions complemented the brightwork of deckhouses and rail, all Honduras mahogany of extraordinary (by modern standards) density, beauty, and closeness of grain. Going below, he descended the main stairway of polished marble, fan-shaped at its foot, past two newel posts crowned with brass lamps, through swinging doors with stained-glass lights, into the spacious saloon. Finished in hand-carved panels of the same fine mahogany, and set off with handsomely engraved mirrors, the main cabin was graced with a granite-topped sideboard, a writing desk, a large table with matching chairs (over which hung a brass chandelier), and a piano. Around the sides extended upholstered settees for the further comfort of her passengers. And in cold weather an open tile fireplace would dispel the chill.

Moving forward, he passed into the paneled centerline passageway onto which the richly appointed staterooms opened. The three largest — there were six in all — contained chests of drawers, mirrors, spacious double beds, and ample storage area.

Such was the quality of this vessel as she took to the water on August 17, 1885, and later received her spars. Aloft, her maintopmast truck was to stand 135 feet above the deck. Outfitted with a variety of sails and upper spars according to her needs as a cruiser or racer, she would spread 8,305 square feet of canvas with "all regular sail set." Whether or not Bush could see it all complete on her launching day, he must still have been a satisfied man. And anxious to try her.

The following year, *Coronet* sailed on her maiden voyage. To England certainly, perhaps some European ports as well, and back; and her owner knew he had something. He had a vessel of no small potential and a captain to match her. And so this New York millionaire had another idea, one that was to secure for the big schooner her first reputation. He decided on a challenge to race her. Not a small man when it came to spending money, he refitted her for the occasion, bringing her total cost to $100,000, and announced a $10,000 prize for the winner. The gauntlet was taken up by none other than Caldwell Colt (of Colt firearms), and his famous schooner *Dauntless* was skippered by the equally famous "Bully" Samuels. The imagination of the New York yachting scene was fired immediately. From New York to Queenstown, Ireland, in March of 1887, it was a race to test the mettle of ships and men. *Coronet*'s victory, by better than 30 hours, secured her status in American yachting and commanded the entire front page of the *New York Times* for March 28, 1887.

The following year, Bush (in the finest 19th-century yachting style) took five or six others on a whirlwind world tour with his new champion. On that voyage, *Coronet* is said to have become the first registered yacht to round Cape Horn from east to west. On that voyage, too, she again demonstrated her ability as an offshore vessel, capable of extensive world cruising under the worst of conditions.

Her fame preceded her. In Honolulu (Hawaii was then an independent monarchy) King Kalakaua visited aboard. And in Yokohama, Emperor Meiji also came aboard — and immediately ordered for himself a boat exactly like *Coronet*'s gig. The Malacca Strait, the Suez Canal, the Mediterranean, and home; and Bush, apparently content, sold her.

Of her seven successive owners, several made the most of *Coronet*'s capabilities. In 1890, Arthur E. Bateman took her for a summer's cruise in western Mediterranean and western European waters. And in 1895 and 1896, Arthur Curtiss James (who called her "the finest

Opposite — In mid-March of 1887, *Coronet* embarked on a transatlantic race from New York to Queenstown, Ireland, against the schooner yacht *Dauntless*. Shown here leaving lower New York Bay, her paid crew crowds on the sail.

245

Hardly more than a casual look is needed to determine that *Coronet* was built by shipwrights who were extremely skilled, not only in making good fits but also in sizing and shaping her timbers so they looked good — both by themselves and as a whole. Wooden yachts this big may never be built again, but many of the techniques used in her construction can be adapted to smaller craft of present and future times. The men who built *Coronet* can, through her, teach us their skills.
— Maynard Bray

1

2

4

3

5

three — Hanging knees complement the lodging knees by supporting the deckbeams from underneath, and they serve also to keep the hull from wracking. Amidships in the living spaces, they are boxed in, but here in the lazarette, one of them is visible in its basic form. Hanging knees are landed on the 3- to 4-inch hull ceiling and are fastened through it into a frame timber. Note that both the beam and lodging knee have been nosed off, even way aft here in the stern, where they are virtually hidden from view.

four — Harmony between a vessel's structure and her joinerwork was a hallmark of old-time shipbuilders, who apparently felt that since the basic structure was nicely proportioned and well fitted and finished, there was no reason to hide it. Beaded staving with tongue-and-groove edges made up the partitions and locker doors in the more plainly finished areas of *Coronet*. Horizontal lodging knees are fitted and it is by this means that the deck structure is tied to the hull and given diagonal strength to keep it from wracking.

five — This is the way intersecting deckbeams and carlings should be joined, no matter what their size, if they are to have nosed-off corners. By cutting down on the molded depth of each beam from the one "upstream" of it, the decorative corner treatment can continue uninterrupted from one end of the beam to the other, in spite of the intersections. Shown here in the background is a main deckbeam, which runs from one side of the vessel to the other, while in the foreground, parallel to it, is an intermediate deckbeam supported on its inboard end by a fore-and-aft carling running on the vessel's centerline between two main beams. Because of their shorter span, the intermediate beams need not be as stiff as the main ones; these measure 5 inches by 5 inches. The centerline carlings are 5¾ inches square and the main deckbeams are molded 7 inches (high) and sided 9 inches (wide).

one — While most of what one sees above deck is not original, there are occasional exceptions. This beautifully shaped cavil cleat is one. The raised elliptical shape that surrounds the opening is part of the cleat itself, fashioned from the same chunk of wood by the hand of its builder. There are a few of the original rail stanchions remaining — mostly up forward — and these show a crisp nosing off of their corners much the same as the beams and knees do below deck.

two — *Coronet* was fitted with cast bronze stanchions aft of the main rigging that supported a lifeline. The owner and his party normally confined themselves to this part of the deck and apparently the lifelines were installed for their safety. The stanchions themselves are of particular interest, being beautifully cast and finished and having a slightly offset mounting spool so as to stand vertically on the cambered railcap.

offshore cruising yacht in existence") took her twice around Cape Horn, en route to Japan and back, on a scientific expedition for Amherst College. Besides her owners on that trip, *Coronet* carried Professor David Todd and his assistants to study a solar eclipse best visible in Japan. The Japan voyage was memorialized by Mrs. Mabel Loomis Todd in *Corona and Coronet*, published in 1898.

In an earlier voyage (1894), James had taken *Coronet* to an unusual cruising ground for a vessel of her size. Through the locks at St. Peters Canal she went, into the Bras d'Or Lakes of Cape Breton Island. His destination was Baddeck, Nova Scotia. *Coronet* and the Jameses spent a day or so at anchor off Beinn Bhreagh, the then-new home of Alexander Graham Bell, and the following evening, *Coronet* was the scene of an "informal reception" for several Baddeck people, including the Bells. An interesting incident occurred the next day while *Coronet*, under the guidance of a Lake pilot, was beating out of the northern end of the Lake. The pilot had apparently elected to use the Little Bras d'Or channel, hardly more than a narrow winding river, and had also passed up the opportunity for a tow. As a result, *Coronet* went hard aground at the seaward end of the estuary. Captain Crosby turned the air appropriately blue to no avail, and James sent overland to North Sydney for a tug. But with the incoming tide, she floated safely off, and no harm was done. A moment's glance at a chart would give anyone nightmares at the thought of beating up such a channel in a 133-foot schooner. Were they mad, or experienced, or both?

This and the others of James's voyages are written up in *Coronet Memories*, a book of composite authorship tied together by the diarists' common love for the vessel they sailed on. By this time, *Coronet* had become flagship of the prestigious New York Yacht Club.

In 1905, she entered American religious history. Twenty years old, she had lived a long and honorable life, and it seemed time to retire her — so, apparently, thought Louis Bossert, her seventh owner. His last voyage (in 1905) had taken her to the Caribbean, but now she was on the block — for $10,000. And in Maine her broker's notice took the eye of Reverend Frank W. Sandford. Her eighth and final owner thus was The Kingdom, a nondenominational Christian organization then headquartered at Shiloh, Maine. Shiloh's history has been ably documented by William C. Hiss in a doctoral dissertation for Tufts University, and by *Coronet*'s present captain, Frank S. Murray, in a book entitled *The Sublimity of Faith*.

Two themes have characterized the story of the big schooner from 1905 to the present: her people loved God, and her people loved her. It has been my fascinating avocation for several years to document her rich and varied history, and I find that her people also had a particular disinclination to answer questions. They were close-mouthed in the best New England tradition. They were careful to mind their own affairs and hoped that others would do the same. And so the vessel and her people were dubbed "mysterious." Accidents did happen, true enough, even tragedy struck; but mystery, I have found, like beauty, is largely in the eye of the beholder.

Led by Sandford, The Kingdom used *Coronet* in extensive worldwide cruising to maintain mission stations in Great Britain, Egypt, and the Holy Land. Like Arthur Curtiss James, Frank Sandford loved the vessel. He was a devout man; *Coronet* in her fearless indomitability spoke to him, perhaps, of the ideal Christian, the Life Triumphant. Her sailors loved her too. Between 1907 and 1909, Reverend Sandford and 29 others sailed her around the world, this time strictly for missionary purposes. Somewhere on her fourth (and last) passage of Cape Horn, in a howling gale and a bad seaway, one of the watch came bursting into the main cabin shouting, "I love the *Coronet*! I do love the *Coronet*! There is not another vessel like her on the water; she rides these waves like a bird." Her captain on that epic voyage was 26-year-old Lester McKenzie, like Crosby also from Nova Scotia. When he was 96, McKenzie still enjoyed chuckling over *Coronet*'s ability. "When the others'd be reefing down or putting into the nearest harbor," he said, "why then she'd be just beginning to enjoy it!"

It was on this same passage of the Horn that she lost her main boom. The great iron boom bail parted, and, completely unrestrained, the huge spar swung away and broke off against the main rigging. In a tangled mass of cordage, canvas, and wind-whipped ocean, McKenzie and the crew wrestled the spar on deck and secured it, unbent the enormous mainsail, dragged it down into the saloon, and cut it off at the first reef. Repositioning the undamaged jaws on the long section of boom, they then rebent the sail (which now fit nicely) and got underway again.

Captain McKenzie recalled their landfall at Melbourne, Australia. It was night, and they were running up the tortuous channel without a pilot. None of them had ever been there before, yet somehow they sailed her into a safe anchorage. In the morning the waterfront was

Previous page — When the Newport-based Museum of Yachting became interested in *Coronet*, artist John Mecray — one of its founders — did this classic painting of her as she appeared about 1888. The museum has had prints made, and the net income from their sale goes toward *Coronet*'s ongoing care and maintenance.

one — A typical panel in the curved partition of the passageway.

two — Locker doors run along each side of the main saloon above the settees, and their panels are hand carved — each to a different pattern.

three — *Coronet* was modeled along pilot-boat lines and her symmetrical below-decks arrangement is also borrowed to some extent from those craft. Beginning at the mainmast, a fore-and-aft passageway runs forward from the main saloon and the state-rooms open into it from either side. Overhead, a skylight is shared by the staterooms and passageway, giving abundant natural light to all.

four — Aft of the mainmast, the passageway opens into the main saloon, its partitions taking on a serpentine shape, as shown here. As with the staterooms, the saloon's overhead has been sheathed. The lowered sheathing panel extending out from the centerline in way of the mast encases the partner timbers.

five — The most comfortable location on board, and also the most privileged, was given over to the owner as a stateroom and an adjoining study. These spaces were amidships, where the motion

in a seaway was less, and to starboard — the higher-ranking side of any vessel. As one might expect, the most elaborate joinerwork (with the possible exception of the main saloon) is to be found here. The overhead is sheathed with paneling and trim in such a way as to suggest the structure of beams and knees, although completely encasing it. Partly connected to the overhead and partly standing free from it are the joiner bulkheads and partitions, such as this one that is built out over the owner's double bed. Although the guest staterooms have the same basic treatment, they are without embellishments such as the hand-carved posts and panels.

amazed that such a feat had been carried off successfully. "We were crazy," said McKenzie. "Why even *today*, when I think of those things, I get gooseflesh!"

The Kingdom took her to the Holy Land three times, once around the world, to the West Indies and Africa, then to the Arctic — all between 1905 and 1911.

Of *Coronet*'s last voyage under Reverend Sandford, it might be best to mention that it does not represent the vessel's major claim to fame. Enough has been written about it to make the matter unnecessary to recount here. The essentials are that the vessel was overcrowded, her rigging and sails were in bad shape, and food was short. She was about 10 days from Portland, Maine, heading north, when the decision was made to return. The situation, though serious, was not unprecedented in the annals of men and the sea. But at this point it became critical: a series of four severe gales drove the staggering vessel far off course; a 10-day run lengthened to 40 days, and scurvy, that age-old menace of sailors, put in its appearance. Good men died. Reverend Sandford had to be held legally responsible. Yet it was the witness of at least one of the crew that through it all he was everywhere doing his bit on deck, and that it was his unflagging courage (along with that of others) that brought them home at all.

But that was the last of his direct involvement with the vessel he loved. *Coronet* was painstakingly reconditioned, below, on deck, and aloft; but her world-cruising days were over. Time, and the great Portland waterfront fire of 1933, humbled her sadly. During the war years she lay unused at Wiscasset, slipping into deeper and deeper decay. Yet even then The Kingdom had not forgotten. Thus it was that in 1946 and 1947 she was hauled at Donaldson's Yard in South Portland, Maine, and given a thorough refit.

It was there that she took on her present appearance. Diesel engines (GM 6-71s), a large deckhouse aft, shortened and altered rig (triangular mainsail), and the complete absence of brightwork on deck make her a dim shadow of her former glory. But down below, a fair amount of her joinerwork remains. You can still get the idea of the way she was. And out of the water she is always beautiful. Some of her planks still measure 40 feet by 14 inches. And the fine run of her lines may yet turn the head of a shipyard visitor.

Today, *Coronet* is by any standard an unusual vessel. The miles she has traveled, the oceans and seas she has cruised, and the far-flung ports she has frequented place her in a highly unusual category. And besides having early carved out a place in yachting history with her victory over *Dauntless* and her subsequent cruising, she is in fact unique for quite another reason. In the last decade of the 19th century, the yachting world saw the pinnacle of the "big yachts." Never again (except briefly, and less for "yachting" than for racing) would the world see their like. *Coronet* is the last of them to survive. Writing in *Sea History*, the journal of the National Maritime Historical Society, John A. Frieman says "*Coronet* . . . is the only big sailing yacht from before the great age of steam, and . . . was for a time the largest sailing yacht in the New York Yacht Club fleet." Her main beam bears her original registry number, 126346, and she has achieved the distinction of being among the two or three oldest American yachts.

She even made a small but noteworthy addition to science in the Japan trip. And her remaining life has seen an immensely dedicated contribution to humanitarian goals in her missionary voyages and in the unnumbered prayers prayed by her passengers in the interests of people less fortunate.

Fittingly, *Coronet*'s lines are preserved in both full-rigged and half-hull models in the New York Yacht Club model room. In 1962 they were taken off by Francis S. Kinney & Co., yacht designers, for the Smithsonian Institution.

Still a viable cruiser, *Coronet*'s recent voyages have demonstrated her enormous appeal to youth. Her traveling has been confined to coastal New England waters in the last few years, but brief as they are, these trips are eagerly sought after by young people of The Kingdom. (By Coast Guard regulations, passengers are limited to nonpaying church members.) Second-, third-, and even fourth-generation descendants of early officers and passengers have returned to experience the deep delight of a large vessel under sail and to rekindle a spark of dedication to a cause larger than themselves.

Her homeport is Gloucester, Massachusetts, and Gloucester has treated her well. One of the snuggest berths in that snug harbor has been hers for more than 25 years. It was in Gloucester that I came to know the old *Coronet* well, and in this case to know her was to love her. Her personality grows on you. I've used the word "indomitable" in describing it; courage is there, too. And, somehow, purpose — a sense of mission.

And yet *Coronet* is living in a hardheaded age. The Kingdom spends several thousand dollars a year on her, in addition to much volunteer labor. What are the returns? The question

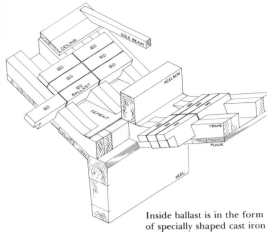

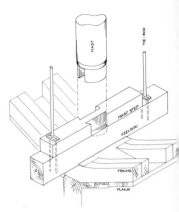

and, taken altogether, this method of ballasting is worthy of adoption in some of the sawn-frame craft being built today. For good fore-and-aft drainage to the pump suction, enough cement was poured into the bilge to cover the lower portions of the frames next to the keelson and form a trough leading from the ends of the vessel to the pump well. *Coronet*'s frames are double-sawn of 6-inch timbers and spaced on what appears to be 26-inch centers.

There are many ways to build mast steps — from a simple mortise cut in the keelson to eleborate and complex affairs that are built from a number of separate pieces — but *Coronet*'s seems to occupy a kind of middle ground. Like much of her other structure,

the step for her foremast, shown here, was soundly based on the wide experience that was available to the builder at the time. It locks the mast in both fore-and-aft and athwart-ships directions and is separate from the keelson so as not to weaken that principal back-bone timber by cutting into it. It is long enough to take considerable fore-and-aft thrust from the mast without fear of splitting, and this length helps spread out the downward force of the mast as well. There are no pockets where water might become trapped, as might happen if the limbers were to get plug-ged up in a mortised step. Of particular interest are the two tie rods with flanges on their ends that are fastened to the step on one end and to the partner, at main deck level, on the other. Such a connec-

tion between the keel and the deck framing has been found necessary on well-thought-out smaller craft, but few builders of large sailing schooners had the foresight to install them. *Coronet*'s mainmast step was inaccessible but is probably quite similar to this one.

Inside ballast is in the form of specially shaped cast iron pigs that nest in the frame bays, their weight being taken by their "wings" which land on frame faces. The planking is thus spared from bearing any of the load. There is a lifting socket cast into each piece for ease of handling,

---

grows insistent as time goes on. To date she has been maintained as a sort of living symbol of what The Kingdom stands for: worldwide out-reach to prepare for the second coming of Christ. She embodied the unflinching willing-ness and ability to go to the limits of endurance on behalf of others. She has been a shrine: she has been to The Kingdom what the U.S.S. Con-stitution is to the United States — a physical link with cherished roots. She is a reminder; she is a spur to courageous dedication in the present.

But the vessel's current condition demands attention. Her last real survey was over 30 years ago. She needs a new mainmast (we built a new

foremast a few years back). She needs a new stem. She needs a lot of things. Most of all perhaps, she needs a friend.

And yet the fine old vessel rides the tide. As I wryly remarked recently to a dockside in-quirer, most of her cruising nowadays is up and down. Surely she deserves better of the maritime world. She should not be allowed to go into neglect. She must not be forgotten. For if, like a quiet and refined old lady, she has lost some of her grace, she has lost none of her charm — or character. For some of us, she never can. For some of us, please God, she never will.

Since 1907, when this plan was drawn, there have been a number of changes to *Coronet*'s arrangement, the most major one being the addition of an engine room in what shows here as the after part of the main saloon. Bulkheaded off from the saloon itself, it is a small space —— a little over 8 feet long — just large enough to squeeze in the pair of side-by-side diesels that provide auxiliary power. Another transformation has taken place in the galley, where, by expansion into the pantry and food storage lockers, additional space has been gained. And for housekeeping convenience, up-

to-date appliances have been installed.

On deck, *Coronet* bears little resemblance to the tall-sparred sailing yacht of 1885. Her masts are shorter and she no longer carries topmasts, a jibboom, or a main gaff. Her deck, most of her bulwarks, and her hatches and skylights have been renewed — according to a more stringent budget than when built originally. With two GM-671 diesel engines she is, perhaps, more motorsailer than schooner yacht. But she's still an unusually fine vessel, well cared for — to the extent finances allow — by people who love her dearly.

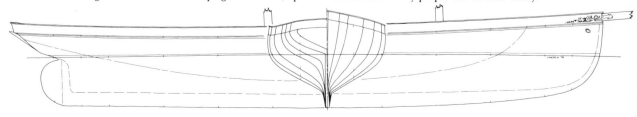

Another *Reality*

Bent Jesperson

A SOMETIMES-*unfair assessment of the wooden boat renaissance labels the movement as reactionary (in the negative sense) as opposed to progressive (in the positive sense). As at least a partial response to this charge, we offer the following piece as a simultaneous celebration of both traditional and the most-modern wooden boat technology. The article discusses a solution to the build-or-rebuild dilemma that can be adapted by nearly anyone in a similar situation. What's more, the piece demonstrates that the skills of many of today's wooden boatbuilders and restorers may be founded on the methods of the past, but they are not bound by them as one would expect. Consider the author, for example. Bent Jespersen is a Dane who apprenticed in his homeland before emigrating to Sidney, British Columbia, and setting up his own boatshop. Here is a man who studied under the old masters, who learned the old ways, who specialized in the traditional construction methods for 29 years, yet who was able to adapt the new wood technologies to a very old problem. His open-mindedness is not atypical for today's wooden boatbuilders.*

In her original form,
Reality was a classically
beautiful 8-meter sloop.

ROLAND BRENER, owner of *Reality*, started it all without knowing, when he entered the 1978 Strait of Georgia Race. The race began with the usual long downwind run to the northernmost mark of the course. The wind was building rapidly and the old 8-meter, built by Camper and Nicholson about 1935, was doing extremely well, since she was not encountering the same control problems the newer boats were meeting. By the time the mark was rounded, the wind was up to 40 knots, and a 25-mile thrash to weather lay ahead. This was the old girl's undoing. The garboard was letting in a stream for its entire length, and water was pouring in through numerous holes in the deck. Headstay sag couldn't be eliminated due to flex in the boat. It was then, between pumping spells, that Roland, the owner, and Jim Ross, a crew member and enthusiastic meter-boat buff, began talking about a new boat, along much the same lines as *Reality*, with slightly higher freeboard and the original 8-meter rig.

Roland was wondering if there was any way of using fiberglass to rebuild *Reality*, or even to build a new boat. Jim, however, suggested a cold-molded wooden hull. They decided to visit me at my shop to discuss the financial feasibility and practicality of building a new wooden hull and using the ballast, engine, and as much rigging as possible from the old boat.

After much discussion, it was decided that the old boat should also be used as a plug or building jig, after modifying the bow profile to match the transom, which had been modified the year before. It was also agreed that the new boat should have more freeboard, which meant that the beam amidships would have to be greater to compensate for the excessive tumblehome caused by higher topsides. I talked with Bill Garden quite regularly during this time. He has always loved meter boats and is open to new ideas. Bill felt our plan was a good one.

We were all caught up with the challenge the job offered, but before starting on it, Roland wanted to race the old boat in the Swiftsure with leaking garboards and all. He and his wife, Dama, also wanted to cruise to the Queen Charlotte Islands and around Vancouver Island before stripping the boat of usable hardware. *Reality* did well in the Swiftsure, and Roland and Dama made their planned trip up north and were more convinced than ever that *Reality* was the kind of boat they wanted. I kept receiving postcards from out-of-the-way places reassuring me that the boat was still hanging together, and that they would keep their promise of bringing the 14,000 pounds of lead ballast back to Sidney.

Reality was lifted out of the water and brought over to my shop on a flatbed truck in the middle of October 1978. Roland already had spent considerable time removing hardware, undoing keelbolts, etc. A crane first lifted the engine out, then lifted the boat off the ballast keel. It took a bit of shaking to break the bedding, but it came free without real difficulty. The next step was to turn the hull upside down and place it on a dolly. This was done with the crane and a double set of slings; a very neat operation.

The hull was then moved into the shop, and the new bow profile was laid out with the help of a few battens and some basic measurements. The extra beam was determined by springing a stiff batten around the sheer and then attaching horizontal fairing pieces every 6 inches to fair the new sheerline into the existing load waterline. A new deck shelf was made out of mahogany and fastened up under the old toe rail with lag screws for easy removal when it came time to separate the halves of the hull from the plug.

The biggest challenge (and worry) was to make the profile pattern for the new backbone. It was to be one lamination 50 feet long, 4½ inches thick, varying in width from 7 inches to 14 inches, and varying in bevel from 10 to 80 degrees. The profile was marked off every 18 inches square with the profile line, and angles were taken with the help of a bevel square and level measurements. All stations thus lifted off the hull were then laid out full size on a piece of plywood. From these lines the planking thickness of three layers of ⅜-inch red cedar was deducted, in order to arrive at the same keel width to fit the old ballast. Of course, doing it this way did not give us a duplicate hull shape, but one slightly deeper in the ends. Since this also added buoyancy, it was thought to be beneficial.

The new backbone would have to be laminated on the shop floor where the boat was standing, so our attention turned to the planking, after we covered the plug with waxed paper to ensure an easy release.

The first diagonal layer of planking, which took three men one week, was done in the following manner. First, a straight veneer was tacked onto the plug amidships; then, a second was placed 1 inch away and marked with scribers. This one was then removed and nailed on top of another, and the two were sawn together on the table saw. This gave us a plank for each side. This procedure was repeated after the previous plank was edge-glued with epoxy and fastened to the plug. The second layer, diagonal to the first, was done in much the same man-

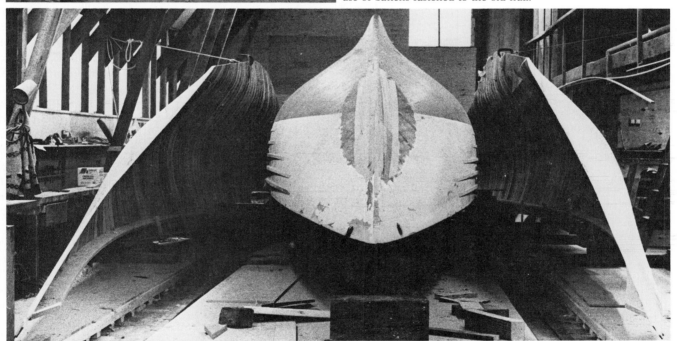

Reality's new hull was created by molding three veneers per side over the inverted old hull. The two inner layers were run diagonally, and the third layer was run fore and aft, a process that required somewhat more time but also was more satisfying. *At the left*, the second veneer layer is nearly all faired off, and *above*, Bent Jespersen applies the glue for the third-layer veneers. *Below*, the finished halves are removed (note the harpins already in place at the sheer). Topside flare in the new hull was achieved by the use of battens fastened to the old hull.

At left, the laminated backbone has been glued and clamped to shape on the floor between the upright halves. *Below*, the faired backbone is braced and the hull halves will be glued and fastened to it.

The new *Reality* nears completion. Ten days after launching, she entered the Swiftsure race, in which she was first home.

Reality, What a Concept

The original 8-meter *Reality* was built by Camper and Nicholson about 1935. European champion in the 8-meter class in the late 1930s, and successful defender of the Queen's Cup against France in 1938, she was of composite construction, mahogany planked with glued splines, galvanized steel frames, and copper fastenings. The frames and floors were badly corroded, and the wood itself was showing signs of electrolysis by the time I decided on the new boat. The garboards leaked to the point that the electric pumps were needed almost constantly. Despite the nearly defunct state of *Reality*, we had enjoyed the boat immensely for five years, racing her with some success under the P.H.R.F. system, and also cruising extensively in the Northwest every year. In fact, my wife and I found her to be an ideal cruising boat, and this confidence in the design prompted us to consider building a new *Reality*. Our experience with the boat enabled us to come up with exact modifications that we felt would improve on the original, at least for our purposes. Our builder, Bent Jespersen, refined and executed them. He proved to be a true artist with a wonderful sense of proportion and cor-

rectness. The new *Reality* was built without any drawings or plans — we simply discussed the project with Bent, and then he went about building it.

We raced the new *Reality* in the Swiftsure 10 days after launching. The boat was untuned and untested, but with a good crew, including Bent Jespersen and Charles Afford (who works for Bent), we were the fastest boat in P.H.R.F., and first home. Though the boat was not tuned for going to weather, which is thought to be her best point of sailing, we were spectacularly fast downwind. At the end of July, my wife, Dama Hanks, and I began a cruise down the California coast, across to Hawaii, and back to British Columbia. The boat attracts a crowd wherever we go and is beautiful either under sail or at the dock. I believe that *Reality* is one idea of an ultimate boat for two people. I designed a seven-eighths rig for the new boat (as opposed to a three-fourths in the original design) and with the increased sail area derived from a larger foretriangle, we do not need a genoa and never have to change headsails. The boat is very fast in all conditions, including very light

winds. The power is a single-cylinder Farymann diesel of 2 h.p. With a Martec folding propeller, it pushes the boat at 6 knots and gives an idea of just how easily driven the hull is. The hull is very light and sits right on her lines, just as I had hoped, when fully laden with all our cruising gear. The motion at sea is extremely comfortable, and the added freeboard and hollow entry have made the boat dry to sail. With her excellent balance and ease of handling, she is always a pleasure, and I singlehand her with ease. It is true that *Reality* can be sailed like a dinghy, can be sailed in and out of crowded harbors due to her responsiveness and ability to turn on a dime, and can undertake extended voyages with ease. This is a boat that does not mind where her crew sits or if they move around. A hard dinghy is carried on the foredeck, and there is more storage space than we shall ever need.

Though Bent did the majority of the work on the new *Reality*, and Dama and I, for the most part, lent a hand with the painting and varnishing, *Reality* cost us a great deal less than most people would guess. It is a concept and project I would recommend without hesitation to anyone who loves this sort of boat.

ner, the only difference being that nails had to be pulled and glue drools faired off before any planking in the second layer could be spiled. The epoxy between the layers was thickened with Cab-o-Sil to discourage any air voids. The third layer of planking, however, was done the conventional fore-and-aft way. This was slightly slower, but a nice change. Next we

faired the entire surface of the hull.

We always get a lot of tourists and know-it-alls coming into the shop, and at this stage we were presented with no end of good advice on how to fair the hull. Some suggested bodyfiles and belt sanders, and some recommended vibrators and disc grinders. After they had finished with their suggestions, we would tell them that we were going to plane the hull by hand, using those old-fashioned-looking wooden planes lying on the bench, and then sand the hull with large sanding blocks. They would shake their heads and tell me about a friend of theirs who had spent 1,000 hours fairing a one-off glass hull. Our whole operation took three men three days for a job well done.

It was an exciting day when the two half hulls were separated from the plug and moved to the sides of the shop. The old hull was then moved out. We now had the two halves in an upside-down position, so we turned them over and interchanged them so they would be ready for joining when the time came.

Forty L-shaped brackets with plywood gussets on either side had been constructed ahead of time. These were nailed to the floor along the full-scale drawing of the backbone. Seven 50-foot-long laminates were each made up by scarfing together four shorter pieces, ¾ inch by 12 inches. These were cut to the exact width of the backbone, then glued and bent around the brackets. The whole assembly was left in clamps for two days before being beveled and erected in the center of the shop. It took about 100 clamps to do the job; all the boatshops in Sidney stopped for two days while we borrowed their clamps.

The two halves were fitted and fastened to the backbone with Coldcure epoxy glue and 2½-inch No. 16 stainless screws, one every 5 inches. After installing the transom and epoxy-sealing everything inside and out, the hull was complete.

We could now breathe a sigh of relief, as the innovative part was over. I personally had done a lot of thinking and worrying up to this point, but the rest was straightforward. Floor timbers were fitted and fastened, and bulkheads, deck-beams, and engine beds were installed. Two layers of ⅜-inch fir plywood covered with Dynel and epoxy were used in the construction of the deck. Honduras mahogany was used for the cabin sides, cockpit coamings, sheer plank, and railcap. Three layers of ¼-inch plywood with Dynel and epoxy were used for the cabintop.

Roland and Dama were burning the midnight oil at this time, doing all the painting and varnishing. When this was done, the time had come to move the boat outside and lift it onto the ballast. The deadwood and rudder were then fitted, and the engine and tanks were installed. Finally, the bottom was sanded and painted.

Launching day was set for May 11. The owner and builder were running around look-

A whole new *Reality* beats across San Francisco Bay. According to her proud owner, she is very dry and fast and a pleasure to sail.

ing confused, but everything went very smoothly. The crane arrived on time, Dama christened the boat, everyone cheered, and the new *Reality* was lowered into the water.

We had been hoping to enter the new boat in the 1979 Swiftsure at the end of May, and although we had everything ready in time, we had had no chance to sail the boat in any sort of breeze before the race. In fact, the only trial under sail was from Sidney to Victoria, the day before the race.

The 1979 Swiftsure turned out to be one of the windiest on record, which was not exactly the kind of weather we had hoped for. However, after slugging along to weather for a couple of hours in 40 knots of breeze and a wild sea, we soon felt more at ease and began to concentrate on winning the 170-mile race. *Reality* was first to finish in the P.H.R.F. fleet and corrected to fourth overall.

I am now sure that no matter how many boats I may build in my lifetime, *Reality* will always be close to my heart. The challenge this job presented and the pleasure of working closely with Roland and Dama will be remembered as two of the true rewards of wooden boatbuilding.

The New York Thirties

P ROBABLY THE MOST ambitious WoodenBoat collection of multifaceted material on a single subject examines the Nathanael Herreshoff-designed New York Thirties, a class of yachts built in 1905 that is still going strong. Indeed, the series is perhaps our most successful collection of new and old text and art.

In celebration of the New York Thirities' 75th year in 1980, we assembled the following stories from individuals who have been, or are, intimately connected with the Thirties. David Kiremidjian describes the inspiration these boats still impart. The late William H. Taylor chronicled their 25th and 50th anniversaries for Yachting magazine, and we were kindly given permission to reprint some of his work for their 75th. What it's like to sail in a New York Thirty is told by Roger Taylor, drawing on his experiences aboard Cockatoo II. Ted Okie tells of the restoration of his Old Timer. Drawings by Sam Manning (describing Old Timer's reframing) and Spencer Lincoln (showing sail plan, arrangement plan and lines) complete our tribute to this unique and outstanding one-design class.

Sheets slacked for reaching. *Banzai* takes off.

Time Is Grace

IN A TIME becoming increasingly aware of its traditions, and increasingly occupied with the preservation and restoration of its finer symbols, it is not unusual to find a classic yacht 75 years old. But it is rare, very rare, to find that out of a class of 18 New York Yacht Club Thirty class sloops built in 1905, at least 13 still exist. We are dealing with a special case. From the beginning, the Herreshoff New York Thirty design was a design set apart, and even after the initial 20-odd-year period of their extraordinary class racing was over, they continued to accumulate the kind of experience that myths are made of — so broad, so varied, that the term "symbol" may not for once be out of place.

The history of the boats is very complex, and now necessarily incomplete. It is difficult to account for their unusual past, but even more so for their continuing present. There are numberless documents, stories, and anecdotes about the boats and the class. By the 1940s, they had become legends to their owners, vessels of incomparable meaning, a feeling well expressed, for example, by Evelyn Mulligan in her lyrical memoir of the charmed life of the *Banzai* (*Motor Boating*, February 1965) or by Bill Wolf, owner of the *Ibis*, who years after having resolved to own a Thirty, sensed that the dream had become reality almost by its own volition, as if the boat had come to him rather than the other way around, magnetized by an almost mystical bond. Other owners have been more straightforward, less romantic, but always acting with great respect for the design and with a strong awareness of the responsibility that age and tradition imposes, regardless of how unusual they felt the whole enterprise to be. Thus Lloyd Bergeson went about the renewal of *Cockatoo II* (ex-*Pintail*, No. 5) in the late 1950s with lucid purpose and method, transforming the boat into a highly successful ocean racer. And Gordon Group, a Cleveland surveyor, asked to evaluate a near-derelict Thirty before she was broken up, not only saved her but, through a tenacity he was at a loss to explain, saw her through three years of trouble and frustration to a complete restoration. In a kind of charmed alternation of near destruction and great good fortune, each of the surviving vessels floats in its own mythical water.

So one searches for the whys and wherefores of such an unprecedented survival. The answers aren't really adequate. Certainly part of it, a great part, is in the origins of the boats themselves, although evidently Herreshoff himself did not intend his creations to last such an extraordinarily long time. It was reported that he considered 20 years a reasonable life expectancy, not surprising since he tended to be unromantic about his creations, and in some ways unhistorical, although very aware of his position in the development of yacht design. We, on the other hand, knowing how long some of his craft have lasted, cannot help speculating about how long they would yet endure if he had intended them to — if, for example, the New York Forties had been given other than galvanized bilge straps.

His was a different era, however, and in asking such questions, we miss something essential about it. Herreshoff, and the other designers of the day, had no need to create for posterity. They produced boats of unsurpassed excellence in materials and craftsmanship simply because that was part of the tradition they belonged to, a self-perpetuating tradition of quality for its own sake, and not for the purpose of braving time. The turn of the century was, after all, a lavish and extravagant era; the exhaustion of great imaginations along with the generous material power to actualize their purposes was hardly thinkable.

But here we are, very definitely "posterity," having barely survived the near-exhaustion of certain traditions in skilled arts of craftsmanship, and the absolute extinction of certain materials. Being very much tuned to survival, any boat or object that has been well preserved or well restored becomes a powerful talisman of our own vital expectations.

When Herreshoff built the New York Thirties (or the "626 class," as they were identified, after the number of the first hull in the series), he was probably concerned only with their success as a rather specialized and transient design experiment. But at the other end of the 75 years, we know that Herreshoff's genius functioned with remarkable consistency in the most varied of design experiments, and that the skills and materials at the Bristol yard justify their legendary status.

Some of the intense interest in the Thirties as a one-design class waned as newer designs began to emerge, particularly the 8- and 10-

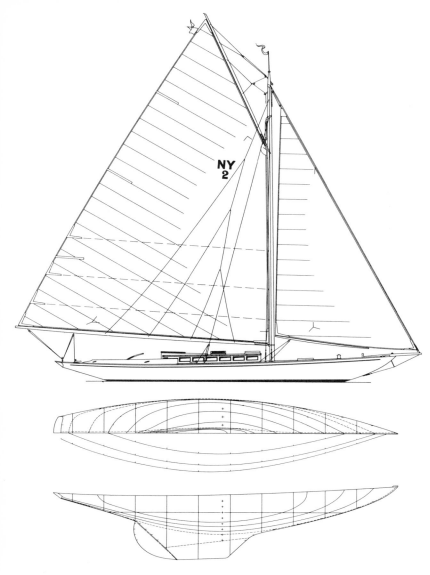

meter classes (although, ironically, class racing in these did not last as long as racing in the Thirties). But as they began to show their age, some were sold out of the club and others were withdrawn from racing altogether. At this point, their history ceases being the collective saga of a privileged and protected era and begins to take on broader, deeper values. Each boat begins a long, solitary, and vulnerable voyage into unknown waters, with only her own intrinsic grace, speed, and seaworthiness to stand her witness. Each encounter with a new prospective owner was a possible chance of neglect, deterioration, and destruction — which is why some fond owners, preferring rather to destroy a favorite vessel themselves than leave a more lengthy butchery to strange hands, specify in their wills that the boat be scuttled. It is true that many fine vessels have been slowly mutilated to death by ignorance and insensitivity. But it is also true that men who have bought boats for nearly nothing with the avowed purpose of scrapping them for ballast and equipment have

found to their amazement that they simply were unable to do the deed when confronted with the reality of the boat itself. The Thirties possessed that requisite harmony of striking line and movement afloat that could make a fatal imprint on anyone at all alive to the subtle elusiveness of beauty and function. After the great care they had received in their early years, they had learned to take care of themselves.

Of all the Thirties, *Ibis*, No. 2 of the class, has met with the most varied fortunes. She was built for C. O'Donnell Iselin, passed to J.P. Morgan, Jr., in 1908, and to Howard Maxwell in 1913, then to six more owners before John Dallett bought her in 1927 and had her shipped to Puerto Rico aboard one of his steamers. He changed her name to *Silhouette* and sailed her back to New York a few years later. During the 1930s, the boat raced on the Sound, and it was during these years that the young Mike Mulligan saw her and resolved to someday own a Thirty. (He subsequently bought *Banzai* in 1940 after the death of Edmund Lang, another of the most devoted Thirties owners, and kept the boat for some 25 years in Manhasset Bay.) But the *Silhouette*, renamed again *Ione* in 1935, went ashore at Throgs Neck in the 1938 hurricane and was purchased by John Rodstrom and Ed Quest. They proceeded with considerable rebuilding, giving her a marconi yawl rig, an engine, and a higher doghouse in place of the distinctive square-windowed trunk cabin. They sailed her until 1945 and sold her to John Hurley. On a cruise out to the eastern end of Long Island in 1946, he anchored one night east of Sag Harbor in the protected bight between Cedar Point Light and Northwest Creek. Early in the morning, he was visited by Bill Wolf, then 16, a sailing instructor at the nearby St. Regis Camp. Wolf reminisces that he had never seen a boat so beautiful as the *Ibis*, and before the day was out, he had vowed that someday he would own that boat.

After Hurley's ownership, the *Ibis* went to Morton Engle of Mamaroneck, who changed her name to *Huntress* and raced her successfully for a few years. In 1954, however, she slipped her mooring in Hurricane Carol and sank in 90 feet of water off Hen and Chickens. Usually that would be sufficient. But not this time, and not for this boat. The *Ibis* was raised and sold to Jack Pomeroy, who removed her lead ballast, most of her fittings, and her mainmast to fit out the 60-foot ketch *Alice*, which he had just acquired. What remained of *Ibis* was then laid up in a yard in Mamaroneck.

And there she lay for nearly four years. She was finally bought for $400 by John Caulfield, a college student. Along with the purchase came the demand from the yard to move the boat "immediately," so John painted her hull grey, launched her, and went to his club at Pelham Manor, where they declined respectfully the honor of receiving so aged a lady. Nothing daunted, she was anchored awash on a mud bank. It was then that Bill Wolf, now Coast Guard licensed and much a part of the life around City Island, heard of her. One night in November, he and a friend, after a quick purchase ceremony with John Caulfield, towed her to Throgs Neck, where she spent the winter high in the water on an 18-pound anchor. Curiously, she leaked hardly at all without the ballast — merely through an old teredo spiral around her rudderstock.

The *Ibis* was rebuilt over the next eight years. Nearly all her frames were sistered, both port and starboard, the horn timber and transom were replaced, a new lead keel was poured and installed, the engine was rebuilt, and new spars were secured or reglued and stepped. The *Ibis* was under sail again in 1966, after 12 years of slow rebirth and 20 years after Bill's first resolve one summer morning near Sag Harbor.

The late 1960s marked bottom dead center for wooden boat activity in general, and in the midst of our national problems and a set of cultural values quite antagonistic to tradition and conservation, the issues of older racing yachts seemed quite remote. But the tide was beginning to turn, and other values were trying to be reborn. The history of *Old Timer*, ex-*Cara Mia*, No. 14, is quite different from that of the *Ibis* and shows well the gathering of other impulses. *Old Timer* had been well owned by H.A. Calahan for the better part of 20 years, and his books on racing and cruising are full of his proud experi-

ence with the boat. He finally sold the Thirty to John Ohl of Sands Point in the early 1950s. Ohl converted her to double head-rigged marconi sloop, installed an engine, and raced her extensively during that decade. After him, the boat fell on some evil days in the middle 1960s, until she was purchased for the yard bill by William Yaro, who was as knowledgeable about turn-of-the-century Herreshoffs as he was devoted to them. Perhaps because *Old Timer* had enjoyed such good ownership and maintenance over the years, she had never been rebuilt (and had also remained in original condition, except for the rig), but now she needed a lot of attention. Yaro took her to Arthur Barstow's yard in Greenport, where some of her framing, planking, and floor timbers in way of the mast were renewed. A hitch in the Navy, and then one in law school, prevented Yaro from completing the work, and *Old Timer* remained largely laid up at Greenport until she was acquired in 1978 by Ted Okie. Okie had acquired a very sharp appreciation of the traditions that *Old Timer* embodies (and has no little command of them himself), and he is having the boat restored at Mystic according to original practice in design and materials. When completed and launched as *Cara Mia*, she will be essentially a new vessel; *Cara Mia*, with *Banzai* and the *Anemone II*, are the only boats still retaining the original design of hull, deck, and house.

It was by means of a series of fortunes and near misfortunes that *Amorita*, ex-*Adelaide II*, No. 9, was spared the chainsaw and the bulldozer. She was one of the boats that went to Lake Erie in the early 1930s. Sometime during the early 1960s, she was fiberglassed and received a new doghouse, but by 1975 she was a derelict in a Cleveland yacht club yard. The

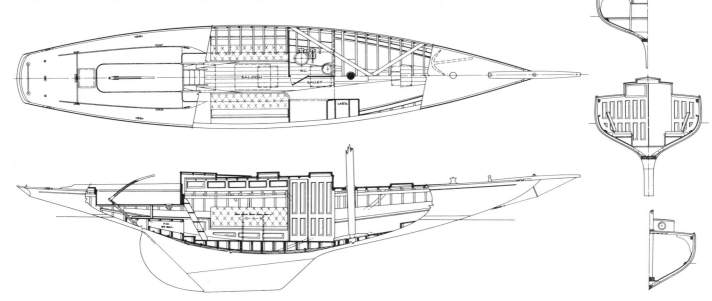

club trustees called on Gordon Group to do a value survey on the boat, but after filing his report, and realizing the old Thirty would be broken up despite her history and superb construction, Gordon Group found he could not sleep. He then proceeded to do exactly what he had advised countless less experienced and certainly less rational dreamweavers never to do — undertake the restoration of an aged wooden boat. Gordon gave the owner his personal commitment to avert the destruction of the boat. He had the vessel moved not once, but twice. He had nearly come to contract with one yard on a rebuilding only to have negotiations collapse, before finally persuading Anthony Musca, a close friend, to underwrite a proper restoration. Over the next two years, he oversaw the long and often delayed process: the boat was first taken down to the wood, then some garboard planking, the horn timber, and a number of floors were renewed, a diesel was installed, and the wiring and plumbing were overhauled. As is sometimes the case, once the job was completed, the connections with *Amorita* were gone. The boat was first put up for sale and eventually donated to a marine historical organization on Long Island.

Only three boats of the original 18 are definitely gone. Two more are missing, but there is a good chance that they may still be sailing, somewhere. The 13 known survivors exist in various forms, all the way from near basket cases no longer in use to well-kept-up craft still under sail each year. Although their condition and appearance aren't what they used to be in most cases, the Thirties have earned the homage they have received over the years as one of the most distinguished of all the racing classes, an embodiment of the best in design, craftsmanship, and devoted ownership.

But what emerges today is not just the story of yet another symbol about to enter a museum, but a record of men who still perceive the life and utility of a creation whose value is intrinsic and enduring, and who possess the sensitivity and the will to insist regardless of conditions that these values be affirmed and reinstated. They represent a form of experience that is indeed privileged, but for no other reason than the fact that they do offer a way of life, as they did not only for their owners but also for many who touched the boats in some fashion. We would hope that the extraordinary anniversary the Thirties celebrated in 1980 will become not only a focus for their particular renewal, but a center of revitalization for many vessels similarly distinguished and similarly placed in our tradition.

At 25,

YACHT RACING classes, be they one-design or built to a rule, are notoriously subject to waves of popularity frequently followed by swift oblivion — a score of boats fighting for a championship for a year or two, and a few years later just a few scattered boats, lost from the racing lists altogether or relegated to the handicap classes. But there is one class now fitting out for its 25th season that has seen the others come and go and which promises to furnish some of the best racing of the coming summer on Long Island Sound — the New York "Thirties."

Undoubtedly the most famous one-design class this country has ever seen, the Thirties should muster close to a dozen boats this year, and their owners have laid out a program of regular and special races that promises sport rivaling that of their first year in 1905.

The agitation of the New York Yacht Club in 1904 for a one-design class of about 30 feet on the waterline resulted in the appointment, in October of that year, of Newberry Lawton, Addison G. Hanan and W. Butler Duncan, Jr., as a committee to arrange for the design and building of such a class.

On November 16th, the Committee accepted the plans and ordered eight boats, and by February 1905, all 18 of the present existing boats had been ordered and their construction started.

Before delivery in the spring of 1905, the class committee drew the numbers of the 18 boats and allotted them to their owners. The racing numbers have never been changed.

The 18 boats were originally white. *Phryne* was painted black after a few races, and at some time in her early career, *Banzai* followed *Phryne*'s lead. One came out blue, one year, and another green, but they look best white.

To go into the racing records of the Thirties — even if you could find them all — would make this article look like Bowditch's navigation tables. They sailed in 51 races the first year, the largest number of Thirties ever on record as sailing together being a fleet of 15 in one race during 1905. From then on, the class has figured prominently in the races of the New York Yacht Club, those on Long Island Sound, and in the old days, in lower New York Bay when that was a yachting center prior to 1916 — now

One of the Best Classes Ever Built

(Excerpted from Yachting, *May, 1929)*　　　　　William H. Taylor

hopelessly ruined by commercial traffic and floating debris.

Not only have the Thirties afforded excellent sport within their own class, but they have won their share of honors in open competition. In their first year, they took three of the great cups on the New York Yacht Club Cruise — two Commodore's Cups and the Rear Commodore's Cup, and they kept it up. As recently as 1927, sailing in handicap competition with the biggest, the fastest, and the most modern yachts in the club, Mr. Davis' *Alice*, sailed by C. Sherman Hoyt (because her owner was busy with his duties on the race committee), performed the outstanding feat of the cruise in defeating a fleet of 30-odd competitors by a wide margin on a run from Vineyard Haven to Newport.

In 1927, J.P. Morgan, now owner of *Phryne*, fitted her with a jib-headed rig and raced, not as a member of the class, but against them for purposes of comparison. The conversion was probably the most successful of its kind. With about 75 feet less canvas, *Phryne* appeared at least as fast as the other nine boats racing in the class that year, and unlike most conversion jobs, the new rig actually added to her beauty. Mr. Morgan's purpose was purely experimental, with the idea that the whole class might be converted if *Phryne* was successful, and a few members now favor such a change. The consensus of opinion among the owners, however, seems to be that the Thirties are as good a class today as they ever were and they see no reason for changing, as not only would the new rigs themselves be expensive, but many of the boats would have to be practically rebuilt to withstand the strains of the taller masts.

A few of the Thirties, of course, have dropped out of the racing lists, and one is now yawl-rigged. They make good cruising boats,

Jammed hard on the wind, this looks like the start of a class race. These longer bowsprits were installed after the first season.

which is one of their charms. But, thanks not only to the boats but to the caliber of the men who have almost invariably owned them, they have always been a strong racing class, and have seen many others come and go in the Long Island Sound racing — the Jewels, the Larchmont one-design, the Qs, the large sloop class of 65s with such boats as *Aurora* and *Winsome*, the Stamford schooners and the Sound schooners, and many more. They were stronger last summer than the Forties or Fifties, although the two latter classes should pick up this year. Ten of the Thirties raced regularly in 1927 and about as many in 1928. Judging from the preseason enthusiasm and the special races for them that have been arranged for 1929 in honor of their silver jubilee, they should be stronger this summer than for many years past. Perhaps they will observe a 30th or even a 35th anniversary, which would be a miracle indeed.

To chronicle the various changes in ownership and names that the 18 boats have passed through would tax the space of a single article, but the record includes many famous yachting names, past and present.

The explanation of the survival and present popularity of the Thirties is, I think, to be found in the type of men who have owned and sailed them. Men and boats make a class. And as to the quality of the boats, you have only to remember how frequently men who have once been in the class and sold out of it have either bought back their old boats — sometimes at a considerable advance in cost — or bought other Thirties.

The Thirties, old as they are, have everything that makes a good racing yacht on the Sound. Fast drifters in the lightest of airs, they can still thrash out to windward in great style in a blow. And yet — most unusual in a modern racing boat — they are really good, comfortable cruisers for their inches, and the class rules keep them so. Last spring, the so-called Eight-meter one-design class was brought out on the Sound, avowedly to replace the Thirties, but while the new class are good boats, equal in speed if not in comfort to the Thirties, I have yet to talk to a Thirty owner who feels that the boats need replacing, or who would trade his Thirty for the best Eight in the class.

One interesting item of note in checking over the list of the 18 original boats is that 13 have been active in the racing during one or both of the past two seasons, and that with one exception (the boat rerigged as a yawl), every one of the original yachts is easily available, if her owner chooses, for the jubilee program that enthusiastic owners are arranging for this summer.

A Salute to the First One-

(Excerpted from Yachting, *March, 1955)*

TWO SCORE and ten years ago, the Herreshoff Manufacturing Company brought forth what was destined to become, in this year of 1955, the first class of one-design racing yachts ever to reach the ripe old age of 50 years — and still be racing. Not, to be sure, still racing as the red-hot one-design class they were for most of those 50 years, as most of them have been rerigged and probably no two are exactly alike now. Nevertheless, most of the New York Yacht Club 30-foot class are still actively sailing on waters all the way from Puget Sound to Chesapeake Bay, and some of them, at least, will be racing among themselves and in mixed company in their 51st season.

It is difficult to remember now that when they were built, these 30-foot-waterline keel sloops were "small boats." They were, in fact, the smallest things that the New York Yacht Club recognized as sailing yachts at all. Men whose boats weren't at least that long on the waterline had no vote in the club, and no smal-

Design Yachts to Reach the Half-Century Mark

William H. Taylor

The dark-hulled *Phryne*, with a reef tucked in, seems to be leading the pack in this 1905 race.

ler craft, even though owned by members, could race in the annual cruise and other club events.

The movement to build such a class came from a group of younger members of the club, but among the 18 original owners were a number of men who could or did own much larger yachts. What they had in mind was "a wholesome, seaworthy craft, free from freak features, about 30-foot waterline, with short overhangs, moderate beam and draft, cabin house, complete with simple outfit for cruising, sail area about 1,000 square feet."

Few, if any, of the original owners have survived the boats, of which at least 14 are still going, some still racing actively, others taking life easier.

Their first race was held by the Manhasset Bay Yacht Club (then only 14 years old) on Long Island Sound early in the spring of 1905. Thirty years later, the same club held an anniversary race for them over the same course—

Matinecock Point was one turning mark—and about half the original 18 turned out. This year, Manhasset is scheduling the Thirties again in the club's annual Fall Series in September. How many will turn up remains to be seen, but some certainly will, as many of the active survivors are owned in the western Sound ports and some may come from farther away.

For 25 years, very few of them were altered in any way, although eventually hard racing and sail carrying — a Thirty skipper rarely reefed, blow high or low—called for some reinforcement in way of the mast step and rigging.

During all those years and well on into the 1930s, the Thirties, in addition to being one of the hottest, most competitive classes on the Sound, were always to be feared by bigger craft in such events as the New York Yacht Club cruises on which, year in and year out, they saved their time to win the major trophies.

The Thirties could go in a hard breeze, and drag what sail they couldn't carry with the aid of their 8,800-pound lead keels. They could also ghost in what seemed no breeze at all. The writer vividly remembers lying becalmed off Execution Rocks all of one hot, seemingly windless summer day in a heavy Friendship sloop — no slouch of a sailer in most weathers. Mel Smith, in the 30-footer *Interlude*, ghosted out of Manhasset Bay past us in the early morning, sailed some 15 miles to Center Island, sailed in and finished a Seawanhaka regatta, sailed home, and late that evening, passed us struggling back into Manhasset Bay.

The boats saw a lot of other classes come and go. When the one-design Eight-meters were built in 1928, we heard they were to "take the place of the Thirties," but a few years later, the Thirties were still racing as a one-design class when the Eights had ceased to do so.

Gradually boats dropped out of the strictly one-design class. Rigs were altered, engines installed, cabin accommodations improved. Gaff mainsails were old-fashioned, though it has yet to be proved that the Thirties are better boats under jib-headed rigs. And while their original accommodations were fine for a stag crew on a yacht club cruise, later owners wanted extra comfort below for family cruising.

Among them, the Thirties have borne quite a collection of names and belonged to a lot of yachtsmen. Only *Alera*, *Linnet*, *Oriole*, and *Banzai* seem to have gotten through 50 years under their original names. The prize name collector was No. 3, which started life as *Atair* was *Atair* when she was lost, and was *Atair* during two other periods in between. In the interim, she was known as *Okee II*, *Hope*, *Carita*, *Lesmone*, *Alberta*, *Alida*, *Nachtan*, *Gray Goose*, and *Our Dream*. Others have rejoiced in anywhere from two to eight name changes. Some have had a dozen owners, others only four or five.

But whatever their names, these boats have remained outstanding testimonials to the art of yacht building, as it was practiced down there in Bristol half a century ago. Look at a lot of other old boats — and a lot that are a great deal younger — and you will see hogged, sagged, and twisted hulls, lopsided, humped up at the chainplates, and running downhill at the ends. The stresses of hard driving, transmitted through light hulls to heavy ballast keels, have done most of it. None of them has been driven any harder than the Thirties have been, and the latter have had their share of groundings, dismastings, and collisions, too. But I can't remember ever seeing a Thirty that did not retain the same handsome, graceful sheer and trim overhangs that were bred into her from old Nat Herreshoff's original model.

With the main eased off so it's partly back-winded by the jib, these boats could carry full sail even in a blow.

A paid hand tends *Nepsi*'s mainsheet as her owners enjoy an afternoon's sail. Her metal fittings gleam from careful polishing earlier in the day.

Recollections Under Sail

Roger Taylor

ON THE OCCASION of their 20th anniversary, Seabury Lawrence wrote in *Yachting* of two Thirties, *Countess* (ex-*Maid of Meudon*, No. 4) and *Lena* (ex-*Pintail*, No. 5), racing from Newport to the head of Buzzards Bay. The 37-mile run before an increasing sou'wester resulted in *Lena*'s crossing the line only three seconds behind *Countess*.

The boats were raced hard and often. All 18 boats changed hands (and names) often, and the longest an original owner kept his Thirty was nine years. They seem to have been a sort of intermediate training ground for highly competitive yachtsmen on their way to bigger boats.

The original rig was a big handsome one: a

generous mainsail with a high-peaked gaff set up parallel to the headstay. On a jib-and-mainsail boat, you can't do much better than this for all-around sailing. Most of Nathanael Herreshoff's boats carried considerable weather helm, and the New York Thirty is no exception. On the wind, the helm will range from light to moderate as the breeze increases. But on a reach in a good breeze, the boats are a real handful (or rather two hands full, with feet firmly placed). In any case, the combination works, for they're certainly fast to windward, and not easily passed on a reach. The racing skippers back then developed a great reputation for never reefing, in spite of the generous rigs, so they sometimes sailed at great angles of heel. Although this didn't seem to slow them down much, I'll bet reefing wouldn't have slowed them down much either, and it would have been considerably more comfortable.

The class went strong for 30 years. By 1935, however, the members of the New York Yacht Club were ready for something new, and they invited several designers to submit proposals for a slightly larger and more modern boat. The Herreshoff Manufacturing Company pro-

duced a 33-foot-waterline model quite similar to the old Thirty but with a marconi rig. In the end, the Club decided in favor of Olin Stephens' New York 32, and the contract was awarded to Henry Nevins, who proceeded to build 20 boats for the 1936 season.

A number of the New York Thirties continued racing and cruising long after the racing class disbanded. The old *Lena*, ex-*Pintail*, became *Cockatoo II* and was owned by a friend of our family, Lloyd Bergeson. I remember being mightily impressed by her one day when Lloyd and his family got underway from East Harbor after lunch and with a single reef tucked into the big gaff mainsail, strapped her down to a hard sou'wester coming right off the land of Fishers Island, and went roaring up the shore like a hunting cheetah.

One day, Lloyd asked me to go racing with him. We went up to the Pine Orchard Yacht Club, and I was so excited to be on one of Nat Herreshoff's New York Thirties that all I can remember about it was a seemingly endless amount of deck space on the boat and the way, in a light air, she ate out to windward away from whatever competition was trying to stay with

Pintail leads *Oriole* in a first season's race. Note the short bowsprits with which the boats were built. *Oriole* is still going strong with a marconi rig and larger cabin, but *Pintail* (as *Cockatoo II*) was lost at sea in 1979 while on her way back from Norway.

her. I thought the *Cockatoo* was wonderful.

As I got to know this remarkable boat, I got to know her remarkable skipper. Lloyd is, among other things, an engineer with an engineer's drive to make his physical surroundings — especially when afloat — work better. He's a dissatisfied improver of things, a trait that led to one of the great shocks of my life. We happened to be "cruising" in our homeport of Camden, Maine, at the time, so my shock was recorded in the log for July 31, 1973: "Lloyd Bergeson sailed in in the *Cockatoo*. He has chopped her stern off!"

While I looked at his handiwork, speechless, Lloyd calmly explained the reason for his action. He reasoned that the last couple of feet of overhang didn't add anything to her sailing waterline length and that its weight added significantly to her pitching moment. So he cut her off and gave her a vertical but radiused transom. The *Cockatoo* pitched less, but she wasn't as pretty after her surgery.

Lloyd has had several rigs in the boat since he took out the original gaff — I think two different marconi yawl rigs and two different marconi sloop rigs. All of them seemed to work well, whether racing or cruising. With their deep keels and plenty of outside lead, the Thirties have great power to carry sail. The time I remember best of all was coming back to Noank, Connecticut, from Shelter Island after an Off Soundings race. The fall northwester brought plenty of very hard gusts. The *Cockatoo* had by then a marconi yawl rig. Coming in through the Race, we had to jam her right up on the wind so the strong ebb tide wouldn't set us down into a big tide rip. I was steering, and I'll never forget what happened when the first big blast of wind hit us after we hardened up. I braced myself to ease her through it, hoping to keep her staggering along all right until it let up again. But instead of staggering, she suddenly accelerated, and I experienced the unbelievable feeling of a boat transforming all the power of the wind into forward motion. She wasn't about to be overpowered, and she certainly wanted no mollycoddling. She looked forward to those great blasts so she could show her stuff.

I was lucky enough to be able to sail in the *Cockatoo* a fair bit from time to time and gradually got to know what to expect on the boat. One thing to expect was apparent chaos at the start of a trip, a chaos that seldom bothered Lloyd and that never interfered with another of his strong traits, managerial ability. Lloyd Bergeson has managed most of the major shipyards east of the Mississippi River. In any given situation, he has a very clear sense of resources, time, and priorities. Orderliness for the sake of orderliness is rather low on his mental list.

I recall arriving at the appointed hour to leave Noank for New London for the start, next day, of an Off Soundings race. Lloyd was sawing a few inches off the main boom. Glancing below, I saw a great array of tools and raw materials. There was no bedding or any food on board. We were going to race next day, and the boat's rating came before housekeeping amenitites, which came before departing at some arbitrary hour.

We went in an Annapolis-to-Newport race. An hour before the start, somebody wanted hot soup. There was no kerosene in the stove. Thirty minutes later, it was concluded that there was no kerosene on board the vessel. We spotted a friendly spectator who would lend us some and maneuvered alongside to get it. In the process, the spectator's main boom fouled our mizzen rigging and a mizzen spreader broke. Ten minutes before the start, Lloyd went aloft with some tape and some fast-acting epoxy mixed up in a little can. Two minutes before the start, he was back at the tiller concentrating 100 percent on beating the competition to the line. I think his repair held for the season. I know it held for the race.

Lloyd rebuilt the *Cockatoo* extensively over the years, installing bronze floors and covering the hull with Dynel. He made a tremendous number of small but significant changes to her construction, always seeking to make her stronger and more durable.

When his top priority is steering, Lloyd Bergeson is the best helmsman I have seen. A New York Thirty is a lovely boat to steer, and he can get more out of one than anybody.

The man is a competitive racer. In that race to Newport, we huddled on the stern, when running, in response to his belief that the increased waterline aft would help her along. In spite of her age, *Cockatoo*, with her modified rig, fared extremely well in nearly every race she entered, winning and placing against far more modern and sophisticated boats. I have seen Lloyd prowl the foredeck for an hour, clew of his ultimate drifter in hand, seeking and finding every breath of air and giving the *Cockatoo* barely perceptible way through the dense fog of a Marblehead-Halifax race.

He is also a compulsive cruiser, participating in every New York Yacht Club cruise that he could, and sailing all over the place in the *Cockatoo* shorthanded or singlehanded. When he was made General Manager of Ingalls Shipyard in Pascagoula, Mississippi, Lloyd and a friend

(continued on page 272)

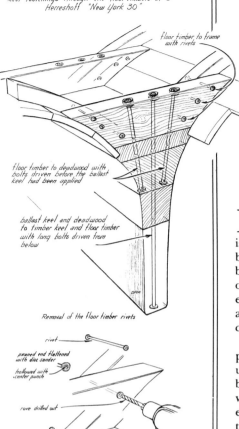

keel fastenings through the floor timbers of a Herreshoff "New York 30"

floor timber to frame with rivets

floor timber to deadwood with bolts driven before the ballast keel had been applied

ballast keel and deadwood to timber keel and floor timber with long bolts driven from below

Removal of the floor timber rivets

rivet

peaned end flattened with disc sander

hollowed with center punch

rove drilled out

shank driven thru with punch

The Restoration of Number 14

William T. Okie, Jr.

HER ORIGINAL NAME was *Cara Mia* and her racing number was, and still is, 14. Her new name will be *Cara Mia*. In between, she carried other names but was best known as *Old Timer* when H.A. Calahan owned her and wrote about her in his several books on boating. I bought her in 1978 and immediately set about restoring her completely.

The premise was to rebuild this boat, replacing any and all members that had given up over the previous 75 years. The process began by removing the house, all joinerwork, rudder, and garboards. A thorough examination indicated that the aft section of the original plank keel had been destroyed by indiscriminate fastening and a hundred caulkings. In addition, we determined that almost all structural members needed to be replaced with the exception of most deckbeams, the fin, forward keel section, bilge

stringers, and sheer clamps. That is, everything from the aft end of the cockpit to several stations forward of the mast. Ergo, we put in a new plank keel from amidships aft, approximately 60 frames, 32 floors, all single planking (four strakes between keel and turn of bilge), new sheerstrakes, and cover boards. We then rebuilt the rudder, replaced the lower members and cornerposts of the house, added a fore-and-aft deck carling under the house sills, replaced eight to 10 deckbeams, the mast partners, five or six deck planks, replaced the transom knees and transom, toerails, cockpit coamings, and a couple of previously botched-up hatches. Then we refastened everything. And I mean everything: all rudder drifts, all keelbolts, floor bolts, stem scarf fastenings, all frame-to-floor rivets, bilge stringer bolts, sheer clamp bolts, hanging knee bolts, deckbeam bolts, every deck

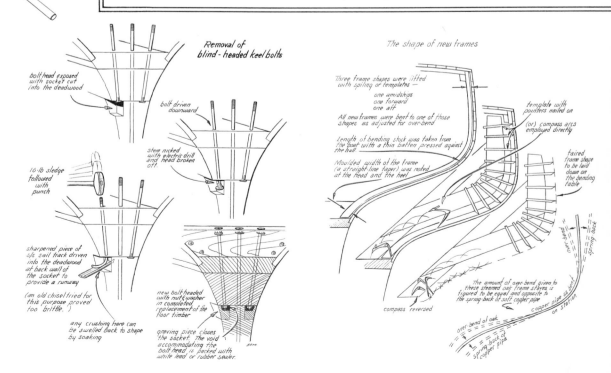

Removal of blind-headed keel bolts

bolt head exposed with socket cut into the deadwood

bolt driven downward

stem nicked with electric drill and head broken off.

16-lb sledge followed with punch

sharpened piece of s/s sail track driven into the deadwood at back wall of the socket to provide a runway

(an old chisel tried for this purpose proved too brittle.)

any crushing here can be swelled back to shape by soaking

graving piece closes the socket. The void accommodating the bolt head is packed with white lead or rubber sealer.

new bolt headed with nut & washer in completed replacement of the floor timber.

The shape of new frames

Three frame shapes were lifted with spiling or templates —
one amidships
one forward
one aft

All new frames were bent to one of those shapes as adjusted for over-bend

Length of bending stock was taken from the boat with a thin batten pressed against the hull.

Moulded width of the frame (a straight-line taper) was noted at the head and the heel.

template with pointers nailed on

(or) compass arcs employed directly

faired frame shape to be laid down on the bending table

compass reversed

The amount of over-bend given to these steamed oak frame staves is figured to be equal and opposite to the spring-back of soft copper pipe

over-bend of oak

spring-back of copper pipe

on station

over-bend

spring-back

copper pipe on station

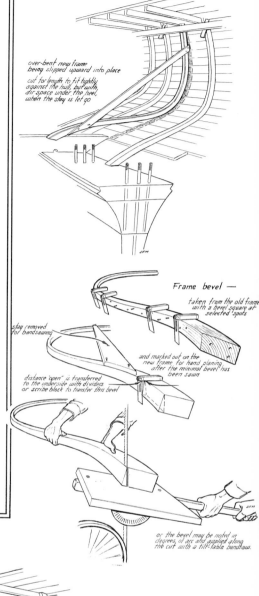

over-bent new frame being slipped upward into place

cut for length to fit tightly against the hull, but with air space under the heel, when the stay is let go

Frame bevel —

taken from the old frame with a bevel square at selected spots

stay removed for bandsawing

and marked out on the new frame for hand planing after the minimal bevel has been sawn

distance "open" is transferred to the underside with dividers or scribe block to transfer this bevel

or the bevel may be noted in degrees, off arc and applied along the cut with a tilt-table bandsaw.

and hull strap fastening, and every plank fastening in the entire boat — bronze below the sheerline and iron in the deck structure — just as Herreshoff had done it.

Following the above, we have recanvased the deck and are now replacing all her old joinerwork, which has been meticulously stripped of paint.

Whenever we could, we put back the same materials we took out. There are probably five or six small changes from her original construction (for example, carling under the house sides, additional vertical cockpit supports, beefed-up deckbeams where running backstays and mainsheet traveler will bear, athwartship keelbolts to prevent fore-and-aft keel fractures).

Other than these minor changes, we have made provisions for a new marconi sloop rig, lifeline stanchions, sheet winches, a different galley location surrounding the companionway ladder, and canvas on the house top in order to make the surface a little more durable and the very dried-out planking waterproof.

All the above is to the credit of Noank Boat Works, who actually did the work. The talent present is: Bruce Madara, executive committee, keeper of the books, job boss, and accomplished boatbuilder; Dennis Souza, jack of all trades, as comfortable bending in a beveled frame as coaxing a 75-year-old deck back to life; Neal Overstrom, who as the most recent member gets stuck with every odd job; and last, but far from least, overqualified, still smiling, member of an endangered species, Paul Stubing, shipwright.

All in all, but for the rig and the absence of a bowsprit, her profile will be New York Thirty; I believe she's now up to the next 75 years! I have reached penury.

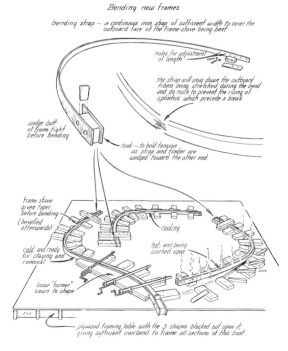

Bending new frames

bending strap — a continuous iron strap of sufficient width to cover the outboard face of the frame-stave being bent

holes for adjustment of length

the strap will snug down the outboard fibers being stretched during the bend and do much to prevent the rising of splinters which precede a break

wedge butt of frame tight before bending

hook — to hold tension as strap and timber are wedged toward the other end

frame stave given taper before bending (beveled afterwards)

cooling

cold, and ready for staying and removal

hot, and being worked upon

loose "former" sawn to shape

plywood framing table with the 3 shapes blocked out upon it, giving sufficient overbend to frame all sections of this boat

2 x 6

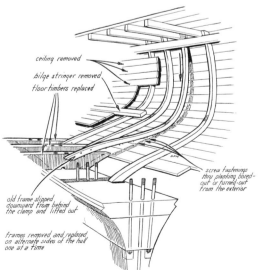

ceiling removed

bilge stringer removed

floor timbers replaced

screw fastenings thru planking bored-out or turned-out from the exterior

old frame slipped downward from behind the clamp and lifted out

frames removed and replaced on alternate sides of the hull one at a time sailed *Cockatoo* from Noank, Connecticut, down the outside route to Biloxi in late fall. Though some predictably heavy weather overtook them at times, the boat and crew arrived safe and sound. Not bad for a vessel of 60-plus years.

When I started getting gray hairs, Lloyd thought I was too old for the foredeck and made me navigator. This speeded up the process considerably, particularly because about that time Lloyd decided to sail mostly in northern waters, so there would always be plenty of fog around. Why is it that the navigator's comeuppances in fog are always so basic? We were coming back to Northeast Harbor, Maine, from an Astor Cup race that a Frenchman's Bay fog bank had canceled, and all the wrong islands began showing up. Just when we were supposed to get to a fat, round island, we'd get to a long, skinny one instead. It was all very confusing, and I wasn't enjoying my lunchtime sandwiches. My digestion improved when I took a hard look at the sandwich container. Lunch had been served in the dish drainer, a regulation rubber-covered wire affair. I smiled at its neat parallel lines of wire-masquerading-as-rubber, moved it aside, and watched the compass swing a good 15 degrees.

One of the good things about sailing with Lloyd in the *Cockatoo* was that sometimes his friend Eric O sen would come along. Talk about your competitive racers. He was with us in the Monhegan Race one time and simply talked the *Cockatoo* out of Hussey Sound ahead of all competitors. Light head wind, head tide. Tricky stuff. Eric stationed himself amidships, where he could talk to all of us more or less simultaneously, whether we were forward or aft, on sheet or tiller. Right from the start, he told everybody what to do. "Head off a little, don't strap that boom down quite so much, there's a puff over there, keep your weight to leeward, we've got to tack, what's that guy doing, there's less tide in there, don't bring that jib across too quick," and on and on. And right in the middle of everything he looked at each one of us and said "BS! BS! BS!" I, for one, was mystified. Nobody had gotten a word in edgewise, so what was *he* saying "BS" to *us* for? It turned out to be racing jargon for Boat Speed. Evidently Eric thought that by fiercely saying "BS!" at all of us, the boat's speed would somehow increase. I'll be damned if it didn't work. He got us out of Hussey Sound ahead of everybody.

The wind stayed light, and we beat all the way to Cape Porpoise, but the minute we got there, the wind shifted 120 degrees, and we beat all the way to Monhegan. That sail was some frustrating, but we finished first in the ocean cruising class and were also first on corrected time, beating the second boat by something over six hours.

There is grace to the way a New York Thirty moves through the water under any conditions. When it is blowing hard, she roars along, the foam of her wake nearly up to her rail at the stern. Going to windward, she eats up through the seas with a minimum of fuss.

The Thirty does better in a light breeze close-hauled than any boat I have been on. Nor does a bobble of a sea — the nemesis of many an otherwise fast boat — bother her unduly when it's light.

It doesn't take much breeze to get her really moving. She's not a particularly quick accelerator, but as the breeze builds, her speed keeps increasing imperceptibly until you suddenly notice that she's going a lot faster than she was.

You get a clear view all around the decks and rail of a Thirty from the helm, so you can enjoy to the fullest the way her slim hull works through the waves. Sitting at the tiller looking aft at her long, lean stern moving swiftly through the water, you get a sense of elegant power.

The helm of a Thirty feels heavy, as if everything about the boat has great momentum: her forward motion, her refusal to make leeway, her reluctance to yaw. You sense that big deep chunk of lead keeping everything going steadily as it should be. There's no doubt the Thirty is a very fast boat, and her speed is made to seem even greater than it is by her low freeboard.

For summer of 1980, the 75th birthday of the New York Thirties, Lloyd Bergeson's plan was to assemble a gang of us who had sailed with him over the years in the *Cockatoo* and do some racing against less historic vessels. He had a higher priority, though, for *Cockatoo*: a voyage to Norway and an exploration of the coastline where his forebears put to sea. This cruise he made, crossing the Atlantic singlehanded in the summer of 1978, cruising in Norway that summer and part of the next, and setting off on the return transatlantic crossing with his son, Henry. Lloyd and Henry lost their vessel but not their lives to the hole behind an ultimate wave in mid-Atlantic.

William H. Taylor called the New York Thirty "the most famous one-design class this country has ever seen." They are some fine boats, boats that deserve to be sailed and cared for by the best seamen around. The *Cockatoo*, for one, got just that.

Peggotty

Jennifer Buckley

WHILE MATILDA D, *the felucca in the next piece, is a replica based on historical documentation, an actual ancient boat inspired* Peggotty's *reconstruction, the subject of this story. Although the boat herself is unique and deserves attention for that reason alone, what makes her story most interesting is the process used to determine her predecessor's actual shape, characteristics, and rig. After all, the evidence her builder, Bob Baker, had to go on was skimpy and ill defined, but such is all that exists for most of the enthusiasts who are trying to revitalize some of the valuable craft and skills of the past. This may be boatbuilding, but it also is nonacademic scholarship.*

PEGGOTTY IS a 17-foot 6-inch fishing cat, probably built at Newport, Rhode Island's Long Wharf. She was built with a fishing well, washboards, and curbing. Even more amazing than her 9-foot beam is her age: *Peggotty* is about 132 years old. Probably about the time the Newport cat began to displace her type of fishing cat, *Peggotty*'s forward thwart was removed and the boat half-decked back to the position of that thwart. After about 25 years of fishing, she went into ferry service. The foredeck was cut back to within 18 inches of the mast and a round-ended house was built over her, leaving a very small standing room aft. *Peggotty* was the last boat to serve at Taggert's Ferry in Little Compton, Rhode Island, where for about 15 years she transported farmers with their eggs, butter, and poultry for the Newport market, across the Sakonnet River to Middletown. Inevitably, the rapid growth of Fall River and New Bedford, Massachusetts, made these cities a better market for Little Compton produce and the ferry was abandoned.

Peggotty sat on the beach at Little Compton until 1906, when Sidney Burleigh, a Little Compton artist, carted her home and planted her in the back garden. He named her *Peggotty*, after the old nurse in *David Copperfield* who was fat and wide and lived in an upside-down boat.

Peggotty in the back garden, used as an artist's studio in Little Compton, Rhode Island.

Burleigh took the top off the house and built a tall house over the entire boat, extending over the guards, standing 5 feet high at the eaves and 8 feet at the peak, with a thatched roof. He knocked out the fish well so that he could put in a new floor, and removed the center thwart to make her roomier inside. Overgrown with roses and honeysuckle, given a Dutch door and windows to let in the sunshine, and a parlor stove set forward for chilly days, she made a studio and teahouse that must have given Burleigh many hours of delight.

Sidney Burleigh died in 1931 at the age of 78, and *Peggotty* sat largely untended until the Little Compton Historical Society acquired her in 1964 and moved her to the Society's historic Wilbur House on West Main Road, where she is now on display. When the Historical Society moved her, they left the keel in the ground and supported her with timbers under the planking.

About two years ago, Mystic Seaport, with the assistance of the Catboat Association's Catboat Fund, asked Bob Baker to take the lines off *Peggotty*. He was familiar with this type of boat, having restored *Button Swan*, a 13-foot Newport fish boat (ca. 1865), for Mystic the year before.

Bob got a good set of lines off the topsides down to a few inches below the copperline. The depth of the hull was arrived at by measuring the forward well ledge (this was loose so Bob could take it home) and by fitting this to the topside measurements at station 5. The angle of the rabbet at the transom, taken off the transom, is the basis of the line of the rabbet aft. By careful fairing and tinkering, referring to the lines of the *Button Swan* boat, Bob developed a set of lines that he believes are quite close to the original.

Inside the original boat, most of the important members are there, but they are out of position and/or broken. The upper portion of the

well and the thwarts were missing (from Burleigh's remodeling). Holes in the ceiling located the thwarts, but the reconstructed well is pure conjecture based on photos, models, and the *Button Swan* boat.

Bob thinks there were parting boards or bulkheads under the thwarts, closing off the area each side of the well, but no trace remains. The width of the washboards was taken at the quarter from a piece of the original that was incorporated into the new deck. The edge of the old washboard was not rounded, indicating that the guard has always been even with the top of the deck. The height of the curbing is speculation, as is the position of the thole pads.

Wooden pins for the sheet were still in place in the quarter knees, and holes for the traveling horse were in the transom. Bob reconstructed the rig from period engravings of Newport Harbor.

Taking off *Peggotty*'s lines involved considerable investigation and speculation. Much of the work was like a puzzle: it was exciting when the pieces fit. In spite of all the answers that Bob found, there were still some teasers, which could only be answered by building another *Peggotty* and seeing how she worked.

When Charles Lee of Newport approached Bob and asked him to build a certain small character boat, Bob wasn't interested in building a boat he didn't like. Probably because *Peggotty*'s drawings were on his desk, he suggested her to Charlie.

There is a sense of simplicity in building a working replica; one does not have to worry about adapting for standing headroom or floating-trailer accommodations — there is simply no question of such things. *Peggotty*'s design fits into a cohesive whole, her ends belong to one another, her sailplan matches the boat, and there is not one "hard" place in her lines. All of these factors appealed to Bob as a designer and as a builder. With a minimum of persuasion, Charlie Lee was convinced and enthusiastic.

Charlie wanted a unique boat, something comfortable and fun to sail. He and his wife, Camilla, have two young sons, and the 9-foot beam of this catboat would give everyone plenty of room. In spite of her extreme beam, *Peggotty* is rather fine-lined and pretty for a working boat, and this was certainly in her favor. Since the new boat was to be built and finished like the original, she would be rugged and simple, with no frills and no varnish to keep up.

The shop at Baker Boat Works looked very roomy when we had it cleared out. When her keel had been cut from an oak timber 4 inches by 20 inches by 19½ feet and set out on the

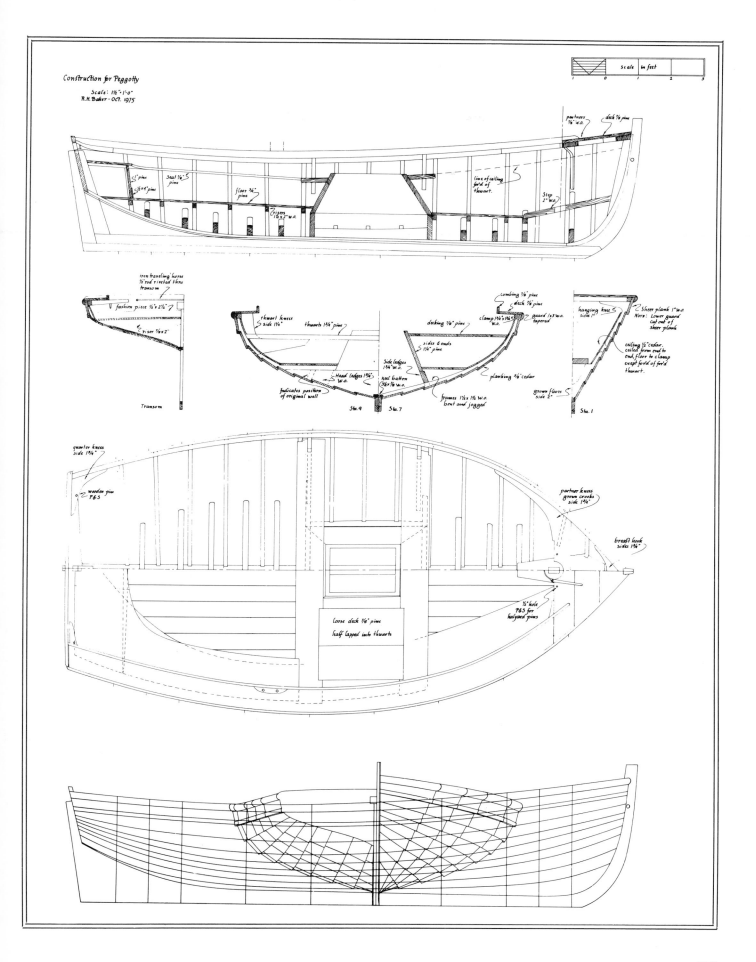

Construction for Peggotty

Scale: 1½"=1'-0"
R.H. Baker – Oct. 1975

The backbone set-up for the new *Peggotty* in Bob Baker's shop.

floor, we had an inkling of how big *Peggotty* was going to be. But when the molds went up, we were aghast!

Working alongside Bob in the shop was Kevin Dwyer of Bristol, Rhode Island. *Peggotty* was the first new boat Kevin had worked on, and the first one Bob had built in a number of years. It was a learning experience for both: Kevin, making practical and tangible the many things he had read about boatbuilding; and Bob, working with an apprentice-carpenter and teaching the things that were almost instinctive in his own work.

An unusual situation came about when *Peggotty* was being lofted on the shop floor. In retrospect, and after pondering her lines for a long time, Bob felt that *Peggotty*'s stern had drooped over the years and that it would be wise to pick it up by ¼ inch in order to have a pleasing sheer. So we did.

From the lofting, molds were built of pine finished only on one side. Patterns for the stem, deadwood, transom, and knees were picked up on plywood. The stem and sternpost were fastened to the keel and the whole works was set up on horses and braced. The original boat's transom was built of one piece of oak, but since we could not find oak wide enough, the new *Peggotty*'s transom is built in three pieces, splined together.

Fastenings for the backbone were forged ⅜-inch iron drift bolts from Newton Millham's Star Forge in Westport, Massachusetts. From studying old boats, Bob has found that wrought iron, not steel, resists rusting and can be used to advantage if you are absolutely sure you are using wrought iron, and take care to red-lead the hole before driving the drifts.

The next step was to set up the molds, brace them to the shop ceiling, and run ribbands around them, following as nearly as possible the plank laps of the original boat.

In the meantime, the search for lumber was on. The oak knees and floor timbers came from woods owned by a friend in Westport. We cut the trees found during a previous day's search; some were dragged with ropes out of the woods over snow, and a Volkswagen bus pulled the ones we couldn't budge. A local sawmill did much of our sawing and was also a source of wood.

Because some of the oak we were working with was still green, we expected a certain amount of shrinkage, so we kept everything well oiled with a 50/50 mixture of raw linseed oil and turpentine. There were no disasters and nothing warped out of control over the months that it took to complete the boat.

Peggotty's original planking was ⅝-inch local cedar, virtually unavailable in the size we needed. It is possible that when *Peggotty* was originally built, very wide cedar planks were used from stem to stern, marked where they came tangent to the molds, and cut to shape and fastened.

Peggotty was not easy to plank. We used southern white cedar purchased from Kiever-Willard in Newburyport, Massachusetts, where we found reasonably clear stock. Her original planks had been bent to their limits, and when we bent the new southern cedar, which is much more brittle than the northern, we did it with prayers.

All *Peggotty*'s planks have a lot of shape and had to be scarfed because we could not obtain lumber wide enough to get them out in one piece. As we cut and fit the planks, we made a matched set for the other side. The forward part of the plank was roughly fitted and cut. Then it was reclamped in place while the after portion was clamped to the molds, marked, and roughly cut. Next, both pieces were clamped to the molds and marked where the scarf would be. We were careful to keep the scarf in the proper position to maintain the shape of the plank. The planks were then removed from the boat, matched, prepared for the scarf, cut, glued, and cured until the next day, when they were fastened on. We used Gougeon Brothers epoxy for the scarfs. It made a very strong bond, and we found it most satisfactory.

Where the going was rough and we had to bend the planks into difficult curves, we ran very hot water over the planks in a sluice box. We decided to try this after the first garboard went in beautifully, but the second exploded! After that, planks went on at the rate of two a day.

Peggotty's sheer plank is unusual: a full inch-thick piece of oak shaped at its lower edge to form the guard rail there. It is 1 inch at the top and tapers to ¾ inch at the lower guard, where it becomes one full inch thick again. Putting in these planks was a challenge, but not as trying as we thought it would be. For insurance, we fashioned a full-size pattern from cedar, then made the sheer planks from it and bent the wet oak right in.

Planks were clinch-nailed with 1½-inch square copper nails from Skookum Fastenings of Anacortes, Washington. The original boat's fastenings were apparently cast bronze nails. Before each plank was bent on and fastened, we ran a bead of polysulfide caulking along the top of the one below as extra insurance for a tight seal. (When she was launched, *Peggotty* did not leak, and the only water we ever pumped out of her was rain water.)

After the boat was planked up, we began framing her with 1½-inch-square white oak frames. Tempers ran as hot as the steambox during this phase of the operation. The frames must be bent hot, then jogged to go over the planking when cold. While they are hot, there is nothing to clamp them to in the boat except the sheer plank. As a result, as soon as you move your foot, they jump away. Bob would give his eye teeth to know how the old-timers managed this without cussing.

The frames were soaked in salt water before they were steamed because wet wood steams better and the salt in the wood helps hold the heat. From midships aft, the turn of the bilge gets tighter and tighter, so the oak is bent to its capacity, quite unwillingly. This was the most trying part of building *Peggotty*, and 15 pairs of frames took three full days' work.

When the frames were cold and hard, they were removed and the jogs were cut. So that water would run by the frames, the jogs were cut about ¼ inch shy of the top edge of each plank, acting like limber holes. The frames were clinch-nailed, as in the original, with 2½-inch to 3½-inch copper spikes.

The sheer clamps were made of white oak 2½ inches square. After being soaked for two or three days, they were bent over a jig on the shop floor and dried for four or five days. The notches were then cut for the frame heads. If they had been cut before the sheer clamps were bent, they probably would have broken. Several calls to the Almighty were heard as these were bent into place — and they made it!

After fastening the frames and sheer clamps, Bob and Kevin began to shape the oak breast-hook and quarter knees. This oak, cut in our

Peggotty was a fishing boat and was fitted with a fishwell. Here a new fishwell is being built for the replicated boat.

friend's woods, was from tree crooks that fit our patterns; all knees were grown-shaped, not "sawn." Fastenings here were copper rivets, and the middle fastening in the breasthook was a wrought iron drift bolt. The floor timbers were fitted and fastened with iron drift bolts and copper nails, as were the two head ledges for the fish well. Risers for the floorboards sit on top of the frames with light fastenings to keep them in place.

Fate smiled just before we began the ceiling for *Peggotty*. The new Parks planer arrived. Before this capitulation to modern technology, all planing had been done by hand. The new planer was a good source of mulch for the vegetable garden and saved hours of work for Bob and Kevin. *Peggotty* is ceiled tight with ½-inch cedar from the aft side of the stem to the face of the transom. After the thwart knees were fitted, the first strake of the ceiling at the line of the thwarts was put in, then the ceiling was fitted up and down from that. Before the thwarts were secured, the rest of the fish well was built on top of the ledges, then the prefitted thwarts were put down on top of the well and secured. The new well was built tight (like the original), but we did not bore the holes in the garboards. This way, it has waterproof storage space aboard. The well has drain holes for bilge water to pass through, but life jackets and picnic paraphernalia can be stored high and dry on a grating above the floor timbers.

A bulkhead was built in the stern for a cuddy, then the stern seats went in, fitting up against the frames on top of the ceiling. Each seat has a fashioned leg under it midway for support.

The two large partner knees were secured with long rivets at this point and the foredeck built, cross planked. The side decks and the

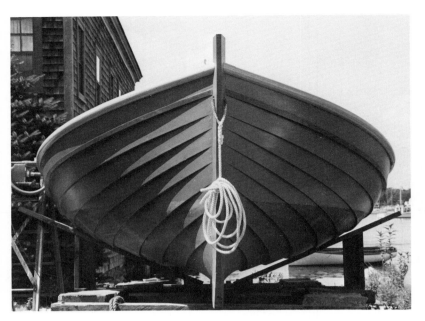

Peggotty sits in her cradle, ready for launching. Her mast will be stepped when she is in the water.

washboards were made with a slight crown from the after end to the forward thwart, where they flatten out to meet the foredeck. The washboards are pine, sawn to shape, made up of three planks to each side with butt blocks underneath.

Half-round oak 1½ inches by 2½ inches forms the upper guard, tapered fore and aft. It is fastened in place with bronze screws to facilitate removal for repair, if necessary. The curbing around the washboards deviated from the drawings. Bob felt that the curbing in the drawings was too low and should be an inch higher. *Peggotty*'s curbings are cedar — Bob's choice, since the originals were long gone.

At about this point in *Peggotty*'s construction, we began painting. Bob is a firm believer in red-lead paint as a wood preservative. Try to find some, and you will discover that it is no longer available. But while it is not available for paint, it is available for agricultural purposes, which seems crazy. We keep our children from teething on boat keels and make our own red-lead paint by mixing agricultural red-lead powder with linseed oil to a proper paint consistency. Several coats of red lead under copper bottom paint is the best life insurance you can get for those planks. Copper paint is extremely drying to bare wood and will suck the life out of it in short order. Red-lead paint helps hold the resins in the wood and acts as a buffer between the wood and the copper paint. At all times, we make sure that there is an *abundance* of ventilation when painting or mixing or sanding.

After red-leading the bottom and priming the topsides, we puttied the fastenings. We mixed whiting, white-lead powder, and linseed oil to make a putty that dries firm and does not shrink. We buy white lead from an art supply place, where it is sold for sizing canvas. Everything is puttied at least twice so that it will be smooth. We use masks, are careful to avoid excessive skin contact with the paint or putty, and wash carefully.

Two good coats of copper bottom paint were used on *Peggotty*. We used oil-based house paint for her topsides. Modern plastic-based marine paints are too hard and brittle for long life. It has been our experience that a softer, oil-based paint wears longer and gives with the wood. It is, however, *not* fast drying, and unexpected rain is a disaster if the boat is in the open and you've nearly finished painting. It takes several days for this paint to dry hard enough for use, but the wait is worth the smooth, semigloss finish you can achieve.

From researching the boat, Bob felt that the original *Peggotty* had grey topsides with a red copper bottom and dark red on the lower guard. However, he found traces of green copper in the laps on the bottom when taking off her lines. Across the transom there is a scribed band the width of the lower guard roughly following the crown of the transom from the lower guard to the bottom of the tiller port. Burleigh incorporated this into his decoration, and Bob feels it was on the boat when Burleigh acquired her. Inside, the oldest paint is yellow ochre, although Burleigh later painted out the inside with dark green.

The new *Peggotty* sports medium grey topsides with a dark brick-red guard, which carries around into the scribed band on the transom. Her upper guard and decks are the same yellow ochre as her inside seats, ceiling, bulkhead, and thwarts. Her floor is dark grey and the inside of the fish well and cuddy are a very dark, flat green. Old fish wells were traditionally painted blue or green inside, presumably to make the fish feel more at home.

Cedar for the mast, boom, and gaff came from local sawmills. Frank Raposa and Ray Clidence shaped and finished the spars, which were then coated liberally with linseed oil and turpentine, mixed half and half. The spars were roughed out with an axe, then shaped with planes and drawknives until sanded to a silky smoothness. They turned out beautifully.

Bob fashioned wooden patterns for castings, which were to be bronze. The original mast gate was probably iron, but as a concession to modern yachting, the new gate was cast in bronze so that it would not drip rust. Since the first *Peggotty*'s fittings were long gone, Bob used the design from the later No Man's Land Boat for the

A Second Look

During a visit to Mystic Seaport, in the late afternoon of a beautiful October day, I saw Bill Doll, who runs the shipyard's stockroom. He was about to cast *Peggotty* off her mooring when he saw me and invited me to go along.

Somehow the tide and wind always seem to be running in the same direction on the Mystic River — against you; they were that day as we set out in *Peggotty*. The wind was light southerly and we had to beat from the mooring off Chubb's Wharf down around the bend at the point. As soon as we rounded it, the wind predictably hauled ahead and required us to keep on tacking as we headed for the shipyard. The tide was down, so we couldn't get too far out of the channel and rather short tacks were necessary. But we made good headway, which, considering *Peggotty*'s design and rig, was surprising to me.

Peggotty is a very wide boat without a centerboard. Her full-length keel is only a few inches deep and her rudder is small. Although there is a lot of area in her cotton mainsail, its seams run up and down and it has no battens. One might expect her to "sail well for her type," as the saying goes. That usually means some forward motion as long as there is a good breeze on the

beam or quarter. *Peggotty* does better. She moves along very nicely, without much leeway, in light air when close-hauled. And she comes about every time, even with the tide against her.

When we ran out of wind in the lee of the big shipyard buildings, and headed back to the mooring, *Peggotty* really flew, first carried on the tide to where the wind was, but then just booming along before the dying southerly.

Peggotty sails well. Her cockpit has more room in it than most 40-footers, and it's good room, largely unobstructed, and close to the water where the action is. She is shallow enough to be run up on the beach for a picnic and can comfortably carry one big family or two small ones. She is stable when you walk around in her and she won't make you hang on for dear life when it breezes

up. When you're sailing, there is only one sheet to tend — and, of course, the tiller. I don't see how one could get a better or simpler dayboat for picnicking or sailing.

Her maintenance would be about as easy as one could imagine in terms of painting, and her lapstrake hull would need little in the way of puttying or caulking, as long as it was not abused in winter storage.

Knowing Bob Baker, I'd expect *Peggotty* to be good — and she is. Bob, more than most people, has a real feel for the way old-time builders did things. He understands that proportion, shape, and simplicity have as much to do with grace and beauty as does the sometimes-distracting glitter of varnish and brass with which many classic reproductions are outfitted. Because he has owned, studied, sailed, and repaired a number of old southern New England small craft, Bob is an authority on how they are rigged and painted. But he is a modest man, and some of this trait carries over into the preceding article. To me it is much too modest in telling how well *Peggotty* was researched and put together. In my opinion, Bob Baker has done an absolutely superb job that is worthy of study by other boatbuilders and scholars.

— Maynard Bray

mast gate. This might not be historically correct, but it works well for *Peggotty*'s telephone pole of a mast. The original rudder hangers, now mostly rusted away, were iron, and bronze was used for the new ones. The pintles were purchased from Wilcox-Crittenden through a local chandler. Bob made patterns for the gudgeons of the old-fashioned square-shanked variety (¾ inch square, 2 inches long), although the originals were the bolt type that passed through the sternpost and set up with a nut inside. The new gudgeons were put in a square-cut hole in the sternpost so that there is a very tight fit, then fastened with copper rivets crosswise.

Peggotty has no cleats. There are wooden pins on the foredeck for the halyard. There is no topping lift, just the halyard and the sheet. There is a pin through the quarter knee to catch a loose turn with the sheet. To belay the sheet, you can take a turn around the traveling horse or through the traveler.

Newton Millham forged the traveler, which was riveted into place after being galvanized to keep it from rusting. Cotton sails for *Peggotty* came from Smith Yacht Sails in Fairhaven, Massachusetts. They fit perfectly, work just right, and look beautiful, so what more could one ask? We bought oak mast hoops from Pert Lowell of Newburyport, Massachusetts, and used manila rope for the rigging. Bob made jaws for the boom, reasoning that goosenecks were not used on small working boats in 1850.

Above – Bob Baker, who took the lines off the original *Peggotty* and built the replica.

Peggotty's single-halyard rig is apparently an excellent setup, although we never see it used today. When we first rigged the boat, we found that the throat block was too close to the mast, and while it lifted the luff of the sail all right, it did not get the peak up. To remedy this situation, we moved the throat block out on the gaff about 8 inches to lift the luff and the peak. It took some experimenting to reach this solution and if he had it to do again, Bob would lengthen the mast by 18 inches so that the peak part of the halyard would be more useful in getting the peak of the sail up.

Midway through construction, Charles Lee accepted a new job in Hong Kong, and Lee's departure date came much too soon, in spite of 14-hour days, seven days a week. The Lees were due in Hong Kong two days after *Peggotty* slid into the water for the first time. There was considerable difficulty with the champagne bottle, but *Peggotty* was successfully launched, the mast was stepped, and the Lees, other builders, and friends sat aboard, bobbing in the river and toasting the new boat with Mount Gay rum. The Lees left for Hong Kong without a sail, but Charlie had a chance to sail her during a business trip in the States.

In the week that followed the Lee's departure, the boat was rigged and final coats of paint were applied with a wary eye on the weather.

We got around to the rudder of the boat next. It was built using the shape of the one on the *Button Swan*. The design came from what can be seen in oil paintings of Newport boats.

Finally *Peggotty* was ready to sail. We picked a medium day, if you know what I mean. To tell the truth, we didn't know what to expect of the old girl. With her long keel and broad beam, we knew she wasn't about to sail herself, and yes, we discovered that she has to *be* sailed. The old Newport fishermen were known as expert sailors, and it was this skill that made them successful fishermen, judging the tides and getting their boats in and out of the rocky ledges around Newport.

Bob was aware of the fact that the rudder does not feel big enough, but if it had been any larger, you couldn't hold onto it. The helm is heavy, but not impossible.

By and large, *Peggotty* is extremely close-winded. On the wind, she makes her course with very little leeway. She will sail well at 40 degrees to the wind without falling off, losing her speed, or causing undue alarm. Off the wind, she goes like an express train! Downwind, she is extremely steady, and even sailing by the lee, there is no rolling or dipping.

When you come around and miss stays, *Peggotty* doesn't get in irons as most boats do. She will fill on the other tack, but not enough to move. Slowly, you can persuade her to go sideways, but occasionally she will go backward. However, if you put the helm down and slack the sheet, she will go off the wind enough to fill the sail and start on the right tack.

Peggotty is a good "ghoster" in light air and if necessary, she rows superbly with one long oar in the tholepins, plenty of muscle, and very little correction with the helm. Although we didn't have a chance to sail her in rough weather, she should be steady. Her sail has three sets of reef points, which were necessary in her fishing days for winter gales. *Peggotty* has about 900 pounds of copper slag for ballast, and with her broad beam, she stands up like a church.

We had *Peggotty* for a couple of weeks of sailing before she went down to Mystic Seaport to be put on display. For our last sail, we took nine friends for a picnic down river. There was room for everyone to stretch out, and the gentle breeze put at least four to sleep in comfort. It was a lazy day of warm sunshine and even a couple of anti-sailers, whom we enticed on board with the picnic basket, said, "Now this is the way to sail." We all agreed.

Ships Such as Those–
Matilda D.

William Gilkerson

MARINE ARTIST William Gilkerson has a friend, Dean Stephens, who built a replica of a San Francisco Bay felucca, a boat type that had once been common around the Bay but had become obsolete. Gilkerson followed the building of the boat carefully, managed to secure her acceptance in San Francisco's Hyde Street Pier maritime exhibit, and played a part in her sea trials. He offered to write the story in a two-part series and illustrate it with a selection of his art, both color and black and white. Given our fascination for feluccas, our wish to acknowledge Dean Stephens' craftsmanship, and our appreciation of Bill's extraordinary talent and ability, we thought the story would be perfect for WoodenBoat. Here is the first part of Matilda D's story.

I UNHOOKED the "No Admittance" chain that blocked the sightseers from the upper level of the old ferryboat *Eureka*, and, hooking it closed again behind me, climbed the steps to the pilothouse. From that height there is a commanding view of San Francisco's Hyde Street Pier and its ancient wooden fleet. There is the *C.A. Thayer*, three-masted schooner of 1895, veteran of the Redwood Coast lumber trade. Tied up alongside her is the scow schooner *Alma*. Launched in 1891, she is the last survivor of a once vast family of her kind. Fully restored, she still sails. Farther up the dock is the steam schooner *Wapama*, 1915, and at the very end of the dock is the deep-sea steam tug *Hercules*, 1907, with her smokestack like an Iowa corn silo. Tallest of all, and matriarchal with her fully rigged masts, the ship *Balclutha* dominates the waterfront to the east, just beyond Fisherman's Wharf.

A northwesterly blew in through the Golden Gate, ruffling the Bay. Grandes Dames all, the old ships with their new paint nodded politely to one another in the gentle swell, seeming very pleased with themselves.

They seemed to say: "Together, we are the best-restored and most representative fleet of our kind in existence, for what other maritime city has saved an example of each of the principal types of craft that served her during the time when sail and steam both flourished? Where but here?"

And yet, it was the gap in this collection that had brought me aboard the old ferryboat that afternoon last spring, and up to the pilothouse office of the master of the ships of Hyde Street Pier, Harry Dring.

To Harry, the old ships are more a string of cosmeticized hussies than elegant ladies, for he knows all their secrets: where their old bones are spongy with rot; where they sag and mildew; where iron sickness and electrolysis have set in; where their metal is thin with rust. He is husband and doctor in one, and he knows them too well to have any illusions about them. With a staff and a budget both too small by far for their complete maintenance, and no shipyard at all, his flotilla of floating anachronisms poses him an endless series of problems. I had come to offer him another.

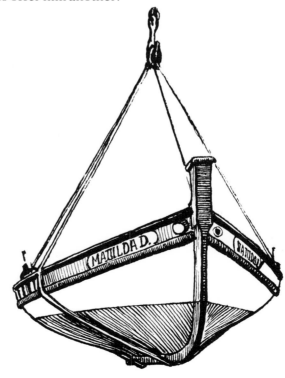

281

Harry was where he is usually to be found, at his old typewriter, hunting and pecking away at one of the never-ending reports to this or that bureau of government.

"Come in and close the door."

I had carelessly entered from the windward side, endangering the stacks of papers, envelopes, file folders, and publications that are piled everywhere. I quickly closed the door. Harry finished typing his sentence, then swiveled around and gazed at me with an inquiring eye.

"Harry, we're going to bring you a boat to add to your collection, and we figured you'd probably want to know so that you can start figuring out where you're going to put it."

Harry stoked his pipe. "Are you aware that there are all kinds of people who want to give us their old boats," he asked mildly, "and that we don't take 'em for lots of very good reasons?"

"Well, it's a new boat, for one thing, and for another, we couldn't afford to give it to you. We'll have to get our expenses out of it, although we're not looking for a profit."

Something that might have been amusement flickered for an instant in the corner of Harry's left eye. He lit the pipe and puffed.

"It's a felucca," I began.

Loosely, a *felucca* is defined as a lateen-rigged craft of the Mediterranean Sea. Specifically, as Harry was aware, I was referring to a vessel that histories and catalogues usually refer to as the *San Francisco Bay Fishing Boat*. In its own day, the vessel was called a Dago Fisherman (by non-Italians), and, properly, a *Silana* by her owner and crew.

In the middle of the last century, many emigrants from southern Italy arrived in northern California, among them fishermen and boatbuilders. Understandably, the boats they built here were those that their ancestors had built and sailed in the Mediterranean since the Dark Ages. Their rig was called lateen by the crusaders, who simply named it after the Latin people who sailed them.

When the Silana made its appearance on San Francisco Bay, it was a foreigner for sure with its low profile, high stemhead, forward-raking mast, long yard, and brightly colored paintwork; a boat obviously from some other time and place. By the time of the Civil War, however, it was a familiar sight, and by the 1890s there were hundreds of them, not only on the Bay, but along the coast from Noyo Harbor in the north to Monterey in the south.

The boats ranged in size from 18 feet to a maximum of 36 feet. They were kept small so that they could be rowed easily. With their double-ended, shallow-draft hulls, they could fish right up on the beach, or in among the rocks of an ironbound coast.

Some feluccas were decked, with a high-coamed hatch forming a kind of cuddy. Others were built as open boats. None had cabins or below-deck furnishings of any kind. When a felucca was kept at sea overnight, as they frequently were, the crew of two or three men took turns sleeping on the catch. In a decked boat there was just enough sleeping room in the hold. Feluccas were not equipped with floorboards, but there was some softness to a mattress of fish. Sometimes boats were kept out as long as three days, and might have stayed longer, but the first day's catch would have reached maximum permissible ripeness by then.

By 1864, the felucca fishermen were being systematically victimized by those to whom they sold their catch, the market operators. These men had conspired with open-pocketed politicians, and ordinances had resulted that forced down the prices the marketeers paid for the fish, but upped the prices for which they sold it. The fishermen rebelled and started their own market, forming a union. It was the organization from which grew today's Fisherman's Wharf Association.

Fisherman's Wharf is today a tiny harbor lost among surrounding restaurants, tinsel shops, and arcades, but once it was the place where the feluccas berthed. The cracked old photos show them there by the dozens, in a long row against the lonely looking wharf. Their decks looked like garage sales, for in harbor, all the gear was brought up from below to dry; line, nets, clothing, sails, boots, ground tackle, lanterns, cooking gear, coal oil tins, floats, buckets, etc.

You could go there and buy fish. The Italian gentlemen were usually to be found among their paraphernalia, generally mending nets.

By the turn of the century, small boat motors had arrived to stay. They were installed in the feluccas, but the two did not get on well together. The Silana was too fine aft. The propeller kicked all the water out from under the stern, causing the after part of the vessel to settle into a hole of its own making, a dangerous thing. Although there are no clear records, it appears that the last feluccas were built around the turn of the century. From its hull form a whole new design had been made. The new boats had broad, buoyant canoe sterns, among other practical innovations. They were called Monterey boats, because the fish canneries at Monterey were now within their range, in a five- or six-day round trip.

Completely obsolete, the feluccas quickly perished and were no more.

All of this Harry knew. I had handed him a

packet of new snapshots, which he was examining. They showed the open door of a large barn. Visible inside was the unmistakable form of a felucca under construction, all her timbers in place, ready to plank. Fiddling around with some clamps was a grizzled-looking character, bearded and wiry, Dean Stephens.

Dean is well known on the West Coast to all there who have anything to do with traditional boatbuilding. For years he cruised the California coast with his family in his Atkin ketch *Charity*, sailing from port to port as an independent contractor, making a hull here, a complete boat there, rebuilding or fixing another somewhere else, doing restorations and building for the San Francisco Maritime Museum between other jobs. By the time he moved ashore and settled on a Mendocino farm to teach woodworking to apprentices, he had earned a well-deserved reputation from Newport Beach to San Francisco as a master boatbuilder.

How had he come to be building a felucca replica? Years before, while looking through a book, he had come across the lines of a Silana, and he had built a couple of half models of the

peculiar hull. ("It just kind of grabbed me, and I always remembered it.")

One day he was approached by Norman Landon Bossini deVall. DeVall ran a marine agency in Noyo and had long had the idea of producing inexpensive wood fishing vessels as a commercial undertaking. One of his ideas was to re-create a felucca. He showed Dean a set of plans he had obtained from marine architect Henry Rusk. Dean was dubious about its commercial possibilities ("Heck, I knew nobody was going to want to fish *that*."), but was nevertheless interested. ("I didn't have much to do for the next couple of months.")

"I had some lumber in the barn. Good stuff. It had been sitting there air-drying a couple of years. So I figured I'd just build the hull, and see what happened. Sort of for the heck of it."

I first heard about the project at Christmas. I had gone over to Dean's Abalobadiah Ranch to hoist a glass.

"Come on out to the barn," Dean said. "I've lofted up a felucca and laid the keel." He had also cut the end timbers. He said his intention was to build just the 24-foot hull, with no deck, and sell it for $3,000. I was taken with its beauty. Would it be an accurate hull, historically?

"Yes, a replica."

Why not deck it and rig it, too?

"Because, for one thing, I don't have the money to buy all the stuff I'd need to finish it, or enough to live on while doing it. The hull's less than a third of the whole boat. Besides, who the heck would buy the darned thing if I did build the whole boat?"

By a fortnight later, three things had happened. Norman had swung a bank loan to "build a fishing boat," I had kicked in another chunk of cash, and together we had talked Dean into going all the way with the replica. We reckoned that with $3,000 cash, plus most of the materials on hand, the project could just squeak by. Dean projected being finished in April.

Norman would be the contact man between Dean and the designer, sailmaker, and whatever research sources might turn up. This is important, because the Abalobadiah Ranch is remote, some 200 miles north of San Francisco, much of it by mountain road. It was a trip Norman made regularly. He would also be able to pick up all the bits and pieces of stuff and bring them north.

I was to keep a record of the project, written and illustrated. As Dean's neighbor, it would be easy for me to pop over and make sketches of the work in progress. As it turned out, I was also to deal with the people who it seemed would most likely buy the boat. (These people were Italians, and Norman suggested he might be best for the job, as one of his middle names is "Bossini," but this was an asset we were never forced to use.)

The idea was that if Norman and I would handle all these other matters, it would leave Dean totally free just to build the boat, which was all he was interested in anyway.

And so the plan shaped up. Our efforts were to bring into being a meticulous replica of an extinct vessel. It was to be finished in the spring, at which time we would immediately need to sell it. None of us could afford to own a felucca, and Dean's investment (his entire winter wage) would be huge. Further, we wanted it to be sailed, and used for the enjoyment of the public.

This meant it would have to be a museum ship, and it seemed the best way to accomplish that would be to get somebody to buy it and make a gift of it to the Historic Ships Display of the California State Maritime Park on Hyde Street Pier. This would make Harry Dring the recipient of the vessel. But who would be the donor?

The Merchant's Association was a prosperous group composed largely of Italian businessmen, many of whom are descendants of felucca fishermen. Would they be interested in our project? The response was enthusiastic. By coincidence, the Association had in mind changing its symbol from a crab to a felucca. We were to send them particulars and photos when the work was farther along. It seemed an auspicious beginning. Later, when the vessel was framed, we would contact Harry and tell him what was afoot.

It was a moment of great expectations, and Norman dreamed of a day when a fleet of feluccas would again sail the bay, racing against one another in regattas, sponsored by the Italian restaurants that would be their owners. Meanwhile, work continued and the problems of building a replica had begun to manifest themselves.

From the standpoint of historical accuracy, the first and biggest problem was that there was no felucca left intact anywhere to look at or copy. The last complete specimen had perished sometime during World War II. Fortunately, its lines had been taken off at Sacramento by Henry Rusk, and it was this draft that had sparked the project and allowed Dean to begin work.

The new boat would duplicate the lines and dimensions of the original. She would measure: 24 feet on deck, 8 feet 2 inches beam, and draw about 18 inches. Her keel, stem, and sternpost were ironbark. She would receive oak frames, beams, carlings, fir decks, and cedar planking.

It was guessed she would weight some two tons unballasted. What amount of ballast she would require, nobody could guess. "I reckon with those lines it'll take about 4 ton inside her to put her down on her marks about an inch," Dean observed.

There were dozens of questions as to details of construction, but few answers. The main source of published data is Howard Chapelle's treatise on feluccas in his *American Small Sailing Craft*, but it was never intended as a builder's guide, and is further flawed by a number of inaccuracies. In compiling his encyclopedic book, Chapelle had of necessity to rely on mountains of data sent him by hundreds of sources, some of them misinformed. In the case of the felucca, there were several obvious mistakes and quite a few points of questionable reliability.

The same was true of other sources of information. Some models exist, but photos of them revealed that they, too, were all inaccurate in one degree or another.

Here and there a few old felucca hulls reportedly survived. San Francisco Maritime Museum Director Karl Kortum reported that two small ones were still being fished in Tomales Bay by the descendants of their original owners. This lead was followed up, and Kortum turned out to be right, as he usually is in such matters.

They turned out to be of some help, but not much. Both the boats were 18 feet long and dated to sometime before World War I. True, they were felucca-type hulls, but both had been repaired and rebuilt so many times that little remained of the originals. Above the waterlines, they had been so altered that it was impossible to get any idea of their original construction. Much of it had been replaced by plywood and fiberglass, and the lines of the boats had been obviously altered.

Also, there were no hatch covers, no coamings, no forward bitts, and no evidence at all that either craft had ever contained a mast, bowsprit, or any kind of sailing rig. Still, some original bottom planking and a few floor timbers and frames were left. These frames were steam-bent, it was noted. Chapelle reported that felucca frames were sawn. In fact, both systems seem to have been used.

Our greatest single source of information was Henry Rusk, marine designer, historian, architect, and patriarch. Henry had been a colleague of the late Mr. Chapelle and had provided him with much of his felucca data.

"I sometimes think I was his only accurate source," harrumphs Henry, who has written a treatise of his own on feluccas. He made the manuscript of this unpublished document

available to us, as well as his extensive photo file of early feluccas, and his drawings. A knowledgeable observer, Henry had in his youth been aboard a working felucca, and it was remarkable how much he had remembered over all the decades. Without his assistance from the beginning, there would have been no felucca replica.

We had settled on a name for the felucca. She was to be *Matilda D*, after Harry Dring's wife, who is the photo archivist at the San Francisco Maritime Museum. Over the years, this lady had made herself tirelessly helpful to an unending line of wooden boat builders and researchers, three of whom were Dean, Norman, and myself.

With the name chosen, and the work well in hand, it was time to take snapshots, head for the city, and spring our project on Harry Dring.

Harry put down the snapshots and leaned back in his chair. "So, supposing the Fisherman's Wharf Association does buy the boat and contribute it to the park here. What am I supposed to do with it, eh?"

It was hoped he would find a crew for it, sail it, exhibit it suitably, and make it available to the Italian community for such appropriate annual festivities as the Blessing of the Fleet Ceremony and Columbus Day.

Harry threw up his arms. "I've got about a hundred pages of reports to finish; we're short-handed; before long we're going to have to move this whole operation to the other end of the waterfront so a new breakwater can be built here; we've got too many boats to take care of already, and now you come along."

His pipe had gone out. He relit it and puffed.

"OK. Maybe it can be done. First thing is to go see the man who has the authority to accept such a gift on behalf of the State of California."

Did Harry think this person would accept it?

"I'll tell him I think the park can use it. After that, we'll find out. What makes you think the Italian community will give it to us?"

And so I became involved in lengthy communications between the Fisherman's Wharf Merchants' Association (which gave us every encouragement short of a commitment to buy the boat) and the California State Parks Foundation (which did make a commitment to receive the boat, were it to be given).

Dean continued building seven days a week. His routine while working on *Matilda D* was to rise at 6 a.m., finish farm chores and breakfast by 8 a.m., then work continuously on the boat until 4:30 p.m. At 5 p.m., there were the cows to milk and other assorted jobs.

By mid-February the boat was framed, and the job of planking had begun. This was a tricky part of the work because the felucca has a bottom that is nearly flat amidships, but a plumb stem and a sternpost almost plumb. There was a lot of spiling. Had one length of plank been used, it would have to have been either edge-set or taken from a piece of lumber 3 feet wide.

Word of the project had begun to circulate, and help came from unexpected places. Bob Larsen, a former student of Dean's, came down from Oregon and helped deck her. Rich Wasserman, another ex-student, brought a fir timber he had cut and dried and from it roughed out the mast. Sailmaker Peter Sutter took on the job of cutting the sails, and loft assistants Jim Leech and Mike Jenkins volunteered to make them by hand. They were to have over 200 hours in them before the work was finished. The goal of accuracy seemed on its way to fulfillment.

"I tried all during the building to assume an attitude that the original builders might have had," Dean recalls. "That may sound kind of funny, but I pretended I was building back in the 1800s. I considered it was a workboat, not a yacht. On the other hand, I wanted it to be as good as a yacht, within the limitations of its type. I had also to consider the people I was building it for. It would be walked on a lot, so I made the hatches to take that, whereas the original would have had much flimsier hatches. I also gave this boat floorboards, which the original would not have had, and *Matilda*'s deck construction incorporates hanging knees. It's hard to say whether they were ever given those or not. They were all built differently."

Unusual and outdated materials had to be obtained: white lead; an old-fashioned bilge pump; hemp; ferdico. Ferdico is the old-fashioned seam pitch that must be heated to a point just short of (but *never* beyond) a boil, then poured, steaming and stinking, instantly into the deck seams before it can cool. Of course, it cools nearly at once.

Problems are inevitable. We were fortunate that ours caused relatively little delay. Norman kept forgetting things, while Henry Rusk kept remembering things. This process did not quite balance out, though, as the things Norman would forget were the bits and pieces Dean needed from the city, while the things Henry would remember were different specifications to parts of the boat that had already been built.

I seemed to be getting nowhere with my efforts to get the Association to make some kind of commitment, however vague, about purchasing *Matilda D* as soon as she was finished, and I took to hissing at the cats and snarling at the dog, a kindly and intelligent animal that deserved better. Dean's temper was put to the test when the ironbark that was delivered for the caprails and rubrails turned out to have been kiln dried, and therefore unbendable. It finally yielded, but only after a week's soaking in Abalobadiah Creek.

April came and found the hull finished, faired, and ready to paint. Designing *Matilda*'s color scheme was my job. I felt constrained to in some way use the intense, hard cerulean blue that was the official color of the Italian Fisherman's Union in the last century, and that survives on the Monterey boats of today. It is an unhappy boat color when used in conjunction with white, as it usually is, but not to use it would deviate from tradition in the replica.

So on went the cerulean blue, but only onto the rubrails, end timbers, and rudder head. The caprail was painted black, the outsides of the rails a paler blue, and the long hatch with its four cover sections were made light grey, as were the insides of the bulwarks. The high-crowned decks were scraped and oiled. The topsides were white. Dean's contribution to the decoration was a gold bead scored the length of the sheerstrake.

Fully dressed in her new paint, *Matilda D* was moved out into the barnyard to be rigged. There, the sunlight reflecting on her new colors gave her a gemlike quality and she looked as though she belonged under glass. And the blue looked OK.

The felucca's mast butts in a slotted step amidships, and is wedged in place. Its forward edge rests on a heavy beam notched to receive it, and is secured by a hinged hasp with staple and pin. The mast rakes sharply forward, at an angle that is adjustable by the positioning of the step wedges.

The long bowsprit pierces the starboard rail alongside the stemhead, and pins to the samson post, a single bitt. The bowsprit may be detached and shipped. On it is an iron traveler ring to which the jib tacks and sets flying.

The 32-foot main yard of *Matilda D* was made of two long poles, flattened for most of their length to overlap one another and lash together, a standard feature of all Mediterranean lateeners. It was to carry a mainsail that would sheet with a single line running through a notch in the afterside of the sternpost just above the upper rudder pintle, then lead over the caprail to a cleat.

All the tackle blocks were built with oak shells, sheaves specially lathed from lignum-vitae, and appropriately Italian hemp strops.

The felucca took no standing rigging as such. A system of gun tackles would stay the mast as well as perform other functions. All of this was rigged to the best of everybody's knowledge, with reference to Henry's plans and old photos, but our best sources were vague. Details were left to be worked out by her first crew.

Who was to sail this boat? It was a big ques-

tion, for we had not managed to turn up anybody who had any experience in traditional lateen rig, and an alien rig it is, to be sure. We knew that a long sweep was sometimes used in conjunction with the rudder for extra steering power, but how that worked, and why, we could only guess. The yard was seized to the mast by a collar-and-lanyard arrangement that would allow the whole yard to be shifted forward or aft, thereby making the center of effort adjustable. How and when was that done? Nobody knew. How was the mainsheet handled when the boat was tacked? For that matter, how was she tacked at all? There were many mysteries to be explored.

The most pressing mystery of all at that time was whether or not the Association was going to buy this fascinating little boat and ensure its place on Hyde Street Pier. All of my telephone conversations with their representative had been very promising. We had lunched together and discussed the matter. He was as enthusiastic as I was. Still, his efforts to convince his own organization had not brought anyone the 200 miles to Mendocino to view the work in progress.

Photos and specifications had been delivered

and approved, however, and the public-relations value of *Matilda D* to the Association was acknowledged. One of their ideas was to buy it and enshrine it on the wharf on a floodlit pedestal, which would revolve slowly. Another idea that had been mentioned was to truck the felucca around the country to various cities, as a traveling exhibit.

Still, there was no commitment, and the moment was fast approaching when we would have to sell *Matilda*. Although her sails had not yet arrived, and there were many details of her rig to be puzzled out, she was for most practical purposes finished. Her building (minus research and errand-running time) had taken 1,400 hours, and cost about $4,500 out of pocket, although most of the materials for her had been on hand at the project's outset. The last of the money in the building fund had been long spent, the debts had piled up, and the wolf was prowling around the door. It was time to take *Matilda D* down to the city, where she would have to be her own best saleswoman. In order to recover expenses, we needed to sell her for $11,000.

On a grey dawn in early June, a truck rolled

onto Hyde Street Pier drawing behind it a felucca, which still smelled faintly of Mendocino barnyard. Her arrival was expected, but without fanfare.

Quickly and efficiently, the boat on its cradle was transferred onto the pier while a few people watched. Harry was among them. He was seeing her for the first time, and it was noticed he permitted himself the luxury of a grin. She was not yet his, but a few hours hence a contingent of Fisherman's Wharf Associates was due to arrive for a viewing, at last, and it was fervently hoped that these gentlemen would arrange for *Matilda D* to remain here with her elderly cousins. If that did not happen, there would be no alternative but to sell her into private ownership as a yacht.

Up went the mast, out went the bowsprit, the long yard was hoisted. There was a glistening of varnish, a stretching taut of new manila, and *Matilda D* was ready to be seen, a seductress for sure. Who could resist her?

The sons and grandsons of the felucca fishermen who came to view her there seemed to fall immediately under her spell. There was a rich flow of the Italian language, good cheer, and much pleased gesticulation. The Association representative with whom I had been working smiled as he translated fragments of the conversations. Yes, they liked the boat very much. It was beautiful. Quite beautiful. Accurate? Yes, yes, very. It looked just as it should.

Had any of them sailed on a felucca, ever? Yes, this gentleman had sailed on his father's felucca, and here were others who had sailed with their grandfathers, all as small boys, 60 years and more ago.

Stories were remembered and related. When the fleet was out in dense fog, and in danger of being scattered, a song would be started aboard one of the boats. One line would be sung. Aboard another vessel, invisible in the mist, another line would be sung, and so on around the fleet, and the little ships would be bound in sage convoy by song.

Sometimes, when the boats were clustered together at sea, races around the fleet would be staged, with the participants leaping wildly from boat to boat, deck to slippery deck. Only the luckiest and surest of foot finished dry, and there was much drinking of red wine to celebrate the winner.

The smiling, nostalgic delegation at last departed, and Dean, Norman, and I left soon thereafter, headed back to the north country. Harry would look after *Matilda D*. Presumably she would soon now be joining his fleet. Until she could be launched, her decks would be covered with wet burlap, and she would be hosed daily with salt water to keep her seams closed.

A month later we were still the owners of a burlap-covered Italian fishing boat.

"I don't understand how you can even consider selling it as a yacht," the voice of the Association representative was saying on the other end of the line. "It's such a work of art, and has such historical importance, it should belong to the public."

Yes, yes. I fully agreed. This man, too, had worked hard to make our dream reality, for it was a dream he shared. He was asking for more time, but the wolf was more than at the door now; he was threatening to break it down. Once again I pointed out that we had waited as long as we could. We had to have a commitment.

The gentleman from the Association explained again that while many of their members were very, very enthusiastic, others saw no sense in buying a boat that would just be given to a museum without visible return. He was sure those who wanted it would prevail, but more time was needed.

I gave the message to Dean. "There isn't any more time," he said. "You tell those guys I'm behind on the rent, I've got a sick cow, a family to feed, and not enough money to buy gas to go to Fort Bragg."

The game was up, and we were a glum crew. There was nothing left to do but put the felucca up for sale as an exotic yacht. Everybody went back to their lives. Norman explained to his bank that the fishing boat had indeed been built, and the loan would soon be repaid. The visions of fleets of feluccas racing on the Bay had long since faded from his fantasies.

Dean busied himself preparing to receive six full-time, live-in students, for the Abalobadiah Ranch was very soon to become one of the nation's few boatbuilding schools. Harry returned to his interminable reports. I crated up my year's production of marine paintings (somehow done in and around the felucca project), packed my pencils and my socks, and left for the East Coast. I had an exhibit scheduled there, to be followed by a summer with boats that were not feluccas.

It was in mid-August that I received my next news of *Matilda D*. Although it seemed she was not to be a museum ship, I was still to write her story for *WoodenBoat* magazine. That and other projects took me to Maine and into the friendly clutter of *WoodenBoat*'s editorial chambers, where Jon Wilson greeted me with: "I understand your felucca has just been bought for Hyde Street Pier by the California State Parks Foundation." And on that we had a drink.

Planking the *Morgan*

Maynard Bray

WOODENBOAT TENDS *to concentrate on the low end of the boating spectrum — small, accessible craft — but occasionally we do publish material on the larger vessels, if only to keep things in perspective. The replanking of Mystic Seaport's whaleship* Charles W. Morgan *is one case in point. We felt that lessons could be learned in the practical restoration of a large ship, and that perhaps large scale should not be viewed with such trepidation. After all, a plank is just a plank, no matter what its size. Maynard Bray felt that if we could get Benjie Mendlowitz to aim his camera at the* Morgan *long enough, he could put together a great story on how big planks are hung — a report, as it were, on the care and feeding of a national landmark.*

Restoration: *One definition — Making an object look like it once did by using the same materials in the same configuration and put together with the same standards of workmanship as the original.*

WOODEN BOAT LOVERS seem to be mostly involved with small craft. The shipwrights' work on larger vessels, however, is interesting and useful, even if you specialize in building skiffs. And if you are a connoisseur of good woodworking, it would be hard to find a better example of quality shipbuilding than in the good fits and fair lines in the new planking being hung on the 139-year-old whaleship *Charles W. Morgan.*

Since 1941, the *Morgan* has been berthed at Mystic Seaport Museum, Mystic, Connecticut, and is a singularly important attraction there. About half a million visitors board her each year to try to understand her career as a whaleship. (She sailed for 80 years in pursuit of whales all over the world and was homeported in both New Bedford, Massachusetts, and San Francisco, California.) The *Morgan* has another story to tell, however. She must be continuously worked on if she is to be kept going, and this work of maintaining, repairing, and restoring her — visible as it is to onlookers — makes a wonderful exhibit in itself. It is hard to beat seeing some of these old-time processes being carried out — it's the next best thing to actually doing them yourself and a whole lot better than hearing secondhand how the artisans used to do it.

The purposeful practice of traditional shipbuilding techniques has kept the old girl going since the day she was built — and this approach

will, we hope, continue long into her future years. Good white oak, heart pine, hackmatack, and black locust have also helped, and these materials are still going into her as the various repairs are made. Some laborsaving power tools are used in the process, but the end result is close to what it was in 1841, when the *Morgan* was built. Philosophically, the approach is to do the job as it would have been done and to make her as strong as she would have needed to be. In part, this means a straightforward, simple approach using proven methods. There are practical limitations, to be sure, but on going aboard, it's doubtful if you'll find any fiberglass, plywood, or Dacron.

The *Morgan* is being retopped, and this process of renewing her hull above the waterline has been going on for several years. More than half of her port side has been finished, and the crew is now framing and planking the starboard side. Later on, she'll be hauled out so her after end can be properly supported while it is being rebuilt. Mystic is extremely fortunate in having a well-equipped and well-staffed working shipyard where all this work can be accomplished — most of it within full view of the museum's visitors. A visit to the Seaport is well worth the time and money for other reasons as well. On its 37 acres are over 200 watercraft besides the *Morgan*, along with first-class maritime-related exhibits and demonstrations, both indoors and out.

Her port side replanked above the waterline, the *Charles W. Morgan* is being fitted with new planking on the starboard side.

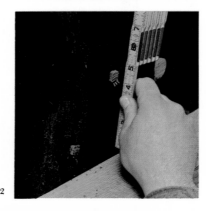

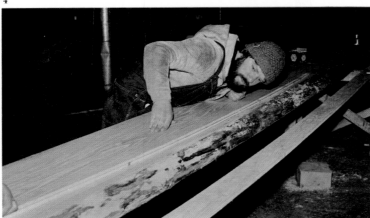

one — Wooden ships were often planked with the logical combination of white oak and longleaf yellow pine (often called heart pine). In the bluff ends, where wide, crooked, and easily bent stuff was needed, oak served well. But the long, straight, clear pine planks, imported from Georgia, northern Florida, and the Carolinas, worked better along the vessel's sides and in much of her bottom. The pine seems to outlast the oak — at least above the waterline — so the adage of "Use pine where you can and oak where you must" for ship planking has probably always prevailed. Here, master shipwright Basil Tuplin takes a spiling for a plank on the starboard bow. One of these new oak planks has already been hung, and it, like the original, has been slit for easier bending.

two — Measuring the width of the new plank to the faired plank line, which is marked along the frames. A good eye is needed for lining planks; that is, in establishing where each edge seam will fall. The seam lines, after planking, are still highly visible, and for good appearance, they must be free of humps and hollows and the planks must all taper evenly in width. At this stage, the frames have been dubbed or planed fair, and the plank lines (each one having been lined out with a long batten) have been inscribed on each frame. Thus, after the shape of the lower edge of the new plank has been established by spiling, the width measurements being taken here will establish the other edge.

three — Few edges are straight in boatbuilding, and it is no different in building a ship. Almost all curved lines, after being marked at intervals, have to be faired by making minor adjustments to the fairing batten until they are eye-sweet, just as shipwright Roger Hambidge is doing here. The basic shape was transferred from the spiling batten, shown at lower right. Only the long-lasting heartwood of this 3¾-inch live-edge oak planking stock is used.

four — From the spiled edge, the width of the new plank is laid off at each frame — the necessary reference marks and width measurements were noted on the spiling batten while it was in place on the vessel. These width marks on the new plank will also be connected and faired with a fairing or lining batten just as for the first edge. The plank is then maneuvered through a big bandsaw, where a cut is made just outside each of the marked lines.

five — Once sawn, the plank edges are planed square and to the marked line, then beveled partway in to form a caulking seam. (Things aren't always that easy on ship's planking. Edges often have to be beveled if the planks are wide and the frames are curving. In such instances, if you're planking upward toward the sheer, you'd probably leave the upper edge of each new plank square and lift bevels from it for the mat-

6

ing (lower) edge of the plank above.) The electric plane shown here is a truly wonderful tool, and one that is found in most professional boatshops as well as in shipbuilding yards. The exclusive use of old-time tools is not a practice at Mystic; there is so much carpentry work to be done on all the watercraft there that the museum can't afford to do it all by hand, even though that would be desirable. There is little difference in the end product, however, and as time permits, Mystic Seaport may well be able to utilize more and more historically appropriate tools.

six — Kerfing, rather than steaming, is the means by which the forwardmost planks make the bend around the *Morgan*'s bluff bow. It certainly takes less time and bother, and, after looking at some of those still-sound original planks, one can hardly argue with the approach. And there are still many of those original planks; the *Morgan*'s bottom — both framing and planking — has been pretty much undisturbed since 1841. Its condition is remarkably good, and there are no plans to renew it.

seven and eight — In place and firmly clamped, the forward end of the plank is bored for a temporary bolt to keep the plank in place while being bent around the frames. The metal clamps were made up from big C-clamps; their ends were cut off, shoulders were welded on, and long threaded bolts were put in their place. They are held fast in temporary holes bored through the ship's ceiling. Temporary holes (to be plugged after use) will also be bored in some of the frames, where iron pins will be placed to provide a means of wedging the plank tightly against its neighbor. A mixture of old and new frame futtocks shows in this photograph, with the futtock butts staggered so they don't all fall on the same plank line.

nine — Another type of clamp is being tightened down here against the butt end of the new plank. It, too, is bolted in through the ceiling, or inner planking, which is as thick as that on the outside. This part of the *Morgan* is quite straight so the flat of the plank lies quite naturally against the frames in full contact. But for a good fit, sawn frames that curve a lot are dubbed off flat in way of each plank (making a series of knuckles in the frames, rather than a smooth curve). By contrast, in a smaller bent-frame vessel or boat, the planks are hollowed to fit the natural curved shape of the frame.

ten — Plank lines marked on the framing show clearly here. Notice also the distance between the butt of one plank and that of its neighbor — a feature needed for strength. The top two planks are of oak and run all the way from the stem. The two under them are of yellow pine and butt against oak planks farther forward. Fastening is mostly by treenails, but bronze spikes are used at the butts.

7

8

9

10

one — Wooden treenails, by and large, hold the planks in place against the frames. There are a few bronze spikes near the ends of the plank where the wedging action of a treenail might cause them to split (the three holes forward of the treenail in this photograph, for example, have spikes in them). These treenails are made of well-seasoned locust, a wood known to be long lived and very strong. Many of the *Morgan*'s original treenails were made by hand and showed an eight-sided shape in cross section. These new ones were turned out on a treenail lathe, a machine that works somewhat like a big pencil sharpener with cutters arranged to produce the correctly sized dowel-like shape. The relation between the hole size and the treenail size is crucial — a good treenail must fit snugly and drive with some resistance, yet not fetch up and buckle when it is partway in. About an inch of penetration per blow is good. Since treenails are turned out well in advance and are expected to shrink or swell a bit, they are made oversize. Because of subsequent shrinkage, some fit OK, but others must be shaved down for a good fit.

two — There are several ways to drive treenails properly, and each yard has its favored method. At Mystic, the practice is to drive the treenail within an inch or so of its final position, cut it off that much proud of the plank, and split the projecting end for a wedge. This takes a bit longer than driving the treenail flush before wedging, but the theory is that, because the wedging of the end takes place before the final drive home, this method pulls the plank in more firmly against the frame.

three — Once split, a locust wedge is driven in to swell out the projecting end. Wedges, like treenails, are made up in quantity ahead of time. Most of these treenails are driven blind; that is, they go through the plank and frame, but not through the ceiling. A small but sufficient number of them are driven all the way through, however, to be split and wedged on the inside.

four — With the wedge sawn flush, the treenail is ready for the final drive to bring it flush with the plank surface.

five — A good-sized iron maul is used here for driving treenails. The nut and washer, shown in all these photographs, is a temporary fastening and will be removed once all the treenails and spikes are driven.

Spikes are specially forged of selnic bronze to match the shape of the original cast ones. The metal fastenings in all of these old ships had to be nonferrous or they would have been eaten up by the copper hull sheathing. Once antifouling bottom paint was developed and marine railways appeared in the major seaports, copper hull sheathing became unnecessary, and the iron or steel below-the-hull fastenings were used in most wooden vessels.

Cirrus: A Treasure from Herreshoff

*W*HEN ALAN BEMIS, *who owns a summer home near our offices in Brooklin, Maine, told us he wanted to throw a 50th birthday party for his boat, we decided to help him celebrate in* WoodenBoat. *The Herreshoff-designed Fishers Island Class represents a timeless construction and design theme;* Cirrus, *one of the class, represents the devotion of an owner toward his boat that is possibly unmatched these days. And* Cirrus *is so beautiful. As an expression of classic perfection, she deserves considerable exposure. Who will ever forget the closing lines of Alan's appreciation, where a Maine fisherman suggested that* Cirrus *was the kind of boat God would have built if He'd had the money?*

Alan Bemis

THE ORIGIN of the Fishers Island Class was briefly described in the April 1928 issue of *Yachting*. This article said, in part:

Many yachtsmen will remember the advent, some fifteen or more years ago, of a one-design class of three boats — *Comet, Dolphin,* and *Mischief,* known as the Newport 29-footers — fine, able, and fast cruising sloops from the board of none other than the genius, Nathanael Herreshoff. At one time the owner of *Dolphin,* Mr. W. Barklie Henry, was highly enthusiastic over the many fine features of these craft. However, Mr. Henry thought that they might be improved upon. Whereupon he went into conference with Mr. Herreshoff, with the result that the Fishers Island Sound One-Design Class of five boats was formed. . . .

The dimensions of the new boats are: LOA 43'8"; LWL 32'; beam 10'8"; draft 6'. In general, they follow the lines of the Newport 29s, with the bow and stern drawn out a bit, sheer straightened to give 6'2" headroom, and increase of draft to 6'. The interior layout was designed to provide the most comfortable accommodations possible for two people aft, with large galley, toilet room, storage space, etc., and good accommodations for a paid hand forward, including a second toilet.

Though the boats are often referred to as the "Fishers Island One-Design Class," Herreshoff usually called them "Fishers Island 31-footers."

They are beautiful boats in every way. They were not designed to "rate well" under any sort of handicap rule, but simply to be ideal sailing vessels under a wide variety of conditions. In developing this class from the Newport 29s, the "Wizard of Bristol" paid little attention to their detail, and much of the design was left to his son, Sidney, and the molding experts.

Cirrus was built for Henry L. Maxwell of Greenwich, Connecticut, and launched August 28, 1930, as *Kelpie,* Herreshoff Hull No. 1157. Maxwell was a distinguished yachtsman, owner of many Herreshoff boats, and commodore of the Larchmont Yacht Club in 1930. The Great Depression kept Maxwell from sailing her as much as he had hoped, and he sold her after four years to a John J. Benjamin, who gave her the inappropriate name *Her Excellency.* Benjamin died sometime in 1934, and she came on the market. I had the good fortune to purchase her on January 19, 1935.

To explain my love for *Cirrus,* I need to backtrack a little. My older brother, Gregg, taught me to sail at an early age. Gregg's sailing skills are well known, and he was an absolutely top instructor. At that time, the family boat was a Manchester 17-foot Knockabout, and I soon developed strong enthusiasm for a sailboat that had good speed for her size on all points of sailing, was responsive, and easy to handle. By

Previous page — In 1980, when *Cirrus* was 50 years old, Alan Bemis (who had owned her for 45 of those years) threw a birthday party in her honor. The highlight was a race with three other visiting Fishers Island 31-footers.

1934, I was happily married and raising a family, but living in Wayland, Massachusetts, too far from the water to be content with a daysailer. Throughout that year, I spent many hours searching for a boat large enough for long cruises, yet one that would handle as well as the Manchester 17-footer. The first time I saw a Herreshoff Fishers Island 31-footer, I fell in love with the boat and asked Parker Converse of John G. Alden's brokerage office to find me one, which he did. That is how *Cirrus* and Bemis came together, a union that has lasted nearly 50 years.

Cirrus, and at least one other boat of the class (*Pinafore,* I think), were built to extra high specifications and may be the finest Fishers Island boats now afloat. Their bottoms were planked with some of the last of the virgin hard pine that only Herreshoff had available. They have teak decks, and all the varnished trim (such as sheerstrakes, toerails, cabin sides, and coamings) is also of high quality teak. Of course the keel, frames, and deckbeams are white oak. Detail is of the finest; the two skylights, for example, are beautiful works of art. Below decks too, all is top quality, with paneled bulkheads and doors and beautiful joinery.

Herreshoff boats up to much larger sizes than the Fishers Island Class were always fitted with tillers, ideal for boats with quick response and excellent balance. Herreshoff fitted most of his sailing auxiliaries with folding propellers of his own design, which were built right there in the shops. I think they are by far the best ever. When folded, they have almost no drag and never foul lobster trap warps or seaweed. The blades lock in the working position and give full reverse thrust. However, any off-center prop makes for difficult slow-speed maneuvering under power, and this is the only characteristic in *Cirrus* that gives us a hard time.

Cirrus has always had red topsides. This was quite a shock to me at first. When the firm of John G. Alden first told me she was for sale, they sent me a standard specification sheet with a photo attached showing the boat with white topsides and without a varnished teak sheerstrake. It was a photo of some other Fishers Island sloop. When I went to New York to look her over, and five or six other possibilities as well, *Cirrus* was in outside storage at the Nevins yard and had a huge canvas cover over her that came way down over her topsides almost to her cradle. We inspected her bottom planking, keel, and rudder, and we crawled around on and below decks. Everything was perfect. There wasn't time to remove the cover.

I knew she was the boat for me and made an

At the start of the Fishers Island Sound class during 1933's Larchmont Race Week, *Kelpie*, under her original rig, leads the way. Henry Maxwell, her owner at the time, is at her helm.

offer for her the next day. Can you believe I bought her for $6,000? As soon as the purchase was complete, I couldn't wait to go to New York again, take off the winter cover, and go over her from stem to stern. I was horrified to find she was red! My first reaction was to have it all removed and changed to white, but her topsides were so perfect, it seemed wiser to keep her red for at least one year. We came to like the idea of red topsides and changed the shade a bit the next year, then added a gold-leaf cove stripe that separated the red paint from the bright teak sheerstrake. Her topsides are now a very special color known as "*Cirrus* Red," supplied by Garvin Willis.

One year I fouled up and failed to get the special red to Frankie Day at his Benjamin River boatyard. Frank said he thought he could mix some that would match. I said, "Give it a try," but I was mighty worried. Two days later, I arrived at the yard to see how she looked. "Do you think we got the right color?" asked Frank. "Well," says I, "it's close, but much too bright a red." "That's strange," said Frank, "because we found just enough left over from last year to do her like she's always been."

The Fishers Island sloops were originally designed with the galley and quarters for a paid hand forward. The first changes we made below deck were to remove the big icebox and bulkhead from the fo'c's'le, making room for a second pipe berth, and to build an icebox aft. We then opened up the galley into the main cabin to make life much more pleasant for the cook, and to let the heat from the galley stove warm the cabin. All of our cruising has been Downeast, where heat from the galley is welcome, and we have always burned hardwood briquets or coal.

The next change was to widen the companionway. I have always felt that the wide companionway on the Concordia yawls made life in good summer weather much more enjoyable for those below. The Fishers Island boats do not have a bridge deck, thus improving access to the cabin tremendously, but the engine, which is off center, was housed in an engine room extended upward all the way to the top of the cabin trunk. This wasted space and made the companionway narrow. We cut down the height of the engine room, put a countertop just above the engine, and widened the com-

SLOOP RIG, KELPIE, 1930   YAWL RIG, CIRRUS, 1930

panionway right across the top of this counter. This makes an excellent spot from which to serve drinks and lunch when most of the crew is in the cockpit, and it also does double duty as a navigating table. This engine cover is removable, so access is even better than before. The companionway is now 4 feet wide, nothing anyone would want to sail with in a big ocean storm, but mighty pleasant in the summertime. The built-in slides and hatch cover are extra strong, so we feel secure in anything short of a hurricane.

I don't feel that the rig is heavy enough for an ocean passage, though Robert Murray of Long Island University sailed his *Patapsco II*

with the original Herreshoff rig around the world in 1960–62. He went the hard way, sailing eastward, and had a particularly rough time crossing the Indian Ocean. His only difficulty of any consequence was a broken running backstay in the middle of the Pacific.

The original sailplans for these boats called for a large mainsail and a relatively small jib, as was usual in the 1920s. The spinnaker, too, was a small one, with its halyard located at the same point as the jib halyard and sheeted inside the forestay. The mast was stayed with only a single pair of spreaders, which were too long to permit sheeting a genoa jib in flat.

The first change we made in the sailplan was a substantial increase in the height of the foretriangle. The original design called for a headstay and a jibstay, the headstay being simply for support of the upper part of the mast and not intended for carrying any sail. We found that the boat definitely could use more headsail in light-to-moderate winds, so we replaced the two headstays with a single one that met the mast about 8 feet above the old jibstay fitting, 41 feet above the deck. Support for the masthead was accomplished with a pair of jumper struts located where the headstay met

A great shift in the manner in which yachtsmen sailed and raced was taking place in the early 1930s, and the Fishers Island sloops got caught right in the middle of it. Like other similarly sized one-design classes, some going back even before the turn of the century, these boats were laid out for a paid hand who took care of the boat more or less full time and who had his living quarters in the forward part of her. Herreshoff had a rather standard arrangement for boats of this size, and the Fishers Island sloops were outfitted with it — a main cabin for the owner with a couple of settee berths and a couple of convertible upper berths, a galley to starboard up near the mast, an enclosed toilet room opposite, and a fo'c's'le forward of the mast for the paid hand, access to which could be gained through a hatch in the foredeck. In 1926, when these craft were designed, there was no reason to vary this arrangement from what had been successful in the past.

But then came the stock market crash of late 1929 and the

hard times that followed. No longer could boats carry paid professionals as a matter of course — that was to be the exception — and for day racing around the buoys and an occasional yacht club cruise, these boats became too expensive to keep up.

Thus *Cirrus* (then *Kelpie*) wasn't the only boat of the class to change hands soon after she was built. After only about five years of one-design racing, the class broke up and the boats were sold. In 1932, there was a move to smaller boats without the expense of a paid hand. These were the Fishers Island 23-footers (34 feet overall), also a Herreshoff product. In time, under subsequent owners, many of the 31-footers were converted for family cruising, just as Alan Bemis did with *Cirrus*.

It has been as cruisers and handicap racers that these wonderful boats have spent most of their lives. For this use they were ideal — seakindly, fast under a wide range of measurement rules, sleeping six in reasonable comfort, affording standing

A Look at

headroom, and being strikingly handsome to look at in spite of changing styles. Of the 13 or so boats built to this model, nearly all are still in use. *Cirrus*, trimmed and decked with teak and somewhat more refined because she was the 11th boat in the series, may be the most elegant, but there are others that also look nearly new after a half century. *Kestrel, Spindrift,* and *Torch* are three that I'm familiar with. Of the others, two are on the Great Lakes, one is on the West Coast, and at least one is on the Chesapeake. I believe *Patapsco II*, in which Dr. Robert Murray sailed around the world in 1960–62, is still around, and I know that *Wild Goose* is being restored in Essex, Connecticut.

The Herreshoff Company went heavily into advertising in the 1930s, but with what appears to have been only marginal success. Among the several "stock" boats offered were the Fishers Island 31s, but the company's construction record indicates

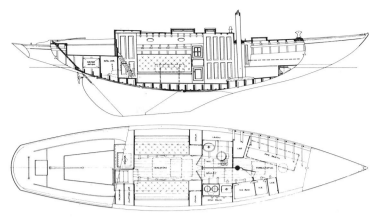

the mast. At the same time, we discarded the upper running backstays and replaced them with a permanent backstay attached to a small boomkin rigged off the stern. This permanent backstay working through the jumper struts and their stays then could carry the headstay load, making the running backstays necessary for mast support only in strong breezes, though we set them up under most conditions just to stiffen the headstay and make her sail better. At this same time, we shortened the main spreaders and rigged another pair above them to carry new diamond shrouds. We also purchased our first parachute spinnaker. All these changes made the boat extremely competitive for racing, as well as a delight to sail at all times.

Back in the 1930s, racing against the Eastern Yacht Club fleet, I found myself in one of the smallest boats. We never did very well, but we had a pile of fun. After the war, and with the larger foretriangle, we were much more competitive, and the average size of the competing boats was smaller. In our first Monhegan races, we were placed in Class A. We won Class A in one Monhegan and usually did well in the others. Farther Downeast, where the competition was not quite so keen, we won a reputation for being the boat to beat. It has always interested me that a boat that was not built to any measurement rule but simply designed to be a fast, able, fine sailing vessel could do so well against boats that were specially designed for speed with a low rating. This is a testimonial to the designer, and to the developers of the rule, too. But in the 1970s, as designers worked harder to "beat the rule" and construction moved toward super-light-displacement skimming dishes, we ceased being very competitive. Now, with the M.D.S. rating in use, we would do very well again.

One extraordinary characteristic of *Cirrus* is

the Class

that only two new boats resulted from this promotional campaign — and both of them seem to have been built on speculation. The first of these was sold in 1936, but it was 10 years later before a buyer was found for the last one. Both boats sold for far less than the $16,000 price prevailing before the Depression.

Although the Fishers Island Yacht Club was involved with the Fishers Island 31-footers by virtue of a few of its members owning them, that class does not appear to have been Club-sponsored. One should think of the letters "FIS" on the sails of these boats as standing for Fishers Island Sound, the body of water in which the boats usually sailed. W. Barklie Henry, of the nearby Watch Hill Yacht Club, originated the idea for such a boat and ordered the first one, *Cyrilla IV*, late in 1926. Three of his friends, thinking that his idea was sound, ordered boats for 1927 delivery. Except for two others, which were built in 1929

and sold elsewhere, the four original boats had things pretty much to themselves for the first three seasons. Then, in 1930, five more boats, some owned in Fishers Island and some in Watch Hill, joined the racing. *Cirrus*, then *Kelpie*, was the last boat of this second batch and wasn't delivered until late August. Ed Maxwell, son of Henry L. Maxwell, the man *Kelpie* was built for, remembers her first race and remembers going aboard her when she had just been delivered to the Maxwell mooring in West Harbor on Fishers Island, fresh and fully outfitted from the Herreshoff yard. For the short time they had her the Maxwells did well with *Kelpie*. In 1931, her first full season, she won the class championship in spite of being one of the heavier boats (a penalty paid for a fancy teak deck instead of a lighter-weight canvas-covered pine one). *Kelpie* didn't go overboard in 1932, but she won Larchmont Race Week the following year and got a second in the American Yacht Club cruise as well. That year was to be her

last under H.L. Maxwell's ownership, and with only a single season intervening, she was destined in 1935 to begin her affair with Alan Bemis.

The Fishers Island 31-footers, although based on the Newport 29-footers and presumed to have been basically laid down from their offsets (a blowup, incidentally, of those for *Alerion*), had some rather significant changes made from the original model. It is likely that the new profile (longer ends, deeper keel, more raking sternpost, straighter sheer) and deckline to match were established by means of a scale drawing. However, the fairing of the lines to these new end points, according to Sidney Herreshoff, was done right on the mold loft floor — full size. Sidney was a most modest man, reluctant to take complete credit for much of what he did, but he did admit (in a taped interview) that his father was in Florida for the winter while this work was going on and that he, Sidney, was in charge of executing the needed changes. I'd say he did well! — Maynard Bray that she sails well against other boats either in very light airs or in strong winds and choppy seas. Only in moderate breezes do we fail to "save our time" against modern, well-sailed boats. A memorable example of her ability in strong winds was the Maine Retired Skippers Race of a few years ago, when a Force-7 NW wind was roaring down Penobscot Bay, kicking up quite a chop. We carried a deep reef in the main and a double-sheeted working jib. The mizzen was furled. *Cirrus* is in perfect balance under this canvas, and she will sail herself to windward as well as a good helmsman can. The seas slow her very little and never knock her off. We got a good start in this race and soon led the whole fleet. Handicaps were at the start. Halfway through the windward leg, the shackle on the jibsheet let go. (I have not used shackles on jibsheets since.) With all that wind, it was 15 minutes before we had another jibsheet bent on and the sail reset. We were in last place then, but again we passed all but two boats and were close behind the winner at the finish. Many cruising boats will douse sail and chug to windward against Force-7 winds, but it is a joy to feel *Cirrus* moving easily into the seas on such a day, and making progress to windward.

Although we often cruise with four or six aboard, Chapie, my wife, and I very much enjoy cruising with just the two of us. As a sloop with the big mainsail, it meant we often had to reef. Even reefed, it was difficult to get away from anchor under rough conditions. *Cirrus* loves to move, and as a sloop she would never hang to an anchor with any sail up. So, I began dreaming about converting her to a yawl. Most of my sailing friends were horrified. They said, "What! You're going to change that boat that loves to go to windward into a yawl that will probably get nowhere?" I felt sure that with her big foretriangle, tall mast, and long mainsail luff, she would go to windward just as well. So, Joel White designed the yawl rig for us, Ike Manchester built the new stays, and Frankie Day built the mizzenmast and put it all together. This was in the spring of 1954. Just a day or two before she was to be launched for the season, I was at Frank Day's yard and asked him when she was going overboard. Frank said, "Well, we have one more little job to do, and that's to shorten the main boom. You said you wanted it 4 feet shorter. Shall we take that 4 feet off the forward end or the aft end, or 2 feet off each end?" We decided on 4 feet off the after end, and Frank measured that off, made a pencil line there, and handed me the crosscut saw.

Easy to Keep

For nearly 50 years, *Cirrus* has had but one owner. Alan Bemis has loved her properly and has seen to it that she was well maintained. For about 20 years, we have looked after her at the Brooklin Boat Yard. Before that, she was in the capable hands of Frank L. Day & Son.

Although she has reached middle age, *Cirrus* is perhaps the easiest boat in the yard to keep up. Her double-planked topsides, Douglas fir over cedar, never show a seam. In the spring, a careful sanding and filling of any little dents accumulated the previous summer is all that is required to prepare the surface for the annual coat of *"Cirrus* Red."

Her deck is laid teak, caulked, with Thiokol in the seams — originally the seams were payed with pitch — requiring very little attention. The only problem in this area is that after more than 50 years, the deck has worn down to the point where the bungs are very thin and a few pop out every year. Alan has started a program to glue in a new one whenever one comes out. Unlike most teak decks I know of, this one doesn't leak very much, I think because it was built of first-quality stuff, with plenty of thickness, and, in 1930, it was laid and caulked by the best craftsmen around.

Her top strakes, cover boards, house sides, coamings, hatches, and rails are all varnished teak. They get a sanding and a coat of varnish in the fall after haulout and another during the summer. About every 10 years, they are cleaned off and built up again. Her bottom requires very little work and leaks for only a day or so when first put in the water in May or June. In all the years that I have known *Cirrus*, both at my yard and at Frank Day's, she has never been recaulked. Her cabintop, originally canvas covered, now fiberglassed., is the one painted surface on deck. Cabintop and spars get a coat of buff paint each spring. Her mainmast, although much modified, is the original spar, built up of eight staves, very much like an elongated barrel. There have been no problems with glue failure. A few years ago we cut off the top 10 feet and glued a more rugged piece on, as the strains of racing were producing some scary bending effects up there. The only other structural work I remember doing was rebuilding the transom planking, which had split and was coming away from the stern frame.

The fact that *Cirrus* hangs together so well after more than a half century of service speaks well of Nat Herreshoff's construction techniques. She is not heavily built (quite the contrary), but in poking around below, one gets an impression of exquisite proportion and a feel for stress under sail, and an idea of how that stress is contained by wood and bronze. She would be considered lightly built by most standards, but experience says it must be just right. —Joel White

"Golly," I said, "I'm not going to cut it off; it will be all crooked." "Well," said Frank, "I won't do it." "Why not?" I asked. Frank said, "With all the changes you've been making on this boat, I figure poor Nat Herreshoff is spinning around in his grave something awful, and I'm not going to make him turn over once more."

The yawl rig was a great success. *Cirrus* went just as fast to windward and was a bit faster off the wind with a mizzen staysail set. Most of all, what I like about the yawl rig is its maneuverability under sail, as well as the simplicity of shortening sail in a breeze of wind. She is very easy and a delight to singlehand.

Not long after the conversion to a yawl, Chapie and I were coming back from a short cruise Downeast and decided to anchor for the night in Cranberry Island Harbor over near the Great Cranberry shore. The forecast called for it to breeze up out of the southeast, and we thought we would have good protection there. During the night, however, it worked up to quite a northeast blow, and we found ourselves on a lee shore with the wind increasing all the time. It was blowing too hard for the little engine and the off-center propeller to push her out of there safely. If we had been a sloop, we would have had to get up a storm trysail or double-reefed main and would have had a really rugged time getting away from the lee shore. But with the mizzen flattened in hard, the engine worked us up over the anchor, and with the anchor on board, we set a storm jib to balance the mizzen and fairly flew into protected Northeast Harbor.

Another time, I wanted to clear a crowded anchorage with a Force-8 gale blowing out of the harbor. Since I was singlehanding, I could not safely turn downwind between all the boats and stretched anchor rodes. But with the mizzen set and auxiliary power on, it was easy to weigh anchor and back clear slowly until I had sea room to set a jib and bear away.

I have often wondered why so many small boat sailors douse sail outside and chug into harbors and out again. Perhaps they don't realize that a 40-foot boat can be as easy to handle as a 12- or 15-footer. When the winds and seas are moderate, it is much easier and more pleasant to set sails at the mooring or at anchor and get underway quietly. *Cirrus* is so nimble that I find her easier to handle than a Herreshoff 12½. I can leave the tiller and let her handle herself for a few moments, even in a harbor.

Center Harbor (Brooklin, Maine) and our nearby Northwest Cove are both completely sheltered from the usual summertime southerly by their little offshore islands. Returning to harbor, one can carry full sail into the lee of the island, drop all the canvas on deck, and carry one's way right up to a mooring or anchorage. It sounds easy, and it is, with *Cirrus*.

Docking, or getting away from a dock, under sail is fun, too, with a boat like *Cirrus*, though I seldom try it alone for fear of gouging her planking. Docking without auxiliary power requires careful preparation. Docklines and fenders must all be in place, particularly the spring- or breastline that will check the forward momentum. It is usually necessary to get all sail doused well clear of the dock and coast in, with accurate allowance for wind and tide.

The aesthetics of any boat, too, are important. With her deep and tapering teak sheerstrake, *Cirrus* is somehow much prettier than most other Fishers Islanders I have seen, and her beautiful smooth topsides and bright teak trim are a joy to behold. The flush deck forward of the mast gives little headroom in the fo'c's'le but it makes a fine working platform and is far more beautiful than any forward-extending cabin trunk would have been. A tall, graceful, tapered spar is not even comparable to the modern uniform-cross-sectioned masts with great clumsy fittings at the truck that look like quarry derricks.

I have always felt that the most important quality of any boat is her sailing and handling ability. *Cirrus* is absolutely tops on all counts here. She seems to move through the water with extraordinary ease whether it be smooth or choppy. She is light enough to accelerate rapidly, yet heavy enough to keep moving through heavy seas. She never pounds and seldom throws any water into the cockpit, even going to windward under breezy conditions. She carries her fullness well astern, so that, in all these years of sailing, we have never been pooped. Her response to the tiller, the way she moves through the water, and the angle of heel are all somehow just right. It's not only myself, a long-time owner, who feels this way about her, but everyone who has ever sailed with me comes up with the same praise for her handling and sailing qualities.

I have been sailing *Cirrus* now for more than 45 years and expect to continue just as long as I can. A large part of the joy of sailing is the beauty of it, and I feel that *Cirrus* is one of the most beautiful sailing craft in the world. We were tied up to a pier in Jonesport one time with an elderly fisherman standing on the pier looking down at us. After several minutes of silence, he said to me, "I do believe that's the kind of a boat God would have built — if He'd had the money."

301

W E INCLUDE this short but enlightening piece on the sloop Lazy Jack as a counterpoint to the refined qualities of Cirrus. Lazy Jack is a very simple but exceedingly satisfying craft within the practical and financial reach of almost anyone. Ed Frost's text is, in a way, a statement about standards — that anyone's boat, or any other possession for that matter, can be beautiful without being extravagant. Ed's illustrations obviously made the difference. We're lucky to have been able to publish this.

W HEN YOU LOOK back and start to add things up, you realize that the satisfaction you got out of a particular boat was in no way relative to her size or cost. As a matter of fact, one of my favorites I built for about $1,000 (in 1954), and I guess we got more pleasure out of her than some people do out of fine yachts costing many thousands of dollars.

The *Lazy Jack* was really just a big flatiron skiff with a beautiful sheerline and a lot of flare in her sides. Instead of a centerboard, she had a long, shallow keel that drew only a little over 2 feet. Her planking was white cedar; frames, white oak; and the keel was locust, almost as heavy and hard as the iron shoe that ran the length of it. This shoe and the weight of the 1½-inch-thick cross-planked bottom were the boat's only ballast. Her spars were solid spruce.

Auxiliary power came from a 5-horse outboard

A Little Ship—
Lazy Jack

Ed Frost

in a well. When it wasn't working or we were going such a short distance that putting it in the well wasn't worthwhile, we could move her with a long oar that was carried along the port cockpit seat. It extended into the cabin somewhat. The door slide was notched out at the bottom so it could be closed without moving the oar. A thwart separated the helmsman from passengers and crew and supported the mainsheet horse, belaying pins, and binnacle box. The horse was bronze so it wouldn't affect the compass.

With the sail on hoops, and the gaff and boom fitted with jaws, all free to move around the mast, you could raise or lower the mainsail without heading into the wind. To take full advantage of this, she was fitted with lazy lifts (quarter lifts and lazyjacks combined), which confined the sail during these operations, preventing it from going overboard even with the boom broad off. The lifts were slacked off when sailing to allow the sail to take its proper shape. This was a handy arrangement; it greatly eased the problems of singlehanding, and the lazy lifts were well worth whatever aerodynamic efficiency they cost.

Although the *Lazy Jack* was only 24 feet overall, she seemed like a bigger boat. I think this was because stove, sink, head, icebox, utensil box, and grub basket were movable. Nothing was fixed in place except the two bunks; everything else was secured with lashings, and we could arrange things to make the most of our space in any particular situation.

A big hatch forward, left open most of the time, ventilated the whole boat. It was a good place to stand when working up forward, and, when we were set up for a day or two layover in some out-of-the-way spot — awning rigged, head forward, and stove in the cockpit — it gave unlimited headroom over the wooden commode that served as the head.

The *Jack* had her faults, but, as with any old friend, we accepted them in exchange for the qualities we greatly admired in her. She was slow in stays due to her long keel, and, for the same reason, very steady on the helm. She would push along all by herself on a close reach. Sailing alone, you could go below, fix a sandwich, take a leisurely look at the chart, or even stretch out for a short nap. When you came back up, she'd be heading within a few degrees of where you left her. And we had shoal draft without the nuisance of leeboards or a centerboard trunk cutting the little cabin in two.

With her low gaff rig and shallow keel, the *Jack* was not very close-winded by today's standards, but when you eased her off a bit, the gaff main pulled like a horse and was without question more efficient than a jibheaded sail would have been on all points of sail except hard on the wind. The *Jack* wouldn't win many races, but she never let us down. After 13 years of hard use, when I sold her, she didn't leak a drop, and there wasn't a soft spot in her. Of course she was never for long ocean voyages; she was not self-righting, and her big cockpit was open to the hull; when it rained, we pumped. She was strictly for summer cruises alongshore, but little voyages, as well as little ships, can be as much fun as big ones, and they are all most of us ever have time for.

The Old Man's Sharpie

Stanley O. Davis

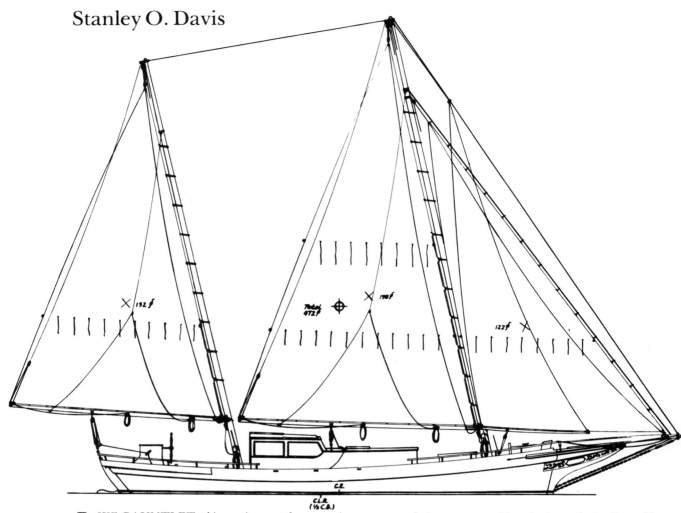

*L*IKE GAUNTLET, *this cautionary tale was an important one for* WoodenBoat. *The article examines the subtle influences that create fallibility. By any advance evaluation of the design's potential, the Old Man's sharpie would have seemed fine. Yet in reality, she failed to perform as intended. Though the nature of her capsize was something of a fluke, she still could not be depended upon in a* range of circumstances. *Though she undoubtedly could have been modified to accommodate her shortcomings, she was, for her designer, too much of a failure. A sad story, to be sure.*

We published this article as a reminder, especially to us at WoodenBoat, *that even in the face of experience there is always the potential for misjudgment in conception.*

---

*A*N ARTICLE on sharpies in *WoodenBoat* set me to reminiscing. I, too, have a deep and abiding affection for yacht derivatives of this venerable workboat type, *but,* if "flat is (truly) back," there are some things the new wave of enthusiasts should know.

Omitted from the article is what I consider to be the most beautiful sharpie yacht design ever conceived. The architect was S. Owen Davis, my father, a protege of Howard Chapelle and lifelong friend of Jim Richardson, the well-known Chesapeake boatbuilder. My father died in 1958, a very young man, never to witness the boom in yachting that was to occur in the next decade. I take this opportunity to affirm that the rather remarkable development of this sport, industry, religion, or whatever, would have enabled him to realize his ambitions. Given more time, he would, as "Chappie" knew and "Mr. Jim" will tell you, have made a much bigger mark than he did. Now, the traces of his work having nearly vanished from the scene, I resurrect this remnant of my "Old Man's" work — bearing the boating torch in those nondescript postwar years — to pass on a few lessons he learned about sharpies. It is a fairly human story — one of tremendous effort yielding mixed results.

Howard Chapelle, as you may know, was a little "nuts" about the sharpie type. This is overstating the case, but he seemed to see, as his friend James R. once remarked in my presence, "a bit of sharpie in everything." Then, too, he was steeped in the heritage of Chesapeake Bay workboats. I haven't set eyes on his scholarly tomes in years, but I am sure they say in effect that Hampton flatties, skipjacks, and the various New England sharpies are in the same tradition. This notion has from time to time been cited as a rationale for combining characteristics of Bay boats and New England watercraft. My father's idea — a sharpie disguised as a bugeye, incorporating the patent stern, unstayed spars, and so forth — seems to have fit some psychological template in Chapelle's mind. He gave the project his enthusiastic support, and, in consequence, its product was widely disseminated in the yachting press of the late 1940s.

The boat was actually built in 1948 or 1949 at Jim Richardson's yard on LeCompte Creek. She was built by my father in a shed near the spot where Mr. Jim's bugeye, the *Jenny Norman*, recently rose from the sawdust and shavings. When I go there nowadays, and I seem to manage the trip once a year, the place evokes kaleidoscopic images in my mind. I was five years old when my father's sharpie was built.

Like the *Jenny Norman*, my father's sharpie seemed to grow from a pile of lumber, emitting, all the while, a cloud of wonderful wood smells. Yet there are, of course, profound differences in the construction of the two. Sharpies are by no means bugeyes, although this one happened to be very bugeye-like in tophamper.

The design, as were so many in those days, was intended for execution by amateur builders; no amateur can build a bugeye. Indeed, it may now be said that no one can build a bugeye save a certain Eastern Shore man whose initials are J.R., but that is a matter of opinion.

It seems to me that traditional construction techniques were employed in producing Owen Davis' version of the bugeye-rigged sharpie, so, like others of the type, she required relatively few man-hours to complete. I am certain that her sides were fabricated in their entirety *first*, then bent to the stem and sternpost. I regret not being able to remember the rest, but tender age is my excuse. In any case, throughout one winter, gestation took place, until by spring she rested under cover with Dad finishing the

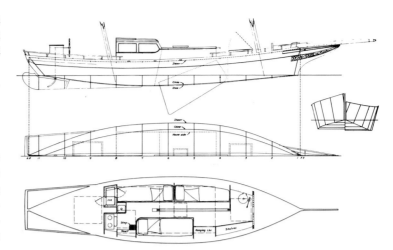

moldings of her cabin sides.

Shortly thereafter, assisted by one of Mr. Jim's tractors, a large dolly, and plenty of Swedish steam, she was moved across the road and launched into LeCompte Creek. I have vivid memories of the first day she was waterborne. For some reason, she slid suddenly down the ways and into the cove, unballasted, floating high above her marks and bobbing like a cork. I can still see my father losing his balance because of the unexpected motion and grabbing for a handhold as she moved sternward, finally coming to rest against one of the pilings that still dot LeCompte's today.

There followed an idyllic period (for me at least) — the bow of the sharpie resting on the marshy shore; me playing with a Richardson toy in the muck near her stem; Dad fitting out the boat. Her copper was "wet" for days and consequently accumulated atop the water surrounding her and along the shore. When I put my feet in the water, my ankles came away rust-red.

After rigging and ballasting were completed, there began a long series of trials during which it came to light that she would require certain modifications. One of these involved installing a skeg between the centerboard trunk and the rudder; another meant shortening the rig somewhat. After a while, she was sailing rather well but still did not meet the expectations of her designer, his mentor, and his closest adviser. There were several Davis-Chapelle-Richardson conferences to figure out why she performed poorly, and what to do. Whatever could reasonably be done, without offending artistic sensibilities, was done; there was the suggestion that she was overcanvased.

I was aboard that boat many times but never sailed in her. The most promising opportunity was lost because of a Choptank River thunder-bumper. The sharpie was anchored in front of

Water Street just downstream from the Cambridge Yacht Club. We took the dinghy and rowed out to her — my father, my mother, and I. It was already breezing up, and she was pitching and tossing, periodically being snubbed abruptly by the anchor rode. As I stood on a thwart in the skiff, her patent stern was alternately above my head and chest high. Dad clambered aboard and made the small boat fast, Mother prepared to lift our cooler to the deck and I fended off. There the adventure came to an end. Sniffing at the air, my father closed and dogged the hatches, replaced the sail stops, and rowed us ashore. Within an hour a storm was rushing up the river, bolts of lightning descended from dark clouds to the water's surface, curtains of rain fell. We ate our picnic in the car.

I must have spent the rest of that summer collecting shark teeth along the bank of the Choptank. A succession of well-dressed visitors were dinner guests at our home, and I gathered — though for some reason it wasn't said outright — that the sharpie was to be sold. Finally she was sold.

Some part of the brokerage action necessitated moving the boat to Annapolis. Dad set off early one fall day from Cambridge; Maryland's capital lies some 30 miles distant by water. Later, Mother and I left in the car to meet him, reaching the destination first, but not by much. In those days a road trip to the western shore of the Bay took many hours — just waiting for the ferry could be a half-day affair.

On entering "Crabtown" we drove over to the Naval Academy Yard, from which location we saw the sharpie at last, with only father aboard, beating into the harbor against a fresh northwesterly breeze. It was, as he often said, pontificating on shoal-draft boats, a matter of "starting the sheets and keeping her footing." He had, and she was. The self-tending rig made the long succession of tacks appear effortless. By the last tack, she fetched a buoy near the Naval Station; there she came about and, close reaching on the starboard tack, foamed into Annapolis Harbor. It was a sight to behold, and every head turned to see the beautiful little boat as she entered. I know the "Old Man" was beaming with pride.

In those days the harbor was crowded with watermen aboard skipjacks and buy boats. You could see them stop their work and point; my father knew that to a man they thought she was a dandy. Three toots sounded and the Spa Creek Bridge began to open its jaws. Dad was headed for his friend Arnie Gay's yard, I now suppose. As usual, the wind for threading that particular needle was dead foul. Still, with all sails set she came on like an express train, and I could see my father hardening up everything as he shot into the breach. As the sharpie emerged shortly thereafter on the headwaters side, he was away from the helm to slack off the sheets when a great gust caught her fair on the beam. She had passed from the bridge's wind shadow into a rush of fresh air.

What followed seemed to happen in slow motion. She rotated majestically from the near vertical until her poles floated like jetsam on the serrated surface of the creek. From our vantage point, now adjacent to the Catholic cemetery, we could see progressively more copper, then even the centerboard, then less and less of the white topsides. As the boat capsized, father climbed across the cabin trunk, finally grasping the weather rail and hauling himself to a perch on the sheerstrake just as the evolution was completed. The sharpie lay where she had fallen, motionless. My father, seated on the rail with his feet on the cabin sides, struck a "Rodin's *Thinker*" pose. Now and then another cat's-paw of autumn air lifted his shirttail.

I don't recall what happened next; undoubtedly he did all the right things. I do know that not many days later, her sails were recut and two more feet came off the top of each spar. My father's later designs were, if anything, under-rigged.

The sharpie was sold to a Texan from Corpus Christi, if memory serves, and was shipped there by truck. I have no idea where she is now; I hope that, like my father, she ultimately "won her battle with the sea."

Ironically, response to the design was overwhelming; literally hundreds of people wrote to inquire about it. My father carefully replied to each suitor, saying that the boat was only marginally successful and that major revisions were required before he could, in good conscience, allow anyone to follow the plans. He went on to other projects and never made the sharpie right — maybe it couldn't be done. Years after his death I asked Howard Chapelle what was wrong with that boat. He just shook his head and, looking at the man to his left, said, "She was twisted, wasn't she, Jim?" I still don't know what he meant by that remark.

The last letter of inquiry arrived just about 10 years ago, which I guess proves that people really do read old boating magazines. The writer, like all the rest, was entranced by her appearance and simplicity of construction. As you can see, she exudes a feeling of power and grace not unlike the "Big Ti," or more recently, *Whitehawk*. Appearances can be deceiving.

The Future of Wooden Boats

Jon Wilson

I N AN AGE of synthetic abundance, it is sometimes difficult to know how wooden boats will fare in the future. To be sure, the harvesting and utilization of wood in boats requires a considerably less sophisticated technology than do other boatbuilding materials. But the proper adaptation of that technology requires — indeed, demands — an absolute measure of skill and experience. Moreover, the design and construction of wooden boats are just the beginning. To assure that they survive the passing of time requires skill and experience. A wooden boat is not an object to be acquired, enjoyed briefly, and then ignored. For that, one must turn to the synthetics (although they also have their quirks), for they are more tolerant of neglect.

The future of wooden boats depends first and foremost upon an understanding of wood itself — its limits and potentials — in the boatshop, on the mooring, and at sea.

This assumes, of course, that we care about wood to begin with, that we appreciate the gift of its presence in our lives, that we are challenged by both its simplicity and its versatility as a structural material. Surely we cannot help but appreciate its renewability in this era of highly developed but finite resources. Surely we have not lost touch with our deep appreciation for the tone and texture of well-worked wood. Surely we do not want to give up altogether the spiritual and physical pleasure of its company. And wood is so wonderfully accessible — we can harvest and work it ourselves or pay others to do so. We need not invest our small fortunes in high technology.

In days gone by, every boatbuilder who had attained the status of master had a thorough knowledge of the woods with which he worked. That wisdom had been imparted over time, had been acquired bit by bit, as he observed the sequence of the standing tree, the squared-up log, the drying lumber, and, finally, the individual pieces taking shape under his own hand. And in his wisdom he became aware of a crucial truth: the shaping and fitting and fastening of these pieces was the culmination of a single process. It was also the beginning of another process — for that piece and for all the others that were fitted and fastened into each new boat. Within that new life would be found demands unmatched by any that had been imposed before upon the wood.

The bottom planks would spend their summers soaking up and their winters drying out. Topsides would be exposed to millpond morning calms and the buffeting of wind and wave. Decks would be drenched in summer rains and baked in summer suns. Spars would bend to the press of whole sail breezes. Beautifully fitted joints would be pulled, pushed, swollen with moisture, and parched in wind and sun. Paint and varnish would strive to keep up with it all, yielding to the inexorable demands of the most powerful forces in the universe. In the old days, these matters were understood well.

I do not mean to suggest that there is no understanding of such matters today, but that the understanding has become substantially less prevalent — among designers, among boatbuilders, and among boat owners. To make matters worse, it has become more difficult to recognize those upon whom such understanding has been conferred, because, more often than not, they are the quiet ones, the ones whose words are barely audible. Their works, on the other hand, speak volumes. The proud owners of such works, if given the opportunity, will do the same.

It would be fair to say that experience of the aforementioned sort is invariably more crucial to the longevity of a wooden boat than the most skillfully executed joinerwork. The individuals and yards that combine the two elements are no longer as plentiful as they once were, but the future of wooden boats lies in good part in the hands of the deeply experienced. And experience can be hard to come by. It has become, like education, a commodity — something to be purchased, not developed. The notion of apprenticeship, as once defined, has become all but extinct in this country. Unfortunately, that system is no longer adaptable to our culture, but it is more lamentable that the attitude —

that experience takes time to acquire — is being either ignored or forgotten.

There are many young builders emerging from educational programs and short-term apprenticeships and self-apprenticeships who have concluded that they would like to make their living building fine wooden boats. They offer varying degrees of energy and commitment, skill and experience, both in the shop and on the water. There are many who have more of one than the other, and many who have less of both. But the latter have something different to offer, for they are the ones who will try harder to make up for what they haven't yet experienced, and the results of their efforts may be exquisite. But exquisiteness is only a portion of what is required. As the marketing experts for the stock wooden boats of the 1950s knew, almost anyone can build a boat that *looks* fantastic as it leaves the shop or showroom. What is needed is to build it so that it *continues* to be fantastic. To build for as many contingencies as possible. To assume that the person who will own the boat may not be fully aware of how best to care for his craft.

To do that, the builder must be constantly aware of the elements with which he is attempting to cooperate. And to be that aware, he must constantly be increasing his understanding of the art and science; he must constantly be developing his experience. This is no easy task for builders today. Knowing all the problems, let alone all the answers, is one of the most difficult obstacles facing the aspiring builder. One of the most effective ways to gain insights, of course, is to intersperse new construction work with repair or reconstruction work. At the very least, this experience offers direct information as to what didn't work and why. Nothing is as forcefully informative as a boat that is falling apart.

Of course, traditional boatbuilding is only a part of the future. It will survive, on at least a modest scale, because it is challenging, gratifying, and economical by comparison with modern boatbuilding. Like other arcane skills, it has been elevated to an art form. As for the more recent developments in the science, cold-molded and sheet-plywood construction, the future is broad and bright. In these technologies lies the potential for light-but-strong hull forms. And these hull forms suggest themselves not only to competitive racers but to the part-time nonprofessionals who need safe and comfortable cruising boats that can be built by their owners at modest cost, and, if necessary, trailed over the road with minimal effort.

These are the wood technologies that produce monocoque shells with few joints and seams — in effect, with few moving parts. But they can be tricky. Both of these technologies depend heavily upon the glues with which they have been constructed, and proper glues are sensitive to temperature, pressure, and moisture in the wood — but insensitive to the need for economy. They are expensive.

On the other hand, if a builder can maneuver through these difficulties in the company of a well-thought-out design, he will find himself the proud owner of a practical, durable, and (hopefully) beautiful wooden boat. It should be easy to keep — although easy means noncomplex, as opposed to effortless. After all, nothing worth one's pride is without effort. But maintenance, of the preventive kind, is simply the process by which the boat — any boat — is nourished. Nothing as dynamic and alive as a well-conceived and well-built boat can survive without nourishment.

Thus, we arrive at the final variable in the future of wooden boats: the presence of grace and good sense in design. Of course, both of these elements suffer from a relative subjectivity: the less one has seen and experienced, the more limited is the ability to discern that which the more experienced observe at a glance. Worse yet, the less experienced individual is unaware of what he doesn't know and is often virtually unable to formulate even the right questions.

The solution, for me, is found in the traditions. It seems foolhardy to ignore the wisdom and experience of those who have gone before us. And not just a couple of decades before us — several decades. It does no harm, in fact, to try to understand the full history of our traditions — not for the romance of it (although that is there in abundance for those who want it) but for the insight to be gained from observing the evolution of solutions to problems in both design and construction. Successful evolution *proceeds* from tradition more than it *departs* from it. If we observe it carefully, then we can understand it clearly. If we can understand it, we can apply it to the development of our own experience. Equipped with an understanding of the traditions of grace and good sense in yacht design, we can proceed to create and establish our own traditions — either as designers and builders or as owners.

It seems almost contradictory to suggest that the future of wooden boats depends in such measure upon our awareness of their traditions. We are so unused to looking back. But it is the fullness of our experience that broadens our vision. It is a kind of catching-up that allows us to look just a little farther out and beyond.

Index

Picture Credits

The Soul of a Wooden Boat: 2: Peter Barlow.

The Man Who Planted Hope: 6-7: Drawing by Tom Parker from the Summer, 1976 issue of *CoEvolution Quarterly*. **8-11:** Drawings from *What Wood is That?* by Herbert L. Edlin, © 1969 by Thames and Hudson, all rights reserved, reprinted by permission of Viking Penguin Inc.

A Boatbuilder's Garden: 12: Courtesy Sierra Club of San Francisco. **15:** Wood engraving by Lynd Ward. **16:** Gordon Lutz.

Milling Your Own: 19-21: Casey Kiernan.

Pete Culler's Workshop: 24: Illustration by Paul Trowbridge. **25:** Drawing by Spencer Lincoln. **26:** Benjamin Mendlowitz. **27:** *Top left* — Benjamin Mendlowitz; *top right* — Kenneth E. Mahler, Mystic Seaport, Mystic, CT.; *bottom* — Claire White Peterson, Mystic Seaport. **28:** *Top left* — Benjamin Mendlowitz; *top right* — Claire White Peterson; *bottom* — Benjamin Mendlowitz. **29:** *Top* — Benjamin Mendlowitz.

From Rags to Riches: 34-39: Matthew Walker.

How to Build *Piccolo*: A Seaworthy Sail & Paddle Canoe: 41: Sherry Streeter. **42-51:** Gail Wills.

Sailing Together Around the World: 63: Victoria Carkhuff. **65:** Mary Maynard. **69:** Redrawn by Spencer Lincoln.

A Second Tri: 62: Jim Brown, The Naked Eye, Inc. **64:** John Pierce. **65:** *Top* — Jim Brown; *bottom* — John Pierce.

In The Classic Spirit: 70: Barbary Coast Yachts. **71:** *Top* — Brian Dowley; *bottom* — Barbary Coast Yachts.

The Genius of N.G. Herreshoff: 75: Bachrach, 1920. **76:** Willard Jackson, courtesy Peabody Museum. **79-83:** Herreshoff Marine Museum. **85:** Drawing by Spencer Lincoln.

The Remarkable Sloop *Shadow*: 86: Willard Jackson, courtesy Peabody Museum, Salem, MA. **91:** Courtesy Foster Collection, Hart Nautical Museum, MIT. **97:** Stebbins, courtesy Foster Collection. **99:** Stebbins, courtesy SPNEA.

Mr. Herreshoff's Wonderful *Rozinante*: 101: Stephen B. Nichols.

Moccasin: Whose Time Has Come: 110-113: S. Woodward.

The Concordia Sloop Boat: 115-117: Norman Fortier.

Peapods Are For Sailing: 118: Maynard Bray. **119:** Anne Bray. **120:** Drawing by Spencer Lincoln.

Sam Wise: A Skiff for All Seasons: 121: Illustration by Paul Trowbridge. **123:** John Erickson.

Swampscott Dories: 130-132: Willard B. Jackson, courtesy Peabody Museum, Salem, MA **133:** Courtesy Peabody Museum. **134:** *Top* — Benjamin Mendlowitz; drawing by David Dillion, courtesy Apprenticeshop/Maine Maritime Museum. **135-136:** Courtesy Peabody Museum. **137:** Drawings by Spencer Lincoln.

Matter of Detail: Rudders & Tillers: 139-141: Drawings by Maynard Bray, redrawn by Spencer Lincoln.

John Gardner: In His Own Words: 142: Mary Ann Stets, courtesy Mystic Seaport Museum. **144:** Kenneth E. Mahler, courtesy Mystic Seaport Museum. **146:** Courtesy Mystic Seaport Museum.

The Dutch Boeier: 151-157: E.H. Bon.

***Boadicea*: 167-173:** Michael Frost.

The Venetian Gondola: 166-168: Renard (Venice). **169:** Bruning.

***Gauntlet*: A Cautionary Tale: 170:** Frank Medeiros. **172:** Beken of Cowes. **174-175:** Frank Medeiros. **176-177:** Benjamin Mendlowitz.

Giffy's Hammer: Surveying Wooden Boats: 178-188: Jerry Kirschenbaum.

Dudley Davidson's Secrets: 193-197: Michael Broom.

Looking Good Again: A Refinishing Story: 198-208: Benjamin Mendlowitz.

***Annie*: 210-215:** Benjamin Mendlowitz.

The Issues of Maritime Preservation: 216: Kip Brundage. **218-219:** Karl Kortum, courtesy National Maritime Museum. **220:** Nicholas Dean. **221:** *U.S.S. Constitution* Museum Foundation. **222:** Kenneth E. Mahler, Mystic Seaport. **225:** South Street Seaport Museum. **226:** Nicholas Dean. **227:** Karl Kortum. **228:** Sandy Johnson.

Ancient Masterpiece: The Royal Ship of Cheops: 231-234: Courtesy Services des Antiquites, Cairo. **235:** *Top* — Services des Antiquites; *bottom* — John Ross. **236:** Services des Antiquites. **237:** *Top* — Services des Antiquites; *bottom* — John Ross. **238:** Drawings courtesy Thames & Hudson, Ltd.

Gathering the Finest: The Herreshoff Rendezvous and the Classic Yacht Regatta: 239-243: Benjamin Mendlowitz.

***Coronet*: Whither Away?: 244:** Courtesy Society for the Preservation of New England Antiquities. **246-247:** Painting by John Mecray. **248-252:** Benjamin Mendlowitz. **252:** Redrawn for publication by Spencer Lincoln based on a lines plan courtesy Smithsonian Institution and arrangement plan courtesy The Kingdom.

Another *Reality*: 253: Beken of Cowes. **255:** *Top left and center* — Roland Brener; *top right and bottom right* — Bent Jesperson; *bottom left* — Bernadette Mertens. **256:** Bernadette Mertens. **257:** Diane Beeston.

The New York Thirties: 258: Morris Rosenfeld & Sons. **260-261:** Drawn for publication by Spencer Lincoln. **263-268:** Morris Rosenfeld & Sons. **270-271:** Drawings by Sam Manning (based on descriptions kindly furnished by Paul Stubing).

***Peggotty*: 273:** Robert Foley. **274:** Little Compton Historical Society. **276-278:** Robert Foley. **279:** Shirley Utterback.

Ships Such as Those: *Matilda D*: 281-289: Illustrations by William Gilkerson.

Planking the *Morgan*: 298-302: Benjamin Mendlowitz.

***Cirrus*: A Treasure from Herreshoff: 295:** Maynard Bray. **297:** Morris Rosenfeld & Sons.

A Little Ship — *Lazy Jack*: 302-303: Illustrations by Ed Frost.